THE HEALTHY MIND

In *The Healthy Mind*, Dr. Henry M. Vyner presents the findings of twenty-seven years of research spent interviewing Tibetan lamas about their experiences of the mind. The interviews have generated a science of stream of consciousness that demonstrates that the healthy human mind is the egoless mind, given the paradox that the egoless mind has an ego. Vyner presents this science and also shows his readers how to cultivate a healthy mind. *The Healthy Mind* features extensive interview excerpts, theoretical maps of the egoless and egocentric mind, discussions of the history of science, and thought experiments that unpack the implications of his findings. This is a useful book for all those interested in the dialogue between Buddhism and psychology and in understanding the nature of the healthy mind.

Henry M. Vyner, MD, MA is an adjunct professor at the Center for Nepali and Asian Studies at Tribhuvan University—the national university of Nepal. He is a physician and cultural anthropologist, and has spent the last twenty-seven years doing a body of research on the nature of the healthy mind amongst Tibetan lamas living in south and central Asia. While in Nepal, he was also a visiting scholar at the University of California at Berkeley, and held a prior position as a research fellow at Tribhuvan University. Prior to his work in Asia, he served as Director of Research at the Radiation Research Institute in Berkeley, California.

THE HEALTHY MIND

Mindfulness, True Self, and the Stream of Consciousness

Henry M. Vyner

Routledge
Taylor & Francis Group
NEW YORK AND LONDON

First published 2019
by Routledge
711 Third Avenue, New York, NY 10017

and by Routledge
2 Park Square, Milton Park, Abingdon, Oxon, OX14 4RN

Routledge is an imprint of the Taylor & Francis Group, an informa business

Library of Congress Cataloging-in-Publication Data
Names: Vyner, Henry M., author.
Title: The healthy mind : mindfulness, the true self, and the stream of consciousness / Henry M. Vyner.
Description: New York, NY : Routledge is an imprint of the Taylor & Francis Group, an Informa Business, [2019] | Includes bibliographical references and index.
Identifiers: LCCN 2018009364 (print) | LCCN 2018026501 (ebook) | ISBN 9781315122649 (eBook) | ISBN 9781138564831 (hbk) | ISBN 9781138564848 (pbk) | ISBN 9781315122649 (pbk)
Subjects: LCSH: Buddhism—Psychology. | Awareness—Religious aspects—Buddhism. | Consciousness—Religious aspects—Buddhism. | Mindfulness (Psychology) | Mental health—Religious aspects—Buddhism.
Classification: LCC BQ4570.P76 (ebook) | LCC BQ4570.P76 V96 2018 (print) | DDC 294.301/9—dc23
LC record available at https://lccn.loc.gov/2018009364

ISBN: 978-1-138-56483-1 (hbk)
ISBN: 978-1-138-56484-8 (pbk)
ISBN: 978-1-315-12264-9 (ebk)

Typeset in Bembo
by Apex CoVantage, LLC

Visit the eResource: www.routledge.com/9781138564831

To all of the lamas that I have interviewed
and
to the freedom of Tibet

CONTENTS

PREFACE

Cultivating the Wild Stream of Consciousness

The journey that took me to Asia to do twenty years of research on the nature of the healthy mind with Tibetan lamas began when I started meditating at the age of twelve. At that point, I didn't know what meditation was. I vaguely knew there was a religion called Buddhism, but again, I knew nothing at all about it. Not even the Four Noble Truths or the Eightfold Path. The journey to Asia began when I spontaneously stumbled into doing what I now know to be meditation.

I would go down to the lake near our small horse farm and let my mind run free out in the space over and around the lake. It was just that simple, and I began to do it regularly. The operative phrase here is "run free." This was the beginning of my pursuit of the wild stream of consciousness and the natural state of mind it engenders.

I let my stream of consciousness run free because I saw it as a way to be as open and honest as I could possibly be with myself about everything that was going on in my mind. That freedom was for me an antidote to the conformism of the life around me, and I wanted to escape that conformism and be what I thought was real.

At that point, I didn't know it yet, but there were two separate traditions in the history of Indo-Tibetan Buddhism that had made a related discovery towards the end of the first millennium AD. They had both recognized that the simple act of letting the stream of consciousness run free, absolutely free, was the key to cultivating an enlightened mind.

Those two lineages still exist today, and they are known as the DzogChen and Mahamudra traditions of Tibetan Buddhism. The DzogChen tradition, in particular, developed and championed meditation practices that allow the stream of consciousness to run free and naturally transform itself into the goodness and self-realization of the egoless mind.

The import of this discovery is that it defines the difference between the egoless mind and the egocentric mind, which causes itself to be unhappy, inauthentic and unhealthy by controlling its stream of consciousness.

DzogChen figured out that when you learn how to let your stream of consciousness run free and remain in its natural state, your thoughts and emotions will spontaneously dissolve and transform themselves into moments of the nondual joy, goodness and self-realization of the enlightened mind, a mind that has no ego. This phenomenon is called self-liberation in DzogChen.

Here's an evocative and beautiful passage from a commentary by the twentieth-century DzogChen lama, the late Dilgo Khyentse Rinpoche, in which he captures the essence of this view of the naturally enlightened mind:

> The wind blows through the sky and flies over continents without settling anywhere. It traverses space and leaves no trace.
> Thus should thoughts pass through our mind. In the natural mind, thoughts are freed by themselves, like the wind.

Here is a passage from a fourteenth-century Tibetan lama named Longchenpa, a seminal figure in the DzogChen tradition, in which he explains in more detail the DzogChen position that allowing the stream of consciousness to run free and remain in its natural state—without repressing, holding on to or modifying anything in the stream of consciousness—is the key to cultivating an enlightened mind:

> Let the Mind be at ease without effort.
> The ordinary mind, unmodified and natural,
> Unstained by the grasping for samsara and nirvana,
> attains liberation in its natural state.
> Let the Mind be at ease without effort.
> The ordinary mind, unmodified and natural,
> attains liberation in its natural state.

For DzogChen practitioners, becoming enlightened is ultimately a matter of learning to let the stream of consciousness run free. Once you are able to let your mind run free, without accepting or rejecting any of your thoughts or emotions, everything else will take care of itself. When the stream of consciousness is allowed to truly run free, this simple act in and of itself will spontaneously generate the wisdom, goodness and compassion of the egoless mind.

When I, myself, first began to let my mind run free down by the lake near my sister's farm, I had no idea that this tradition of letting the stream of consciousness run free already existed in a religion called Buddhism. Nor did I understand that the wild stream of consciousness was the crux of the healthy mind. Nor did I realize that stumbling upon and discovering the virtues of the unfettered stream of consciousness would lead me to do more than twenty years of scientific research with Tibetan lamas that would generate a body of data that could one day change our notions of the nature of the healthy mind. But all of these things have happened.

At the time, I was just trying to be real and find an alternative to the egocentric conformism in which we are all brought up. As I began to let my own stream of consciousness run free, I realized right away that something worthwhile was going on. I always felt more at peace and more authentic whenever I did this thing that I was doing with my mind.

Being the son of an academic psychiatrist in a family in which we discussed Freud over the dinner table, I decided to try and understand what it was I was doing with my mind, and what it all meant. I wanted to figure out how to make the positive states of mind that I was experiencing last, and although I didn't have the words to say it at the time, I also wanted to live a life of self-realization. I wanted to be my genuine self, and I wanted to live amongst people who were also being their true selves. This was the beginning of my research on the nature of the healthy mind.

I began making systematic observations of the things that I was seeing in my stream of consciousness right then and there as a kid. I also began to derive, from those observations, a small body of theory, and then I used that theory to guide my meditation.

One of my first theoretical ideas, which came early, was that it is important to let the stream of consciousness run free and remain in its natural state. At the time, I thought that this meant not repressing any of my emotions and thoughts, and later on I would learn that this also meant not holding on to or believing them either.

By the age of twenty, I realized that what I was actually doing was pursuing the cultivation of an egoless mind. I can still see in my mind today the exact moment in college when I first had that realization. I didn't entirely understand it at the time, but I was beginning to see that allowing the stream of consciousness to run free is really the essence of cultivating an egoless mind. They are one and the same thing.

In medical school, that epiphany gelled into the conviction that I wanted to practice a psychiatry centered on the healthy mind. It began to seem to me that the goal of therapy should be to restore a person to a healthy state of mind. I also began to wonder if it might be possible to prevent mental illness and perhaps even create a healthier society by cultivating healthy minds.

Then, to my genuine astonishment, I found that no one was interested in, much less doing, research on either the healthy mind or the stream of consciousness! It actually took me another decade and a half to find other scientists with whom I could collaborate on this line of work.

I couldn't find anyone right away because no one in the behaviorist department of psychology in which I studied as an undergraduate was studying the mind or the stream of consciousness, much less the healthy mind. Nor was there anyone studying the healthy mind or the stream of consciousness in the Freudian department of psychiatry in which I later trained.

Nonetheless, I continued to hold dear the conviction that my life's work was the pursuit of the healthy mind, and I continued to pursue this work on my own time. While I was looking for a way to do research on the healthy mind, I went on to also get a degree in cultural anthropology, and then I did a body of research on the psychological effects of ionizing radiation at the Radiation Research Institute in Berkeley.[1,2,3]

In the fall of 1990, I finally found a group of scientists with whom I could collaborate and do research on the healthy mind. Not only were they studying the same group of phenomena that I had been investigating—the phenomena that appear in the stream of consciousness—but they had also come to several of the same theoretical conclusions about the nature of the healthy mind.

These scientists had developed a systematic science of the stream of consciousness, and they also understood the import of letting the stream of consciousness run free. They had described the processes by which the mind becomes healthy when you let the stream of consciousness run free, and the processes by which the mind becomes unhealthy when the ego does not allow the stream of consciousness to run free.

I found these scientists when I stumbled upon and read a book called *Buddha Mind*, which is an anthology of writings by the fourteenth-century Tibetan lama I mentioned earlier, Longchenpa.

As I read *Buddha Mind*, it became apparent right away that Longchenpa was describing many of the same phenomena and states of mind that I myself had observed and found crucial to understanding what I thought might be a healthy mind. Not only that, Longchenpa seemed to have developed precise theories of the nature of the healthy and unhealthy mind that were similar to my own theories. Most of all, he seemed to know much more about the healthy mind than I did.

I then learned that Longchenpa had long been, and continues to be, a seminal figure in one of the four principal schools of contemporary Tibetan Buddhism: the Nyingma school. Nyingma means the "ancient ones" in Tibetan.

This turned out to mean that Longchenpa's observations and theories of the healthy mind were, and still are, common knowledge among present-day practitioners of the Nyingma school. Longchenpa's writings are the foundation

1. H. M. Vyner. (1988). *The Psychosocial Effects of the Invisible Environmental Contaminants*. Lexington: Lexington Books.
2. H. M. Vyner. (1983). The psychological effects of ionizing radiation. *Culture, Medicine and Psychiatry*, 3: 241–261.
3. H. M. Vyner. (1988). The psychological dimensions of health care for patients exposed to radiation and the other invisible environmental contaminants. *Social Science and Medicine*, 27: 1097–1103.

of contemporary Nyingma philosophy and mind science, and they are core texts in the curriculum taught in their monastic universities.

In my own mind, this raised the possibility that the phenomena that Longchenpa was describing were universal phenomena, phenomena that appear in the minds of all meditators, and perhaps even in the minds of all human beings. Longchenpa had experienced them. I had experienced them, and now it seemed possible that perhaps many of the present-day practitioners of the Nyingma school were familiar with them as well.

This also raised the possibility that Longchenpa's theory of the healthy mind, and my own similar theory, might be empirically correct; and that these theories might actually provide a foundation upon which one could cultivate a healthy mind.

Was this a science of the healthy mind buried in a religion?

Within months, I left everything I was doing, got a small grant and headed off to Asia to find and interview contemporary Nyingma lamas who were living in the Tibetan diaspora that had sprung up in Nepal and India after the Chinese invasion of Tibet in 1950. Later on that search would take me to Ladakh, Sikkim and Bhutan.

To do this research, I have traveled to, and lived in, villages and monasteries all over Nepal, Bhutan, Ladakh, Sikkim and India. I have often trekked a week or more to get to sixteenth-century villages and monasteries to do interviews with a lama. Before my recent return to America, I trekked eight days to get to a sixteenth-century village in north central Nepal to do a round of interviews with a lama living at the foot of Mount Manaslu (26,781 feet).

The interviews that the lamas and I have been doing together are generating a science of both the healthy mind and the stream of consciousness that will, with time and further work, change the way that we see the healthy mind.

For one, this science is establishing that the egocentric mind, the type of mind that almost all socialized human beings have, is an unhealthy mind. The study of the stream of consciousness has made it altogether clear that the egocentric mind is a mind that imposes upon a human being an ongoing sense of unhappiness, conflict and inauthenticity.

Second, our findings are also establishing that the egoless, or natural mind, is a healthy mind, given the paradox that you have to have an ego to become egoless. We have found that the egoless mind is a mind that forgoes the conflicts, fictions and moods of the ego; and that at the same time, it is a mind lives in an authenticity born of joy and goodness.

I chose to interview Tibetan lamas for this research on the healthy mind for two pivotal reasons. For one, many lamas are accomplished scientists of the healthy mind and the stream of consciousness. It is part of their religious tradition.

Second, as advanced practitioners of Buddhism, the central purpose of their life is to cultivate the wisdom and goodness of the egoless mind, which they call an enlightened mind. The cultivation of the egoless mind has been the central concern of the Buddhist tradition ever since its inception, and the lamas know a great deal about it.

The lamas are a living cultural experiment, if you will, that tests whether or not the egoless mind is a healthy mind. By studying the lamas, we can determine whether or not the egoless mind is a healthy mind. Interviewing the lamas is not quite as empirically elegant as it would be to do controlled experiments with a group of people who grew up on another planet where everyone is raised to be egoless, but they are an excellent second best.

When I first began to do this work, I was fully aware, of course, that I was treading outside the paradigmatic and methodological boundaries of contemporary science. There was, and still is, a taboo against directly studying the mind and the stream of consciousness. That taboo is evolving, but still very present. It is now acceptable to study the brain, cognitive behavior, verbal reports of cognitive and emotional states and computer models of the mind; but not the phenomena that appear in the stream of consciousness.

Once I committed myself to the decision to do this healthy mind research, it became clear that it would go better if I abandoned a traditional career. In additional to the paradigm problem, there was an immense amount of work to do, and I felt that it would not be possible to do it all in a life of occasional research junkets.

Even though it meant abandoning a traditional career as an academic psychiatrist, it was an easy decision to go ahead and pursue the study of the healthy mind for the simple reason that I believed in it. I chose to take this path with the hope that if the work was done well, that a time would come when it would bear fruit and be accepted by both the scientific community and the larger public.

That time to broach that possibility has now come. Enough data has been accumulated to bring this research back in from the cold. *The Healthy Mind* is going to present an overview of our findings and make the case that (1) the healthy mind is the egoless mind; (2) the egocentric mind is an unhealthy mind; (3) it is possible to empirically study the phenomena that appear in the stream of consciousness; and (4) the structural conflict of the egocentric mind may well be the template upon which the sociopolitical conflicts of racism, religious intolerance, terrorism and war are built.

SEMANTICS AND SYNONYMS

The Healthy Mind is an inquiry into the nature of the healthy human mind. It assesses the nature of the healthy mind by comparing the egocentric state of mind and the egoless state of mind.

It compares these two states of mind by constructing maps that describe the structure and dynamics of both the egocentric mind and the egoless mind.

Both of these states of mind are mediated by phenomena that appear in the stream of consciousness, just as the phenomenon we call electricity is mediated by the flow of electrons. Given that this is the case, the maps have been derived from a descriptive science, or typology, of the phenomena that appear in the stream of consciousness.

This descriptive science is systematically presented with empirical definitions of each phenomenon in Chapter 6, "Ode to the Stream of Consciousness." Many of the technical terms that are used in *The Healthy Mind* are defined there.[1]

However, as I was writing *The Healthy Mind*, I realized that a potentially confusing profusion of synonyms was piling up, and that it would be a good idea to forestall confusion by listing and explaining the synonyms.

In the following list, synonyms are separated by an equal (=) sign. Terms that are antonyms are separated by a not equal (≠) sign. After each group of synonyms,

1. When Tibetan terms are presented, they are all spelled phonetically to make it easier for you to hear and pronounce them—which is to say the English spellings are not direct transliterations of the Tibetan spellings.

there are a number of entries that explain, and give context to, the meaning of the synonyms:

1. Identity ≠ Self ≠ Ego

    a. The word *self* has different meanings in different contexts and different bodies of thought in the history of Western ideas. In Jung's Analytic theory, for example, the term can be said to refer to the totality of who a person really is. In Hartmann's Ego Psychology, the term refers to a person's self-concept. Both of these notions embody the idea that that a person has a character that is more or less permanent.
    b. A person's identity, on the other hand, is a concept or image of a person's self that purports to define that self. It does so by defining a person's permanent character and place in society.
    c. Because of its translation history, Buddhism is said to ascribe to the doctrine that a person does not have a "self." But this is probably a mistranslation that would at this point in the history of Buddhist translation take an act of Congress to change.
    d. As I, and I think others, understand the Buddhist tradition, what it actually says is that a person does not have a permanent identity.
    e. In the work being presented in *The Healthy Mind*, the term self is used to refer to who a person really is in any given present moment. Please see Chapter 12 for a thorough discussion of this idea.
    f. In addition, *The Healthy Mind* defines an egoless mind as being a mind that (1) does not see itself as having a permanent identity, and that as a result (2) does not control its stream of consciousness to maintain a belief that it has an identity.
    g. An egocentric mind, in contrast, is a mind that (1) does believe it has a permanent identity, and that as a result (2) does control its stream of consciousness to maintain its belief that it has the identity it thinks it has.

2. Meaning = Phenomenon (in the context of the stream of consciousness)

    a. A meaning is a construct that articulates the mind's cognitive, emotional and intentional response to an experience.
    b. The phenomena that appear in the stream of consciousness are meanings. Indeed, the stream of consciousness is a temporal sequence of meanings.
    c. The stream of consciousness presents meanings to the watcher as thoughts, feelings, emotions, epiphanies, mind-films and moods.

3. Watcher = Awareness

    a. The experience of knowing the stream of consciousness is one in which it seems as though there are two entities present in that experience: the stream of consciousness and the awareness that knows and responds to the stream of consciousness.

b. The science of the stream of consciousness has given the term *watcher* to the awareness that knows the stream of consciousness, and the two terms can be used interchangeably.

4. Suchness = As It Is = As It Really Is

   a. To know the suchness of a meaning is to either know its content as it really is or to know it as nondual egoless awareness itself.
   b. There are two aspects to knowing the suchness of a meaning:
      1. Knowing that meaning without projecting any egocentric concepts *onto* it.
      2. Having nondual awareness of that meaning.

5. Nondual Awareness ≠ Dual Awareness

   a. The mind can have two kinds of awareness of the phenomena that appear in the stream of consciousness: dual awareness and nondual awareness.
   b. The egocentric mind has dual awareness of phenomena.
   c. The egoless mind has nondual awareness of phenomena.
   d. Please see Chapter 6 (and many other chapters as well) for an extensive discussion of dual and nondual awareness.

6. Stream of Consciousness = Mind Stream
7. Individual Moment of Consciousness = Primordial Meaning

   a. Meanings appear in the stream of consciousness in several different forms.
   b. The individual moments of consciousness (iMoC) are one type of meaning, and they attribute meaning to one specific experience.
   c. For a number of reasons that will be explored in Chapter 6, the individual moments of consciousness are also called primordial meanings.

8. Mind-Film = Ego Narrative = Involuntary Stream of Consciousness = Mind Wandering

   a. A second type of meaning is the mind-film.
   b. The mind-films appear as recursive cycles of thoughts that tell stories that have the same themes over and over again.
   c. In contrast to the primordial meanings, the mind-films are active for long periods of time and as a result, give contextual narrative meaning to many experiences.

9. Egoless Mind = Enlightened Mind

   a. There are two egoless states of mind, as defined by the science of the stream of consciousness: the completely egoless mind (CESoM) and the partially egoless mind (PESoM).

b. The completely egoless mind is the same state of mind as the enlightened mind of Buddhism.
c. Please see the section titled "Overview" in Chapter 12 for further discussion of the difference between a completely egoless mind (CESoM) and a partially egoless mind (PESoM).

10. Egoless Mind ≠ Enlightened Mind

a. Once again, there are two egoless states of mind: the completely egoless mind (CESoM) and the partially egoless mind (PESoM).
b. The partially egoless mind is not the same state of mind as the enlightened mind.
c. Once again, please see the section titled "Overview" in Chapter 12 for further discussion of the difference between a completely egoless mind (CESoM) and a partially egoless mind (PESoM).

11. Egoless Mind = Natural Mind = Natural State of the Mind

a. The egoless mind does not control its stream of consciousness. It allows its stream of consciousness to run free and remain in its natural state because it does not attempt to create and maintain an identity.
b. When the stream of consciousness is allowed to run free and remain in its natural state, the mind as a whole settles into its natural state, and it is in this sense that the egoless mind and the natural mind are synonyms. Please see Chapter 11 for an extensive discussion of the natural state of the mind.

12. Egoless Awareness = Egoless Watcher

a. Egoless awareness is the subjective aspect of the egoless mind.
b. The egoless watcher has nondual awareness of the phenomena that appear in its stream of consciousness, and in addition it does not grasp those phenomena.

13. The Watcher = Egocentric Watcher

a. The watcher is the subject of the egocentric mind.
b. The egocentric watcher grasps the phenomena that appear in its stream of consciousness and as a result has dual awareness of them.

ACKNOWLEDGMENTS

First and foremost, I want to thank all of the fifty-four lamas whom I have interviewed for this research on the nature of the healthy mind. Given that it is indeed unusual for a scientist to come and ask a lama to discuss their experiences of their own mind, it was exceedingly open and generous for the lamas to participate in our interviews. There would have been no science of the healthy mind or of the stream of consciousness without the lamas.

In addition, there are several lamas I would like to single out for the particular insights they gave me into the nature of the egoless mind: the late Tulku Peygyal, Khenpo Thubten of the Kullu Valley, Khenpo Tsewang Gyatso of Namdroling Monastery, Lopon Tegchoke of Sikkim and Bhutan, the Bön lama Lopon Tenzin Namdak of Swayambhu, the late Penor Rinpoche of Namdroling Monastery and His Holiness the Dalai Lama.

Perhaps the most important contribution made to this study by a lama was made by the fourteenth-century lama Longchenpa. Reading Longchenpa is a great joy, and I was inspired to do this research by reading his work. In particular it was reading his description of the two modes of self-awareness in *Treasury of Word and Meaning* that launched this work. I also want to thank the two scholars who introduced me to Longchenpa: the late Herbert Gunther in two seminars on *Kindly Bent to Ease Us*, and the lama Tulku Thondup Rinpoche in his book *Buddha Mind/The Practice of DzogChen.*

There are Western scholars to be thanked as well: William James and Jerome Singer, both of whom opened the door, in their own way, to empirically studying the stream of consciousness.

There were several people who did the important work of introducing or connecting me to lamas who they thought would make good subjects for interviews. These include DzogChen Rinpoche, Khenpo Thubten Gyatso, Babu

Sherpa, Karma Phuntso, a monk named Tamdin, Dasho Pema Tenzin and Dasho Sherab Gyaltsen of Bhutan, Marguerite Swift and finally Jigme Lama of the village of Samma in north-central Nepal. Marguerite also read and critiqued many of the chapters for *The Healthy Mind.* Bidur Dongol of Vajra Publications in Kathmandu did me the very good turn of overhearing me discuss my work at a gathering and then coming up with the idea of publishing a series of volumes that collect and annotate my research interviews: *The Healthy Mind Interviews.*

I want to thank the Gurung family, Hari Khanal and Uttam Phuyal of the Moonlight Hotel of Kathmandu Jim and Stephanie Carpenter for their turn-of-the-century log cabin and Zoe de Bray for the Hallaby House—for providing excellent places to write *The Healthy Mind.* Thank you as well to the folks at Routledge: George Zimmar for engaging with my original proposal; Lillian Rand for shepherding the proposal through to acceptance; and Lillian Rand, Emma Starr, Jamie Magyar, Kate Fornadel and Peter Lloyd for bringing the book through production.

Finally, friends and family. I have been extraordinarily lucky to have the unstinting friendship of both Roger Behnken and Adrian Smith during the time I was doing the research for and the writing of *The Healthy Mind.* If it were not for my uncle Robert M. Taubman and my sister Lynne, *The Healthy Mind* would never have been written. Thank you to all.

PART I
Introduction

1

EGO AND WAR

9/11

FIGURE 1.1 Achilles Dragging Hector Before the Walls of Troy[1]

Imagine for a moment that the president of the United States at the time of the terrorist attacks of September 11, 2001, had been a person who sees life as a stage upon which there is a perpetual struggle between the forces of good and evil. Suppose that he, himself, was a man who had experienced his own life as being a conflict between the good and evil within himself, and that at one point the forces that he called evil had threatened to overtake him and ruin his life.

He had gone somewhat astray in his youth, and he had done things that a future president should not have done—things that were both illegal and unworthy of his family and origins.

Then one day, as the story often goes in America, he saw the light, and he redeemed himself. The forces of good within him triumphed and took control of his life, and he resolved to do his best to become a good and righteous man.

When this future president turned his life around, it instilled within him a deep conviction that the central dynamic of life is a battle in which good is in

1. F. Matsch. (1892). *Triumphant Achilles.* Achilleion, Corfu, Greece.

perpetual conflict with evil. He came to believe that all human beings endlessly wage this war within their soul in which good and evil brawl with one another for control. He came to feel that in this endless moral struggle, sometimes the forces of good prevail, and sometimes the forces of evil win. This was the universe in which he now lived.

After his redemption, this president-to-be was of course grateful that good had triumphed in his own life, and it was only natural that the moral narrative of good and evil became the frame of reference that he brought to understanding much of what happened around him. Now he had a clear and simple way of making sense of life's complexities.

Having already found that this moral narrative gave coherence and meaning to the events of his own personal struggles, he would now use the same framework to comprehend the larger events of the world with which he would have to deal when he became the president of the United States.

He saw the play of good and evil in almost everything that happened around him. He saw it in the issues of abortion, gun control, welfare and homosexuality in domestic American politics. He saw the international face of evil in the form of terrorism, Islamism, communism and more.

He came to see life itself as one grand jousting match in which the righteous and good people of the world are continually picking up the cudgel of goodness and doing battle with the evil that is present in both themselves and the greater world around them. "Bring it on."

Now if this kind of man had been president of the United States when the terrorist attacks of 9/11 killed almost three thousand people in New York, Pennsylvania and Washington, DC, how would he have seen those attacks? How would he have reacted to them?

His response, of course, would have been predictable. This president, a well-intended man whose only concern in this context would have been to protect the country he loves, would have plugged the attack into the dominant narrative of his life—the narrative of good versus evil. He would have seen the attack as nothing less than the act of an evil cabal that had to be eradicated from the face of the earth, like all evil.

Acting on this narrative premise, he would have rallied the country to take part in and support a series of what he would call just and necessary wars to eliminate that evil, and this of course is just what he did.

In the wake of the 9/11 attacks, this kind of narrative about good and evil did, to be sure, resonate with a large portion of the American public. The reason that it struck a chord within the hearts of so many Americans is that most human beings, not just Americans, carry around some version of this moral narrative of good and evil within their own hearts and minds. And certainly if anything can be called evil, the attacks of 9/11 were.

Thus it was that the president was not the only person in post-9/11 America that brought a narrative of good and evil to the task of comprehending the events of that day. Many, if not most, of us wanted to go to war and destroy the evil that had struck us such a severe blow, and we wholeheartedly backed the president when he took us down the path to holy war.

But history also records that we Americans were not the only ones to bring a moral narrative to the events of that day. To say the very least, the terrorists saw themselves as righteous warriors engaged in a steeped moral combat as well. They flew the planes that they hijacked into the World Trade Center because they saw America as an imperial country of infidels that was bent on destroying Islam and imposing the American way of life on the Muslim world.

They saw themselves as moral and righteous actors because they felt they were protecting their Islamic religion and their God, and in turn, they saw us as being the evil ones. This was the basic moral narrative that moved them to attack us without any seeming sense of remorse. There can be no doubt that it was this narrative that caused 9/11 itself, and has caused countless other terrorist attacks and wars as well.

What are we to make of the fact that both the terrorists and ourselves brought narratives of good and evil to the events of 9/11? What does it tell us about who we are as human beings?

The ubiquity of this type of moral narrative is a reflection of the fact that most, if not all, of the world's peoples are brought up to live in a universe that is defined by the presence of good and evil. Even just a cursory look at the world's religions will tell us that it is the very nature of the socialized human psyche to construct and live in cosmologies that sunder the world into good and evil. We all do it.

Although the details of these morality tales differ from one society to the next, from one culture to the next, and from one era to the next, we all partake of them in our own way. There is God and Satan. Ram and Ravana. Ahura Mazda and Ahriman. The Capitalists and the Communists. Conservatives and Liberals. Believers and Infidels. Pro-choice and Pro-life. White supremacists and people of color.

By and large, humanity lives in stories of good and evil, and we live in these narratives day in and day out even though they drag us off to war, and into lives in which we seek out and thrive on conflict.

How has it come to pass that the vast majority of our species lives in a dualistic moral universe in which good survives by essaying forth every day and projecting itself into a life of eternal combat in which it destroys the forces of iniquity that inhabit both ourselves and the universe? How did this dualistic morality become a universal structure in the human mind? How did these cosmologies that channel us into racism, religious intolerance, terrorism and acts of war become the milieu in which we live our lives?

I just recently watched a video in which a three-hundred-pound mother gorilla is sitting in the sun with her newborn infant on her chest being as tender with that infant as any human mother could ever possibly be. There is much we have in common with the other great apes. Yet despite our similarities, it goes without saying that none of the other members of the animal kingdom—not even our close cousins the great apes—create and live in mythologies that institutionalize a good that requires the righteous destruction of an evil.

In this chapter, we are going to open our investigation into the nature of the healthy mind by first taking a look at the means by which the ego creates a state of mind that is conducive to conflict and even war. In essence, we will be examining the mechanism by which the ego creates the narratives of good and evil that move human beings to commit acts of terrorism and warfare.

After we take a look at this issue, we will then continue our exploration into the nature of the healthy mind by doing a systematic investigation of the structure and dynamics of both the egocentric mind and the egoless mind, and this inquiry will be grounded in the science of the phenomena that appear in the stream of consciousness. *The Healthy Mind* will evaluate both of these states of mind for the purpose of determining which state of mind is healthier. But first, for now, we will take a look at the ego and its propensity for conflict.

Many of the great personality theorists of the twentieth century have asserted that the ego causes a considerable amount of individual pain, conflict and suffering.[2] As part of our inquiry into the nature of the healthy mind, *The Healthy Mind* is going to focus on describing the broad spectrum of individual psychopathology created by the routine machinations of the ego.[3]

However, there is also a sociopolitical dimension to this story that is relevant to our task of evaluating whether or not the egocentric mind is a healthy mind, and it is an interesting place to begin our investigation of the healthy mind. Why? Because once you map out the structure and dynamics of the egocentric mind, as we have done, it is difficult to avoid concluding that the conflict that sits at the core of every egocentric mind—think of Freud's structural theory of the ego and id, for example—is the psychological cause of humanity's identity-based conflicts: religious intolerance, racism, terrorism, war between nation-states and so forth.

This conclusion has been derived from our theoretical maps of the egocentric mind, which have in turn been derived from our observations of the phenomena that appear in the stream of consciousness (SoC).[4] These observations have generated two lines of evidence that support and establish the validity of this hypothesis.

The first line of evidence is the discovery that humanity's identity-based sociopolitical conflicts have precisely the same structure and dynamic as the egocentric mind's conflict with itself. As we will be seeing, these two realms

2. See for example Freud (2010) and Kernberg (1975).
3. Please see Chapters 2 through 6 for a systematic presentation of the science of the phenomena that appear in the stream of consciousness, and Chapters 8 and 9 for a systematic discussion of the structure and dynamics of egocentric mind.
4. Please see Chapter 6 for a systematic presentation of the descriptive science, or typology, of the phenomena that appear in the stream of consciousness. This descriptive science has been derived from the lama interviews, and it is the foundation of the research on the nature of the healthy mind that is being presented in *The Healthy Mind*.

of conflict have homologous structures and dynamics.[5] This finding suggests that our sociopolitical conflicts are replications of the endemic conflict of the egocentric mind—just as the DNA molecule replicates itself to form new DNA molecules that will pass on genetic information to subsequent generations.

This hypothesis is given further credence by our second line of evidence: we have found the mechanism by which the egocentric mind replicates its structural conflict and transfers it to its social and political relationships with other people. We are going to describe that mechanism in the remainder of this chapter, and we will begin this exposition by first taking a look at the ego itself.

The Ego

The history of personality theory depicts the ego as being a structural entity within the human mind.[6] A more colloquial definition of the ego is that it is our self-esteem. If we say that someone has a big ego, we tend to mean he or she has high self-esteem. Or if we say that someone has a huge ego, we mean that they have grandiose self-esteem.

To be certain, self-esteem is both created and lost by the ego, but actually, the ego is much more than an emblem for our self-esteem. The ego is a functioning part of the mind, just as the heart and brain are functioning parts of our body.

If the function of the heart is to pump oxygen and nutrient rich blood to the body, the core function of the ego is to socialize a person by controlling their mind and behavior. In the course of the process of socializing you, the ego does indeed create your self-esteem and identity.

Human beings don't have an ego when they are born, but our family and society place one inside us as we grow up. The ego that we are all given controls our thoughts, emotions and actions so that we will find a place in and become a well-behaved part of our family and society.

We all have egos because we live in egocentric societies[7] that have institutionalized the ego, and employ it for the purpose of socializing its members. As matters stand now, all societies are, to the best of our knowledge, egocentric societies.

However, despite its ubiquity, the ego is problematic. It creates illness within us even as it socializes us. The most fundamental pathology that the ego creates is that it divides the mind in two, and in so doing, it turns each of us into two people: the person you really are and your ego.

5. Please see Chapter 14 for both a case study of the dynamic homologies that exist between the egocentric mind and the sociopolitical conflicts it generates, and further discussion of the cause of those homologies.
6. Freud, of course, introduced the idea that the ego is a structural entity within the mind, and almost all personality theorists since his time have continued this theoretical tradition.
7. By egocentric society, I mean a society that organizes itself around the ego by teaching its young to have an ego, and by propagating the egocentric mind from one generation to the next.

This division, in turn, creates conflict within the mind, and to make matters worse, the ego exports that conflict to its relationships with other people. The ego is, if you will, a factory that manufactures conflict both within its own mind when it looks inward, and between people when it looks outward. As we will be seeing, this is one of the several normal pathologies[8] that the ego routinely creates within the mind.

The story of the ego begins with the true self. Everybody, every human being, has a true self. Your true self is the person you really are moment to moment.[9]

As you grow up, your society and family ask you to be somebody different than the person you really are. We are all given an identity, or self-concept, and then told that this received identity is the person we really are, as well as the person we should be. This is something we all experience.

That identity, in turn, becomes the center of your ego, and it defines your place in society[10] (Erikson, 1980). The primary function of the ego is to control your mind, actually your stream of consciousness (Vyner, 2007–2008), so that you will become the person that has, or at least to some extent resembles, your given identity.

Once you have an ego, you become two people. First you were just yourself. With an ego in place, you become two people: your true self and your ego. To have an ego is to have a second person in your mind who wants you to be somebody other than the person you really are.

Societies and families do not mean any harm by cultivating an ego within the minds of their youth and turning them into two people. In fact, they mean well. They put this second person into your mind for the purpose of shaping your behavior so as to help you find your place in society. This is simply the way that living in an egocentric society works.

Egocentric societies work on the implicit premise that giving a person an ego and identity will accomplish two basic ends. One, an identity will shape you into becoming a person that will serve a good and useful function within your society—as a teacher, parent, cardiologist, carpenter, politician, cellist, football player or whatever it might be.

The ego also works on the premise that adherence to an identity will sculpt us into being a person who will fit in with the morality and ethos of our society. An ego is designed to keep you from doing things you are not supposed to do, as defined by your society.

8. The normal pathologies are a group of maladies that are generated by the routine workings of the ego. See Chapter 9 for a systematic description of the normal pathologies of the ego, the psychological mechanisms that create them and the state of mind they produce.
9. Please see the second half of Chapter 12 for a thorough discussion of the true self.
10. Erik Erikson was a wise human being who is perhaps our most profound student and theoretician of identity. He took the view that identity is "a social function of the ego" (1980, p. 161). He defines identity as "the accrued confidence that one's ability to maintain inner sameness and continuity (one's ego in the psychological sense) is matched by the sameness and continuity of one's meaning for others" (1980, p. 94).

In both of these senses, the ego seems to serve a useful purpose. But as irony would have it, the ego also makes your mind an unhealthy mind.

The most fundamental problem created by the ego is the duality and conflict that it constructs within the mind. Once again, it turns each of us into two people, and those two people tend to fight with one another. They fight with one another to determine who you are going to be. Your true self simply wants to be the person you really are in the moment, and your ego wants you to be the person who has the identity your society has asked you to have. This is the primordial duality of the mind, and this duality gives birth, in turn, to a number of other maladies within the mind: the normal pathologies of the ego.

Freud of course made the case that this egopoietic conflict exists within the mind of all human beings. In his Structural Model of the mind, the Ego is in perpetual conflict with the Id. Freud was not, however, alone in realizing that the egocentric mind is a mind that lives in conflict with itself. Long before Freud and a multitude of twentieth-century personality theorists wrote about this egopoietic conflict, Plato, Augustine and Hegel also described this ubiquitous inner quarrel and placed it at the center of their own theories of the mind.[11]

In other words, both the ego and the conflict it routinely creates within the mind are something we have known about and experienced for a long time. It is a conflict that inhabits the minds of everyone who has an ego. Much of the time that conflict is unconscious, and we are unaware that it is taking place; but there are also times in which we are more than aware of it.

Monkey on Your Back

To get a feel for who the ego really is, for the place that this other person has in your life, we can think of the ego as being like an invisible monkey on our back, a monkey that is constantly chattering and whispering things into your ear.

Then imagine that the monkey's utterances become the thoughts, stories, emotions and moods that appear in your stream of consciousness. You think they are your own thoughts and feelings, but in fact, almost everything that appears in your stream of consciousness is the stuff that this monkey is surreptitiously mumbling into your ear.

Given that the monkey's words appear in your stream of consciousness as your thoughts, it is only natural that you would think that they are our own, but they are not. They belong to the monkey, or excuse me, to your ego. They are definitely not the still quiet voice of your genuine self. They do not tell you how you see and really feel about the present moment.

11. The idea that I want to convey here, and will return to later, is that there is a wealth of literature in the history of ideas that indicates that humanity has long recognized that the egocentric mind experiences itself as being two minds that are in perpetual conflict with one another. See for example Plato's *Phaedrus* (1995), Augustine's *Confessions* (2013), Hegel's *The Phenomenology of Spirit* (1977) and Freud's *The Ego and the Id* (1960).

The sole job of this monkey-ego is to control your mind so that you will become the person that he wants you to be. His goal, his singular Sisyphean task, is to make you become the identity that your family and society have given to you. That's why he is on your back chattering into your ear in the first place. He wants to feed you thoughts, moods and stories that will make you want to become, and think that you actually are, that person. That is his principal purpose in the life of your mind.

This monkey-ego controls your mind by controlling your stream of consciousness, and he does four different things to control your stream of consciousness. He judges the meanings that appear in your stream of consciousness. He represses thoughts and emotions that he does not like. He holds on to thoughts and feelings that he does like, and most of all, he makes up stories that he is perpetually breathing into your ear. First the monkey creates your stream of consciousness; then he controls its contents.

He spends the bulk of his time telling you stories that make you believe that you are somebody different than you really are. He will criticize you when you are not being the person he wants you to be, and he will be quick to lavish flatteries upon you when you are being the person that he wants you to be.

These stories that the monkey tells you are the phenomenon that the science of the stream of consciousness calls the *mind-films*. The mind-films are the noisy cascade of thoughts and emotions that are constantly running through the back of your mind. Once again, we think that these stories are real and that they are our own thoughts, but actually they are the creation of the monkey.

Perhaps ninety-eight percent of the stuff that appears in your stream of consciousness is the ego's monkey chatter. The great bulk of the stories and emotions that appear in your stream of consciousness are not expressions of your true self. This includes the stories that drag us off to war, the stories that turn the world into a place in which there is constant combat between good and evil.

The Mind-Films

It turns out that this duality of ego and true self is the ground from which our cosmologies of good and evil grow; the cosmologies that create within us the psychological impetus to commit acts of terrorism and go to war. To understand how this happens, let's back up for a moment and take a look at the mind from the perspective of the findings of the science of the stream of consciousness.

One of the cardinal findings of the science of the stream of consciousness, a finding that shows up in many other disciplines that investigate the mind, is that the egocentric mind carries within itself a small repertoire of mind-films that it displays to itself over and over again (Vyner, 2009–2010). These films appear in the stream of consciousness, and we are vaguely aware of these narratives as the cascade of thought noise that is perpetually running through the back of our minds day in and day out. The mind-films are one of the sixty-four phenomena that the science of the stream of consciousness has found, to date, within the stream of consciousness.[12]

If you take a careful look at this more or less constant noise in your mind, which you can easily do in meditation, you will see, as clearly as you can see your own face in a mirror, that this noise is actually a small clutch of stories that you keep telling your self over and again. Every egocentric mind has within itself a projection booth, if you will, that is stocked with a small repertoire of thought films that it projects into its stream of consciousness, and then onto its experience of the world, over and over again. The egocentric mind lives within the narratives of these mind-films as if they were real.

These films appear within the mind as recurring loops of thought, and they appear in tandem with matching emotions and moods. Given that they are endlessly recursive, it is easy to discern, with experience, that you are watching the same basic movies over and over. Modern cognitive neuroscience is beginning to recognize the existence of these films, and it refers to them as mind wandering (Smallwood and Schooler, 2006).

The existence of the mind-films has been recognized by a number of other disciplines as well. They are called fantasies and defense mechanisms in psychoanalytic thought; habitual patterns of thought (Tib.: *bak-chaks*) in Tibetan Buddhist mind science; and scripts in Beck's theory of cognitive therapy. These recurring narratives really are just like movies. They are the movies of the mind, and because we all have egos, we all live in the stories that these films tell us day in and day out.[13]

A mind-film might be a story in which you see yourself as a hero à la Walter Mitty. Or it might be a film in which you see yourself as a beautiful woman capable of conquering any man she wants. Or it might be a film in which you remember an event in your life in which you were exactly the kind of person you want to be. Or a moment in your life for which you feel survivor guilt because your best friend died in an avalanche in Tibet, and you survived only because you got lucky and ran the other way.

The egocentric mind believes that the realities portrayed by these movies are real, and it actually lives in them as though they are real. It is like watching a movie in a theater and getting so caught up in the action that you forget that you are watching a movie, as you become, vicariously, the hero of the film.

In the case of mind-films, however, the movie is in your head, and the forgetting is far more complete. So complete that most of us don't even realize

12. Once again, please see Chapter 6, "Ode to the Stream of Consciousness" for a presentation of the descriptive science of all of the phenomena that appear in the stream of consciousness, as known to date.
13. My intent here, in citing the range of literature that has recognized the phenomenon of the mind-films is to begin to show you that they are a universal phenomenon, a phenomenon that is present in all minds that have an ego. We will be discussing the mind-films at greater length in Chapter 6 and in several other places in *The Healthy Mind.*

that we are living our lives within these narratives that are created by our egos. As we will be seeing, the primary function of the mind-films is to create stories and realities that help us believe that the identities that our ego thinks we have are both real and sacred.

To my eye, one of the reasons that cinematic movies have become such a rich and prominent presence in modern life is that they mimic the movies of the mind and serve some of the same functions. Like the mind-films, cinematic films help us distract ourselves from what is really going on in our mind, and they empower us to pretend that we are someone different than the person we really are.

This is what is happening when kids come home from a movie and pretend that they are the heroes and villains that they have just seen on the screen. If you have an ego, and we all do, you are constantly pretending to be someone else, to be someone different than the self you really are. We all become, to one degree or another, the lead characters in the movies created by our ego instead of being ourselves. "All the world's a stage."

Mind-Films and the Moral Universe

When your ego projects its mind-films onto your experience of the world, those films create the moral universe in which you live, which is simply a transfer of the function they serve in the egocentric mind into your social world.

The mind-films are the medium in which the egocentric mind makes judgments of itself. A film might tell you that the chapter you are writing right now is brilliant. Or a film might criticize you and tell you that you are gaining weight and not getting enough exercise.

When the ego projects these films onto its social life, they become the medium in which you make judgments about other people; in particular, about people you see as being different than yourself.

A film might condemn someone else for being considerably more flamboyant than you are. Or a film might tell you over and again just how lovely that woman you met tonight was.

The reason that the egocentric mind judges itself, in the first place, is that these judgments are a crucial part of the dynamic by which it resolves the conflict between its identity and its true self. Bear with me for a moment while I explain.

In essence, the ego resolves this conflict between its identity and true self by eliminating those portions of its mind that do not match its identity. This is the eliminative dynamic of the egocentric mind.

The ego eliminates the non-identity portions of its mind by first dividing itself into two moral moieties—self and non-self—and then eliminating the non-self. It is indeed the very nature of the egocentric mind to partition itself into these two different selves.

The egocentric mind creates this division by sorting the meanings that appear in its stream of consciousness—its thoughts, feelings, emotions and so forth—into two moral categories: self and non-self, which are often thought of as simply "good" and "bad."[14]

The ego defines good and bad relative to its identity. It sees the thoughts, emotions and impulses that match its sense of identity and morality as being good, and it sees the thoughts and feelings that are at odds with its morality and identity as being bad.

This division is the foundation of the mechanism by which the egocentric mind controls its behavior and makes itself adhere to both its identity and, in one and the same motion, to the ethos and constraints of the society in which it lives.

The ego accepts, and thus allows itself to both know and express, those thoughts and emotions that it deems good, which are the thoughts and emotions that are congruent with its sense of identity.

On the other hand, the ego represses, and thus does not allow itself to know and express, those thoughts and emotions that it deems bad. It eliminates thoughts and emotions that it deems non-self because they are at odds with its identity.

This is a simple dynamic, but in its perpetuity, it is an endless and thankless labor that the gods would have been just as content to use as their punishment for Sisyphus.

This uncomplicated control dynamic is an observable process, and often we are aware of it as it unfolds. For example, we have all had the experience of fighting with ourselves to keep ourselves from expressing a hot emotion or a tendentious idea.

This omnipresent egocentric labor in which we divide our thoughts and emotions into two moral categories gives birth, in turn, to the mind-films that infuse our lives with a sense of moral combat. Here's how it happens.

The mind-films have many functions. One of them is to motivate, and provide a rationale for, the ego's eliminative dynamic. The films serve the function of convincing the ego that it should eliminate these thoughts, emotions and impulses that it sees as non-self.

The mind-films carry out this function by creating judgmental stories that help a person believe, among other things, that (1) they are a virtuous person when their actions and thoughts adhere to the moral categories created by their identity, and (2) they are a bad person when their actions and thoughts do not adhere to the moral categories created by their identity.

In other words, one of the things that our mind-films do is enact judgments on our own mind and behaviors. This is not, as we will be seeing, the only function of the mind-films, but this is definitely their role in the eliminative dynamic.

In this capacity, your ego might narrate a story that tells you that your family and friends will think you are self-destructive if you quit your prosperous corporate job to become a dirtbag mountain climber living out of a truck. Or it

14. Please see Chapters 8 and 9 for a systematic description of the ego's control dynamic.

might fabricate a film that tells you over and again that you will go to heaven if you kill infidels.

Once again, the ego creates these mind-films for the purpose of judging your mind and behavior relative to the moral categories fostered by your identity. Much of what the mind-films do in this capacity is criticize "bad" impulses and esteem "good" ones—both in your self and in others.

The designed effect of the critical mind-films is to discourage you from expressing thoughts and emotions that are contrary to your identity; and the effect of the positive mind-films is to encourage you to express thoughts and emotions that match your identity.

In essence, these films express and enforce the moral mandates of your identity. They do so by submerging you, if you will, in a moral universe—a universe that is created by the narratives of your mind–films, a universe that is an echo chamber that is constantly telling you what to do and what not to do. We all live, to varying degrees, in an ethical cosmos of our own creation, a universe that has been created by the narratives of our ego's mind-films.

To create this universe, it is necessary to have these films running incessantly, and indeed they do. They must run constantly because they have a never-ending task to complete. Their portion of the ego's Sisyphean burden is the perpetual work of keeping alive the illusion that you have the identity that you think you need to have.

The mind-films sustain this illusion by constantly enfolding all of your experiences into a narrative that matches your identity. It is a lot of work, and this is the reason why we all have a constant stream of thought noise running through the back of our mind.

In other words, the ego deploys these films to paint, for itself, a world that corroborates its conception of its identity. This is one of the primary functions of the mind-films. They construct a narrative world that confirms that you are the brilliant, loving, beautiful or worthless human being that your ego wants you to be.

In the process of constructing an identity-confirming world with its mind-films, the ego invariably projects the moral categories it uses to judge itself onto its experience of the world. This means that in addition to constructing a cosmos that enforces and confirms your conception of yourself, these same films also frame and enact your judgments of other people as well.

What all of this amounts to, simply enough, is that the ego and its mind-films have two spheres of operation: (1) one's own mind and (2) the larger world in which you live. The ego utilizes the same films to give contextual meaning to both realms of experience.

When you and your ego look inward, your films serve the purpose of both judging your mind and shaping you into being a person who has your identity. When the ego looks outward, its films serve the purpose of judging other people in the same light, and thereby framing your perceptions of them.

It is in the ego's projection of these films onto our experience of the world that we see the first hint of how these films create the moral cosmologies in which we live. They are not just the medium in which we judge ourselves.

When the ego projects its films onto the world, they become the frame of reference within which we judge other people too.

Given that the mind-films frame our judgments of both ourselves and others, they literally create for us the moral universe in which we live, a moral universe within which those judgments are framed relative to our own identity. People of one religion want nothing to do with people of a different religion. People of one ethnicity subjugate people of a different ethnicity and so forth.

Ultimately, this means that the cosmologies of good and evil that move us to reject and even eliminate people we regard as non-self, as different than our identity, are simply a projection of our ego's mind-films onto the larger canvas of life.

The egopoietic morality tales that we use to fabricate judgements of ourselves are also the fabric from which we stitch together the judgments that encourage us to dislike, be intolerant of and even eliminate people that we see as being different than ourself: people of other ethnicities, religions, communities and nation-states. Just as our mind-films move us to judge and eliminate the non-self in our own selves, they move us to eliminate the non-self in our sociopolitical sphere as well.

First we divide ourselves into two moral moieties so that we can repress and eliminate from our mind the thoughts and emotions what we deem non-self, and then we divide the world and the people in it along the same lines. This is the eliminative dynamic of the egocentric mind, and as we will be seeing, the egocentric mind brings this same dynamic to its interactions with people.

In the course of mapping out the dynamics of the egocentric mind, the science of the stream of consciousness has realized that social groups composed of egocentric people with a shared group identity behave just like the ego of the individual mind.

The individual egocentric mind and the egocentric group both seek out and create conflict with entities that it regards as non-self—in one case with non-self thoughts and emotions, and in the second case with non-self people. Furthermore, they both use exactly the same tactics to resolve the identity based conflicts that this dynamic creates.

Once again, one tactic they share in common is the elimination of non-self. In addition, they both create narrative realities for the purpose of instigating and justifying their eliminative behavior.

The egocentric mind eliminates thoughts, feelings and emotions that are non-self. Egocentric groups seek to disempower and remove non-self human beings from their social sphere. Sometimes, they even seek to eliminate them, period.

Apartheid, slavery, terrorism, war and genocide are close to hand examples of the eliminative tactics that are employed by social, religious and political groups.

In other words, the sociopolitical conflicts engendered by the eliminative dynamic have precisely the same structure and dynamic as the egocentric mind's structural conflict with itself. These two realms of conflict have homologous structures and dynamics, just as a human arm and a whale fin have homologous bone structures.

These homologies suggest, once again, that our sociopolitical conflicts are simply replications of the conflict that the egocentric mind has with itself.

In other words, just as the DNA molecule is the template that guides the synthesis of proteins, the egocentric mind is a template that guides the fabrication of sociopolitical conflict. The intermediary template that guides the synthesis of sociopolitical conflict is the ego's mind-films, just as the messenger RNA molecule mediates the synthesis of a protein. *The Healthy Mind* will explore these homologies and the ego's role in creating them at greater length in its final chapter.

Mind-Films Become Culture

The hypothesis that is being presented in this chapter is that humanity's sociopolitical conflicts are replications of the conflicts of the individual egocentric mind. This hypothesis proposes that the ego replicates its inner identity-based conflicts by transferring them to its relationships with other people. This transference is initiated by a process in which an individual person's judgmental mind-films become shared moral culture.

There are excellent anthropological studies of premodern societies that support this theory. These studies describe the visible processes by which a society transforms individual mind-films into cultural myth, and in so doing they establish that there actually are societies that create cosmology by transforming mind-films into shared myth. Unlike our own societies, the bare bones of this transformational process are naked and more visible to the eye in these premodern societies.

Take the Tukano, for example, who are a tribal people that live on the floor of the Amazonian jungle along the Vaupés River and its tributaries in Colombia and Brazil. They are hunter-gatherers and horticulturalists living traditional lives in longhouses built on stilts, and we know about them from the writings of the very able Austrian-Colombian anthropologist Reichel-Dolmatoff (Reichel-Dolmatoff, 1975).

Every seven to ten days or so, the men in a Tukano community will spend an entire night up doing a ritual that Reichel-Dolmatoff calls the Yaje Ceremony. They drink an hallucinogenic tea that they make from a vine called Yaje, and then they interpret their hallucinations together. When a hallucination comes to one man, he will stand up and describe it out loud as it is happening, and instead of going to a psychiatrist, everyone will gather around—including the women—and try to divine what the hallucination means.

In general, the Tukano decipher their hallucinations by interpreting them in the context of myths that they already have: "That is the god of the hunt coming down to tell you to be braver when you go hunting." "That is the goddess of creation coming down from the sky in her chariot to tell us that we have gone astray, and that we must move back across the river and return to the traditional way of life that our ancestors lived."

These hallucinations are mind-films that have been made visible by the Yaje. They are stream-of-consciousness narratives that have become visible as hallucinations because of the biological effects of the alkaloids of the Yaje vine.

Sometimes, the Tukano will incorporate a particular hallucination into their mythology, and they do so in ways that are remarkably concrete. The Tukano paint scenes from their hallucinogenic narratives onto the walls of the longhouses in which they live. Or they might paint symbols or scenes from a hallucination onto their cooking utensils. Or they might tell the story of their hallucinations to one another over and over again. In this way, their mind-films become part of the cosmology in which they live their daily lives. The Tukano literally live in the midst of myths that are representations of their individual mind-films.

In this vivid and visible transformation of hallucinations into mythology, we see the actual workings of the process by which individual mind-films are transformed into a society's mythology. We see this same transformative process in the rituals of many other societies as well, including, for example, the vision quest of the Plains Indians, the peyote hunt of the Huichol—and perhaps on cable television too, as we watch our political pundits scramble to extend their ideologies to the events of the day.

As we proceed further with our investigation of the dynamics of the egocentric mind we will find that this is a universal process; that the ego's mind-films play a central role in generating the belief systems that form the moral context in which we make judgments of not only ourselves, but of everyone else as well. Once these films become shared belief systems, they can, in turn, cause an egocentric society to replicate the eliminative behavior of the individual egocentric mind.

Social Control

It is worth remembering for a moment that the ego's eliminative dynamic, and the mind-films that propel and endorse it, all happen in the name of social control. The ego is a social institution that is embedded within the individual mind. It fabricates an identity; divides the mind in two in the name of that identity; and it creates mind-films all for the purpose of exercising social control over a person's mind and behavior.

Ultimately, this tells us how and why we have created the moral cosmologies in which we live. We human beings did not create our identities and cleave our minds and universe into two moral halves so that religions could be raised upon the foundation of the mystery of duality. Nor did we divide ourselves in two so that philosophers could ponder for centuries the origins and nature of duality. Nor did we splice the mind in half so that psychoanalysts could spend years trying to stitch it back together by analyzing the transference that embodies and enshrines this duality.

The findings of the science of the stream of consciousness show that we human beings have created identities and divided the contents of our minds into two morally opposed entities for the more down-to-earth purpose of simply controlling and socializing ourselves. The moral duality of the egocentric mind, and the mind-films that are the handmaidens of that duality, are simply two elements of a larger psychological system that the ego has developed, over probably countless millennia, to control humanity's behavior.

When the mind-films are projected onto our experience of the world, they become the stories of duality and moral combat that take us to war. These conflict-engendering narratives are created by the ego. Once again, they are simply one of the components in the repertoire of psychological processes that the ego employs to govern and socialize the individual mind.

The moral narratives created by both the individual and collective egos of a society bind a people together into a collective identity, but in doing so, they also draw us into wars and an endemic intolerance of people who are different than ourselves.

We could have responded differently to the events of 9/11, but we allowed the narratives of our national ego to well up into a non-negotiable demand that as a nation we had to take revenge and find justice by taking recourse to war. It was a reenactment of both the revenge that Captain Ahab sought to take on Moby Dick, and the revenge that Hamlet had hesitated to take. In the wake of 9/11, however, our thirst for revenge went virtually unquestioned.

The Egoless Mind

Despite the fact that the duality created by the ego is deeply problematic and almost certainly plays a role in taking us to war, duality is also an important and fascinating phenomenon. Theologians, philosophers and psychologists have long pondered the many different species of duality: ontological duality, metaphysical duality, epistemological duality, moral duality, experiential duality and, perhaps most of all, the structural duality of the human mind.

This polyphony of dualities yearns to be understood and resolved. When one engages in the process of trying to understand this cascade of dualities, one intriguing question will invariably arise: What is the primordial duality of the human mind? Is there one particular duality that gives birth to all of the other dualities; and, in particular, to the structural conflict that sits at the center of the human psyche?

Different bodies of thought have, of course, posited different primordial dualities. For many religions, including our own Judeo-Christian tradition, the primordial duality of life is the duality between good and evil. In psychoanalytic theory the primordial duality is a conflict between a person's biological impulses and the rational constraints of society.

Buddhism sees the duality of the mind as being a fictitious duality between our conceptions of our self, which it sees as an illusion, and everything else. For Descartes, there was, of course, the duality of mind and matter. For many contemporary scientists and philosophers, finding the mechanism by which the material brain produces consciousness is a holy grail and so forth.

The promise of this quest for the primordial duality is this: if one could just locate the primordial human duality, we could perhaps nip all duality in the bud and eliminate the internal and interpersonal conflict it engenders.

This is a tantalizing prospect, and it is a quest that seems, especially to the young intellect, to be a pursuit that has the potential to make the world a better place. Certainly, the elimination of duality would be a more refined means of resolving conflict than the ego's solution of having one half of the mind conquer the other half of the mind.

However, upon further inspection, it turns out that thinking about duality sustains duality. The more you analyze duality, the more you fortify its place within your mind. It is ultimately a fruitless endeavor.

At first glance, this might seem to be an unjust rent in the fabric of the universe. How could it possibly be that the well-intended intellectual search for the origin of duality nourishes duality and conflict?

Actually, though, it is not an injustice. It is simply one of the lessons along the way to learning that there is a non-conceptual, or non-intellectual, means of both preventing and transcending the dualities and conflicts created by the ego.

Indeed, the findings of the science of the stream of consciousness make it clear that the only really healthy and effective means of resolving the abiding conflicts of the egocentric mind is to prevent them from coming to life in the first place.

One prevents the birth of duality and conflict within the mind by cultivating a state of mind in which the mind has nondual awareness of itself, to be more precise, by cultivating the mind's ability to have nondual awareness of its own stream of consciousness.

The egoless mind has consistent nondual awareness of itself. This is crucial. As we will be seeing in Chapters 8 and 9, the egocentric mind creates perpetual conflict within itself by having dual awareness of the thoughts and emotions that appear in its stream of consciousness.

In contrast, the egoless mind has nondual awareness of its thoughts and emotions, and as a result, the potential for conflict dissolves and disappears in every moment. This is epistemological nonduality, and it is one of the defining qualities of the egoless mind.

The egoless mind is nondual in other respects as well. For one, if you don't have an ego, then there is only one of you: your true self.

Another sense in which the egoless mind is nondual is that it is a mind that forgoes the folly of dividing itself into two moral entities. It abstains from the egocentric enterprise of dividing its thoughts, emotions and feelings into different moral categories.

The egoless mind has no need to morally cleave itself in two because it does not take up the ego's interminable labor of trying to maintain an identity that is different than its true self. Once again, it resolves duality by not creating it in the first place.

Given that it has no permanent identity to maintain, the egoless mind does not engage in the ego's ploy of divide and conquer. It does not divide the mind in two moral halves and eliminate the "bad" half. Ultimately, this means that the egoless mind is able to abstain from creating the internal conflicts that plague the egocentric mind and take us to war and many other dark places as well.

Which brings us back to the president and 9/11. If we had all been brought up in a world in which we were taught to be egoless, 9/11 would never have happened in the first place. Without egos, human beings would not feel the need to destroy people who are different than themselves, just as the egoless mind does not feel the need to repress, or destroy, thoughts and emotions that are different than its identity.

But given that we are all raised to have egos, there is a sense in which the president was not to blame for his administration's bellicose response to the attacks of 9/11. The dynamic that took us to war was much larger than the president. The president, his aides and the American public, like all of the rest of humanity, were brought up to have egos, and as a result, they all possessed conflicted minds that seek out strife and war—just as the terrorists of 9/11 did.

We seek out war and the superiority of racism, sexism and religious intolerance because we live in egocentric societies in which we are all taught to wear and live behind the mask, the persona, that we call the ego. The world really is a stage upon which we are all acting because we live in societies that have accepted the implicit, unexamined and incorrect position that the egocentric mind is a healthy mind.

As *The Healthy Mind* will make clear, embracing the institution of the ego has been and continues to be a profound mistake. The egocentric mind creates a whole host of humanity's most divisive and enduring problems. Duality and conflict engendering narratives are but two of them.

In all fairness, it should also be said that the institution of the ego definitely has its virtues. As human beings living in society, we certainly need to have a means of controlling our behavior so as to ensure that we will be good to one another; but as *The Healthy Mind* will make evident, there is a far healthier way to go about it than putting the monkey of the ego upon our backs.

In some respects the institution of the ego has served us well, but the monkey has also taken a toll. It takes this beautiful phenomenon—our stream of consciousness—and fetters it in the name of creating an identity and maintaining social control. In doing this simple thing, it has endowed *Homo sapiens* with a vast spectrum of endemic dysfunction and pathology. We have taken the stream of consciousness—the fount of our conscious creativity—and we have chained and debased it for the more trivial purpose of controlling our behavior.

It is an understandable mistake. Somewhere along our evolutionary path we evidently decided that we would have to control our minds to live together peacefully with one another in community. It must have seemed to early humanity that controlling the thoughts and emotions that appear in the stream of consciousness was a reasonable approach to cultivating self-control. After all, this approach does have its tangible successes, as we can see in a moment in which we successfully repress the emotion of anger.

But as we are about to see, it turns out that we made a mistake when we decided to control our minds by taking on identities and controlling the ebb and flow of the stream of consciousness—by damming and polluting the stream of consciousness, if you will.

To be sure, if creating an identity and constraining the stream of consciousness were the only means that we have at hand to make ourselves behave with some semblance of goodness, if this were the only means available to cultivate lives in which we live in harmony with one another in society, then so be it. It would have to be acceptable.

But as the science of the stream of consciousness that is being presented in *The Healthy Mind* will make abundantly clear, there is a second and far healthier way to go about cultivating the goodness that we need to live together in genuine harmony with both our own mind and with one another.

If the basic strategy of the egocentric mind is to inculcate decency between people by controlling our thoughts and emotions, the egoless mind takes a fundamentally different approach to ensuring that we treat one another well. The egoless mind controls itself by not controlling itself! It leaves the thoughts and feelings and everything else that appears in its stream of consciousness in their natural and thus unaltered state. It allows the stream of consciousness to run its natural course, and herein lies the crux of the matter.

By allowing its stream of consciousness to run free, the egoless mind creates within itself a palpable reservoir of goodness. When the mind abstains from being an ego and lets its stream of consciousness run free, a tangible sense of goodness will arise spontaneously within the mind. If you persist in letting their stream of consciousness run free, that goodness will grow stronger and become a stable presence within the mind. You will actually be able to feel it.

This is, it turns out, a basic law of nature. It carries the same empirical weight as saying that DNA molecules convey genetic information from one generation of organism to the next. Or that all matter is composed of atoms. If you leave your stream of consciousness in its natural state, it will create a reservoir within your mind and fill that reservoir with goodness and joy.

This is what meditation and mindfulness are ultimately all about. Meditation, if pursued for the sake of cultivating an egoless mind, generates a totally open state of mind in which you allow your stream of consciousness to run free and remain in its natural state; and by doing so you will allow your mind to generate a deep well of goodness within itself, and to realize your true self moment in and moment out, day in and day out.

When that sense of goodness comes to abide within your mind, it becomes both the ground of, and the context for, everything you think, say and do. Indeed, goodness permeates the egoless mind, and this is literally the means by which it controls itself. The egoless mind controls itself by instilling within itself a goodness of intention that gives a person an almost preternatural ability to treat other people and themselves well.

This is one of the most fundamental discoveries of the science of the stream of consciousness, and if all goes well, it will become a finding with which we will all become more familiar.

All of which is to say is that we have, as a species, made a simple mistake. We have chosen for ourselves a means of self-control and socialization that is unhealthy. We have chosen to use a mechanism of social control that has turned us into a conflicted species of unabating battles and constant sorrows, and we have done so even though a healthier means of self-control was and continues to be available to us.

Fortunately, this is a mistake upon which we can now build. In fact, it may have even been a necessary mistake. It turns out that one of the countless paradoxes of the egoless mind is that the egoless mind has an ego.

This, then, is an introductory sketch of what *The Healthy Mind* is all about. It is going to take us on a scientific journey to Nepal, Bhutan, Ladakh and India in which we will experientially and empirically investigate the nature of the healthy human mind. Is the healthy mind the egocentric mind? Or is it the egoless mind?

Our point of departure for this scientific journey will be right here: if you want to empirically understand the nature of the healthy mind, it is necessary to first understand the stream of consciousness. There is no other way to go. The causes of both the healthy and unhealthy mind are to be found in the stream of consciousness, just as the cause, and perhaps the cure, of cancer is to be found in the mutations that occur in the DNA of the cancerous cell.

References

Augustine. (2013). *Confessions: St Augustine*, trans. Fr Benignus O'Rourke O.S.A. London: DLT Books.

Erikson, E.H. (1980). *Identity and the Life Cycle*. New York, NY: W. W. Norton and Company.

Freud, S. (1960). *The Ego and the Id*. New York, NY: W. W. Norton.

Freud, S. (2010). *Civilization and Its Discontents*. New York, NY: W. W. Norton and Company.

Hegel, G. W. (1977). *Phenomenology of Spirit*, trans. A. V. Miller. Oxford: Clarendon Press.

Kernberg, O. F. (1975). *Borderline Conditions and Pathological Narcissism*. New York, NY: Aronson.

Matsch, F. (1892). *Triumphant Achilles*. Achilleion, Corfu, Greece.

Plato. (1995). *Phaedrus*, trans. A. Nehamus and P. Woodruff. Indianapolis, IN: Hackett Publishing Company.

Reichel-Dolmatoff, G. (1975). *The Shaman and the Jaguar: A Study of Narcotic Drugs Among the Indians of Colombia*. Philadelphia, PA: Temple University Press.

Smallwood, J., and Schooler, J. (2006). The restless mind. *Psychological Bulletin*, 132(6), 946–958.

Vyner, H.M. (2007–2008). The dialectical phenomena and processes of the mind. *Imagination, Cognition and Personality*, 27(2), 163–196.

Vyner, H. M. (2009–2010). A preliminary theory of the defining dynamic of the healthy human mind. *Imagination, Cognition and Personality*, 29(3), 225–270.

2

THE HEALTHY MIND ASSUMPTION

If you were so unlucky as to need a surgery in the middle of the nineteenth century in Europe, you had almost a fifty percent chance of dying. Fifty percent. For example, the mortality rate after amputations at the Glasgow Royal Infirmary from 1864 to 1866, when Joseph Lister first began to do surgery there, was forty-five percent. It was fifty percent in Edinburgh hospitals, and thirty-eight percent at the best hospitals in Paris (Ashhurst, 1889).

The problem was that medicine had not yet discovered that the little animals that we now call bacteria cause disease. It was thus routine, even at the best of hospitals, for a surgeon to leave his dissecting laboratory and come do surgery on a patient in blood-stained clothing without even washing his hands.

This all changed when Joseph Lister read Pasteur's work. Lister immediately understood the implications of Pasteur's microbiology for the practice of surgery, and he initiated the practice of operating under antiseptic conditions. At his instigation, his surgical ward at the Glasgow Royal Infirmary began to use carbolic acid to cleanse their instruments, wash their hands, cleanse a patient's wound or incision, and cleanse the wards in which the patients stayed. Three years later, the mortality rate on Lister's surgical ward had fallen to fifteen percent (Lister, 1870).

This is not, of course, an isolated example. It is in the nature of scientific progress that sometimes science, a society, or even our entire species, through no fault of our own, have taken part in practices or have held beliefs, sometimes beliefs of great consequence, that were wrong; wrong in the sense that they were empirically incorrect. Before the advent of science, and of course sometimes even now, we cobble together whatever ideas we get our hands on to make sense—as best we can—of the mysteries of the universes within and without.

We created a flat earth; an earth in the center of the universe; gods that controlled the weather, the sun, the moon, our destinies, our minds; demons and devils that tormented our minds; the pseudo-scientific theories of phlogiston and the aether; and somewhere along the way we adopted the theory, at least in practice, that the egocentric mind is a healthy mind.

We didn't necessarily make up these theories because we were stupid or dishonest. We needed to understand our universe and our mind, and these ideas seemed to work at the time that we first put them together. We created these theories to help us make sense of our world and our lives.

With the advent of science, our criteria for truth changed. Over the centuries, science has picked off and discarded, one by one, the elements of our beliefs that were not empirically correct. *The Healthy Mind* is going to take a look at yet another anachronism: the implicit, unexamined and incorrect assumption that the egocentric mind that we are all brought up to have is a healthy mind. *The Healthy Mind* is going to examine this long held belief in the light of a new body of scientific evidence that establishes that it is incorrect.

In other words, we are living in the midst of yet another self-imposed blind spot in which we have, as a species, long misunderstood the nature of the healthy mind. Just as surgeons did not appreciate that there were invisible little animals that cause disease until the second half of the nineteenth century, science, and thus our species, has not yet recognized that the ego is a pathogen too. As a result, generation upon generation of children have been unwittingly and unintentionally brought up to have fundamentally unhealthy minds.

In addition, there is the further possibility that egocentric mind is the psychological foundation of several of humanity's most pervasive and intractable problems. What if science were to establish that the ego is the cause of the moods, inner conflict and inauthenticity that make many a human life uneasy and unhappy? Or that the ego is the seed from which much mental illness grows? Or that the ego is the psychological foundation of organized warfare, religious intolerance, racism and the caustic belief that there is only one truth and one good way of life?

If science were to unequivocally establish that the egocentric mind that we have all been brought up to have is actually an unhealthy mind, what would we do about it? Would we not, like Lister, take matters in hand and find a way to stop propagating the egocentric mind from one generation to the next? Would we not also set out to find out whether or not there is another type of mind that is a healthier mind?

Of course we would, and that is what *The Healthy Mind* is all about. This book is going to take up one fundamental question: what is the nature of the healthy human mind?

The Healthy Mind is going to address and answer this question by marshaling the findings of a new field of scientific inquiry—the science of the phenomena that appear in the stream of consciousness. We will employ the findings of this field to map out the egoless and egocentric states of mind, and to evaluate which state of mind is healthier.

In sum, *The Healthy Mind* will present a body of data that establishes that (1) the egoless mind is a healthy mind that is genuinely happy because it allows a person to realize and become their true self, and that in contrast (2) the egocentric mind is a profoundly unhealthy mind.

In essence, we will see that the egocentric mind is an unhappy and unhealthy mind because (1) it keeps a person from being their true self and (2) it creates a spectrum of psychopathology that is inherent to, and universally present in, the egocentric mind.

Finally, *The Healthy Mind* will also describe the rudiments of cultivating an egoless mind, and conclude with a contemplation of the future of the egoless mind.

Happiness, the True Self and Original Sin

Genuine happiness is much closer to home, and much simpler than we allow ourselves to think it is. The greatest joy and goodness in life come from simple act of just being your true self, the person you really are, as opposed to being an ego. "To thine own self be true" (Shakespeare). "Know thyself" (Socrates).

Being your true self brings, of course, the satisfaction of integrity, but the process of being yourself also brings unencumbered happiness. To be your true self generates a happiness that is deeper and far more resilient than the transient joys of sensual pleasure, fortune and fame. To live a life of self-realization is to create within yourself a happiness that is bone deep.

If you have been raised in an egocentric society and as a result have an ego, as we all do, you become your true self by letting go of your ego. This might sound more difficult than climbing and traversing the west ridge of Mount Everest, as Hornbein and Unsoeld did in 1963; but it is almost as easy as simply ceasing to believe the judgments, stories, emotions and moods created by your ego. First you learn to identify these elements of your ego, then you let you let go of your belief in them in meditation, and then you transfer these skills to the day-to-day course of your life.

The principal virtue, although not the only one, of just simply ceasing to believe in your ego's judgments, stories, emotions and moods is that as you let them go, they will spontaneously transform themselves into egoless mind on their own.

Here, for now, is a sketch of how those transformations happen: as you let the stories and emotions of your ego go, you will have nondual awareness of them and they will dissolve. As we began to see in Chapter 1, when thoughts and emotions dissolve in the light of nondual awareness, they are spontaneously transformed into moments of goodness, joy and self-realization (Vyner, 2009–2010). And as these transformations continue to occur, reservoirs of goodness and joy will build up within you.

These feelings of joy and goodness are, in and of themselves, happiness. They feel good. At the same time, they also unite with your awareness. As they unite with your awareness, they become the egoless awareness that makes it possible for a person to know and be their true self in every moment. In other words, both self-realization and happiness are simultaneously generated by the process of letting go of your ego. Self-realization and happiness go hand in hand in the egoless mind.

The feeling of goodness has a delightfully surprising quality to it, even though you will be constantly aware of it once it has established itself in your mind. It is surprising in the sense that you will find yourself being good to people without even trying to be good, or thinking about it. This goodness expresses itself in words and deeds that you did not know were in you. They will just pop out of you naturally.

Perhaps the most gratifying thing of all about this sense of goodness is that is leaves you feeling that you want other people to become happy and realize their true selves just as much as you want it for yourself. To become one's self is to take genuine delight in, and even yearn for, everyone else's self-realization as well. Indeed, it is impossible to become your true self unless you genuinely want the same for everyone else.

Nonetheless, the bulk of humanity is brought up to abandon their true self and become the ego that our well-meaning but misguided families bestow upon us. We have been giving ourselves egos for countless centuries, and we do it because this is the way we socialize ourselves.

In the course of institutionalizing the ego, we have also stigmatized the act of becoming our true selves. It is our Original Sin, if you will. After all, Adam and Eve's Original Sin was that they ate an apple from the tree of self-knowledge. In this impulse to give ourselves egos, we have meant well, but it has also been a tragic mistake that has shaped the course of human history much for the worse.

The De Facto Healthy Mind

As matters stand now, the egocentric mind is the de facto healthy mind of our species.

It seems that all human societies insert both an identity, and an ego that preserves that identity, into the minds of their young. In a traditional society, that identity might be a specific kinship role in a clan, or your tribe's notion of womanhood or manhood.

In our own day, an identity might be your profession, your nation-state, your political ideology or the subculture to which you fancy yourself to belong. Or it might be a more individualistic identity that you have fashioned for yourself.

We don't know when human beings first began to teach themselves to have egos, but in our present day, having an identity and an ego is simply the nature of life in human society. To the best of our knowledge, all societies are egocentric societies—societies that are organized around the propagation of the egocentric mind. We have yet to receive any anthropological reports of the existence of any egoless societies.

It is also true that our individual ego and identity are not the only ones we acquire. If you live in an egocentric society, you are also brought up to have a group ego in addition to your individual ego. There are national egos, religious egos and ethnic egos. There are also ideological egos—one might identify as a communist or a conservative, and of course there are more than a few of us who identify with athletic teams, or an alternative way of life.

Given that egocentric societies transmit egos from one generation to the next, the ego is a social institution. If an egocentric society is functioning as it should, generation after generation of boys grow up to become like their fathers, just as young girls become like their mothers.

The ego is a social institution because it is the means by which a society accomplishes two tasks that are crucial to the survival of any society: (1) the ego is the means by which we create a sense of direction and ambition in our lives and (2) it is also the means by which a society controls the behavior of its people. In both of these respects, the ego is a fundamentally moral institution. It is the means by which we teach ourselves to know and keep our place in society.

To those of us who have an ego, and again that would be just about all of us, it seems utterly necessary to have one. For one, we believe that the ego is the means by which we create greatness, and indeed it is the instrument that an egocentric society uses to create the accomplished athletes, scientists, artists and statesmen that are its heroes and heroines.

The rest of us believe that we need to have an ego because it is the means by which we give direction to our more ordinary lives. I cannot tell you how many times people have told me that they need to have an ego because they feel that they would not have the drive to get up, get out of bed and go to work in the morning if they did not have one.

It is true, to be sure, that an ego can move a person to accomplish both the little and great things of life, but as we will be seeing, the science of the healthy mind makes it clear that there are far healthier ways to move an individual to accomplish their goals and make manifest their destiny.

Nonetheless, we acquiesce to this Faustian bargain in which we barter away our true selves in exchange for an ego because we think we need to have an ego. We accept our egos even though we sense that having one can make us foolish, throw us into conflict with both ourselves and others, and constrain us to a life in which we sacrifice our destiny and happiness. Indeed, the institution of the ego is the reason that there are so many people among us who do not know who they are, or what they really want to do with their lives.

Despite the fact that we can intuit that there is something amiss with this institution of the ego, we have never sat down together, as either individuals or a society, to evaluate whether or not the egocentric mind is a healthy mind. Our scientists have not yet systematically taken up the question of determining the nature of the healthy mind. Neither have our philosophers, theologians or psychiatrists. We live in a world in which we have simply long assumed that the mind with an ego is a wholesome and healthy mind.

On the other hand, no one has ever explicitly declared that the mind with an ego is a healthy mind. Henry V did not stand at the gates of Agincourt and exhort his troops to take up arms by declaring the virtues of the ego. Nor do our parents or our schools teach us that the egocentric mind is a healthy mind. We are all just simply brought up to have an ego.

In other words, the egocentric mind is both our de facto and unexamined notion of the healthy mind. It is our de facto notion of the healthy mind in the sense that this is simply the way we do things. We all live in societies in which we are taught to carry on our lives with the mask of an ego fixed firmly upon our faces.

Given that we have, for millennia, propagated the ego from one generation to the next, it looks as though we have implicitly assumed that the egocentric mind is an acceptable and healthy mind. In acting on this assumption we have unintentionally transmitted a powerful pathogen from one generation to the next without having ever considered whether or not it is a healthy thing to do.

The Healthy Mind is going to take up this issue and present a body of data that empirically assesses whether or not the egocentric mind is a healthy mind. To make this assessment, we will describe (1) the defining dynamic of the egocentric mind, (2) the state of mind created by that dynamic, and in particular (3) the normal pathologies of the ego—a group of pathologies that are indigenous to, and appear to be present in, every mind that has an ego.

The Healthy Mind will not, however, be content to confine itself to empirically chronicling the shortcomings of the egocentric state of mind. It will also describe the workings of the egoless mind and the healthy state of mind to which they give birth.

The Healthy Mind Research

For the last twenty-seven years now, I have been interviewing Tibetan lamas who live in south Asia, away from the celebrity of being a lama in Europe or America, in depth about their experiences of their own mind in meditation for the purpose of (Vyner, 2003, 2004a, 2004b, 2005, 2007, 2007–2008, 2009–2010, 2018):

1. Developing a basic science of the phenomena that appear in the stream of consciousness.
2. Deriving from that science an empirically valid theory of the nature of the healthy human mind.

To do this work, I have traveled to, and lived in, villages and monasteries all over Nepal, Bhutan, Ladakh, Sikkim and India. Often these villages and monasteries have been so remote that trekking was the only way to get to them. Before my most recent return to America, I trekked eight days to get to a sixteenth-century village in north central Nepal to do a month of interviews with a lama living at the foot of Mount Manaslu (26,781 feet).

In the course of doing these interviews it has often been necessary to live in traditional and thus premodern conditions. I have lived in unheated stone houses without windows in which the only light was the orange glow coming from a fire in the hearth; in houses in which there was no indoor plumbing; in homes in which livestock lived in and roamed through the house; in houses in which cooking was done over an open fire indoors, and in which we ate the same staple foods two or three meals a day—day after day.

This way of life might sound difficult and perhaps even distasteful to the modern ear. Nonetheless, it is an understatement to say that as a rule, the people with whom I have been fortunate enough to share this way of life were more often than not happy people whose sense of self was bone deep. I myself much enjoyed sharing this way of life with them, although I found it prudent to be careful about hygiene.

It has also been a joy and privilege to live amongst people who goodheartedly and unquestioningly live in their religious beliefs as though it were a thousand years ago. It has also been inspiring to have the feelings that living amongst 25,000-foot mountains can awaken within you. Most of all, I have enjoyed giving medical care to villages and monasteries that are days and weeks by foot away from the nearest clinic.

Sometimes I interview a lama for an hour or two at a time. On some occasions, interviews have lasted a whole sprawling day. Sometimes I would do one interview with a lama, and then a year or more might pass before it was possible to come back and do a second interview with that same lama. At other times, I have done ten and more interviews with a lama over the course of a single month. It would all depend.

I have interviewed lamas in opulent sun-filled rooms in well-to-do flatland monasteries, and in unbelievably primitive mountain monasteries as well. I once interviewed a revered and famous lama for weeks on end in the simple hut in which he lived an unadorned and uncelebrated life on the margins of his mountain monastery; and as we talked, wild rhesus monkeys with huge incisors would often come to his open window and eat food right out of his hands. (Perhaps this is where the Buddhist metaphor for taming the monkey mind originated!)

I once interviewed another lama every single day for a month in the midday sun in the small adobe courtyard of his rude mountain dwelling because at 12,000 feet in December it was the only warm and well-lit place we could find to work together.

This work that the lamas and I have been doing together has been generating both a science of the healthy mind and a science of the phenomena that appear in the stream of consciousness. The theory of the healthy mind that this work has generated has been derived from the lama's observations of the phenomena that appear in the stream of consciousness.

I believe that with the passage of time both of these sciences will bring about a change in the way that both science and laypeople see the healthy mind. The empirical study of the stream of consciousness makes it altogether clear that the egocentric mind is a mind that imposes upon a human being an ongoing sense of unnecessary unhappiness, conflict and inauthenticity.

Secondly, our findings will also establish that the egoless mind is, in contrast, a healthier mind, given the paradox that you have to have an ego to become egoless. For instance, our findings show that the egoless mind is a mind that both forgoes conflict and lives in an authenticity born of joy and goodness (Vyner, 2009–2010).

I chose to interview Tibetan lamas for this research on the healthy mind for two pivotal reasons. For one, many Buddhist scholar-meditators are accomplished scientists of both the egoless mind and the stream of consciousness. These sciences are a long-standing part of their religious tradition.

Second, as advanced practitioners of Buddhism, the central purpose of a lama's life is to cultivate what they see as the wisdom, goodness and compassion of the egoless mind. The cultivation of the egoless mind has been one of the central concerns of the Buddhist tradition ever since its inception, and as a result, Buddhist monks often know quite a lot about the egoless mind.

This means that the lamas are a living cultural experiment, if you will, that explores whether or not the egoless mind is a healthy mind. Interviewing the lamas is not quite as scientifically elegant as it would be to study an experimental group of people living on another planet where everyone is raised to be egoless and then comparing them to a control group from an egocentric planet; but interviewing the lamas is a very good second best.

As the entirety of this book is about to make clear, the science of the healthy mind and the stream of consciousness that the lamas and I have been putting together bears a distinct relationship to the ancient proto-science of the stream of consciousness that has long lain at the heart of the Buddhist religion.

The modern science of the stream of consciousness that we have been developing together evaluates the findings of this traditional Buddhist mind science, and it does so by using the methods of modern science to empiricize, replicate and expand upon that traditional science.

However, we should take a moment to notice that this science is not a Buddhist science per se. Its findings and theory are the findings of a science—the science of the stream of consciousness. The observations that are the foundation of this science have been recorded from a group of men who have had extensive experience observing both the phenomena that appear in the stream of consciousness and the egoless state of mind. They just happen to be Buddhist monks. They are probably the most sophisticated observers of the stream of consciousness and the egoless mind alive, and that is why they were chosen to be participants in this study. Christian, Hindu, Moslem, Jewish and atheist observers of the stream of consciousness would certainly see, if they looked, much the same repertoire of phenomena and causal sequences as the lamas interviewed for this study have seen.

The Healthy Mind and the Science of the Stream of Consciousness

The science of the stream of consciousness is indispensable to the empirical study of the healthy mind; if one wants to empirically understand the nature of the healthy mind, it is imperative that you study the stream of consciousness (Vyner, 2009–2010). This is the same as saying that if you want to decipher and comprehend nature's genetic code, you have to study DNA and RNA molecules.

The investigation of the stream of consciousness is requisite to the scientific exploration of the healthy mind for one very straightforward reason: the phenomena that determine whether or not a given mind is healthy or unhealthy are phenomena that appear in the stream of consciousness, and only in the stream of consciousness. The phenomena that make the egocentric mind an unhealthy mind appear in the stream of consciousness, as do the phenomena that make the egoless mind a healthy mind.

Our work has shown that the principal determinant of whether or not a given mind is healthy is its mode of self-awareness—the way in which it knows the phenomena that appear in its stream of consciousness. The egoless and egocentric minds employ two very different modes of self-awareness to know and control their streams of consciousness. One of those modes of self-awareness produces a healthy state of mind, and the other does not.

To review what we already know about the egocentric mode of self-awareness, the egocentric mind controls itself by literally governing the contents of its stream of consciousness. For example, the egocentric mind might employ the act of repression to eliminate a thought or emotion from its stream of consciousness. The repression of a moment of anger to keep yourself from being either aware of or expressing that anger is an example of an action taken by the egocentric mode of self-awareness. The egoless mind does not repress emotions and thoughts.

You might say, well it is a good thing to repress and abstain from expressing anger, and there is of course an element of truth to this assertion. The point that we will be making though, is that there is a healthier way to deal with anger and all of the other emotions.

A second means by which the ego controls the contents of the stream of consciousness is that it narrates mind-films and inserts them into the stream of consciousness. These films are recurring cycles of thoughts. A mind-film might be a narrative in which you tell yourself—over and over again—that the people in your life think you are lovable, or brave, or ridiculous. Or that someone else is wonderful or intolerable.

The egoless mind, in contrast, controls itself in a profoundly different way. It governs itself by not controlling itself. The egoless mind does not manipulate the contents of its stream of consciousness in any fashion at all. It allows its stream of consciousness to run free and remain in its natural state. It controls itself by not controlling itself.

This must surely, at first glance, seem to be at the very least counterintuitive. How can the mind possibly control itself by abandoning self-control? The first answer is that this is simply one of the many interesting and gratifying paradoxes of the egoless mind.

As we have already begun to see, one of the fundamental findings of the science of the stream of consciousness is that the simple act of allowing your stream of consciousness to run free and remain in its natural state will invariably cause a reservoir of goodness and joy to build up within your mind and body. The egoless mind controls itself by instilling an abiding sense of goodness within itself.

Which brings us full circle. Herein lies the reason that it is imperative for a science of the healthy mind to study the stream of consciousness: the workings of the egoless and egocentric streams of consciousness are fundamentally different from one another, and as a result, they create two very different states of mind, one of which is healthy and one of which is not.

Given that the pivotal differences between the healthy and unhealthy mind lie in their respective streams of consciousness, the only way to observe and understand those differences is to study the stream of consciousness. This is where the differences between them appear, and this is the only place at which they can be directly observed by a human being and by science.

The Science of the Stream of Consciousness

This brings us up against a large paradigm problem. Even though science is beginning to open itself to the prospect of studying consciousness per se, it does not, as it is presently configured, allow itself to study the phenomena and processes that appear in the stream of consciousness. Which is kind of crazy, if you will allow me a moment of colloquial hyperbole.

Certainly if anything is obvious in life, it is a matter of common sense that our thoughts, inner narratives, emotions and moods have a profound impact upon the way we lead our lives. I think, therefore I am. I feel and emote, therefore I do. It is the better part of wisdom to recognize that we need to understand the workings of the stream of consciousness, and its impact upon our lives.

Consider all of the moment to moment ways in which your thoughts and emotions create your state of mind and how they affect the way you behave.

You do not have to be a scientist or an enlightened Tibetan lama to appreciate that your thoughts and emotions play a huge role in determining whether or not you are happy. We all know that when we are in an irritated mood, we act differently than when we are feeling happy or in love.

But there is more to understanding the stream of consciousness than just this. As we shall be seeing, the way in which we respond to and know the meanings that appear in our streams of consciousness are perhaps the most important determinants of whether or not we are happy and healthy human beings. And yet we are ignorant of much of this.

Our ignorance is a product of the fact that science has held itself in abeyance and claimed that the phenomena and processes that appear in the stream of consciousness cannot be empirically studied. This claim rests on two basic assertions that are well known and easy to comprehend: (1) the phenomena of the stream of consciousness are said to be "subjective phenomena" and (2) two human beings cannot simultaneously observe the thoughts and emotions that appear in one given stream of consciousness. Only you can see your stream of consciousness, and only I can see my stream of consciousness. This causes the problem that is known as the problem of interpersonal verification.

These claims raise genuine methodological problems. However, as we will be seeing in later chapters, both of these positions are oversimplifications that are only partially correct. In addition, the issues they raise are more than surmountable.

The bottom line is this: if you take a careful look at the science of the stream of consciousness that we are developing, you will find that it works just like every other field of scientific inquiry.

The Healthy Mind is going to establish that: (1) this field of inquiry uses the same scientific method as every other field of scientific inquiry; (2) the phenomena that appear in the stream of consciousness are objective phenomena that can be studied by science because they are paradoxical phenomena that are simultaneously objective and subjective phenomena; and (3) it is indeed possible to achieve interpersonal verification of observations of these phenomena.

However, please know that although *The Healthy Mind* will engage with these philosophy of science issues, it will not dwell on them at length. *The Healthy Mind* will, instead, make its case by presenting both our data and the theory of the healthy mind that had been derived from that data. It is felt that the best way to make the case that it is possible to do valid empirical studies of the phenomena that appear in the stream of consciousness is to go ahead and do them.

Given that the science of the stream of consciousness is, in a modern context, a new and contested science, I want to briefly, for now, introduce you to this science, so that you can begin to appreciate that it works in precisely the same manner as every other field of scientific inquiry.

Science is, at its most fundamental level, the study of natural phenomena for the purpose of understanding the mechanics of the processes that occur in the natural systems to which those phenomena belong (Descartes, 1983; Chalmers, 2004).

For instance, in the middle of the twentieth century, physicists studied the movement of galaxies and the phenomenon of cosmic microwave background radiation to come to an understanding of the origins and genesis of the system that we call the universe. Biologists examined hemoglobin molecules to determine that their function is to carry oxygen to the tissues of the systems that we call plants and animals. And for almost a century now, science has been investigating the effects of antibiotics on the small systems that we call bacteria.

Like all natural phenomena, the thoughts, emotions and epiphanies that appear in the stream of consciousness are phenomena that participate in the workings of a larger system. Just as quarks combine to form protons and neutrons; just as atoms come together to form molecules; and just as molecules come together to form cells; thoughts, feelings, emotions and moods come together to form the system that we call the stream of consciousness. The stream of consciousness is, of course, part of the larger natural system that we call the human mind.

The science of the stream of consciousness has established that the phenomena that appear in your stream of consciousness—your thoughts, emotions, moods, repressions and so forth—mediate two objective natural processes that are fundamental to the functioning of the larger system that is the human mind. The stream of consciousness mediates (1) the processes by which the mind knows itself (self-awareness) and (2) the processes by which the mind controls itself (self-control).

In keeping with this analysis, the science of the stream of consciousness observes, describes and analyzes the phenomena that appear in the stream of consciousness for the purpose of understanding both the mechanics of the processes of self-awareness and self-control, and the effects that they have on the larger system to which they belong: the mind.

The primary tool this science uses to observe and study these phenomena is meditation. Meditation is the microscope, if you will, that we use to study the phenomena that appear in the stream of consciousness.

To give you a preliminary idea of the kind of phenomena that are studied by the science of the stream of consciousness, here are six quick examples for now: (1) the *involuntary stream of consciousness* (ISoC)—which is called mind wandering by contemporary cognitive science; (2) the *individual moments of consciousness* (iMoC), such as a feeling or an epiphany; (3) the *dissolution* of a single moment of consciousness; (4) the *repression* of a thought, emotion or mind-film; (5) *dual awareness*; and (6) *nondual awareness*. Notice that these phenomena are all defined by their form, as opposed to their content. This is an important detail, and we'll return to it later.

To date, the science of the stream of consciousness has already delineated sixty-four different phenomena that appear in the stream of consciousness, and it is our full expectation that many more phenomena will be discovered and delineated in the future.

"Ode to the Stream of Consciousness," which is Chapter 6 of *The Healthy Mind*, will present a technical description of each of these sixty-four phenomena. This comprehensive descriptive science is the foundation of the modern science of the stream of consciousness, and it has been generated by the lama interviews (Vyner, 2003, 2004a, 2004b, 2005, 2007, 2007–2008, 2009–2010, 2018).

The scientists who study the stream of consciousness are both indigenous and Western meditator-scientists who have received extensive theoretical and applied training in meditation and the stream of consciousness. They use meditation as a research tool to (1) observe and describe the phenomena that appear in the stream of consciousness; (2) investigate the causal relationships that exist between these phenomena; and (3) develop a body of theory that is derived from its observations of these phenomena and causal processes.

Data can be collected in one of two ways. A meditator-scientist can record their own observations of the stream of consciousness. Or a second scientist, who would also have to be an experienced meditator and observer of the stream of consciousness, can elicit and record the observations of other observers of the stream of consciousness.

The theory that is generated by the science of the stream of consciousness—including its theory of the healthy mind—is derived from its observations of the stream of consciousness. The theory that has been developed to date explains both the healthy mind and the functions of the stream of consciousness by reducing them to the psychological elements of which they are composed. It does not explain them by reducing them to the material processes of the brain, although it is fully anticipated that the neurological processes that mediate these psychological processes might well be the subject of future studies.

Interestingly enough, there has been, in the Buddhist tradition, a long history of empirically studying the stream of consciousness and the egoless mind. Indeed, their ability to successfully practice meditation has been built upon what they have learned about the stream of consciousness.

The Buddhist tradition seems to have understood, from its very inception, the need to comprehend the stream of consciousness. For example, the very first systematic school of Buddhist philosophy and psychology, which carries the name of *Abhidharma* in Sanskrit, contains a proto-science of the phenomena that appear in the stream of consciousness (Hirakawa and Groner, 1990). This tradition was carried forward, and most of the subsequent schools of Buddhist psychology were also grounded in both a basic and applied science of the stream of consciousness.

Buddhists practitioner-scientists have also applied their science of the stream of consciousness to the task of investigating the egoless and egocentric mind, and they have come to the conclusion that the egoless mind is a healthier state of mind.

In sum, contemporary Tibetan lamas often are, as students and practitioners of this tradition, accomplished scientists of the egoless mind, the egocentric mind, and the stream of consciousness. They come from a tradition that has studied the stream of consciousness and the healthy mind for centuries, and as a result, they know more about these subjects than the modern science of psychology does. This is one of the principal reasons that I chose to make Tibetan lamas both my subjects and colleagues, if you will, in the scientific study of the healthy mind.

The Empirical Ego

This brings us to the ego. What is the ego? The history of personality theory tends to portray the ego as a theoretical entity within the mind. However, the ego is also an observable entity that is easy to see when you look at your mind. I'm going to present a quick experiential introduction to the ego in this section, so that as we go along you'll have a clear and precise idea of the empirical entities within the mind to which the term ego refers, as it is presently understood by the science of the stream of consciousness. In later chapters, we'll be describing the structure and dynamic of the ego at greater length.

Every important theorist in the history of personality theory—Freud, Jung, Klein, Winnicott, Hartmann, Kernberg, Kohut and so on—has put forth their own theory of what the ego is and what it does. Different theorists have used the term ego to mean somewhat different things.

However, despite the diversity of ego theory, the history of personality theory has, in general, converged upon one central idea: the ego is the entity within the mind that controls the workings of the mind. For example, in Freud's Structural Theory of the mind, the ego controls the biological impulses that emanate from the Freudian id—sex and aggression—at the behest of the superego. In Plato's vision of the dialectical mind, reason controls the spirit and the passions, and in Winnicott's Object Relations Theory of the personality, the false self overrides the true self.

This basic idea of the ego as the controlling entity in the mind is usually combined with the notion that the ego represents the interests of society within the mind. A vast amount of personality theory has taken the position that the ego's function is to exercise social control over a person's desires and wishes.

The science of the stream of consciousness is in accord with this consensus theory of the ego. It sees the ego as being the entity within the mind that controls and socializes the mind. It goes three steps further, however. First, it finds the observable entity within the mind that is the ego. Second, it describes the observable actions that this entity takes to control the mind. Third, it describes the effects that these actions have upon the mind. In delineating the effects of these actions, it simultaneously describes the state of mind that is created by the ego.

It is crucial to find the entity that is the ego because if your plan is to empirically study the workings of the ego and the effects that it has upon the larger system that is the mind, you must first locate the actual entity that is the ego. This is much the same as saying that if you want to study the behavior of chimpanzees in the Tanzanian jungle, you must first find chimpanzees so that you can actually observe their behavior. In addition, it is also true that if you are interested in cultivating an egoless mind, it is crucial to identify the constituents of the ego so that you can let them go.

To find your own ego, close your eyes for a moment and take a look at your mind. The first thing you'll notice is that it seems as though there are two basic entities present in your experience of your mind: (1) your stream of consciousness and (2) the awareness, or watcher, that looks at and knows your stream of consciousness. This awareness is the entity within your mind that thinks it is you. It is your awareness.

This duality of watcher and stream of consciousness is the basic structure of the mind's experience of itself. It is much the same experience as standing on the bank of a river and watching that river flow by.

If you observe the watcher and the stream of consciousness for a while, it becomes apparent that in addition to watching the flow of the stream of consciousness, the watcher is constantly taking actions that alter and thus control the stream of consciousness.

For example, one can easily see the watcher repress the thoughts and emotions that appear in your stream of consciousness. It is also an easy matter to see the watcher attach, or hold on to, thoughts and emotions; and with more experience, you can also discern that it is the watcher who narrates the thought films that recursively cycle through the stream of consciousness.

This means that the watcher is the ego in the egocentric mind. The watcher is the ego because it is the actual agent that controls the egocentric mind, which it does by controlling the stream of consciousness.

The watcher is also the ego in the more primordial sense that it sees itself as being both the subject of your experience and the author of your actions. It sees itself, for instance, as being the entity within your mind that is the person that is reading this book right now.

Another sense in which the watcher sees itself as being you, is that it is the entity within your mind that thinks it has your identity. It is the person, if you will, within your mind that thinks that you are a pacifist, or a Frenchwoman, or a person of middling intelligence, or a cellist or whomever it is that you think you are. Take a look and see right now. Close your eyes for a moment and figure out who it is that believes that you are you.

The watcher, then, is the center of the ego. However, the watcher and its conception of its identity are but two of the five principal components of the ego. The ego is a system that is composed of five fundamental entities:

1. The watcher
2. The stream of consciousness

3. Meanings created by the ego
4. The identity that the watcher believes it has
5. The control dynamic that takes place between the watcher and the stream of consciousness.

In sum, given that the science of the stream of consciousness has been able to observe the entire repertoire of actions that the watcher employs to control the stream of consciousness, it has come to the conclusion that the watcher is the ego—the entity within the mind that governs the behavior of the socialized mind. As we will be seeing, the watcher exercises social control over the mind by first constructing for itself an identity, and then controlling the stream of consciousness so that a person's thoughts, emotions and behaviors conform to that identity.

The Ego's Control Dynamic and Its Effects

In this analysis, the watcher is the ego because it is the agent that carries out the defining work of the ego: controlling the mind. The watcher is the empirical entity within the mind that both carries your sense of identity, and controls your mind and behavior for the purpose of making it appear as though you actually have that identity.

To the watcher falls the daunting and virtually impossible task of trying to ensure that everything a person thinks, says and does conforms to their identity.

The watcher has a repertoire of four fundamental actions that it employs to preserve the conception of self that is a person's identity: (1) it judges the meanings that appear in your stream of consciousness; (2) it represses thoughts and emotions that contradict its identity; (3) it holds on to thoughts and feelings that match its identity; and (4) it writes, directs and acts out a cluster of mind-films that construct realities that support its sense of your identity (Vyner, 2007–2008).

This is an immense amount of work, and it is a never-ending vigil that takes a lot of time and energy. Thus the watcher is a mental Sisyphus. He is constantly rolling the stone of identity up the hill of perfection, only to have it fall down over and over again. He never seems to be able to get that stone to the top of the hill and keep it there. Sometimes he almost gets the stone to the crest of the hill, and then he will invariably think or do something that is at odds with his identity. Then the stone will roll all the way back down to the bottom of the hill again.

For our purposes of understanding the healthy mind, the most important thing to grasp at this early juncture about the pathogenicity of the ego is this: it is the ego's Sisyphean control dynamic that makes the egocentric mind an unhealthy mind. The actions that the ego takes to preserve its identity—the judgments, repressions, attachments and stories that it narrates—initiate causal sequences within the mind that make the egocentric state of mind unhealthy. This is one of the cardinal findings of the science of the stream of consciousness, and it is key to understanding why the egocentric state of mind is an unhealthy one.

The control dynamic of the ego engenders an unhealthy state of mind for one basic reason: it creates the *normal pathologies of the ego*. The normal pathologies of the ego are a quartet of maladies that occur, to varying degrees, in every mind that has an ego. As described by the science of the stream of consciousness, they are as follows: (1) conflict, (2) loss of self, (3) moods and (4) the mind-films and the existential ruts they engender (Vyner, 2009–2010). It is these pathologies, in turn, that make every egocentric mind an unhealthy mind.

These egopoietic pathologies are so commonplace in our lives that we do not see them as being unhealthy because their ubiquity causes us to see them, to varying degrees, as being a normal part of life. Nonetheless, despite the fact that these pathologies are all threads in the normative fabric of the egocentric mind, they are also significant problems that cause pain and inauthenticity within the individual mind. They also create the psychological ground upon which larger sociopolitical problems are apt to grow.

The Egocentric State of Mind

In Chapter 9, titled "The Vicissitudes of the Ego," *The Healthy Mind* will present a systematic description of the normal pathologies of the ego and the state of mind that they create. For now, though, by way of presenting a quick introduction to the egocentric state of mind, this section is going to present a few down to earth examples of how these pathologies manifest in everyday life.

For example, if you should ever find yourself in conflict with your self, this is a state of mind that has been produced by your ego. If you should ever feel superior or inferior to another human being, or for that matter to your self, these feelings are also the creation of the ego, as are the great majority of the judgments you make of both yourself and other people.

If you are the Speaker of the House of the United States, and you explode in narcissistic indignation because the president relegates you to the back of Air Force One and ignores you, this is ego. If you are a famous television personality in America, and you throw a temper tantrum when you find yourself turned away from an elite department store in Paris because you have arrived a few minutes past their closing time, and if you then proceed to loudly demand that the store allow you to come in and go shopping anyway because you are the famous person you are, this too is ego. The basic principle at work in both of these cases is that a person with an ego cares how other people see his or her self, and they will even demand to be treated in a way that is commensurate with their own image of their self.

The act of repression, which is of course regularly deployed by the socialized human mind, is another example of ego process. When you repress your thoughts or emotions, this is almost certainly an action that is being taken by your ego.

Ultimately, and this might come as a surprise, the vast majority of the thoughts, emotions and stories that rush by in your stream of consciousness are ego process. They are ego process in the sense that they are meanings that the ego creates to help you believe that you have the identity that you think you have, and to ensure that your behavior accords with that identity.

This cascade of egopoietic thought noise is not benign. It plays a central role, for example, in causing what is perhaps the most disheartening of the normal pathologies of the ego: the loss of one's true self. This noise buries the goodness and joy that are the natural state of your mind, and it also covers over and obscures the nondual meanings that are your true self in any given moment.

A second dynamic that causes a person with an ego to lose their true self is the conflict that the ego creates within the mind. It is a conflict about whether or not you are going to be your true self or become the identity, or false self, that is championed by your ego.

People often experience this conflict as a fight about whether or not they will be the person that they feel they really are, or the person that their family and society wants them to be. This is a quarrel that has been described by a multitude of thinkers in the history of ideas, and it is a perpetual presence in the inner landscape of the egocentric mind.

In the face of this conflict and the loss of self it engenders, the ego usually prevails over the self. It wins by raising the stakes, which it does by creating the illusion that its identity is sacred and thus worth fighting to preserve. And fight it does. A person with an ego will fight to the death to preserve their identity—be it a national identity, a religious identity, an ethnic identity, a tribal identity or a personal identity.

Unfortunately, this also means that the inner conflict of the ego is contagious. If you get angry with your spouse because you are in conflict with your self, this is an example of this contagion. If you then transfer that anger to your children, or to someone at your office or to another nation-state, this too is evidence of just how contagious the ego's conflicts with itself can be. The ego's inner conflicts are, unfortunately, disseminated to a person's relationships with other people, as much of the history of humanity testifies.

In the end, these conflicts are all part of the mask of having an ego. To have an ego is to put on one or more masks for your entire life, and to pretend that you are someone different than the person you really are moment to moment. As a result, a person with an ego lives in conflict with, and loses the ability to know and be, their true self. To have an ego is to enter into a Faustian bargain in which you literally lose your soul.

The Egoless Mind

There are myriad ways to describe the healthy contours of the egoless state of mind. It is a mind that lives in the present moment. It is a mind that abides in the goodness and joy that are the natural state of the mind. It is a mind that is free of the noisy stream of thoughts that wanders endlessly through the egocentric mind. It is a mind that refrains from indulging in bad moods and so forth.

To give you a concise introduction to the underlying reasons that the egoless mind is a healthy state of mind, here are three of the core dynamics that make it a healthy mind:

1. The egoless mind allows its stream of consciousness to run free and remain in its natural state.
2. The person with an egoless mind is able to know and be their true self because the egoless mind knows itself as it really is in every moment.
3. The workings of the egoless mind do not generate the normal pathologies of the ego, and as a result, the egoless mind does not cause itself to experience psychological pain.

The first trait—the act of allowing the stream of consciousness to run free—is the foundation of, and causal dynamic of, the egoless mind. This simple act of allowing the stream of consciousness to remain in its natural state generates the entire egoless state of mind, including its abilities to realize its true self and abstain from incarnating the normal pathologies of the ego.

Indeed, the egoless mind is able to both realize its true self, and abstain from creating the normal pathologies of the ego, precisely because, and only because, it allows its stream of consciousness to run free. To cultivate a state of mind in which the stream of consciousness is allowed to remain in its natural state is the crux of developing an egoless mind and becoming one's true self.

The freedom of the egoless stream of consciousness is also the dynamic that defines the difference between the egoless and egocentric minds. Whereas the egocentric mind perpetually controls and alters the contents of its stream of consciousness for the purpose of maintaining its sense of identity, the egoless mind allows its stream of consciousness to run free.

It is this act of allowing the stream of consciousness to run free that makes the egoless mind a fundamentally healthy mind. Allowing it to run free generates a cluster of causal sequences that give birth to egoless awareness; and egoless awareness, in turn, engenders the entire egoless state of mind.

Here, for now, is a quick introductory overview of the sequence of causal processes that generate egoless awareness. The first step is this: when the mind allows its stream of consciousness to run free, it causes itself to have nondual awareness of the meanings that appear in its stream of consciousness.

1. Allow the Stream of Consciousness to Run Free → Nondual Awareness of Meanings

When the mind has nondual awareness of meanings, they dissolve and are transformed into moments of joy, goodness and self-realization. These spontaneous metamorphoses are the *nondual transformations* of the egoless mind, and they play a central role in generating the egoless state of mind. Here is a description of the basic causal process that leads to the occurrence of the nondual transformations:

2. Nondual Awareness of a Meaning → Nondual Transformation of that Meaning Occurs

As these transformations continue to increasingly occur over time, the palpable reservoir of goodness and joy that was mentioned earlier will build up within the mind. Which is to say that these feelings of joy and goodness will become a stable and conscious presence within your mind. You will be continually aware of them as you go through your day. Here is the causal sequence that describes the broad strokes of this process:

3. Sustained Occurrence of Nondual Transformations → Reservoir of Joy and Goodness Appears Within the Mind

These causal sequences are laws of nature. Just as leaves turn red and gold every autumn because the days are growing shorter, and just as the stars at the center of a galaxy collapse to form a black hole, when the mind emancipates itself from the ego's control dynamic, and allows its stream of consciousness to run free, a palpable reservoir of goodness and joy develops within the mind.

The import of this reservoir of goodness is that it unites with and becomes your awareness. It becomes the egoless awareness that has nondual awareness of your thoughts, emotions and stories; which causes them, in turn, to dissolve and be spontaneously transformed into even more moments of joy, goodness and self-realization. The ongoing creation of these moments of joy and goodness fortifies and stabilizes egoless awareness, and this strengthens your ability to know the nondual suchness of the meanings that you give to the present moment.

In the egoless state of mind, this reservoir of goodness and joy also becomes the ground of everything you say and do. This is why the egoless mind has no moral need to control its stream of consciousness. Once again, the egoless mind controls itself by instilling within itself this sense of goodness.

Does allowing one's stream of consciousness to run free mean that a person who has an egoless mind acts out and expresses every thought and feeling that comes into your mind? The answer to this question is no, of course not.

Does this mean that if science and society were to accept the notion that the egocentric mind is an unhealthy mind and abandon the ego, that humanity would also abandon self-control and descend into a nightmarish jungle in which we abandon all notions of morality and social contract? Once again, the answer is no.

Allowing your stream of consciousness to run free is a skill that is very different from the act of allowing yourself to express everything you are thinking and feeling. You can, once you know how, allow your stream of consciousness to run free without wanting or needing to express all of the thoughts and emotions that come and go within it.

The Healthy Mind is going to describe in detail all of the mechanisms by which the unfettered stream of consciousness generates a healthy state of mind in Chapters 11 and 12. These chapters will also map out and describe the egoless state of mind itself.

Once we have understood the egoless state of mind, *The Healthy Mind* will then discuss the means by which one cultivates an egoless mind, and in its final two chapters, we will contemplate two different aspects of the future of the egoless mind.

Is the egoless mind a state of mind that is within ready reach of the average person? If we teach our children to become egoless from an early age, would it be a feasible goal for a general population? What would an egoless Congress and an egoless foreign policy look like?

References

Ashhurst, J. (1889). *The International Encyclopedia of Surgery*, Volume 1. New York, NY: W. Wood, p. 623.

Chalmers, D. (2004). How can we construct a science of consciousness? In M. S. Gazzaniga (Ed.), *The Cognitive Neurosciences III*. Cambridge, MA: MIT Press, pp. 1111–1120.

Descartes, R. (1983). *Principles of Philosophy*. Dordrecht: D. Reidel.

Hirakawa, A. and Groner, P. (1990). *A History of Indian Buddhism: From Śākyamuni to Early Mahāyāna*. Honolulu: University of Hawaii Press.

Lister, J. (1870). Effects of the antiseptic system of treatment upon the salubrity of a surgical hospital. *Lancet*, 1, 4–6 and 40–42.

Vyner, H. M. (2003). The descriptive psychology of Tibetan Buddhism and the nature of the healthy human mind. *Anthropology of Consciousness*, 13(2), 1–25.

Vyner, H. M. (2004a). *The Healthy Mind Interviews, Volume 1: Khenpo Nyima Wangyal*. Kathmandu: Vajra Books.

Vyner, H. M. (2004b). *The Healthy Mind Interviews, Volume 2: Khenpo Tsewang Gyatso*. Kathmandu: Vajra Books.

Vyner, H. M. (2005). *The Healthy Mind Interviews, Volume 3: Lopon Tekchog*. Kathmandu: Vajra Books.

Vyner, H. M. (2007). *The Healthy Mind Interviews, Volume 4: Dalai Lama, Lopon Tenzin Namdak, Lopon Tekchog*. Kathmandu: Vajra Books.

Vyner, H. M. (2007–2008). The dialectical phenomena and processes of the mind. *Imagination, Cognition and Personality*, 27(2), 163–196.

Vyner, H. M. (2009–2010). A preliminary theory of the defining dynamic of the healthy human mind. *Imagination, Cognition and Personality*, 29(3), 225–270.

Vyner, H. M. (in press, 2018). *The Healthy Mind Interviews, Volume 5: Penor Rinpoche and Khenpo Tsewang Gyatso*. Kathmandu: Vajra Books.

3

LOPON TEGCHOKE INTERVIEW

The Primordial Wisdom of the Natural Mind

For centuries, there were four independent border kingdoms between Tibet and India. From east to west, they were Bhutan, Sikkim, Nepal and Ladakh. Nepal was and is a syncretistic melange of Hindu, Buddhist and shamanic cultures, whereas Ladakh, Sikkim and Bhutan have long been Buddhist kingdoms.

In the winter of 1997 I went to Gangtok, the capital of Sikkim, on a fishing expedition, if you will, to look for new lamas to interview. I had introductions to a few lamas, and I was lucky enough while I was there to get two difficult to get visa extensions that made it possible to scour the landscape and do first interviews with sixteen lamas in that short period of time. The idea was to assess if it would be worthwhile to come back to Sikkim at a later time and interview those lamas in depth.

I was at Deorali Monastery one day doing an interview with the elderly but still daunting lama Dodrupchen Rinpoche. Afterwards, my translator—a Ladakhi monk named Thubten Gyatso who is now an abbot, and who had previously translated for me when I did a series of interviews with the renowned Longchenpa scholar Khenpo Thubten when the Khenpo was guest teaching at DzogChen Monastery in the winter of 1992–1993—suggested that a lama named Lopon Tegchoke might be an excellent lama to interview.

Lopon Tegchoke was, at the time, the head teacher at the Deorali Monastery, and Thubten Gyatso arranged for me to meet with him. I can still see in my mind's eye that first meeting in a spacious and somehow well-lit room deep in the damp and otherwise poorly lit subterranean bowels of Deorali Monastery.

I could see right away that Lopon Tegchoke was an extraordinary man. When he opens his mouth, stories, metaphors and figures of speech that feel ancient and wise come pouring out. They are figures of speech that are the fruit of an ancient wisdom civilization, figures of speech that you might easily have heard if you had visited Bhutan or Tibet in the sixteenth century.

I interviewed Lopon Tegchoke twice during that first visit to Gangtok, and from his mouth I heard things that I had never heard before. I immediately resolved to interview the Lopon as much as I possibly could, but every time I would return to Gangtok, he was always away in his homeland of Bhutan. He had grown up in eastern Bhutan as the child of two itinerant and renunciate yogis who devoted their entire lives to wandering around the kingdom of Bhutan seeking teachings and enlightenment. Now Lopon was the head teacher of one of the great monasteries of the Tibetan Buddhist world.

In the late winter months of 2004, I was in Bhutan at the invitation of the Secretary of the Ministry of Finance. It was my first visit to Bhutan. On my very first afternoon in Thimpu, Bhutan's capital, I met with the secretary, and I mentioned to him that I was looking for a lama named Lopon Tegchoke. I asked the secretary if he knew him. A look of incredulity and pleasure crossed his face as he said that he had known Lopon Tegchoke since their childhood, and he mentioned that he had the phone number at Lopon's retreat home on him!

I think my eyes must have widened and grown as large as grapefruits. He gave me the phone number right then and there, and I immediately walked over to the front desk of the hotel, picked up the phone and called the number. I explained who I was to the monk who answered the phone, and also explained that I had interviewed Lopon in Gangtok and that I was hoping to interview him again here in Bhutan.

The voice on the other end of the line said, "Do you know who this is? I'm Thubten Gyatso!" It was a wonderful moment. We talked like the old friends we were, and as we talked I was certain that this meant that I would be able to come see and interview Lopon Tegchoke.

But when I asked if I could come see Lopon, Thubten Gyatso explained that Lopon was in retreat and that it would be impossible to see him. He suggested I call back in a week to see if it might be possible then. I called back, but the answer was still no.

Time passed, and then I got an idea. The Secretary of Finance was a devout and caring Buddhist, and he understood how important it was to me to see Lopon Tegchoke. I called the Secretary, and I asked him if he would be willing to just get in his car and go down to Lopon's retreat in West Paro with me, knock on Lopon Tegchoke's door and see if would be possible to see him. To my great surprise, he said yes! We went the next day.

It turned out that Thubten Gyatso was there, and that he was Lopon Tegchoke's personal attendant. Despite being astonished to see us, he greeted us with great affection. He also told me immediately that it would not be possible to see the Lopon.

As I sat there in a sort of waiting room outside of the Lopon's chambers wondering what I could possibly do next, a large Teddy Roosevelt of a man with a radiant and honest smile emerged out of the Lopon's room. He turned out to be the governor of Thimpu - the capital of Bhutan. The governor was and still is a student of Lopon Tegchoke's, and I have heard him say many a time since that day that he sees the Lopon as a "Buddha."

The governor sat down with us, and he became curious about my work. As we talked I could see that he was a remarkable human being; remarkable for both his strength and dignity of character, and his devotion to Buddhism. About an hour later we were all sitting in front of Lopon!

Over the next year, I returned to Bhutan two more times, and I interviewed Lopon perhaps a dozen times at great length, once for an entire day. I remember feeling sort of stunned by all of my good luck.

Those interviews all took place at Lopon's small retreat beneath the world famous Tiger's Nest Monastery in the West Paro valley, and every single interview was remarkable. Tiger's Nest is well known in the West because there are many stunning photos of the entire monastery, which is a small compact monastery that is perched improbably on the tiniest of ledges on the side of a sheer cliff in the mountains above the floor of the Paro valley.

Nondual Awareness

One of the many remarkable things about Lopon Tegchoke was that once we got to know one another, he was willing to talk openly about the experience of nondual awareness, which is the essence of the enlightened, or egoless, mind.

Nondual awareness realizes, and is a synonym for, the revered Buddhist experience of emptiness. The import of realizing the emptiness of one's own mind is that when the mind realizes its own emptiness, it knows itself exactly as it is. The mind that realizes its own emptiness knows its true self.[1]

In general, there is a reluctance among lamas to talk about nondual awareness and the experience of emptiness. Lamas have traditionally forgone talking about the content of their nondual experiences of the mind, and they do so for real and substantive reasons that we will discuss at length in Chapter 11. But again, Lopon Tegchoke was willing to talk about nondual awareness, as were many of the other lamas I interviewed.

Understanding nondual awareness is of considerable import to the work of mapping out the egoless state of mind and empirically evaluating whether or not the egoless mind is a healthy mind. It is crucial to fathom what actually happens in nondual awareness because the egoless mind is a mind that has sustained nondual awareness of itself. As it turns out, it is the egoless mind's ability to have nondual awareness of itself that makes it a healthy mind. As we will be seeing, the egoless mind is a mind is able to know and be its true self precisely because it has nondual awareness of the meanings that appear in its stream of consciousness.

1. Please see Chapter 11 for an empirical discussion of the true self and its equivalence to the nature of mind.

There is a long-standing and important debate in the history of Buddhist philosophy about whether or not nondual awareness has content, and it is entirely relevant to understanding what actually happens when the mind has nondual awareness of itself. Another way to frame this philosophical issue is as follows: when the mind has nondual awareness of itself, does it know something or does it know nothing?

One school of philosophical thought has said that nondual awareness does have content, and a second school of thought said that it does not. These two positions are easier to understand and evaluate if we render them empirically:

1. The first position, which is the position that there is content in the mind's nondual experience of itself, can be rendered as follows: when the mind has nondual awareness of the meanings that appear in its stream of consciousness it realizes the suchness of their content. It knows the content of each of those meanings exactly as it is.
2. The second position, which is the position that there is no content in the mind's nondual experience of itself, is that when the mind has nondual awareness of itself, it knows nothing. Nondual awareness has no content, and thus there is no content to experience.

This issue of whether or not nondual awareness has content is of considerable import because it raises the question of whether or not the egoless mind gives meaning to its experience.

If you contend that nondual awareness has no content, then you are taking the position that the egoless mind does not give meaning to its experience, which is both counterintuitive and inconsistent with the fact that one of the basic functions of the mind is that it gives meaning to a person's experience.

If, on the other hand, you hold that nondual awareness does have content, you are asserting that the egoless mind does give meaning to its experience.

This, then, is the context within which Lopon's descriptions of nondual awareness take on importance. In the following excerpt, Lopon confirms that the nondual mind does have content, and he does so by actually talking about the experience of knowing one specific type of nondual meaning.

In this passage, Lopon tells us that in his experience nondual meanings do appear in the egoless stream of consciousness, and he does so by describing one species of nondual meaning—a type of meaning that he calls "suchness primordial wisdom."[2] This assertion is, in and of itself, an important observation of the egoless mind, especially coming from Lopon.

However, if you read the passage carefully, it has much more to say about the egoless mind, including how to cultivate one. I could write a whole book of annotations to unpack the meaning of this passage. Please read the passage first, and then I'll explain the larger picture it gives us of how the egoless mind works.

2. Tib.: day khona nyid togpai yeshe.

Finally, the intent of presenting this interview with Lopon Tekchoke at his point in *The Healthy Mind* is to (1) introduce you to the egoless mind and (2) show you how the interviews generate the data of the science of the science of the stream of consciousness.

Suchness Primordial Wisdom[3]

HMV: There are times when there are countless thoughts running through my mind. At other times, there are long interludes in which there are but a few thoughts coming and going. During these periods of relative quiet, I become increasingly aware of the appearance of single thoughts in my mind that appear and then instantly dissolve and disappear just like that (I snap my fingers).

LTC: At that time, you are on the path.

HMV: It has been my experience, that four different kinds of things can happen immediately after a single thought dissolves like that. Sometimes, for example, a feeling of joy will arise after a thought dissolves. Sometimes a feeling of compassion will appear. Sometimes there will be a temporary cessation of all inner appearances; a single thought will dissolve and then nothing new will arise for a period of time.

LTC: Yes.

HMV: The fourth thing that can and does happen after a single thought dissolves, is that a large insight of one kind or another will immediately arise in my mind. It might be an understanding of the nature of mind, or perhaps an understanding of nondual awareness. It could be any number of things.

LTC: That insight is suchness primordial wisdom, enlightened mind.

HMV: Do you mean that it would be enlightened mind if those insights were present all of the time, as opposed to coming and going for moments at a time?

LTC: Yes. The enlightened mind is a permanent chain of nondual moments. If you are in dharmakaya,[4] there are no thoughts. It is like the permanent nature of the sky. There is a permanent stream of nondual moments.

HMV: Would that be the same thing as saying that enlightenment is a permanent stream of nondual moments of primordial wisdom?[5]

3. H. Vyner. (2005). *The Healthy Mind Interviews, Volume 3: Lopon Tegchoke.* Kathmandu: Vajra Publications.
4. Dharmakaya is a Sanskrit term, and it is one of what are traditionally called the three bodies, or kayas, of the Buddha. Kaya is usually translated as body. The kaya doctrine is a key theory in the history of Buddhist ideas, and there have been a number of different formulations of the kaya doctrine since the beginning of Buddhism. The kaya doctrine says, essentially, that a Buddha has more than one aspect, and different schools of Buddhist thought have defined those several aspects in different ways. Empirically, the kayas are the defining aspects of the enlightened mind.
5. Tib.: yeshe.

LTC: Yes.

HMV: Thank you. That's very helpful. Given that these temporary moments of insight (on the path) are not enlightened mind, what would you call them? Are they simply moments of primordial wisdom?

LTC: Yes. Initially, primordial wisdom lasts for a very short while. Gradually, as you go on practicing, the primordial wisdom, the gap, increases. At the same time, the deluded minds will decrease. When you reach Buddhahood, then the deluded appearances will cease altogether.

HMV: Then only the kayas[6] and primordial wisdom will appear.

LTC: Yes. [Emphatic] When the recurring patterns of ego thought[7] are no longer being created, then the delusions of the samsaric mind will, over time, gradually subside. And then the primordial wisdom will increase.

Annotation: In this passage, Lopon says that the mind creates at least one type of nondual meaning, which is called day khona nyid togpai yeshe, or suchness primordial wisdom, in Tibetan. He describes suchness primordial wisdom as being a moment of insight that arises after the dissolution of a single thought.

Lopon also says three more very interesting things here about the nature of the completely egoless, or enlightened, mind.

1. Dual, or deluded, appearances cease to arise in the egoless mind. This would include thoughts, emotions, moods and mind-films.
2. Only the kayas[8] and primordial wisdom appear in the fully realized egoless mind.
3. The egoless mind is a permanent stream of nondual moments of togpai yeshe.

Finally, it should be said that the kayas and primordial wisdom are observable, or empirical, phenomena. In this passage, Lopon has described the experience of knowing one particular type of primordial wisdom: suchness primordial wisdom.

HMV: Would it be correct to say Lopon, that on the path, in between moments of primordial wisdom, that thoughts and emotions continue to appear?

LTC: Yes.

6. Once again, kaya is a Sanskrit term that refers to the several aspects of a Buddha's body and mind.
7. "Recurring patterns of ego thought" is a non-literal translation of the Tibetan term "bak-chak."
8. Empirically, the kayas refer to nondual egoless awareness, predual primordial meanings, and the nondual realizations of the egoless mind. All of these phenomena will be described and discussed at length at several places throughout the book, and especially in chapter eleven.

HMV: But that once primordial wisdom becomes permanent, thoughts and emotions no longer appear in the mind?

LTC: Yes. That's correct. You have thought it out very well.

HMV: One more question in this vein. When a person is experiencing moments of primordial wisdom, what is it that holds them back from having a permanent stream of nondual primordial wisdom?

LTC: It is prevented by the delusions created by the recurring patterns of ego thought. The power of these recurring patterns is very strong, and they prevent you from staying in a longer stream of suchness primordial wisdom.

HMV: Are you saying that following[9] your habitual patterns of ego thought will keep you from remaining in a permanent stream of nondual primordial wisdom?

LTC: Yes.

HMV: Thank you very much. Finally, for now, does suchness primordial wisdom always appear as a large insight? Or can they appear in some other way as well?

LTC: Suchness primordial wisdom is always an insight like that. While you are on the path, primordial wisdom has to be continuously appearing. They are essential.

HMV: Why?

LTC: To attain enlightenment. That is the path.

HMV: Is it true, then, that one progresses along the path to enlightenment by having increasingly frequent moments of primordial wisdom?

LTC: Yes.

HMV: How does the realization of these moments of primordial wisdom by egoless awareness[10] on the path help a person realize fruition egoless awareness?[11]

LTC: You have yet to see the essence of egoless awareness face-to-face. On the path, you still believe you have an identity. The sole responsibility of primordial wisdom is to destroy that ignorance of self-conception.

Annotation: Lopon says here that the difference between being in the process of developing an enlightened mind, and the final state of becoming fully enlightened, is that when you are still developing an enlightened

9. To "follow" a stream of thoughts is to believe and live in the story that they narrate.
10. "Egoless awareness," here, is a translation of the Tibetan term "rigpa." Rigpa is usually translated as "awareness" and can also be translated at "nondual awareness." Please see Chapter 11 for an extensive discussion of egoless awareness and its place in the egoless mind.
11. "Fruition" egoless awareness refers to the stable egoless awareness of the completely egoless, or enlightened, mind. It is stable in the sense that it does not disappear. Please see Chapter 12 for a discussion of the difference between the completely egoless mind and the partially egoless mind.

mind, you still believe you have an identity, or self-concept. It is this sense of identity that holds one back from becoming fully enlightened.

HMV: Ahh.

LTC: Egoless awareness and primordial wisdom clean off the dirt of self-conception.

HMV: How does primordial wisdom cleanse the mind of the ignorance of self-conception?

LTC: Primordial wisdom is actually the same as egoless awareness. When nondual awareness appears, ignorance decreases; it gradually dissolves and disappears.

HMV: Let's try an example. I think of myself as having many different identities, or self-concepts, to which I am attached. For example, I see myself as a doctor. I see myself as a mountaineer. I see myself as a person that has a big heart. And so forth. Now when you say that the ignorance of self-conception decreases with the realization of moments of primordial wisdom, are you saying that in a moment of primordial wisdom that a person abandons one of their identities?

LTC: Oh yes. [Emphatic]

HMV: So let's say that maybe I carry around fifty identities. Are you saying that as a result of having an experience of primordial wisdom, that I will let one of those identities go; that in my heart, I will really let one of them go?

LTC: Oh yes.

HMV: And then there are forty-nine more to go.

LTC: Oh yes. It's like this. When you go into the mountains, when you are at the base camp, at that time you are a doctor. Now when you climb the first step, you abandon the doctor at the base. When you climb another step, you get further away from being that doctor. As you go higher and higher up the mountain, the doctor you abandoned at the base camp is farther and farther away. So as your primordial wisdom increases, a conception of self is abandoned more and more.

HMV: Thank you. That's very helpful.

The phenomenon that Lopon Tegchoke has described here—suchness primordial wisdom—is one specific type of nondual meaning that the egoless mind creates in response to its experience; just as thoughts are a type of dual meaning that the egocentric mind creates.

In essence, suchness primordial wisdom is a moment of awareness in which you know your self as you really are. As described here by Lopon Tekchoke, it is a moment of insight in which you let go of a meaning created by your ego and get a larger picture of how you really see the world. The science of the stream of consciousness calls this type of nondual meaning a *realization*, which is equivalent to what our Western tradition would call an epiphany.

It is remarkable enough to have before us an empirical description of this type of nondual meaning, but there is more to be learned about the egoless mind from Lopon Tekchoke's description of this phenomenon.

For one, Lopon makes it clear that for the person who has an egoless mind, every day is full of endless realizations—both small and large—in which you constantly know yourself as you really are moment to moment.

As Lopon Tekchoke says in this interview, the enlightened mind is an unending series of moments of nondual awareness. Imagine what life would be like if you knew your true self in every moment because your mind was a perpetual stream of self-revelations. Or even if you simply had a large number of epiphanies in the course of every day.

In contrast, if you have an egocentric mind, epiphanies only occur every once in a great while. I have several times asked a dinner table full of friends how often they have epiphanies. The usual and most frequent answer is something on the order of three or four epiphanies a month.

This disparity in the frequency of epiphanies points us towards a larger understanding of both the egoless mind, and the differences between it and the egocentric mind.

The egoless mind is able to live in a constant stream of realizations because it has nondual awareness of itself. It has nondual awareness of the thoughts, emotions, feelings and mind-films that appear in its stream of consciousness, and this leads to a continual harvest of nondual realizations.[12]

The egocentric mind, in contrast, has but rare access to realizations because it has dual awareness of itself. It has dual awareness of the meanings that appear in its stream of consciousness.[13]

To put it another way, the egoless and egocentric minds have different modes of self-awareness. The egoless mind has what we will be calling an egoless mode of self-awareness, and the egocentric mind has an egocentric mode of self-awareness (Vyner, 2009–2010).

The import of these two modes of self-awareness is that they engender two very different states of mind. The egoless mode of self-awareness creates the egoless state of mind, which is healthy; and the egocentric mode of self-awareness generates the egocentric state of mind, which, as we will be seeing, is unhealthy (Vyner, 2009–2010).

These two states of mind are very different. The dual self-awareness of the egocentric mind generates a cluttered stream of consciousness. The egocentric mind peers at itself through veils of thoughts and emotions, and those veils block

12. Please see Chapter 11 for a discussion of how and why the egoless mind's nondual awareness of itself leads to a continual harvest of nondual realizations.
13. Please see Chapter 9 for a discussion of how and why the egocentric mind's dual awareness of itself renders it unable to have a continual harvest of realizations.

its ability to become aware of the epiphanies that would otherwise reveal its true self to itself in every moment. It's like looking for a small road sign on an unlit country road in a blizzard that's a whiteout.

In contrast, there is no blizzard in the egoless mind because it has nondual awareness of the meanings that appear in its stream of consciousness. It's just one well-lit road sign after another. This makes it possible for the egoless mind to live in a constant stream of nondual realizations/epiphanies.

The egoless mind has the clarity to see its epiphanies clearly, and have nondual awareness of them, because its stream of consciousness is not cluttered with a contrapuntal plethora of thoughts, films and emotions that have nothing to do with the present moment.

The second half of *The Healthy Mind* is going to explore at length nondual awareness, dual awareness, the egoless mode of self-awareness, the egocentric mode of self-awareness, the egoless state of mind and the egocentric state of mind.

However, before we can describe and analyze these states of mind, we have more work to do. We must first acquaint ourselves with the basic science of the phenomena that appear in the stream of consciousness.

Our introduction to the science of the stream of consciousness will begin with (1) an explanation of its methodology, (2) a discussion of why it is a valid field of scientific inquiry and (3) an account of why I chose to study Tibetan lamas.

The culmination of this introduction to the science of the stream of consciousness will be a presentation of the descriptive science of the stream of consciousness that has been generated by the lama interviews—which is a typology of all of the dual and nondual phenomena that appear in the stream of consciousness as they are known to date. It is important to first familiarize ourselves with this descriptive science of the stream of consciousness because both our descriptions and theory of the healthy mind have all been derived from it.

References

Vyner, H. M. (2005). *The Healthy Mind Interviews, Volume 3: Lopon Tegchoke*. Kathmandu: Vajra Publications.

Vyner, H. M. (2009–2010). A preliminary theory of the defining dynamic of the healthy human mind. *Imagination, Cognition and Personality*, 29(3), 225–270.

PART II

Science of the Stream of Consciousness

4

TIBET

Entering the Stream of Consciousness

In the summer of 1994, I found myself wandering, on my own, through the Chang Tang of northern Tibet. Chang-Tang means Northern Plain in Tibetan, and it is a sere, high plateau that bottoms out at 14,000 feet and rises up to more than 23,000 feet in the many mountain ranges that run through it. The mountains create large closed basins—like in Utah or southern Colorado, except everything is much higher and more remote.

The Chang Tang stretches through large swathes of the northern portion of the Tibetan plateau, and altogether it is about the size of Germany and Poland combined. The only people who live there are the occasional clan of Tibetan nomads. They live year-round in dark black tents made of yak hair that are invariably guarded by ferocious mastiffs that range up to 125 big-chested pounds of unfriendly guard dog whose first instinct is to invariably come after you for the kill. I know from personal experience.

When you are on the Chang Tang, you are deeply aware of the sky, because it is, after all, closer. Water is scarce in the Chang Tang and several times, while trekking there, I ran out of water, and would then find groundwater only to discover that it was saltwater because it had accumulated in a closed geological basin. It wasn't as salty as ocean water, but it definitely was not drinkable. The Chang Tang is an unforgiving place, and that is part of its charm.

To trek alone for a month in the Chang Tang, I had to first elude the Chinese system of controlling foreigners traveling in Tibet. This, in and of itself, felt like an accomplishment.

The Chinese carefully manage the presence of any and all foreigners in Tibet. It's part chess game, part police state. For one, the Chinese are constantly changing the rules for getting a visa and traveling in Tibet. Sometimes they just plain close the border for a while if they don't want foreigners to come in and see what is going on—like they did in 2008 when Tibetans demonstrations sprung up all over the plateau to leverage the Beijing Olympics to make a desperate and despairing hue and cry against the Chinese occupation of Tibet.

You often have to get several permits to go where you want to go in Tibet, and then when you're just about there, a young soldier at a checkpoint, with a rifle in his hands and peach-fuzz on his face, will tell you that you don't have the right permits. I don't remember ever needing to get a permit to breathe, but sometimes it felt like the time might well come when it might be necessary to do just that.

Sitting down and talking too long with a Tibetan in a cafe can get that person brought in for questioning, or even thrown in jail. The last time I was in Lhasa there were closed circuit video cameras mounted on lampposts that kept track of people. To be in Tibet is to feel like you are definitely dealing with a civilization that has had 4,000 years of experience with suppressing dissent and keeping foreigners out. Think of the Great Wall of China.

You learn to fight fire with fire. Once I changed the date on the newsprint visa extension that was stapled into my passport, and as I was doing so, a drop of ink from my not so modern Chinese pen fell on the paper and was totally absorbed before I could do anything about it. And there it was. It was completely obvious that I had doctored, if you will, the visa. I can remember pushing it through the window at the border check post feeling certain in my gut that something bad was about to happen, but somehow I came out of that one OK.

I've been taken into custody by Chinese soldiers, and on two occasions I have actually had to fight minor skirmishes with soldiers to defend myself. Chinese soldiers like to yell at the top of their lungs when they fight. It's meant to be unnerving. I have had to outsmart the Chinese upon many an occasion. Maybe it's true that I have even snuck across the border into Tibet a couple of times.

One time I made arrangements to go to Kham—the eastern portion of Tibet—to interview a well-known and deeply respected lama. After months of preparation, six days before I was scheduled to start the long journey to get to his monastery, it came to my attention that the Chinese army had just occupied and taken over his monastery. They knocked down buildings, forced monks and nuns to flee for their lives in every direction of the compass, and they took the lama I was coming to interview to Sichuan and imprisoned him there for the remainder of his life. The remainder of his life. Several years later he was put in a hospital where he died of what the Chinese called an "illness." I never did get the chance to meet or interview him.

These kind of experiences are not at all unique to my own travels in Tibet. Many, if not most, of the scholars and serious travelers that I know who have tried to do their work in Tibet have similar stories to tell.

So when the time came, I was pleased to find myself finally trekking alone on the Chang Tang so that I could see nomadic life in Tibet as it really is. Sometimes on the Chang Tang you find yourself standing at the base of some of the most beautiful snow-covered mountains in the world looking up at a ridge line trying to figure out if you can locate and then possibly navigate your way through a 19,000-foot pass that your impossibly inadequate map says is somewhere in there just to the north of you. At other places the Chang Tang is an utterly barren yellowish-brown moonscape strewn with rock and rubble.

One day, as I was making my way through some moonscape, I thought I saw something moving and perhaps even coming my way several miles ahead. What in the world could this possibly be?

It turned out to be a lama traveling all alone on horseback. He was wearing a lama's robes, and I'm going to say he was about thirty-eight years old. He had the ruddy wind burnished cheeks of a Tibetan living in the open at high altitude in the wind and sun.

He was sitting astride a quintessential thirteen-hand Tibetan pony with his feet almost touching the ground. There was an archetypal rainbow-striped wool Tibetan horse blanket between the pony and his saddle, and the saddle was the typical wooden saddle you see being sold in small town markets all over Tibet and northern Nepal.

The foundation of the Tibetan saddle is two flat pieces of wood that form its sides that are surmounted by a wooden arch that forms horns—like the horn on the front of a Western American saddle—but in this case there are horns on both the front and back of the saddle. There were some pieces of leather on top of the wood to provide at least some cushioning, and then a Tibetan blanket on top of that.

The lama was out there all alone out in the middle of nowhere. He had no entourage, and he was just as puzzled to see me as I was to see him. He was curious enough to get off his pony, and we sat down and talked a while.

He was a lovely man, and he had the spirited wild look and topknot of a young lama from a school of Tibetan Buddhism called the Nyingma school. He was carrying a few meager supplies, but most of all, his saddle was festooned with the religious texts he was carrying. His priorities were unmistakable.

My Tibetan wasn't so good, but we were able to talk a little, and we gestured a lot. A lot of our time together was spent trying to figure out what our words meant. He showed me texts, and we even talked a little bit of philosophy. We traded food. We chanted and smiled together. And then we packed everything up, said our goodbyes and commenced to once again going our own ways. Our meeting was like a single epiphany in an egoless stream of consciousness. It popped up, quickly dissolved and then left no trace.

That experience has become a metaphor for me about what it must have been like to come to the Tibetan continent from afar—maybe at the beginning of the nineteenth century—and begin the task of translating Tibetan into another language.

It has also served as a metaphor for what it has been like to do scientific research on the stream of consciousness and the healthy mind with Tibetan lamas at the turn of the twentieth century. It's a complicated business, and you have to start at the beginning—even though, thank goodness, people have been translating Tibetan into Western languages for almost two centuries now.

First of all, there is the issue that lamas are not accustomed to talking about the finer nuances of the stream of consciousness and the egoless mind with a foreign doctor. Historically, in Tibet, a lama might have those conversations, if they were had at all, with only a few of their more advanced students and fellow lamas.

Having a scientist come and ask to talk with a lama about the egoless mind was not exactly something that happened in traditional Tibet! A Western scholar or mountaineer might occasionally show up and ask questions about customs or geography. Or a priest might come and try to convert everyone to Christianity.

Nowadays it is more likely that language scholars from the West will come to talk about the meaning of religious texts they are trying to translate. But for a scientist to come for the purpose of having scientific discussions about the stream of consciousness? To the best of my knowledge, there are no records of anything like that ever happening before.

This means that there were a couple of times that I was politely asked to leave, and once or twice, when I first began to do this work, the asking was not so polite! It has been an adventure. There was so much to learn.

Then there was the reality that we were talking about phenomena that can only be seen with the mind's eye. The subtlety of these phenomena means that Tibetan mind science is every bit as sophisticated and complex as elementary particle physics. Most of the things that I'll be writing about in *The Healthy Mind* are the more rudimentary aspects of what the lamas and I have talked about. I would be glad, even gratified, to present the more complicated aspects of our interviews to you, but I don't want to lose you, dear reader, or put you to sleep!

Often, it would, understandably, take a while for a lama to get to know me and decide if it might be worthwhile talking to me. For example, the first four times I asked the late lama Khenpo Thubten of Manali if there was such a thing as nondual phenomena, and whether or not such phenomena could appear in the stream of awareness, he just said no. This was long ago in 1993 when I was first starting out. The fifth time I asked the Khenpo that question he all of a sudden said yes, and then we got on with things. We ended up having many long and fruitful conversations about nondual phenomena from which I learned much.

Another complexity was that I would also have to start at the beginning each time I began to interview a new lama. I have long had a little twenty-minute talk that I would give to a lama at the beginning of our first interview to explain what science is, and what it is I had come to do.

Often, among my first questions, I'd actually ask lamas, who are much more accustomed to talking about the nuances of the enlightened mind, if in their experience there is a stream of consciousness in the mind. Or if there is a watcher that watches and knows that stream of consciousness! This is akin to asking Einstein in 1954 if there are electrons in an atom.

Here is an example of me asking elementary questions of this kind of the late Penor Rinpoche at Namdroling Monastery in south India in an interview in the late winter of 1997 (Vyner, 2018):

HMV: If the mind is the faculty that knows external appearances, when we know inner appearances,[1] is that also mind?

PR: That is also mind.

HMV: In other words, self-awareness[2] is also mind.

PR: Yes.

HMV: Is a moment of mental consciousness[3] a mind?

PR: Yes.

HMV: Why?

PR: It is because the mental consciousness is thinking, and that is why it is the mind.

HMV: Thank you. Is a mental consciousness a temporary mind or a permanent mind?

PR: A mental consciousness is not necessarily permanent. It has to go through the process of changing.

HMV: Is an emotion a mind?

PR: It is also an aspect of the mind.

HMV: Is it also temporary?

PR: Yes.

HMV: Is the stream of consciousness a mind?

PR: Yes.

HMV: Is the stream of consciousness many minds, or just one mind?

PR: Mind is generally one. It has all of its different aspects.

HMV: Thank you. The reason that I am asking you this line of questions is that in the West we generally think of the mind as being one thing—one large system. We see the mind as a whole system that does many things: it learns things; it remembers experiences; it creates the stream of consciousness; it creates thoughts; and so forth. Is it the same in Tibetan psychology? Or is it different?

PR: Yes. It's the same.

HMV: Are you saying that Tibetan psychology sees the mind as being one large system?

PR: Yes.

1. The technical term "inner appearance" is a translation of the Tibetan term nang-gyi-nangwa. It refers to all of the different kinds of phenomena that appear in the stream of consciousness: thoughts, emotions, feelings, moods, mind-films, epiphanies and so forth.
2. Self-awareness is a translation of the Tibetan term rang-rig.
3. Moment of mental consciousness is a translation of the Tibetan term yid-gyi shespa. Buddhist psychology sees the egocentric mind as a stream of moments of consciousness that is composed of six types of sensory moments of consciousness, and the moment of mental consciousness is one of them.

HMV: What is the word for that larger system in Tibetan?

PR: There is no specific name. But depending upon the activity in which the mind is engaged, it will have a name.

HMV: But again, there is a larger system.

PR: Yes. It's the ground.[4]

HMV: By ground, do you mean the Tibetan term "gzhi," the ground of awareness?

PR: The mind is like a mirror in which all different kinds of things can appear. The mind is like that.

HMV: Are you saying that the whole larger system that is the mind is the ground of awareness, *gzhi*?

PR: Yes. From that, all of the thoughts and afflictive emotions like hatred and so forth arise.

HMV: When you say that the ground, or *gzhi*, is the larger system, are you also saying that the mandala at the ground is the larger system?

PR: Yes. The virtuous thoughts, the non-virtuous thoughts just normally arise from the ground that is the mind.

HMV: Thank you very much.

Another thing that I learned along the way is that lamas, as a rule, much prefer talking about more advanced matters, just as scientists sometimes prefer to talk about advanced matters, as opposed to talking about basics with a layperson. There was a period of time when I made an assiduous effort to focus on systematically discussing the workings of the egocentric mind, and this is when I discovered that lamas were not all that uninterested in having extensive discussions of the workings of the unhealthy mind.

At times, the reverse can be true as well. Lamas have at times been reluctant to talk about more advanced matters—especially at first, if we didn't yet know one another well. Talking about the egoless mind, once again, was something that a lama would normally do only with a colleague or an advanced student. Tibetans lamas believe that a person can lose their wisdom if they talk about their nondual experience too much. They also believe that it is not a good idea to talk about such matters with people who do not have the ability to understand them.

Then there were linguistic issues. There were times, especially in the beginning, when I would have hours of conversation with a lama about the meaning of one single Tibetan word. As a scientist, I needed to understand, if possible, exactly what type of empirical phenomenon a given term referred to.

Take for example, the essential Tibetan term "yeshe," which is often translated into English as "primordial wisdom." Primordial wisdom is a very important term in Tibetan psychology. The term has many meanings, most of which refer to one aspect or another of the nondual experience of knowing your mind

4. Tib.: gzhi. I usually translate it as "ground of awareness."

exactly as it is. It is a moment of nondual awareness in which the mind knows itself without projecting any egopoietic concepts onto itself.

I knew that this was the general meaning of the term when I first started interviewing lamas about primordial wisdom, but I still had to figure out if the term "yeshe" refers to nondual awareness itself, to the nondual phenomena of which that nondual awareness is aware, to both or to something else altogether.

Furthermore, there are many different kinds of primordial wisdom, and indeed sometimes the term can refer to nondual awareness itself, and at other times to a nondual inner appearance—a moment of nondual awareness that appears in the stream of awareness. Here is Lopon Tekchoke again explaining just this point (Vyner, 2005):

HMV: I'd like to turn now to yeshe, or primordial wisdom. Is primordial wisdom a nondual inner appearance?

LTC: Yes.

HMV: Thank you. Is primordial wisdom the same thing as an empty appearance, or chos-nyid?

LTC: Primordial wisdom is the awareness that actually knows the empty appearances; the nature. When primordial wisdom realizes the emptiness of an appearance, it dissolves into and becomes nondual awareness.

HMV: What is the difference, then, between nondual awareness and primordial wisdom?

LTC: There are two kinds of primordial wisdom. There is one kind of primordial wisdom that is primordially there. It is always present. Then there is another kind of primordial wisdom that appears when you see an object without any delusion. That is also primordial wisdom.

HMV: What is the term for the primordial yeshe, the primordial wisdom that is always there?

LTC: That primordial yeshe is called naturally occurring primordial wisdom, or rangjung yeshe. In DzogChen,[5] naturally occurring primordial wisdom is the same as primordial nondual awareness.

HMV: Ahh. And then what is the Tibetan term for the primordial wisdom that knows a specific object the way it is?

LTC: Suchness primordial wisdom.[6] Suchness primordial wisdom is the wisdom that knows a phenomenon as it is.

5. DzogChen is the name of a meditation, philosophical and literary tradition that appears in two of the religions of the Tibetan Plateau: Tibetan Buddhism and the indigenous Tibetan religion that is called Bön. Almost all of the lamas that I interviewed for this work have been practitioners and scholars of DzogChen.

6. Tib.: de khona nyid togpa'i yeshe. In Buddhist epistemology, to know the suchness of a phenomenon is to know that phenomenon as it is; to know it without projecting any additional constructs onto it. Nondual awareness knows the suchness, or emptiness, of a phenomenon. Dual awareness does not. Suchness primordial wisdom is a moment of nondual awareness in which the mind knows the suchness of a phenomenon, or meaning.

Yet another complication was that different lamas often use the same Tibetan word to refer to different empirical phenomena, and it was of course important to learn those variations, and keep all of that straight as well.

All of this could sometimes be tedious work, but there was never any question in my mind that it was both essential and worthwhile to cover all of this rudimentary ground, and much more. It had to be done if I was going to establish a proper science of the phenomena that appear in the stream of consciousness. So I did it, and to be honest, I loved this part of the work. It was a pleasure to do it, and it was even more gratifying when this early work made it possible to move on to more profound matters—like describing in detail the workings of the egoless state of mind.

Buddhism and Science

It has become fashionable over the last few decades to say of Buddhism that it is a science of the mind. Conferences abound in which it is declared that Buddhist philosophy and modern science have much in common. Sometimes it seems as though the functional MRI was invented for the sole purpose of proving that meditation is good for the brain. Forty years have now passed since we were first told by Fritjof Capra that quantum mechanics and Buddhism seem to have the same worldview (Capra, 1975).

The vogue of this trend has gathered so much momentum that it has become part of popular culture, which in and of itself is enough to make any serious scientist skeptical of the merits of the idea.

Nonetheless, it is true that there lies, within the history of Buddhist ideas, a proto-science of the mind. To be more exact, this Buddhist mind science is a science of the phenomena that appear in the stream of consciousness. Indeed, ever since its inception, Buddhism psychology has always been, at its core, a science of the stream of consciousness.

The first systematic school of Buddhist psychology—the Abhidharma—was a proto-science of the stream of consciousness. In addition, many of Buddhism's philosophical positions have been derived from its observations of the stream of consciousness; just as William James himself derived philosophical positions—for example, his five characters of thought—from his observations of the stream of consciousness (James, 1890, pp. 224–290).

This Buddhist science of the stream of consciousness has been applied to the task of answering a considerable spectrum of questions about the mind. Of relevance to our inquiry into the nature of the healthy mind, Buddhism's maps of the egoless and egocentric mind, for example, have been derived from its observations of the phenomena that appear in the stream of consciousness.

This science of the stream of consciousness is not a trivial part of the Buddhism. It lies at the very heart of the Buddhist tradition, and this chapter will present some of the observations of the stream of consciousness that it has made over the centuries.

This does not mean that the Buddhist practitioners who first created this science were familiar with our modern notion of what science is; or that they thought of themselves as scientists; or that they wore long white coats and worked in laboratories. Certainly it does not mean that they were brain scientists. They were scientists of the mind.

What it does mean, however, is that countless Buddhist practitioners and scholars have, over the centuries, studied the mind in a scientific fashion and discovered empirical truths. They have made systematic observations of the phenomena that appear in the stream of consciousness, and they derived from those observations theories of cognition, the healthy mind and much more.

This, of course, is exactly what every field of science does: it makes methodical observations of a specific group of phenomena, and then it derives from those observations a body of theory about those phenomena.

My experience interviewing lamas that has shown me firsthand that Buddhist philosophy is grounded in observations of the stream of consciousness. I found, in our interviews, that the lamas often used the language and theory of Buddhist philosophy to describe their experiences of their own mind. We will delve into examples of this phenomenon is a moment.

My task as a scientist has been to empiricize the lama's philosophical descriptions of their experiences of their own mind; to transform their philosophical descriptions of the mind into experiential descriptions of the workings of the mind.

The foundation of my approach to empiricizing the lama interviews has been to choose crucial technical terms from the Buddhist literature and ask the lamas to describe the mental phenomena or states of mind to which those terms refer. Invariably, the lamas described their experiences of the mind in terms of either (1) a phenomenon or a group of phenomena that appear in the stream of consciousness or (2) the awareness that knows those phenomena.

In other words, when the lamas presented their descriptions of the phenomena of the mind in the language or theory of Buddhist philosophy, we would explore those descriptions in a way that would transform them into experiential, and thus empirical, renderings of those phenomena. Let me give you a concrete example of what I mean.

The DzogChen tradition of Tibet (Klein, 2014; Thondup, 1996) is regarded as an advanced school of meditation and philosophy, and it is found in both the Tibetan Buddhist and Bön traditions.[7] DzogChen is particularly adept at

7. Bön is the name of the indigenous religion of the Tibetan plateau. It was practiced in Tibet before the coming of Buddhism in Tibet, and it is still practiced to this day.

empirically describing the experience of having an egoless mind, and I would also say that DzogChen is the most empirical of all the Buddhist schools of psychology. These are the principal reasons that I chose to study DzogChen lamas.

The DzogChen theory of the ground of awareness[8] is perhaps the most fundamental and distinctive theory of DzogChen philosophy, and although it is not at all obvious to the untrained eye, it is actually a theory of self-awareness—the mind's awareness of its own stream of consciousness.

The next several pages are going to present a series of excerpts from interviews with three DzogChen lamas—the late Penor Rinpoche, Khenpo Tsewang Gyatso and Lopon Tekchoke—in which we worked together to empiricize the DzogChen theory of the ground of awareness.

Each of the lamas use the term "ground of awareness" to refer to the phenomenon of nondual self-awareness. Once again, nondual self-awareness is the specific type of awareness that the egoless mind has of its stream of consciousness. In contrast, the egocentric mind has dual awareness of the phenomena its stream of consciousness.

Once again, and as we will be seeing, the egoless mind is actually defined by the fact that it is a mind that has nondual awareness of itself, and this is why I carefully pursued the description of nondual self-awareness with these lamas and many other lamas as well. Understanding nondual self-awareness is a key part of understanding the dynamics of the egoless mind.

Eliciting and understanding a description of egoless, or nondual, self-awareness went forward in several steps. In this first excerpt, the late Penor Rinpoche, who was at the time the head lama of the DzogChen tradition, simply confirms my hypothesis that the DzogChen theory of the ground of awareness is actually DzogChen's theory of self-awareness.

This was a crucial step forward at the time, because the DzogChen texts that discuss the ground of awareness do not come right out and say that their descriptions of the ground of awareness are actually descriptions of the process of self-awareness (Vyner, 2018):

HMV: It seems to me that there are three main theories of self-awareness in the history of Buddhist ideas, and I'd like to ask you some questions about those theories.

PR: OK.

HMV: First of all there is the Abhidharma theory of self-awareness. It says that self-awareness occurs when one thought remembers a previous thought. Is this a correct understanding of the Abhidharmic theory of self-awareness?

PR: Yes. But every individual yana has its own explanation.

HMV: Yes. I think the principal Mahayana theory of self-awareness is the Yogacara theory, which says that self-awareness occurs when a single moment of consciousness is aware of itself.

8. Tib.: gzhi.

PR: Yes that's correct.

HMV: Finally, it seems like the third basic theory of self-awareness is the DzogChen theory of the ground of awareness and of appearances of that ground.[9]

PR: Oh yes.

HMV: Would it be correct, then, to say that the theory of the ground of awareness is a theory of self-awareness?

PR: Yes. If the self-awareness recognizes appearances of the ground, then it is OK.

In this next excerpt, Khenpo Tsewang Gyatso, of Namdroling Monastery in south India, confirms that the theory of the ground of awareness is DzogChen's theory of nondual self-awareness, which is also called wisdom self-awareness and egoless awareness.[10] The Khenpo then goes on to describe the basic structure and dynamic of nondual self-awareness (Vyner, 2018):

HMV: The last time we talked, you said that the DzogChen theory of the ground is actually a theory of self-awareness. Did I understand you correctly?

KTG: Yes.

HMV: If I understood you correctly, you also said that this DzogChen theory describes self-awareness as being a process in which egoless awareness knows itself.[11]

KTG: Yes.

HMV: When the nondual mind, or egoless awareness, knows itself . . . what kind of appearances does that awareness know?

KTG: The appearances that it knows are rigpa's nature, the display of egoless awareness.

HMV: What type of appearances does egoless. awareness know when it knows itself?

KTG: The display of rigpa's nature includes the appearances of primordial wisdom, the three aspects of the enlightened mind, and all of the qualities the enlightened mind.[12]

9. Tib.: gzhi nang.
10. "The terms nondual self-awareness (Tib: rang-rig), wisdom self-awareness (Tib: rang-rig yeshe) and egoless awareness (Tib: rigpa) are synonyms. They are synonyms in the sense that empirically all three of these terms refer to the same phenomenon: the awareness of the egoless mind that realizes its true self because it has nondual awareness of the meanings that appear in its SoC." Please see chapter eleven for a systematic description of this phenomenon.
11. Once again, the technical Tibetan term "rigpa" is usually translated into English as "awareness," but I often translate it as "nondual awareness" because empirically it is nondual awareness, as opposed to dual awareness.
12. Here the Khenpo is listing the three types of phenomena that nondual self-awareness knows: (1) the "three aspects of the enlightened mind" (Skt: trikaya; Tib: sku sum) (2) primordial wisdom (Tib: yeshe) and (3) the qualities of the enlightened mind (yonten).

HMV: Thank you. Does that mean that it would be correct to say that wisdom self-awareness is the same as awareness?

KTG: Yes.

HMV: Does that mean that wisdom self-awareness knows and realizes primordial wisdom?

KTG: Yes.

HMV: What kind of primordial wisdom does it realize? Does it realize any particular kind of primordial wisdom?

KTG: It realizes all of the different kinds of primordial wisdom. Nondual self-awareness is inseparable from all of the different kinds of primordial wisdom.

HMV: Does nondual self-awareness also realize the three principal aspects of the Buddha's mind, the three kayas?

KTG: Yes.

HMV: Does this mean that the enlightened, or egoless, mind itself can be defined as this special and distinct mode of nondual self-awareness?

KTG: Yes.

HMV: Is this the same as saying that the enlightened mind is actually a type of self-awareness in which the mind realizes its own emptiness?

KTG: Yes.

HMV: Does nondual, or DzogChen, self-awareness realize the nature of the mind?

KTG: Yes.

HMV: Of course. Is that the same thing as saying that nondual self-awareness leaves the mind in its natural state?

KTG: Yes. That's the same thing.

HMV: Thank you. What does it mean to leave the mind in its natural state? What is the natural state of the mind?

KTG: When the mind is in its natural state, it abides in its primordial pure nature—as it is. There is a sense of complete awareness and of just abiding.

HMV: What do you mean by just abiding?

KTG: Not having any kind of disturbance. Not having any kind of conceptual thoughts or dual minds of any kind.

HMV: So the natural state of the mind is non-conceptual and nondual. Would it also be correct to say that the natural state of the mind is a state of mind in which awareness does not accept or reject or follow inner appearances?

KTG: Yes.

HMV: Is that an important aspect of it?

KTG: Yes. Yes. [Emphatic]

HMV: Does that mean that the natural state of the mind is a state of mind in which awareness leaves all inner appearances in their natural, or unaltered, state?

KTG: Yes.

This remarkable passage provides us with a description of the basic structure and dynamic of the nondual self-awareness of the enlightened, or egoless, mind. In this description, Khenpo confirms that:

1. The subjective aspect of the egoless mind is wisdom self-awareness (Tib: rang-rig yeshe), which is also called egoless. awareness (Tib: rigpa), in DzogChen mind science.
2. The objective aspect of the egoless mind are the nondual phenomena that wisdom self-awareness knows: primordial wisdom, the primordial meanings and the three aspects of the Buddha's mind.
3. Nondual self-awareness leaves the mind in its natural state. It does not alter the stream of awareness in any way.

The final step in the empirical mapping of nondual self-awareness is to describe the nondual phenomena that it knows. Here is a passage from a 2005 interview with Lopon Tekchoke, in which the Lopon describes one of the nondual phenomena that is known by nondual self-awareness: the phenomenon that is called an "appearance of the ground of awareness"[13] by DzogChen mind science. The science of the stream of consciousness calls this phenomenon a "primordial meaning." In this passage, Lopon starts off by referring to a primordial meaning as the phenomenon that nondual awareness knows when it knows itself (Vyner, 2005):

LTC: Oh yes. In the state of nondual awareness, when nondual awareness knows itself, you know and understand the attributes of nondual awareness.

HMV: What are the attributes of nondual awareness?

LTC: The attributes of self-illumination.[14]

HMV: What is self-illumination?

LTC: Self-illumination is an appearance that illuminates one's self.

HMV: When you see a moment of self-illumination as an inner appearance,[15] does it actually look like light rays?

LTC: Yes.

HMV: Can an appearance of self-illumination create intention or meaning?

LTC: Yes. It can provide both meaning and intention.

HMV: Does self-illumination always appear as rays of light, or can it appear in some other way as well?

LTC: Only as rays.

HMV: Thank you. Once again, then, what does it mean to "know the attributes of self-illumination?"

13. Tib.: Gzhi snang.
14. Tib.: Rang dang.
15. Empirically, the term "inner appearance" (Tib.: nang-gyi nang-wa) refers to any dual, predual or nondual phenomenon that appears in the stream of consciousness.

LTC: It means understanding the exact meaning of that illumination in a moment. [Lopon claps his hands]

HMV: Do the appearances of self-illumination give nondual meaning to experience? Are they nondual inner appearances that give meaning to a person's experience in the same way that the dual inner appearances such as thoughts give dual meaning to experience?

LTC: When self-illumination appears to nondual awareness, it is like a reflection appearing in a mirror. It is like this.

HMV: Are the images that appear in the mirror inner appearances, external appearances or both?

LTC: They are primordial meanings.

HMV: Ahh. And once again, does a primordial meaning give meaning to a person's experience?

LTC: Oh yes.

HMV: Thank you very much.

Over decades of research, the lamas and I have used this same approach to systematically empiricize countless technical terms from the larger corpus of Buddhist psychology and philosophy. In the process, we have identified and described many of the phenomena that have been delineated by the centuries-old Buddhist proto-science of the stream of consciousness, and there are still a vast number of phenomena waiting to be identified and described.

The fruit of this empiricizing enterprise was that it gradually generated a descriptive science of the phenomena that appear in the stream of consciousness. This was the first step in our investigation of the healthy mind.

The second step was to construct maps of the structure and dynamics of the egoless and egocentric states of mind. These maps are descriptive theories of how the various phenomena of the stream of consciousness interact with one another to create the egoless and egocentric states of mind.[16] As such, they were derived from our descriptive science of the phenomena that appear in the stream of consciousness.

The Buddhist Science of the Egoless Mind

The ultimate reason that I chose to do twenty plus years of research on the healthy mind with Tibetan lamas is that: (1) Indo-Tibetan Buddhism has long had, at its core, a sophisticated proto-science of both the stream of consciousness and the egoless mind; and (2) the DzogChen descriptions of the egoless and egocentric mind rang true with my own experience of these states of mind.

16. Please see Chapters 8 and 9 for the theoretical map of the egocentric mind, and Chapter 11 for the theoretical map of the egoless mind.

It makes perfect sense that Buddhist practitioner-scholars developed a proto-science of the stream of consciousness and the egoless mind. The heart of Buddhist soteriological practice is to change the way one's mind works as a means of cultivating an egoless mind. Given that their aim is to change the dynamics of the mind, Buddhist meditators have had a genuine need to empirically study the mind and figure out how it works.

To understand the mind, Buddhism chose to study the stream of consciousness—which probably happened because of course you constantly experience the stream of consciousness in meditation. To wit, the very first systematic Buddhist psychology—the Abhidharma—was centered around an elaborate typology of the phenomena that appear in the stream of consciousness; and to this day, Buddhist psychology continues to be a science of the stream of consciousness.

By focusing on the stream of consciousness, Buddhist psychology discovered that the defining differences between the egoless and egocentric mind are differences in their stream of consciousness. Indeed, the egoless mind has a very different stream of consciousness than the egocentric mind.

In the long run, this has turned out to mean that Tibetan lamas know far more about the healthy human mind than modern science does, and they do so precisely because they come from a tradition that has been exploring the stream of consciousness, the egoless mind and the egocentric mind for more than two millennia.

The proto-science of the stream of consciousness that is found in the Buddhist literature is actually humanity's first science of the stream of consciousness.

In our own Western tradition, there was indirect mention of the stream of consciousness in the writings of Homer and Plato for instance, but the first unmistakable mention of the stream of consciousness in the world's literature, as well as the first attempt to systematically describe the phenomena that appear in the stream of consciousness, appears in the Abhidharma literature of early Buddhism. This literature dates back to roughly the third century BC. In the modern scientific tradition of the West, we have yet to develop a systematic science of the stream of consciousness.

This early Abhidharmic science of the stream of consciousness was used as a soteriological guide by Buddhist meditators. The first Buddhists practitioners believed that the central task of the path that leads to an enlightened mind was to eliminate a group of phenomena that they called defilements from the stream of consciousness. The Abhidharmic science of the stream of consciousness was used to identify and eliminate those defilements from their mind. It was also used as a guide to understanding the basic mechanisms of how the mind works.

The meditator-scholars of the Abhidharma made systematic observations of the phenomena that appear in the stream of consciousness, and they published their observations as long lists, or typologies, of the different types of phenomena that they saw in the stream of consciousness. Each of the phenomena that they described was a specific type of moment of consciousness, and their typologies of those phenomena tended to be fifty to seventy items long.[17]

It is tempting, in retrospect, to see those typologies as descriptive sciences of the phenomena that appear in the stream of consciousness, and many people do. After all, the first step in the scientific method, and thus any scientific investigation, is to make systematic observations of the phenomena that one is purporting to study. The Abhidharmic typologies are a record of the early Buddhist observations of the stream of consciousness.

The Abhidharmic typologies appear to be empirical in the very real sense that many of the phenomena they delineate do indeed appear in the stream of consciousness. Here are just a few examples of the type of phenomena that were described by the Abhidharmic scholars (Hirakawa and Groner, 1990):

1. Desire
2. Wisdom
3. Perception
4. Equanimity
5. Anger
6. Conceit.

The Abhidharma scholars did more, though, than just make observations of phenomena. They also derived, from their observations, a vast array of mechanical, and thus seemingly scientific, theories about several aspects of how the mind works. Among many others, the Abhidharmic scholars developed theories about:

1. The mechanics of the process of sensation
2. The mechanics of the process of perception
3. The mechanics of the process of self-awareness
4. The nature of the stream of consciousness
5. The defilements of the egocentric mind
6. The qualities of the enlightened mind
7. The fundamental nature of a human being
8. How to attain nirvana.

In retrospect, some of these theories appear to be scientific in our modern sense, and some of them do not.

Over the course of many centuries, this early Buddhist science of the stream of consciousness blossomed into a more sophisticated and empirical science of

17. There were nineteen different schools of Abhidharma, and although there was a great deal of overlapping between each of the schools, each school is thought to have produced their own typology of the phenomena that appear in the stream of consciousness.

the stream of consciousness. With the passage of time, new phenomena were observed and added to the Buddhist science of the stream of consciousness.

In addition, many causal sequences were delineated as well. As just one example for now, it was observed that when the mind grasps[18] a thought, many more thoughts would immediately appear in the mind. Another basic finding was the discovery that when the mind does not grasp thoughts or emotions, those thoughts and emotions will dissolve.

This Buddhist science of the stream of consciousness became, in turn, the foundation of a sophisticated science of the egoless mind. Buddhist meditator-scholars systematically applied their basic science of the stream of consciousness to the task of describing and analyzing the egoless state of mind.

This Buddhist proto-science of the egoless mind has delineated, over the course of almost twenty centuries of inquiry, several of the cardinal qualities of the egoless mind. Here are some of those cardinal qualities:[19]

1. The egoless mind does not see itself as having a permanent personal identity. The egocentric mind, in contrast, does see itself as having an essence that is usually articulated as a permanent identity, or self-concept (Hirakawa and Groner, 1990) (*The Emptiness of Person*).
2. The Theory of Defilements: This theory asserts that there are moments of consciousness called defilements—among them for example the emotions—that appear in the egocentric mind and cause it to both suffer and lose access to its true nature.
   a. This theory also asserts that defilements do not appear in the stream of consciousness of the egoless mind, and that as a result, the egoless mind does not suffer or lose access to its true nature (Cox, 1992) (*Defilements*).
3. The phenomena that appear in the stream of consciousness of the egoless mind do not have a permanent identity. They do not have an identity because the egoless mind does not attribute a conceptual identity to them in the process of knowing them (Dalai Lama, 2015) (*The Emptiness of Phenomena*).
   a. In contrast, the egocentric mind does see the phenomena that appear in its stream of consciousness as having an identity.

18. In Buddhist psychology, the term **grasping** refers to a mode of knowing a phenomenon in which the mind attributes a concept of self to a phenomenon in the process of knowing it. The egocentric mind grasps thoughts and emotions in the process of knowing them, and it does so for example, by repressing or holding on to them when they appear in the stream of consciousness. The egoless mind, in contrast, does not grasp the meanings that appear in its stream of consciousness.
19. The list of qualities of the egoless mind being presented here are presented in their empiricized form. However, the references attached to each of these qualities will take you to a text that explains each quality in the terms in which they were originally articulated in Buddhist philosophy. In addition, there is a second parenthesis attached to each listed quality, and it contains the name—in italics—of the Buddhist theory that the listed empiricized quality articulates.

4. The egoless mind has nondual awareness of the phenomena that appear in its stream of consciousness (Makransky, 1997) (*Nondual Awareness*).
   a. In contrast, the egocentric mind has dual awareness of the phenomena that appear in its stream of consciousness.
5. By virtue of the fact that the egoless mind has nondual awareness of the phenomena that appear in its stream of consciousness, it knows them as they really are (Brunnholzl, 2014) (*Buddha Nature*).
6. The egoless watcher allows the stream of consciousness to run free and abide in its natural state. It leaves the stream of awareness in its natural state by virtue of the fact that it does not try to alter it. This means that it does not judge, repress, attach or follow any of the meanings that appear in its stream of consciousness (Longchenpa, 2001) (*Effortlessness*).
7. By allowing its stream of consciousness to run free, the egoless mind causes the phenomena that appear in its stream of consciousness to spontaneously transform themselves into either the nondual awareness or nondual meanings of the egoless mind (Thondup, 1996) (*Self-Liberation*).
8. A very effective way, perhaps the most effective way, to cultivate the egoless mind is to practice meditations that cultivate a state of mind in which the watcher leaves the stream of consciousness in its natural state (Longchenpa, 2001; Namkhai Norbu, 2000) (*Effortless Meditation in Which the Meditator Rests in the Nature of Mind*).

After many centuries of development, the Buddhist science of the egoless mind has become a refined body of knowledge. The observations listed here are all empirically correct, and they have been evaluated and incorporated into the larger theory of the healthy mind being presented here.

Given, as we will be seeing, that the egoless mind is a healthier mind than the egocentric mind, it is fair to assert that there is much that modern science can learn from Buddhist mind science about the nature of the healthy mind.

Over the course of many centuries, Buddhist meditator-scholars have systematically applied their basic science of the stream of consciousness to the task of understanding the nature of the healthy mind. They have harnessed that science to the tasks of (1) mapping out the structure and dynamics of the egoless and egocentric minds; (2) understanding the differences between these two states of mind; and (3) learning how to best apply meditation to the task of cultivating an egoless mind.

It is important for modern science to notice that Buddhist mind science has this extensive knowledge of the healthy mind precisely because, and only because, it has allowed itself to study the stream of consciousness. If it had not studied the stream of consciousness, it would never have understood the defining dynamics of either the egoless mind or the egocentric mind.

Buddhist scholars somehow understood that the science of the stream of consciousness is the key to understanding the nature of the healthy mind; the royal road, if you will, to scientifically understanding the nature of the healthy mind.

Given that at present modern science does not yet allow itself to study the phenomena that appear in the stream of consciousness, this is a crucial point for us to appreciate if we are to take up the study of the healthy mind. We will have to allow ourselves to study the stream of consciousness if we want to empirically understand, for ourselves, the nature of the healthy mind.

My intention in doing the lama interviews has been to learn what the Tibetans know about the healthy mind and the stream of consciousness, and to both empiricize and empirically evaluate their knowledge so that it could be welcomed into, and become part of, the canon of modern science.

In the interviews that the lamas and I have been doing together, we have distilled Tibetan Buddhist psychology, if you will, and condensed out from it a modern science of both the healthy mind and the stream of consciousness. This is the larger sense in which we have been empiricizing Buddhist philosophy and psychology.

In the course of pursuing this distillation, we have been replicating, empirically evaluating and expanding upon the Buddhist proto-science of the egoless mind and the stream of consciousness.

This does not mean, however, that the science being presented in *The Healthy Mind* is in any sense Buddhism. It is simply a science of the phenomena that appear in the stream of consciousness, and the theories of the healthy mind that have been derived from that science.

I have been interviewing Buddhist lamas to record their observations of these phenomena because they are probably the most sophisticated observers of the stream of consciousness on the planet. They are accomplished scientists of the stream of consciousness who have made countless observations of the phenomena that appear in the mind stream. They also have a deeply empirical understanding of the egoless and egocentric states of mind.

In our interviews, I have been recording the lamas' observations of the stream of consciousness, and I have done so for the purpose of putting together a typology of phenomena that will serve as the foundation for a modern science of the stream of consciousness.

I have focused on applying the science of the stream of consciousness to the investigation of the nature of the healthy mind, but the expectation is that the science of the stream of consciousness will be germane to the investigation of many other issues as well.

The remainder of *The Healthy Mind* is now going to present the essence of what has been learned from more than twenty years of working together with the lamas. The next two chapters of *The Healthy Mind* will present both the descriptive science of the stream of consciousness that has emerged from the interviews, and an analysis of our methodology. Subsequent chapters will then present the theory of the healthy mind that has been derived from that science.

References

Brunnholzl, K. (2014). *When the Clouds Part: The Uttaratantra and Its Meditative Tradition as a Bridge Between Sutra and Tantra.* Boston and London: Snow Lion Publications.

Capra, F. (1975). *The Tao of Physics: An Exploration of the Parallels Between Modern Physics and Eastern Mysticism.* Boston: Shambhala Publications.

Cox, C. (1992). Attainment through abandonment: The Sarvastivadin path of removing defilements. In R. Buswell and R. Gimello (eds.), *Paths to Liberation: The Marga and Its Transformation in Buddhist Thought.* Honolulu: Kuroda Institute, University of Hawaii Press, pp. 63–105.

Dalai Lama. (2015). *The World of Tibetan Buddhism: An Overview of Its Philosophy and Practice*, ed. Thubten Jinpa. Somerville: Wisdom Publications.

Hirakawa, A., and Groner, P. (1990). *A History of Indian Buddhism: From Śākyamuni to Early Mahāyāna.* Honolulu: University of Hawaii Press.

James, W. (1890). *Principles of Psychology.* New York, NY: Henry Holt and Co.

Klein, A. (2011). DzogChen. In J. L. Garfield and W. Edelglass (eds.) *The Oxford Handbook of World Philosophy.* Oxford: Oxford University Press, pp. 265–278.

Longchenpa. (2001). *A Treasure Trove of Scriptural Transmission.* Junction City, CA: Padma Publishing.

Makransky, J. (1997). *Buddhahood Embodied: Sources of Controversy in India and Tibet.* Albany: SUNY Press.

Namkhai Norbu. (2000). *The Crystal and the Way of Light.* Ithaca, NY: Snow Lion Publications.

Thondup, T. (1996). *The Practice of DzogChen.* Ithaca, NY: Snow Lion Publications.

Vyner, H. M. (2005). *The Healthy Mind Interviews, Volume 3: Lopon Tekchog.* Kathmandu: Vajra Books.

Vyner, H. M. (2018). *The Healthy Mind Interviews: Volume 5: Penor Rinpoche and Khenpo Tsewang Rinpoche.* Kathmandu: Vajra Publications.

5

A CULTIVATED BLIND SPOT

A Phenomenon Is a Phenomenon Is a Phenomenon

We have no idea of whether or not the people who painted animals on the walls of the caves at Lascaux seventeen thousand years ago had a stream of consciousness, and we'll probably never know if the people who built the first fires had a stream of consciousness. Nor do we know if the poet who wrote the *Gilgamesh* a slight five or so thousand years ago had a stream of consciousness, although judging from the dualities of the *Gilgamesh*, my guess is that he or she probably did.

We simply have no way of determining when thoughts and emotions first appeared as knowable objects within the human mind. Which is to say that we have no idea when the stream of consciousness first became a presence within the mind.

Nor do we know *why* the stream of consciousness first appeared within our minds. The science of the stream of consciousness has established that the modern mind uses the stream of consciousness to control its behavior and socialize itself (Vyner, 2007–2008), and this suggests that the stream of consciousness might have appeared as a response to the circumstance of living with social constraints in large social groups.

It seems entirely possible that social constraints, and their handmaiden repression, forced the stream of consciousness to emerge, and that as it became visible it gave the mind a way to look at and control the meanings that it was giving to its experience. But again, we do not know for certain that this was the case. There are no bones or stone tools that could provide us with evidence to prove this hypothesis.

Even today, we have no way of determining whether or not we are the only species that has a stream of consciousness. Chimpanzees use blades of grass to collect the termites they eat. We often feel as though our golden retrievers and horses, and even wolves in the wild, have the same kind of feelings and sense of purpose that we have; and there can be no question that often it looks as though they do.

But still, we have no way of knowing whether or not they actually have a stream of consciousness—a flow of thoughts, intuitions, feelings, emotions and epiphanies that appear as discrete and knowable phenomena within the inner space of their mind and only within their mind.

How would we determine whether or not a non-human animal, or for that matter another human being, has a stream of consciousness? In a world in which science has imposed upon itself an ignorance of the stream of consciousness, this is called the other minds problem in the philosophy of mind.

I wrote a short story in medical school that created a fictional solution to the problem. That story grew out of my early yearnings to empirically study the stream of consciousness. I knew back then that it was something I would be doing.

In the world in which that short story was set, every single human being had a small digital readout on the side of their head that displayed exactly what was going on in their stream of consciousness. The readout was sort of like one of those moving digital advertising banners in Times Square, and it sat on the left temple—the same side as the speech centers of the brain.

These readouts were capable of telling you exactly what a person was thinking, what they were repressing and more. In this world, science was able to study the phenomena that appear in the stream of consciousness. After all, the digital readouts made interpersonal verification of the happenings of the stream of consciousness possible. Two scientists could simultaneously observe in real time what was happening in another person's stream of consciousness. With this added advantage, the mind scientists of that fictional world knew much more about the mind than the psychologists and psychiatrists of our own day do.

In the world in which we really do live, science does not yet have a biological or physical means of determining whether or not a non-verbal animal, or for that matter another human being, has a stream of consciousness. As matters stand now, a functional MRI is not capable of telling us whether or not a person has a stream of thoughts running through his or her mind. Neither is an EEG. Or a person's genome. Nor, of course, will an x-ray, a lumbar puncture or a blood test tell us whether or not a person has a stream of consciousness.

Short of having a digital readout on the side of our heads, the only direct way we have of knowing if another person has a stream of consciousness running through the inner landscape of their mind is to ask them if they have one.

I have asked a lot of people if they have a stream of consciousness. It is, for one, part of my work. Every single human being I have ever asked, has told me that they do have a stream of consciousness. It is a universal characteristic of the human mind; just as every human body has a brain, a pancreas and ribosomal RNA that guides the manufacture of proteins in its cells.

I have even posed the question to auditoria full of people: "Is there anyone in the audience who does not have a stream of consciousness?" No one has ever, in earnest, raised their hand and said that they do not have a stream of consciousness. Although I have to be honest: I have never asked Daniel Dennett or the Churchlands. Nevertheless, I feel safe in saying that all healthy human beings do have a stream of consciousness.

Modern science has unnecessarily deepened the mystery that surrounds the stream of consciousness by not allowing itself to study the phenomena that appear in the stream of consciousness. Science has exiled the stream of consciousness.

Nonetheless, it is both important, and an easy matter, to scientifically study the phenomena that appear in the stream of consciousness, as the entire history of the Buddhist science of the stream of consciousness makes abundantly clear.

In addition, our contemporary studies of mind wandering and the lama studies of the healthy mind that are being reported in this book are both inaugurating a modern science of the stream of consciousness.

Our study of the healthy mind has led us to an empirical understanding of the nature of the healthy mind, and it will also hopefully make it clear that it is more than a little important that we scientifically understand the stream of consciousness.

The study of the stream of consciousness is the key to understanding such disparate issues as the nature of the healthy mind, and to finding the psychological equivalent for the anatomical lesion of somatic medicine—which would put the diagnoses and treatments of the fields of psychiatry and clinical psychology on an empirical par with those produced by the fields of cardiology and pediatrics. The only impediment to empirically studying the stream of consciousness is scientific convention.

The Strong Argument

Perhaps the strongest argument for scientifically studying the stream of consciousness is that it is of the utmost importance that we understand it. Forgive me for a moment while I belabor the obvious.

The psychological processes that appear in the stream of consciousness are a group of natural phenomena that have a profound impact upon the quality of a human being's life. It is simply a matter of common sense that our thoughts and emotions have an extensive effect on everything that we say and do.

A single prescient thought might solve a national problem. Or give you an idea for a gift that will delight a friend. Or put your mind at ease, or give birth to a string quartet.

In a less healthy vein, a person can get lost in and live in, to their detriment, the recursive thought narratives that cycle endlessly through the egocentric mind. Or an emotion can get stuck in consciousness and become a foul or foolish mood. All of the emotions—including sadness, anger, pride and jealousy—can linger in consciousness for long periods of time and become moods that color everything a person thinks, says and does.

Evidence of the import that our society attaches to reversing the impact of the negative moods is to be found in the fact that there are vast classes of professional people and whole industries that are devoted to medically altering the moods that are created within the stream of consciousness.

American physicians prescribed antidepressants to 13.3 million patients in 1996, and to 27 million patients in 2005 (Olfson and Marcus, 2009). Eleven billion dollars were spent on antidepressants in the United States in 2010 (Smith, 2012), and that doesn't include the self-administered anti-depressants like alcohol and recreational drugs.

The prevailing paradigm of biological psychiatry tells us that neurotransmitters cause the moods of depression and mania, but a simple study of the stream of consciousness shows that actually moods are created by the way we relate to our stream of consciousness. Moods appear in the mind when the egocentric watcher represses or holds on to an emotion that has appeared in its stream of consciousness (Vyner, 2009–2010).

This is a phenomenon that can be easily observed by even a beginning student of the stream of consciousness. The veracity of these observations are further confirmed by the fact that the major neurotransmitter theories of depression—the catecholamine hypothesis and the serotonin hypothesis—have never, after more than a half of century of research, been shown to be correct (Kirsch, 2010).

The emotions and the moods are not the only phenomena in the stream of consciousness that can negatively impact our lives. Our thoughts can create problems, too. If a sad or angry cycle of thoughts keeps cycling through a person's mind over and over again, the greater likelihood is that the person will act out those thoughts and become the sad or angry character in the story that they are narrating. Research and clinical experience with these inner narratives is beginning to show that they are the cause of the dysfunctional interpersonal relationships that define the character disorders (Beck et al., 2004; Kanske, 2016).

In this passage from an interview that we did together in 1994, the Tibetan Bön lama Lopon Tenzin Namdak expressed the opinion that a thought film can even take a nation to war (Vyner, 2005):

HMV: How do thoughts appear in the stream of consciousness?

LTN: Well in the normal way. They just spontaneously appear. And if you don't touch them, if you don't follow anything, it will not be long before those thoughts will be liberated. You don't need to do anything else. But if you do something to them, then more and more thoughts will develop. Continuously.

HMV: When you say "do something," what do you mean?

LTN: If you don't care when the thought comes, it will disappear by itself. There's no trace. If you do something, then everything is created. If you are a national leader, first of all you will have very simple thoughts coming up, and then you give an order. You immediately take action. You say something. You give an order to the next person, and they do something more and more and then you have created the Second World War.

In addition to asserting that the contents of your thoughts can start a war, Lopon Tenzin Namdak is also hinting at a much larger principle here: the way in which a human being relates to the thoughts that appear in their stream of consciousness will have a large impact on their life. As we will be seeing, it determines nothing less than whether or not you will be a happy and healthy human being.

For example, in the preceding passage, the Lopon describes the consequences of two different ways of relating to your thoughts. The first one is this: if you try to "do something" and control your stream of consciousness, "more and more thoughts will develop," and you will find yourself mired in the mind-films that cause the normal pathologies of the ego.

On the other hand, if you leave your stream of consciousness in its natural state, your "thoughts will be liberated" and become moments of your true self. In addition, the normal pathologies of the ego will not arise within your mind. As we will be seeing, it really is that simple.

In much the same way, the way you handle your stream of consciousness will also determine whether or not you are a tolerant or intolerant human being. If you are intolerant of your own unwanted thoughts and feelings, you will be intolerant of people that you see as being different than your self. On the other hand, if you are open to your own thoughts and emotions, you will probably be open to other people as well.

The basic principle at play here is this: the way in which a human being relates to their own thoughts and emotions will shape the way in which they perceive and resolve their differences with themselves and with other people.

Most of all, the way in which a person manages their stream of consciousness will determine whether or not they will be able to realize their destiny and become their true self. As we will be seeing, if you try to control the flow of your stream of consciousness, you will simply not be able to know and be your self. On the other hand, if you leave the flow of your stream of consciousness in its natural state, you will be able to become the person you really are moment to moment.

For all of these reasons and more, the psychological processes that appear in the stream of consciousness have a profound impact upon our lives. They play an immense role in shaping both our individual lives and perhaps even the nature of the societies in which we live. We owe it to ourselves to understand them and do our best to make them healthy.

Fukushima

Despite the fact that the stream of consciousness has an immense impact upon our state of mind and what we say and do, we are living in a time in which science has turned a blind eye to the stream of consciousness. With but a few exceptions, the scientific community has abstained from studying the stream of consciousness, and it does so because it ascribes to the belief that it is not possible to do valid empirical studies of the stream of consciousness. The scientific stream of consciousness has decided that it cannot study itself.

This is a cultivated scientific blind spot, if you will, and it is a mistake. It has placed humanity in a cognitive predicament that is similar to the type of predicament that can develop in the wake of a nuclear power plant accident. Take for example, the nuclear power plant meltdowns that occurred at Fukushima in Japan in 2011.

Three of the four nuclear power plants at Fukushima melted down and released massive amounts of radioactivity into the environment after an earthquake and tsunami devastated the Japanese nation in February 2011.

First came the earthquake. The earthquake completely cut off the supply of electricity to the Fukushima plants. This was dangerous because the water pumps that cool the Fukushima nuclear power plant and keep them from exploding run on electricity, just as they do at all nuclear power plants. If the water-cooling system of a nuclear power plant fails, the radioactive fuel rods of the reactors will overheat and melt. If this happens, the danger of explosion exists, and radioactivity will find its way into the environment.

The Fukushima plant had backup diesel generators on-site. When the electricity failed, the backup generators immediately went online, but they were promptly knocked out of commission by the tsunami that followed upon the heels of the earthquake.

This meant that it was no longer possible to cool the nuclear reactors at the Fukushima site. There was no further backup for the diesels. Three of the four Fukushima reactors overheated and melted down, and the owners of the site were reduced to using helicopters for days on end to dump seawater on the reactor buildings to try and cool the reactors.

The situation got so out of hand that the operators of the Fukushima power plants simply lost control of their reactors for weeks and months on end. There were multiple explosions, and massive amounts of radioactivity were released into the environment. It took three years to bring those reactors under some semblance of genuine control.

During this whole crisis, there were and continue to be long periods of time in which the engineers at Fukushima had absolutely no idea what was going on inside of their reactors. The instruments they would normally use to monitor their reactors were rendered useless by the loss of electricity, and on top of that, high levels of radioactivity made it impossible for them to actually go inside the reactor buildings to see what was going on.

They could not go in, of course, because the levels of radiation in the reactors was many times greater than the dose of radiation that would kill a person. As of February 2017, the radiation levels are still increasing in the reactors, and the level in Reactor Number One was measured at the overwhelmingly lethal level of 530 sieverts per hour (*Japan Times*, 2017).

As a result, the engineers at Fukushima simply did not know what was happening inside of their reactors. They did not know what structures had been broken or compromised inside of the reactors. Nor did they know what other kinds of destructive processes had been unleashed by the meltdowns. Even now, they are just beginning to learn, with the help of fiber optics, where the fuel rods are and what state they are in.

They were simply flying blind. They did not know with any precision what was actually going on inside of their reactors as they melted down. Years passed before they were able to begin threading fiber-optic cameras into the reactors to try and find out what was going on. As of July 2017, it has just become possible to confirm with fiber-optic cameras that large masses of melted fuel might be lying on the floor of the Fukushima reactors (*The Guardian*, 2017).

The engineers needed a wealth of information to be able to stop the disasters that were unfolding in their reactors, but they simply could not get access to the information that might have made it possible for them to perhaps stop the reactors from exploding, burning and releasing prodigious amounts of radioactivity into the environment.

The information they needed was there to be had in the reactors, but they could not get inside of their reactors to harvest that knowledge. It was absolutely essential that they determine what was going on in their reactors, but they were unable do so.

Fukushima and the Stream of Consciousness

The cognitive quandary that bedevils the scientific study of the stream of consciousness is much the same as the cognitive dilemma that confronted, and continues to confront, the nuclear engineers at Fukushima. Just as it was beyond crucial for the engineers to understand what was going on inside of their reactors, it is a matter of great import that science and humanity find a way to empirically study and understand the workings of the stream of consciousness.

Nevertheless, science has backed itself into a corner in which it has made it impossible to find out exactly what is going on "in there." Basically, science has convinced itself that the phenomena that appear in the stream of consciousness cannot be studied by science because they are both private and subjective phenomena that are hidden from the human eye. Only you can see your stream of consciousness, and only I can see my stream of consciousness.

Psychology allows itself to do studies in which subjects verbally report upon the contents of their mind, but for the most part, it still does not allow itself to study the actual psychological phenomena and processes that appear in the stream of consciousness.

In this kind of scientific climate, the amount of research being funded or done on the psychological processes that occur in the stream of consciousness is minuscule. Work on the stream of consciousness can sometimes get published in respected scientific journals and books, but this genre of research is still a long way from being either accepted by, or influential within, the larger scientific community.

As a result, we do not yet have a systematic body of scientific knowledge about the stream of consciousness that has attained the stature that will allow it to have a beneficial impact upon our lives. For example, this impasse has kept us from understanding, among many other things, the nature of the healthy human mind.

The information we need to understand the nature of the healthy mind is right there in the stream of consciousness, just as the answers were there to be found inside of the Fukushima reactors. We will be better off as a species once we have allowed ourselves to empirically study both the processes that occur in the stream of consciousness and the larger issues to which those processes speak.

In the case of the Fukushima accidents, it was and continues to be an objective radiation danger that has kept the Japanese engineers and their international consultants from gathering the information they need. In the case of the stream of consciousness, it is simply scientific convention that is keeping us from getting the information we need to establish the nature of the healthy human mind.

I want to emphasize this next point: there are, to be sure, methodological difficulties that are unique to the empirical study of the phenomena of the stream of consciousness. The most obvious problem, of course, is that they are private phenomena.

Nonetheless, given that the stream of consciousness plays such a substantial role in shaping our lives, it would be far wiser for science to acknowledge that these difficulties exist and then devise the best way possible to study the stream of consciousness in light of these difficulties. In the lama studies that are being presented in *The Healthy Mind*, this is precisely what we have been doing.

The Traditional Objections

Why, then, has science backed itself into this corner? What are its objections to studying the stream of consciousness? Are they valid objections? Is it really impossible to empirically study the stream of consciousness? Or is it possible to find a way to address and surmount the concerns that the paradigm holds dear?

The abandonment of the study of the mind by science began, of course, in 1913 with John Broadus Watson's Behaviorist critique of the Introspectionist school of psychology—the first school of scientific psychology (Watson, 1913).

The Introspectionist school was, to be sure, a confused mess, and Watson was right to criticize it. The Introspectionists did not even understand what type of phenomena they were studying (Vyner, 2009–2010). However, in his insistence that psychology could only study behavior, and not the mind, Watson threw the baby out with the bathwater. This was a mistake, and it continues to cloud our definitions of what phenomena can and cannot be empirically studied to this very day.

Traditionally, there have been two principal objections to scientifically studying the phenomena that appear in the stream of consciousness:

1. *The epistemological-ontological objection*: The phenomena that appear in the stream of consciousness—thoughts, emotions, feelings, epiphanies and so forth—are subjective phenomena. The claim here is that given that science only studies objective phenomena, it cannot study the phenomena that appear in the stream of consciousness.
2. *The methodological objection*: The phenomena that appear in the stream of consciousness are not public phenomena. Only you can see your stream of consciousness, and only I can see my stream of consciousness. The claim here is this: given that it is impossible for two people to simultaneously observe the same phenomena and achieve what is called—by the philosophy of science—the interpersonal verification of observations of the stream of consciousness, valid empirical studies of these phenomena cannot be done. This is a genuine problem because the interpersonal verification of observations is certainly one of the cornerstones of the scientific method.

In addition, several metaphysical objections to the study of consciousness have been assembled over the last several decades.

These objections are metaphysical in the sense that they are speculative, as opposed to empirical, positions. They are usually positions that have been taken by scholars who are wholeheartedly committed to the materialist explanation of mind and behavior. They have rummaged around in the cedar chest of metaphysics to come up with positions that buttress the stance that it is not possible to scientifically study the mind and the stream of consciousness itself. One of those positions is the view that not only is not possible to empirically study the mind or the stream of consciousness, it is not necessary. Here are two examples of this type of position:

1. There is no such thing as mind. Our thoughts and feelings do not really exist. They are just the way we experience the neurophysiological processes that occur in the brain (Churchland, 1998; Dennett, 1978).
2. Human beings are just biological machines, and consciousness is only an epiphenomenon that does not affect the functioning of these machines that are us (McLaughlin, 1994). In a different era, Thomas Henry Huxley took an earlier version of this position by famously arguing against the efficacy of the soul: "The soul stands related to the body as the bell of a clock to the works, and consciousness answers to the sound which the bell gives out when it is struck" (Huxley, 1874).

With the exception of Huxley, who was arguing in a different time, one has to be amused with these arguments and wonder if their proponents really believe what they are saying. Or if they have a healthy acquaintance with their own mind. Or if perhaps they might be amusing themselves by indulging in the naughty pleasure of aggravating their opponents with specious and nonsensical theory that has the outer appearance of intellectual coherence and respectability. Whatever the case may be, one thing is for certain. These are not empirical positions; nor are they positions that move science forward.

Despite the fact that these arguments verge on being polemic, an important scientific issue is at stake here. The issue at stake is this: do we or do we not need to study the mind itself to understand the mind?

At Second Glance

To a proponent of the empirical study of the stream of consciousness, it would seem, at first glance, to be prudent to address and refute these paradigmatic objections to the study of consciousness and the stream of consciousness. One might think that by doing so, that we could convince the scientific community that they have misjudged the situation, and that there are remedies to the genuine concerns that they raise.

At second glance, however, it becomes clear that it would be but folly to spend any more time addressing this traditional list of concerns at this point in the history of the dialogue. A century of conversation about these issues has proven to be nothing but a fruitless and self-defeating conversation for proponents of the scientific study of the stream of consciousness.

Decades of ink and words have been spilt in the effort to both legitimize and delegitimize the empirical study of both consciousness and the stream of consciousness. Generations of scientists who have proposed to study consciousness have been put on the defensive.

Many proponents of the study of consciousness have allowed themselves to get mired down in the well-intended but endlessly recursive process of trying to elaborate a philosophy of science that would somehow pacify the naysayers, and move the scientific community to confer its imprimatur upon the study of the stream of consciousness. However, this dialogue has gotten nowhere, and it has become, to borrow a term from Freud, a ritualized repetition compulsion.

This dialogue has given birth to a small cottage industry of philosophers and scientists who have carved careers out of lobbing philosophical objections across the bow of scientists who wish to study the mind itself. Despite the fact that they are wrong, I am convinced that these people mean well and are acting out of a sincere belief in what they are saying and doing. They also speak, to be sure, for the larger scientific community, and for the belief systems that are embedded in its dominant paradigms.

Recycling and Solar Airplanes

The same arguments have been revisited and recycled over and again in the twentieth and twenty-first centuries to make the case that it is not possible to empirically study the stream of consciousness. The result has been that proponents of the empirical study of consciousness and the stream of consciousness have been repeatedly stymied.

Meanwhile, the stream of consciousness remains in the scientific dark, and one consequence of this cultivated blind spot is that we continue to live with a disabling misconception of the healthy mind. We are, in essence, denying ourselves an empirical understanding of the nature of the healthy mind.

Instead of getting on with the business of studying the stream of consciousness, advocates of the scientific study of consciousness have been trapped into making an eternal return to the quest of trying to establish the legitimacy of the scientific study of consciousness. This ritualized process has gotten us nowhere. We still do not understand the bulk of the psychological processes that appear in the stream of consciousness or their impact upon our lives.

It is as if a newly designed and as of yet untested featherweight solar airplane was sitting on a runway near the coast of New Hampshire, and two engineers are standing next to the plane arguing about whether or not it will ever fly all the way to Europe.

The traditional engineer argues confidently and disparagingly that the plane will crash into the ocean the moment it leaves the ground. The solar engineer literally pleads that it can fly, and that it will make it to France once a few more improvements have been made to the plane. She makes her case by showing the other engineer graph after graph on her laptop.

Meanwhile, a pilot in full aviation regalia strides up, gets into the plane, taxis it down the runway, takes off and flies it non-stop all the way across the Atlantic Ocean to Paris.

In the research that the lamas and I have been doing on the healthy mind and the stream of consciousness, we have essentially chosen to take the same course as our pilot. We have simply gone ahead and done our work.

A decision was made that it would not have been fruitful to stand on the tarmac for another century and argue about whether or not it is possible to scientifically study the stream of consciousness. The time had come to simply go ahead and do the work, and then subject it to collegial scientific scrutiny and see how it fares. It has been a good decision. We have learned a great deal.

Had we gotten sidetracked into engaging in the now century-old ritual of addressing, yet again, the traditional philosophical objections to empirically studying the stream of consciousness, we would not have done our work. It was decided that the best way to address these objections was to simply go ahead and do the work, and then see if it would be able to withstand peer review.

However, given the genuine merit of the arguments against studying the stream of consciousness, and given that the lamas and I are now more than twenty years into doing this work, I would like to take a brief moment to introduce you to the solutions that have been developed to the traditional critique of the study of the stream of consciousness. I would like you to understand that it is indeed possible to empirically study the stream of consciousness and how it is done.

Implications

There is much at stake in the question of whether or not science can study the stream of consciousness. The rejection of the study of the stream of consciousness has had a devastating effect on the fields of psychology and psychiatry, and in turn on society.

Those who reject the study of consciousness have saddled psychology and psychiatry with a methodological purism that has become the tail that wags the dog of these sciences. We are permitting ourselves to study only those phenomena that our present conception of the scientific method allows us to study. This purism has channeled the scientific study of the mind into a narrow defile in which only the study of behavior and the brain is considered valid. The mind itself—the mind that we experience as the stream of consciousness—cannot be studied directly.

The collateral damage that has been done to the fields of psychiatry and psychology by this entrenched position has two fundamental dimensions: (1) there is much of import—perhaps the most important things—that we do not yet know about the mind; and (2) we are turning human beings into machines in both our own eyes and in clinical practice. The mind we are told is simply a computer embedded in the flesh of our brains.

We have truly abandoned the mind. Psychiatry has essentially become the practice of modulating the neurotransmitters in the central nervous system—just like maintaining a proper oil level in an automobile. The cognitive sciences see the human mind as being a computer, and they analyze our cognitive behaviors for the purpose of understanding how that computer works. The cognitive neurosciences take that metaphor one step further and are attempting to ascertain how that computer has been hardwired into the substance of our brains.

I would go so far as to say that by adopting this methodology that forces us to abandon the study of the mind, we have debased the sciences of psychology and psychiatry, and turned them into fields that are grounded in two debilitating premises:

1. Psychology and psychiatry have become the study of behavior and the brain, and not the study of the mind itself.
2. The central task of psychology and psychiatry is to understand the mind as a Cartesian machine—as either a computer or a brain—so that the machine can be tweaked and repaired to make it behave like a better machine.

The overwhelming effect of these presuppositions is that the fields of psychology and psychiatry are both in the midst of a long night in which they have renounced the study of the mind and as a result, limited their own ability to understand it. Again, one of the several untoward consequences of this self-imposed ignorance is that we are still saddled with the belief that the egocentric mind is a healthy mind. In a more general sense, we are depriving ourselves of the wisdom that we could gain from truly studying and understanding the mind. The kind of wisdom that an Erik Erikson, for example, brought to the study of the mind.

I would like to see the fields of psychology and psychiatry take off their blinders, withdraw from the purely mechanistic and materialist approach to the mind that has taken root in the wake of Watson's critique, and move in a healthier direction. It would be far better for both science and society if psychiatry and psychology became fields that are grounded in a healthier set of principles that would at least include:

1. Psychology and psychiatry are the study of the mind, the stream of consciousness, behavior and the nervous system.
2. One of the central tasks of the fields of psychology and psychiatry is to understand both the nature of the healthy mind and its cultivation.
3. The principal goal of the clinical practice of psychiatry and psychology is to help unhealthy people cultivate a healthier mind.

In this context, it is essential that we restore psychology to the study of the mind and stream of consciousness, if for no other reason than to give ourselves a proper understanding of the healthy mind, and to reorient psychology, psychiatry and perhaps even our societies to the cultivation of a healthy mind.

Subjectivity and Paradox

In the course of doing the lama studies, solutions to the traditional objections to studying the stream of consciousness—subjectivity and interpersonal verification—were developed.

The first objection to the study of the phenomena that appear in the stream of consciousness—the idea that they are subjective phenomena—is partially true and thus worthy of serious consideration. The gist of this claim is that given that science is the study of objective phenomena, consciousness—which is, from this perspective, a group of subjective phenomena—cannot be studied by science.

At first glance, this argument would seem to have merit and call into question the validity of scientifically studying the stream of consciousness. After all, there can be no doubt that thoughts and emotions are subjective phenomena. They are by their very nature meanings, and meanings are of course subjective phenomena.

Thoughts, emotions and mind-films are subjective because different human beings can and do, of course, give different meanings to the same experience. In other words, the meanings that we each give to our experiences are not universals. Given that they are not universal phenomena, they are not objective, like the speed of light or the structure of DNA. If ten human beings watched the movie *Rashomon* together, they might well interpret the meaning of that movie in ten different ways.

However, when you actually study the stream of consciousness empirically, one of the things that becomes apparent is that thoughts, emotions and mind-films are also objective phenomena. They are objective in the sense that they are phenomena that participate in and mediate a specific group of natural processes that occur universally in the mind of all human beings. To be precise, they mediate the objective processes by which the mind knows and controls itself. Every healthy human mind knows and controls itself.

Given that these processes are universals that appear in the minds of all human beings, they are also objective phenomena they can be studied by science. They are simply another group of natural phenomena.

This, then, is the solution of the problem of subjectivity. The phenomena that appear in the stream of consciousness are, to be certain, subjective phenomena; but they are also objective phenomena as well.

In other words, they are paradoxical phenomena. Every single thought, emotion, mind-film and epiphany that appears in the stream of consciousness is simultaneously a subjective and objective phenomenon (Vyner, 2007–2008), just as visible light is simultaneously a particle and a wave.

Knowing the Stream of Consciousness

Furthermore, and this is where things get interesting, given that the phenomena of the stream of consciousness are both subjective and objective phenomena, there are two ways of knowing the stream of consciousness. To put it another way, there are two different types of knowledge that one can acquire in the process of knowing the phenomena that appear in the stream of consciousness. A human being can have either *subjective* or *empirical* knowledge of these phenomena.

On the one hand, every thought and emotion that appears in the stream of consciousness is a construct that contains content that gives meaning to the mind's experience of both itself and the world. As constructs that endow meaning, they are, by definition, subjective phenomena.

When as a human being you know the content of your thoughts and feelings, you are knowing them as meanings that are subjective phenomena. In this case, you are acquiring subjective knowledge of the phenomena that appear in your stream of consciousness.

Knowing the contents of your mind in this way can also be called *self-knowledge.* To acquire accurate and genuine self-knowledge is one of the most important things a human being can do, and it is the province of self-realization, psychotherapy, soteriology, art and life itself.

On the other hand, one can also know the form, function and behavior of the phenomena that appear in the stream of consciousness, as opposed to knowing their content.

You can observe, for example, that thoughts will sometimes appear as an individual moment of consciousness that dissolves right away; or that at other times thoughts will appear as an ongoing sequence of thematically connected thoughts that create a narrative. Or that the repression of an emotion will cause a mood to appear and remain present in awareness. And so forth. The findings of the science of the stream of consciousness suggests that these are universals that occur in the mind of all human beings with a healthy central nervous system.

To know the phenomena of the stream of consciousness in this way is to know them as the objective phenomena that mediate and participate in the natural processes of self-awareness and self-control. This type of knowledge of the stream of consciousness is empirical in the sense that you are knowing processes and phenomena that are universally present in the minds of all human beings. To know them in this way is to acquire *empirical knowledge* of these phenomena.

This, then, is the second way in which a human being can know the phenomena that appear in the stream of consciousness, and this is the kind of knowledge that the science of the stream of consciousness acquires about these phenomena. This is the solution to the issue of subjectivity.

Homo sapiens veritas and Interpersonal Verification

Let us now turn our attention to the second issue: the issue of interpersonal verification. Once again, this is a genuine problem. It is an inescapable fact that the experience of the stream of consciousness is a private one: only I can see my thoughts and feelings, and only you can see yours.

The two of us can watch a full moon rise over the nearby mountains together, and as it lights up the valley through which we are skiing, we can agree that it is an inspiring experience. But only you can actually experience what you see and feel as you ski under the moon, and only I can know what I have experienced.

This privacy of experience generates the methodological problem of *interpersonal verification*. The issue of interpersonal verification is usually articulated like this: given that it is impossible for two people to simultaneously observe the phenomena that appear in any single person's stream of consciousness, it would seem to be impossible, *in principle*, for one scientist to independently verify that a second scientist's observations of the stream of consciousness are either correct or incorrect.

This is not a trivial point. Interpersonal verification is rightfully regarded as being one of the cornerstones of the practice of modern science. Indeed, it is one of the sacred tenets of the scientific method.

However, it is also true that scientists are not in the habit of actually going to one another's laboratories to witness and verify one another's observations in real time. Scientists usually verify one another's work by repeating it in their own laboratories. This is how interpersonal verification works in the real world of the day-to-day practice of science.

If you extend the same principle to the study of the stream of consciousness, this means that it is not necessary for scientists to get inside of one another's heads to verify their respective observations of the stream of consciousness. They can test and verify another scientist's observations by looking at their own stream of consciousness—by replicating one another's work in their own laboratory, if you will. That is indeed what the Tibetans have been doing for centuries.

Ultimately, science's methodological objections to the study of consciousness can, once again, be boiled down to the simple and direct issue of honesty. If we could find a way to determine whether or not a person is or is not giving an honest and accurate report of what is happening in his or her stream of consciousness, the science of the stream of consciousness would flourish and be regarded as a valid science by the scientific community.

Consider this thought experiment for a moment. Imagine that human evolution had taken a slightly different course, and that after our species first appeared as *Homo sapiens sapiens* in east Africa about roughly 170,000 years ago, that one more important evolutionary step occurred soon thereafter in the development of the human brain and mind.

Suppose that there was a mutation, or perhaps a group of mutations, that turned us into a slightly different species: *Homo sapiens veritas*. Imagine further that the sole evolutionary difference between *Homo sapiens veritas* and *Homo sapiens sapiens* is that a person who is a *Homo sapiens veritas* is completely incapable of being dishonest about the contents of their stream of consciousness.

In other words, a *Homo sapiens veritas* would be a person who would always tell the truth about what was going on in his or her mind. If there were thoughts running through his mind, he would not tell you that his mind was quiet. If she were in love with a man that did not love her, she would not hide her feelings. If a subject of a scientific study told you that his emotions were dissolving in the instant that they appear in his stream of consciousness, you would know that he was telling you the truth and so forth.

This would, to say the least, change a lot of things in our lives, including the prospect of scientifically studying the stream of consciousness. A scientist studying the stream of consciousness of a *Homo sapiens veritas* would be able to have no doubt that his subjects were producing empirically accurate reports about what was actually going on in their stream of consciousness.

If we knew that our subjects were incapable of being dishonest, there would be no impediment to establishing a science of the stream of consciousness. Under these circumstances, the scientific community would surely embrace the idea that the study of the stream of consciousness is a valid science. Once again, the point here is that honesty is the issue.

Much the same thing would and will come to pass when science discovers an infallible neurological signature for either honesty or dishonesty. If we were to discover, for example, that there is a specific fMRI finding that indicates that a person is being dishonest, or if on the other hand it were found that a specific PET scan finding indicates that a person is being honest, then once again, it would be possible to know in real time whether or not a subject in an experiment is telling the truth about what was going on in their stream of consciousness.

Once it becomes possible to tell in real time whether or not a person is giving honest reports about their stream of consciousness, the question of interpersonal verification will disappear. With the rapid advances that are now occurring in the use of these imaging techniques, that day could come soon.

In the meantime, though, I have been pursuing an option that is a very fine second best. I have been doing research on the workings of the stream of consciousness with an exceptionally honest group of human beings. Once again, for almost the last twenty years now, I have been interviewing Tibetan lamas about their experiences of their own minds in meditation for the purpose of:

1. Developing a descriptive science of the phenomena and processes that appear in the human stream of consciousness.
2. Deriving from that descriptive science an empirically valid theory of the defining characteristics of the healthy human mind.

The lamas that I have been interviewing have all been men, as almost all Tibetan lamas are, and they are men who have spent their entire lives pursuing the religious life. Many of them have little or no ego, which means they have almost none of the usual incentives that one would have to be dishonest or misleading about what is going on in their stream of consciousness.

Here is an example of how that honesty comes into play. There is a vein of Buddhist literature that takes the position that thoughts cease to appear in the enlightened mind. The complete cessation of thoughts is said to be an important and elevated spiritual attainment.

In this context, I once asked the Dalai Lama in an interview in 1994 whether or not there were still thoughts appearing in his mind. Here is what happened (Vyner, 2007):

HMV: The involuntary stream of consciousness, which is one phenomenon, is the constant stream of thoughts and emotions that are constantly going through a person's mind.

HHDL: Yes.

HMV: The cessation of the involuntary stream of consciousness is another phenomenon.

HHDL: What do you mean by cessation?

HMV: The stopping of the flow of thoughts and emotions.

HHDL: Temporary?

HMV: Yes, temporary.

HHDL: Not permanent cessation.

HMV: No, not permanent cessation. As far as you know, does anyone ever attain permanent cessation?
HHDL: Should be.
HMV: It is possible.
HHDL: That is the goal. Amongst practitioners, that is the goal. [Laughter]
HMV: Have you experienced that?
HHDL: No. [More laughter]

In this situation, the Dalai Lama could easily have shown himself in what would seem to be a more accomplished spiritual light by answering that he no longer has thought noise running through his mind. By being honest and saying that he still has thoughts, he risked leaving the impression that he might not be as enlightened or as spiritually accomplished as he is. Nonetheless, he told the truth. The Dalai Lama freely and lightheartedly admitted that thoughts still appear in his stream of consciousness.

Another consideration that makes the lamas exceptionally good subjects for these early studies of the stream of consciousness is that they tend to have exceptionally clear minds. Their minds are clear because their meditation practices have profoundly diminished the amount of thought noise that runs through their stream of consciousness, even if they have not brought that noise to a complete and final halt. This, in turn, makes it possible for a lama to see and remember with a great deal of clarity what is actually going on in their mind.

A third virtue of doing this research with the lamas is that they are scientists. They are scientists of the stream of consciousness. They have spent almost their entire lives observing, analyzing, and doing meditative experiments on their own stream of consciousness. I have come to see them as scientific colleagues that I have been interviewing to find out what they have observed and inferred from their experiences with the stream of consciousness.

Indeed, the work that the lamas and I have been doing together is creating, in a modern context, a new field of scientific inquiry: the science of the stream of consciousness.

When I, myself, originally took the decision to do this work, I did so with my eyes wide open. I knew that it could not be done within the traditional institutional confines of science. Twice in the course of my training in psychiatry, I presented my ideas for pursuing this work on the healthy mind and the stream of consciousness to well-meaning mentors, and both of them actively discouraged me from doing so.

Nonetheless, I decided to go ahead and pursue this line of research anyway as an independent scientist, and make it my life's work. It was the prospect of practicing a psychiatry that was grounded in the cultivation of the healthy mind that held my abiding interest and moved me to make this decision. It was, for me, a matter of integrity.

I was, and still am, convinced that the practice of psychiatry should be built upon an understanding of, and the cultivation of, a healthy mind. I also felt that for myself it would not be morally correct to practice a psychiatry that was not centered around the cultivation of the healthy mind.

As I began to do this work on the healthy mind, I did so with the belief that if it was done well, that a time would surely come when it would bear fruit and be accepted by both the scientific community and the larger public. I had confidence that eventually it would be possible to accumulate a body of data and theory that would, like the flight to Paris, render irrelevant the arguments taking place back on the tarmac.

That time has now come. Enough data has been accumulated to begin the task of making the case that (1) the healthy mind is the egoless mind and (2) that it is possible to empirically study the phenomena that appear in the stream of consciousness.

Our findings to date, although preliminary, leave no doubt that the egoless mind is a healthy mind and that the egocentric mind is not. Our work also makes it abundantly clear that it is possible to empirically study the phenomena that appear in the stream of consciousness. Solutions to the traditional problems of interpersonal verification and subjectivity have been found. We have, if you will, gotten the science of the stream of consciousness off the ground.

Finally, while it is true that after more than twenty years of work I have considerable confidence in our data and theory, it should also be said that the modern science of the stream of consciousness that we are creating is, in many respects, just in its infancy. The findings that are being presented in the remainder of *The Healthy Mind* are but the initial findings and stumblings of a new field of scientific inquiry. There is much more work to do.

Inevitably, replications and additional studies will have to be done to develop a body of data that will be strong enough to incontrovertibly establish the validity of our early findings and hypotheses. Surely, mistakes will be found along the way, and it is also anticipated that new phenomena and theories will emerge as this work proceeds. This is just the beginning.

Perhaps it would be useful to think of our work in this way: the science of the stream of consciousness is in roughly the same place now as astronomy was in Galileo's day. In the same way that Galileo was using the new tool of the telescope to study the basic structure of our solar system, we are using the new (to science) tool of meditation to investigate the healthy mind and the stream of consciousness. We are just beginning to accumulate a body of observations that will hopefully be a foundation for further research.

Just as it took a while for the Catholic church and Europe to accept Galileo's confirmation of the Copernican theory that the earth orbits around the sun, it will surely take time for the scientific community to accept that that it is possible to empirically study the phenomena that appear in the stream of consciousness, and for the larger public to accept that the counterintuitive notion that the healthy mind is the egoless mind.

The research being presented in this volume is, in the context of our contemporary paradigms, a pilot study that aspires to open doors and inspire further research into the nature of the healthy mind and the workings of the stream of consciousness.

It is in this spirit that the remainder of *The Healthy Human Mind* is now going to present an overview of the findings and theory of this new field of inquiry.

References

Beck, A. T., Freeman, A., and Davis, D. D. (2004). *Cognitive Therapy of Personality Disorders.* New York and London: The Guilford Press.

Churchland, P., and Churchland, P. (1998). *On the Contrary: Critical Essays, 1987–1997.* Cambridge, MA: MIT Press.

Dennett, D. (1978). *The Intentional Stance.* Cambridge, MA: MIT Press.

The Guardian. (2017). *Fukushima: Robot Images Show Massive Deposits Thought to be Melted Nuclear Fuel.* www.theguardian.com/environment/2017/jul/23/fukushima-images-show-massive-deposits-thought-to-be-melted-nuclear-fuel

Huxley, T. H. (1874). On the hypothesis that animals are automata, and its history. In *Collected Essays: Volume I, Method and Results.* London: Macmillan, pp. 195–250.

Japan Times. (2017). *Highest Radiation Reading Since 3/11 Detected at Fukushima No. 1 Reactor.* www.japantimes.co.jp/news/2017/02/03/national/fukushima-radiation-level-highest-since-march-11/#.WJSGobYrLOY

Kanske, P. (2016). *Profiles of Mind Wandering Activity in Psychopathology.* Talk presented at 50th Congress of the German Society for Psychology (DGPs). Leipzig, Germany.

Kirsch, I. (2010). *The Emperor's New Drugs.* New York, NY: Basic Books.

McLaughlin, B. (1994). *Epiphenomenalism: A Companion to the Philosophy of Mind*, ed. S. Guttenplan. Oxford: Blackwell, pp. 277–288.

Olfson, M., and Marcus, S. C. (2009). National patterns in antidepressant medication treatment. *Archives of General Psychiatry*, 66(8), 848–856.

Smith, B. L. (2012). Inappropriate prescribing. *Monitor on Psychology*, 43(6), 36.

Vyner, H. M. (2005). *The Healthy Mind Interviews, Volume 3: Lopon Tekchog.* Kathmandu: Vajra Books.

Vyner, H. M. (2007). *The Healthy Mind Interviews, Volume 4: Dalai Lama, Lopon Tenzin Namdak, Lopon Tekchog.* Kathmandu: Vajra Books.

Vyner, H. M. (2007–2008). The dialectical phenomena and processes of the mind. *Imagination, Cognition and Personality*, 27(2), 163–196.

Vyner, H. M. (2009–2010). A preliminary theory of the defining dynamic of the healthy human mind. *Imagination, Cognition and Personality*, 29(3), 225–270.

Watson, J. B. (1913). Psychology as the behaviorist views it. *Psychological Review*, 20, 158–177.

6

ODE TO THE STREAM OF CONSCIOUSNESS

It goes without saying that the observation of phenomena is the cornerstone of the scientific method. The first step in the scientific study of any phenomenon or natural system is to make systematic observations of the phenomena or system that has drawn your interest.

Perhaps you might be making systematic observations of the behavior of cathode rays in a cathode ray tube and one day serendipitously discover x-rays, as Roentgen did. Or perhaps you might dig, sift and brush your way through acre upon acre of soil for months on end in the Great Rift Valley of east Africa to find a few bone fragments that might dramatically alter our conception of the origins of humanity.

No matter what it is you are studying, though, every scientific quest is of course rooted in the making of systematic observations, and the purpose of making these observations is to search for natural phenomena that are universals within the system you are studying. Science is the study of phenomena for the purpose of understanding the structure and dynamics of the natural systems to which those phenomena belong.

William Harvey studied the heart in the sixteenth century and came up with the new idea that it was part of a larger system that circulates blood throughout the entire body. Newton studied the motion of the planets in our solar system to come to the understanding that a force he called gravity governs their movements around the sun. Faraday studied a human-made system—a wire circuit that included a coil—and found that moving a magnet in and out of that coil induced an electrical current in the circuit. Science studies systems and the phenomena that mediate the structure and dynamics of systems.

In our inquiry into the nature of the healthy mind, we will be investigating two natural systems: (1) the human mind and (2) a subsystem of the mind: the stream of consciousness.

Sometimes it takes only a single observation to change the course of scientific history. In the summer of 1928, Alexander Fleming left a stack of uncovered petri dishes in a corner of his laboratory at St. Mary's Hospital Medical School in London while he went on vacation with his family. When he came back from his vacation, he found that a contaminant had grown on one, just one, of the petri dishes on which he had been growing *Staphylococcus* bacteria.

Upon further inspection, Fleming noticed that the *Staphylococcus* colonies in the area surrounding the contaminant had been destroyed. One thing led to another, and it turned out that the contaminant was a *Penicillium* fungus. Within six months Fleming had discovered the first modern antibiotic: penicillin.

Galileo used one of the first telescopes ever made to discover that there were moons orbiting around Jupiter, and this single discovery threw into question the entire Aristotelian cosmology in which Europe had been living for centuries. The universe that Aristotle had given us was composed of nine crystalline spheres that were said to rotate around the earth—the center of the Catholic universe—and that cosmology was simply not compatible with the finding that there were moons orbiting around Jupiter.

When Michelson and Morley discovered that the speed of light was identical in all directions relative to the motion of the earth, it led directly to the formulation of the special theory of relativity.

Sometimes, however, it takes thousands upon thousands of observations to establish a new scientific theory. Darwin and Kepler, for example, built their respective theories of evolution and planetary motion upon countless observations of animal species and planetary motion.

It can even take a century for science to understand a single phenomenon. The DNA molecule was first isolated in 1868, but it took almost a century of biochemical, genetic and histological research to determine its chemical composition, structure and function.

The study being presented here has been eliciting observations of the stream of consciousness from Tibetan lamas for more than twenty-five years now, and innumerable observations have been recorded. It was necessary to start at the beginning, and in a sense, we are still at the beginning.

We began our research by first delineating as many dual and nondual phenomena as we could find in the stream of consciousness of both the egoless and egocentric minds. The goal all along has been to develop a comprehensive typology of these phenomena, and I was particularly interested in those phenomena that were relevant to mapping out and understanding the egoless and egocentric states of mind. Once again, we have to date delineated sixty-four phenomena and causal sequences.

Many of the phenomena that we have described are probably universals that appear in the stream of consciousness of all human beings; that would include, for instance, the involuntary stream of consciousness—or mind wandering as it is known by contemporary cognitive science, primordial meanings, mind-films, emotions and moods, the repression of emotions and thoughts, epiphanies and so forth.

It is possible that some of the phenomena that we have described might only appear in the stream of consciousness of seasoned meditators, but it will take further research to determine whether or not this is the case. This group of phenomena might include nondual awareness, the cessation of thoughts, abiding nondual joy and many more.

The remainder of this chapter is now going to present a typology of the sixty-four phenomena that we have observed and delineated to date, and they are the observations upon which the modern science of the stream of consciousness is being built. Once again, it is fully anticipated that additional phenomena that are not being reported here will be discovered in the future.

The Phenomena That Appear in the Stream of Consciousness

The descriptive science being presented here is a comprehensive list of all of the phenomena that have been delineated to date. Given the contested status of the empirical study of the stream of consciousness, I am presenting the entire typology of phenomena in hopes that it will make it possible for readers to:

1. See for themselves that many of the phenomena that have been delineated by the science of the stream of consciousness are phenomena that you yourself already know from your experiences of your own mind. Many of these phenomena are the common experience of humanity.
2. Experience firsthand the scientific consequences of something that you already know: it is possible to recognize and describe the discrete phenomena that appear in the stream of consciousness.
3. See, as you read the theory of the healthy mind being presented in the later chapters of *The Healthy Mind*, that this theory has been directly derived from these observations.
4. Become familiar with these phenomena because (a) they will become the foundation of future research into the stream of consciousness and (b) they will help you understand how one pursues the cultivation of the egoless mind.

Here then, is the descriptive science of the phenomena that appear in the stream of consciousness that has been generated by the lama interviews. This typology of phenomena has been derived from observations of the stream of consciousness that have been reported by the lamas (Vyner, 2003, 2004a, 2004b, 2005, 2007, 2007–2008, 2009–2010, 2018).

Please read carefully and remember the phenomena listed here. We will be referring to them over and over again as we map out the egoless and egocentric states of mind en route to investigating the nature of the healthy mind.

The Structure of the Experience of the Stream of Consciousness

1. Experiential Duality
2. The Watcher
3. The Stream of Consciousness

The basic structure of the mind's experience of itself is familiar to all of us. It is a situation in which you look at your mind and see the appearance and disappearance of a whole multitude of phenomena as they flow by in your stream of consciousness. Thoughts, emotions, epiphanies, mind-films and more appear in the stream of consciousness.

This is a universal experience of the mind that we all have, and the science of the stream of consciousness has delineated three phenomena that describe the fundaments of this experience of knowing the stream of consciousness.

When the mind knows its own stream of consciousness, it actually seems as though there are two different minds present within that experience. There is one mind, the stream of consciousness, that presents thoughts, emotions and more to the mind's awareness, and there is a second mind, which is awareness itself, that knows and responds to those meanings.

In the science of the SoC that is being presented here, the technical names for these two minds are the *watcher* and the *stream of consciousness.*

The stream of consciousness is a temporal sequence of meanings.[1] This stream of meanings appears within the inner space of the mind as a constant flow of thoughts, images, emotions, feelings and more.

The watcher is the awareness that knows the meanings that appear in the stream of consciousness, and as we will be seeing it also responds to them. For example, the watcher might repress an emotion or hold on to a thought.

In addition, the watcher has two modes of self-awareness: an egoless mode and an egocentric mode.[2] Each mode embodies a different approach to knowing and responding to the meanings that appear in the stream of consciousness.

The watcher is also the entity that experiences itself as being the subject that is having your experience. It experiences itself as being the subject that knows both your stream of consciousness and the world in which you live.

1. A **meaning** is, in our context, a construct that the mind creates to express its cognitive, emotional or intentional response to a given experience.
2. The two modes of self-awareness play a key role in defining the difference between the egoless and egocentric minds, and they will be explored at length in several forthcoming chapters.

The watcher and the stream of consciousness seem to be different minds to us because they often want different things at the same time. This difference in intention is apparent to us, for example, when we see the watcher repress desires that arise as thoughts and feelings in our stream of consciousness. The thought or feeling expresses a desire, and the watcher represses it because it does not, for some reason, want to express that desire.

The experience of watching one's mind and having the impression that two separate minds are present is, in and of itself, another phenomenon. The science of the stream of consciousness calls this phenomenon *experiential duality.*

The Defining Dynamic Between the Watcher and the Stream of Consciousness

Given that there are two entities present in our experience of the stream of consciousness, there is also a recurring dynamic that defines the relationship between them. This dynamic is a circumscribed process in which three basic things happen over and over again: (1) the stream of consciousness presents meanings to the watcher; (2) the watcher becomes aware of and responds to those meanings; and (3) the watcher's response sets in motion a causal sequence that changes the stream of consciousness.

The stream of consciousness presents meanings to the watcher in the form of thoughts, images, narratives, feelings, emotions and epiphanies. The watcher, in turn, responds to these meanings, and it does so in a number of well-defined ways. Once again, the watcher might repress an emotion, hold on to a thought or do absolutely nothing at all.

Every single response that the watcher makes to a given meaning causes, in turn, a sequence of events to occur that will determine what will happen next in the stream of consciousness. Different actions inaugurate different causal sequences that have, in turn, different consequences.

For example, when the watcher represses a moment of sadness, this will cause the emotion to remain present in awareness as a sad mood. Or if the watcher holds on to a single angry thought, this will cause a whole cascade of angry thoughts to appear in stream of consciousness.

These are the fundaments of the dynamic that is perpetually unfolding between the egocentric watcher and the stream of consciousness. As we will be seeing, this is a dynamic in which the watcher controls the stream of consciousness. The watcher represses thoughts and emotions that it does not want you to know or express. It holds on to moods that it likes. It creates and holds on to stories that the ego narrates. And more.

In keeping with this basic analysis, the phenomena that appear in the stream of consciousness can be divided into four basic categories:

1. *Meanings* that appear in the stream of consciousness.
2. *Actions* that the watcher takes in response to those meanings.

3. *Causal phenomena*: the phenomena that appear in the stream of consciousness as a result of the responses that the watcher makes to a given meaning.
4. *The causal sequences*: Causal processes that are initiated by the watcher's responses to the phenomena that appear in the stream of consciousness. These causal processes cause the causal phenomena to appear.

The remainder of this chapter is going to present a descriptive science, or typology if you will, of these phenomena. Each phenomenon will be described as they are known and experienced by the watcher.

This typology will be presented in four sections. Each section will correspond, in sequence, to one of the four categories of phenomena that have just been listed above. In addition, each of the phenomena described in a given section will be listed at the beginning of that section.

Before we start, I would like to emphasize, one more time, that the descriptive science that is being presented here is but the early findings of the field of the modern science of the stream of consciousness. Even though I am certain that most of the phenomena being reported here will stand the test of time and further research, it will take years and perhaps decades of additional study to establish a definitive and comprehensive science of the phenomena that appear in the stream of consciousness.

This early work of identifying the phenomena that appear in the stream of consciousness is akin to the work of finding and describing species at the beginnings of the fields of botany, zoology and paleoanthropology. The greater likelihood is that many more phenomena and causal sequences will be discovered in the future, and I look forward to it.

I. Meanings

1. The Involuntary Stream of Consciousness (ISoC)
2. Individual Moments of Consciousness (iMoC)
3. The Voluntary Stream of Consciousness (VSoC)
4. Mind-Films
5. Emotions[3]
6. Moods[4]
7. Primordial Meanings
8. Nondual Realizations[5]
7. Diminution
8. Cessation

3. Emotions will discussed in the "Actions" section of this chapter.
4. Moods will be discussed in "The Egocentric Transformations" section of this chapter.
5. Nondual realizations will be discussed in "The Nondual Transformations" section of this chapter.

9. Egopoietic Meanings
10. Egoless Meanings.

The most elemental function of the stream of consciousness is that it presents meanings to the watcher. A *meaning* is a construct that the mind creates to express its cognitive, emotional or intentional response to a given experience. For example, when you walk in the front door of your house after a long day at work and your laughing children run up and hug you, the love you feel for them in that moment is a meaning. When you continue thinking about a dangerous situation in which you almost lost your life in the mountains, those thoughts are all meanings too.

The meanings fall into categories. The *egopoietic meanings* are meanings that are created by the ego, and they only appear in the egocentric stream of consciousness. They are (1) the *involuntary stream of consciousness*, (2) the *emotions* and (3) the *moods*. The *egoless meanings* appear only in the egoless stream of consciousness, and they are the *nondual primordial meanings* and the *nondual realizations*.

1. The Involuntary Stream of Consciousness (ISoC)

We will begin our discussion of meanings with the involuntary stream of consciousness (ISoC) because it is the phenomenon that you will see the most of as an observer of the stream of consciousness. If you have an ego, the involuntary stream will be a constant presence in your experience of your mind. Close your eyes for a moment now and take a look.

The ISoC is a perpetual and unsought flow of thoughts, images, feelings and emotions that is a more or less constant presence in the inner space of the egocentric mind. You don't have to meditate to be familiar with the ISoC. Most people know it as the endless stream of thoughts that is the background noise that is constantly flowing through their mind. Cognitive science has recognized the presence of the ISoC in the mind, and it has given it the name of mind wandering (Smallwood, J. and Schooler, J., 2006).

The ISoC is involuntary in the sense that the watcher experiences it as not being under its control. This is true in two respects. For one, the ISoC starts and stops of its own accord. The watcher does not control when the involuntary stream appears or disappears.

Second, the watcher does not control the contents of the involuntary stream either. It does not experience itself as choosing the contents of the thoughts and emotions that appear in the ISoC. The ISoC has, if you will, a mind of its own.

If you have never consciously known your own ISoC, try meditating for a moment. You will find that it is a woefully easy matter to observe the ISoC in meditation. The involuntary stream is a constant presence in the mind of a meditator, and it is most often observed, although not always, against the background of trying to do an assigned meditative task.

For example, try for a moment to focus your awareness on the sensation of your breath as it moves back and forth across the tips of your nostrils. As you attempt to keep your mind focused on your breath, you'll find that your attention will wander off, over and over again, into a rather complete fascination with the robust stream of thoughts that is your ISoC.

It's much the same as sitting in a movie theater and forgetting that you are watching a movie. You can get so completely absorbed in your thoughts that you forget that you are supposed to be paying attention to your breath. It happens to everyone who meditates, and it happens a lot.

You might find yourself thinking about the last time you trekked around Mt. Kailash in western Tibet. Or you might think over and over again about a wonderful time you once had with someone you love. Or perhaps you'll find yourself continuing to criticize yourself for a mistake you made last week. Or you might be aware that you are thinking, and yet not even know what it is you are thinking about. This is the involuntary stream of consciousness.

Meditation is not the only circumstance in which the ISoC appears in the mind. If you have an ego, the involuntary stream runs through your mind almost all of the time. The ISoC is a constant presence in the egocentric stream of consciousness, but it virtually never appears in the egoless mind.

The ISoC can manifest in a number of different ways. Your dreams are the way you experience your involuntary stream of consciousness while you are sleeping. Your daydreams are one way of experiencing the ISoC while you are awake, and the distracting thoughts you feel racing through your mind when you are in an uncomfortable situation are also the ISoC.

Chosje Rinpoche

Here is a passage from an interview with Chosje Rinpoche, a Ladakhi lama, whom I interviewed in Ladakh[6] in the summer of 1998. In this passage Chosje Rinpoche discusses the involuntary stream of consciousness and several of the other phenomena that we have just described as well.

HMV: When you meditate, does a stream of thoughts ever appear in your mind?
CJR: Yes.
HMV: How do the thoughts appear? Do they ever appear in your mind as images?

6. Ladakh, was, until 1842, an independent Buddhist kingdom located on the western edge of the Tibetan plateau. In 1842 it was conquered by an Indian prince and incorporated into the British Raj, from whence it became part of the Indian state of Jammu and Kashmir.

CJR: Yes.

HMV: Do they ever appear as words?

CJR: Yes.

HMV: Do they ever appear as emotions?

CJR: Yes.

HMV: Do they ever appear as feelings?

CJR: Yes.

HMV: Are there other kinds of appearances as well?

CJR: All kinds of phenomenal experience. There is no limit to what will arise and what will not arise. It can be feeling. It can be emotion. It can be trying to think that red is yellow and yellow is red. [Laughter]

HMV: Is this stream of thoughts involuntary? That is, do you have the feeling that you make those thoughts appear, or do they appear on their own?

CJR: They just appear.

HMV: Do you choose the contents of those thoughts, or does the content choose itself?

CJR: If you know how to make your mind open, then it will come like a wave and dissolve by itself. But if you try to observe more than is necessary, you will start to make up all sorts of things. Then you will make a pattern and start to create certain past habits or past thoughts. Or try to fit that with the future. Then we can just create a movie. It's like being at a movie.

HMV: There are movies in the mind aren't there.

CJR: Yes. We can make a whole movie.

HMV: When a movie comes do you have the feeling that you are in control of its content?

CJR: When you make a movie, you are not really in control. You are not in control. But we create a reference point and pretend we are in control, and that's what ego is all about. The ego thinks it's in control, but it's not really in control.

HMV: In your experience, does the stream of thoughts ever disappear?

CJR: Yes it can disappear.

HMV: How long does it disappear? Seconds? Minutes? Hours? Days? Months?

CJR: Sometimes it can be short time. Sometimes it can be long time.

HMV: Can you observe all of this?

CJR: Yes. You know it.

HMV: When the stream of thoughts appears in your mind, does it seem like there is an awareness that is watching the thoughts, a watcher?

CJR: Yes there is. That's the experience. But in one way we know that the watcher and the watching are both none other than our mind. They are not really two. But it seems to be that there is a watcher and watching. And instead of being in a nondual state, we spend years watching the watcher and the watching. [Laughter] Which is an experience. One is trapped in experience. So one needs to know how to meditate to cut through those delusions.

HMV: When are you watching the stream of thoughts, does it ever seem to you that the watcher acts upon, or responds to, the stream of thoughts? For example, does the watcher ever grasp[7] thoughts?

CJR: Yes.

HMV: Is that a fair way to put it? Is it true that within the experience of this apparent duality of watcher and stream of consciousness that the watcher sometimes grasps thoughts?

CJR: Yes. The watcher grasps thoughts. The watcher grasps projections. And actually they are both thoughts.

HMV: The subject and object are both thoughts.

CJR: Yes. Both subject and object. The watcher grasps the projection and the projection is a thought.

HMV: Does the watcher ever reject a thought?

CJR: Sure. It will reject something unpleasant. It will also accept something pleasant.

HMV: Does the watcher ever follow[8] thoughts?

CJR: It will do, and it will also let all of them go.

HMV: How does the watcher experience the phenomenon of rejection? How would you describe that experience?

CJR: The watcher is not a neutral state. You see. Basically the watcher takes sides. All of the watcher's rejection and accepting is ego process.

HMV: OK. So that's all ego.

CJR: Yes. It's all ego process.

HMV: Does the watcher in the mind with an ego reject thoughts that are inconsistent, or disagree with, its self-image or self-concept?

CJR: Oh sure. Sometimes you try to work against your habitual thought patterns. Yes. It could definitely play that trick.

HMV: Now on the other hand, could the watcher accept, or hold on to, those thoughts or inner appearances that support its picture of itself?

CJR: Absolutely. It does that most of the time. [Laughter] Much more than it does the other one. [Laughter] Most of the time it will try to work how it wants to be.

HMV: The ego is very busy, isn't it?

7. To grasp a meaning—whether it be a thought, emotion, mind-film or epiphany—is to attribute a concept of self to that meaning in the process of knowing it. The watcher is the entity that grasps meanings, and it does so by taking one of four different types of action: (1) judging the meaning; (2) rejecting or repressing the meaning; (3) accepting, or holding on to, the meaning; and (4) following, or believing the narrative theme of, a stream of thoughts or a mood. Please see the discussion of grasping in the "Actions" section of this chapter.

8. Following, once again, is a response that the watcher makes to a mind-film. When the watcher follows a mind-film, it believes and lives in the story being narrated by its thoughts. The Tibetan term translated as following is jay-soo-drong.

2. *The Individual Moments of Consciousness (iMoC)*

One of the basic experiences of meditation is that with the ongoing practice of meditation, the ISoC slows down and become less of a presence within the mind. The speed and intensity of the thoughts of the involuntary stream will decrease, and gaps will begin to appear in the involuntary stream. By gap, I mean that periods of time occur in which thoughts and emotions will cease to appear in your mind.

This slowing of the ISoC is a phenomenon: the phenomenon of *diminution.* Meditation causes the diminution of the ISoC to occur. This is an easy to understand example of one of the casual sequences that have been delineated by the science of the stream of consciousness. This causal sequence can be schematically described as follows:

MEDITATION → DIMINUTION OF THE ISOC[9]

Sometimes the ISoC will totally disappear for longer periods of time. This is the phenomenon of *cessation.* Some schools of Buddhism have claimed that the cultivation of permanent cessation is a necessary accomplishment on the path to enlightenment.

Empirically, however, cessation seems to be a temporary phenomenon. In all of the interviews that I have done so far with lamas, I have yet to have anyone say that they have experienced a permanent cessation of their ISoC, and this includes His Holiness the Dalai Lama.

Nonetheless, there definitely is something about the practice of meditation that causes both the diminution and/or temporary cessation of the involuntary stream of consciousness. This diminution of the stream of consciousness is often accompanied by the experience of the mind becoming more peaceful. You will feel more at peace as your ISoC slows down.

As the ISoC slows down and becomes less of a distraction, it also becomes apparent that there is a second more subtle type of meaning that appears within the mind.

If the first type of meaning is the ISoC, which presents meanings to awareness in a dream-like sequence of many different thoughts and images, the second type of meaning is the *individual moment of consciousness (iMoC).* As the involuntary stream recedes, the individual moments of consciousness become more apparent.

It is as if a San Francisco fog bank were to dissolve and disappear under the warmth of the afternoon sun, and that as it dissolves you can all of a sudden see that there is one other boat sailing on the bay and that it is coming right at you from underneath the Golden Gate Bridge. The involuntary stream is a

9. From here on out, *The Healthy Mind* will schematically describe causal sequences as an independent variable and a dependent variable with a one-directional causal arrow between them.

fog, if you will, that makes it difficult to see the subtler iMoCs, and when it disappears, it becomes much easier to see them.

The individual moments of consciousness appear within the mind as a single subtle thought, or feeling and they are important because they are the *primordial meanings* of the mind.

They are primordial in two respects: (1) they are the first meaning that the mind gives to any given experience and (2) they articulate how a person really feels about the experience they are having in the present moment.

When the primordial meanings first appear in the stream of consciousness, they are pre-dual meanings. They are pre-dual in the sense that they have not yet been grasped by the watcher and become a dual meaning. Nor have they been known by nondual awareness and become a nondual meaning.

When a primordial meaning is grasped by the watcher, it is transformed into an egopoietic meaning. When the watcher has nondual awareness of a primordial meaning, it becomes an egoless meaning.

With the sustained practice of meditation, a person begins to experience more and more iMoCs. It seems as though they are appearing in your mind more often. This is another causal sequence:

SUSTAINED MEDITATION → INCREASED AWARENESS OF IMOCS

As the fog of the involuntary stream lifts, it becomes easier and easier to see the individual moments of consciousness.

As the fog dissolves, it will also become easier for the mind to have nondual awareness[10] of the primordial meanings, and this too will happen more often. Nondual awareness transforms the primordial meanings into realizations, or epiphanies.[11]

However, one does not have to meditate to experience epiphanies. People who do not meditate experience them as well. Non-meditators know them as a quick moment of poetic realization, or as a large insight into something. However, the diminution of the ISoC makes epiphanies a much more frequent occurrence:

DIMINUTION OF ISOC → INCREASED NUMBER OF EPIPHANIES

3. The Voluntary Stream of Consciousness

Finally, there is a second type of stream of thoughts within the mind, and it is called the *voluntary stream of consciousness* (VSoC). The voluntary stream of consciousness is a temporal sequence of thoughts that the watcher experiences

10. The phenomenon of nondual awareness will be explored and explained at length in the "Causal Phenomena" section of this chapter.
11. These epiphanies are called **realizations** by the science of the stream of consciousness. They are also the same phenomenon as the phenomenon that was called suchness primordial wisdom by Lopon Tegchoke in chapter three. Please see "The Nondual Transformations" below for a discussion of the phenomenon of realization.

as being under its control. The voluntary stream of consciousness does not, if you will, have a mind of its own.

The watcher experiences itself as being the source of the voluntary stream of consciousness, and it sees itself as being in control of the appearance, disappearance and contents of a voluntary stream of thoughts.

In the life of the mind, the VSoC is the means by which a person voluntarily thinks about, analyzes and consciously gives meaning to their experience. It is a deliberate cognitive process in which it seems as though you are initiating a chain of thoughts and choosing its contents. For example, I might note to myself, in the midst of a conversation with a friend, that he has a particularly keen look in his eyes, or that he knows an incredible amount about the French Revolution or that he seems distracted.

4. *Differences Between the Involuntary Stream of Consciousness and the Individual Moments of Consciousness*

1. Dissolution
2. Mind-Films.

There are a number of significant differences between the ISoC and the iMoCs that are important to understand. The first one of course is their mode of appearance. When an iMoC appears in the stream of consciousness, it appears for an instant, and then it will quickly dissolve and disappear if it is not grasped by the watcher. This is the phenomenon of *dissolution.*

In contrast, when the involuntary stream is active, a cascade of thoughts and emotions continues to run on and on within the mind one right after another.

A second difference between the individual iMoC and the ISoC is the way in which they give meaning to a person's experience. An iMoC gives meaning to one specific event—the immediate experience in which a person is presently involved. An iMoC tells you how you feel about that experience and how you want to respond to it.

A single MoC might be an insight into Chekhov's conception of love. Or it might tell you what you want to say to the person who is standing in front of you. Or how you feel about what you just said to that person.

The ISoC, in contrast, does not give meaning to one specific event or experience. It tends to run on and on for long periods of time, and in the process of doing so, it projects contextual narrative meaning onto all of the experiences that a person has while the ISoC is active.

The ISoC projects contextual meaning onto a person's experience by telling stories. The narrative of these stories, which are called *mind-films* by the science of the stream of consciousness, is presented, or carried along if you will, by the thoughts and images that appear in the mind-film. This happens in much the same way that thoughts and images carry the narrative of a dream or a movie.

For example, suppose a good friend has asked you to meet her in a nearby park, and as you talk she gently tells you that your spouse has fallen in love with, and is having an affair with, a mutual friend. In that moment in which you find out that the person to whom you have given your life and heart is now in love with someone else, a film composed of angry thoughts and bitter emotions might well start running through your mind.

That film would probably become a recurring loop of thoughts centered around the themes of anger and betrayal, and it might remain active in your mind for hours or days or even longer. While that film is active within your mind, you will live in the narrative of that film. Everything you see and do will take on meaning by becoming part of the anger, bitterness and betrayal being narrated by the story in that film. This is how a mind-film works.

After you have done a lot of meditation, and have watched the ISoC course through your mind for hours upon end, you will eventually realize that you are basically watching the same films, the same stories with the same themes, over and over again.

It is as if the egocentric mind is a projection booth that contains a small repertoire of perhaps five or six films, and that it keeps projecting those same films onto your experience over and over again, ad infinitum.

Sometimes your mind might project an angry warrior film. Sometimes it might project a proud or narcissistic film. Or it might project a recurring cycle of thoughts and emotions in which you are consumed with despair. Or it might even project several films at once.

The story of a mind-film is narrated by the thoughts and images that are the compositional elements of that film. These thoughts and images are presented by and appear as an ISoC.

A mind-film often appears in tandem with a mood that matches its narrative. The mood epitomizes and amplifies the meaning of the story being presented by the film's images and thoughts. A proud film will be accompanied by a proud mood, and so on. The mood is the soundtrack, if you will, of the film.

When an ISoC film is active within the mind, it gives meaning to a person's experience of the world by coloring that experience. The narrative and mood of a film become, in a very literal sense, the setting or context within which the events in a person's life take on meaning. Once again, those events take on meaning by becoming part of the narrative and mood of that film.

If a proud film is playing, your mind will tend to give proud meanings to your experience. Seduction films will predispose to seductive meanings and behaviors, jealous films to jealous meanings and so forth. This is the mechanism by which the mind-films color and give contextual meaning to the mind's experience of the world.

II. Actions

1. Judgement
2. Repression
3. Attachment
4. Following
5. Grasping
6. Nondual awareness
7. Egoless awareness
8. Nondual transformation.

The second dimension of the dynamic between the watcher and the stream of consciousness is that the watcher responds to all of the meanings that appear in its stream of consciousness. The egoless and egocentric mind respond to meanings with a very different repertoire of actions.

The egocentric watcher has a small repertoire of actions that it can and does take to control the stream of consciousness: *judgment, repression, attachment* and *following*, which are all different types of *grasping*. When the watcher takes any one of these actions, it projects concepts onto a meaning in the process of knowing it.

The egoless watcher, in contrast, has but one action in its repertoire: *nondual awareness*. Nondual awareness knows the meanings that appear in its stream of consciousness without projecting any concepts onto those meanings, and as a result, nondual awareness is a non-conceptual awareness that knows the content of a meaning as it really is. In addition, when the egoless watcher has nondual awareness of a meaning, that meaning dissolves.

Finally, the watcher experiences itself as being the source of all of these actions. Here now are descriptions of these actions as the watcher experiences them:

1. Judgement

The egocentric watcher judges all of the meanings that appear in its stream of consciousness. It likes some meanings, and it dislikes others.

The watcher evaluates meanings by attributing a judgmental concept of identity to each of them in the process of knowing them: This is brilliant idea. This anger means I am a bad person. This is a foolish story that I'm telling myself, and so forth.

The watcher experiences itself as being the source of these judgments, and they appear in the stream of consciousness as positive and negative emotions. These *emotions*[12] are the observable aspect of the phenomenon of *judgment.*

2. Repression and Attachment

Repression is an action that the watcher takes to try to keep itself from becoming aware of, or expressing, a meaning that appears in its stream of consciousness. Sometimes the repression of a meaning is automatic and you aren't aware of it as it happens; and sometimes the watcher is aware of itself as it goes through the act of repressing a meaning.

For example, in a moment in which you are consciously struggling with yourself to not express your jealousy when you suspect your spouse is having an affair, you can feel the jealousy and you can feel that you are struggling to push the jealousy down so that you won't give vent to your feelings. This is a moment of repression.

The action of *attachment* is just the opposite. It's a process in which the watcher holds on to a meaning that it likes and keeps it present in awareness. For example, if the watcher attaches a feeling of excitement, that feeling will remain in awareness as an excited mood. Or if the watcher attaches a single flattering thought, that thought will become a sequence of flattering thoughts that remain present in awareness as a flattering mind-film.

3. Following

Sometimes the mind believes and lives in the stories contained in its mind-films. When the mind lives in the narrative of a mind-film that is recursively coursing through its stream of consciousness, this is the phenomenon of *following*. The mind is following the mind-film.

When the mind follows a film, it believes and lives in that film in the sense that (1) the mind believes that the story that the film is telling is true; (2) the mind acts out and plays a role in that story and (3) the mind participates in, and is thus not separate from, the mood of the film. The watcher finds itself immersed in the narrative mood of the film, and when that happens, the mood colors the watcher's experience of both the mind and the external world.

For example, suppose a thought comes to mind that reminds you of something that you once said to a group of friends that was really clever. If you attach that

12. Emotions serve several functions in the mind. In the context of the ego's actions, they are expressions of the judgments that the egocentric watcher makes of the meanings that appear in its stream of consciousness.

thought, a whole series of thoughts, images and feelings that recall your bon mot and your friends' response to it might well probably start running through your stream of consciousness.

As this process snowballs, the thoughts become a mind-film that will keep coursing through your mind over and over again. As this happens, you find that you have become a rather apt, and even appreciative, audience of this story, and you become a total believer of the narrative it portrays.

As you get lost in this film, you come to believe that you are a most clever person, and this will even make you act as though you think you are clever. This is what it means to say that you are following and living in the story that a mind-film is narrating.

This is actually the state of mind in which most of us live day in and day out. We think we are living in the world, but actually we are living in our mind-films as we make our way through the world.

This is the deeper meaning of Chuang Tzu's famous expression, "Now I do not know whether I was then a man dreaming I was a butterfly, or whether I am now a butterfly, dreaming I am a man."

The import of the mind-films, in the context of assessing the nature of the healthy mind, is that they play a role in causing much of the normal pathology of the ego.

1. Grasping

Grasping is a technical term in Buddhist psychology. Grasping refers to all of the different actions that the egocentric watcher takes in response to the meanings that appear in its stream of consciousness. This would include judgment, repression, attachment and following.

The defining essence of the grasping actions is that when the watcher grasps a meaning, or phenomenon, it attributes a concept of identity to that meaning in the process of knowing it. In the late Penor Rinpoche's words (Vyner, 2018):

HMV: And what do you mean by grasping? What does it mean to grasp a thought?

PR: Thinking that "this is this" and "this is that."

HMV: Ahh. So grasping is attributing a self-concept to a thought. Is that what you mean?

PR: Yes. If you don't meditate much, when you see something, then you say "this is this, this is that." That is called grasping.

For example, when the watcher judges an emotion and decides that it is either a bad or good emotion, that is an act of grasping. Or if you hold on to a good feeling, this too is a grasping action.

5. Nondual Awareness

Nondual awareness is a response to a meaning. It is a response in which the mind knows the suchness of a meaning because the watcher does nothing at all to alter that meaning in the process of knowing it.

The watcher does nothing in the sense that it does not commit any of the egocentric acts of judgment, repression, attachment or following. In other words, the watcher abstains from grasping meanings, and as a result, it allows the mind to have spontaneous nondual awareness of all of the meanings it knows.

Nondual awareness is experienced as the phenomenon of *dissolution.* When the mind has nondual awareness of a meaning, that meaning dissolves into awareness. This is the sense in which nondual awareness is ontologically nondual: awareness and the meaning it knows are not ontologically separate from one another.

In contrast, when the mind has dual awareness of a meaning, the meaning remains separate from awareness, and it remains present in the stream of consciousness as a mind-film or mood.[13]

Given that nondual awareness is an action that is a response to a meaning, the actor that takes this action is *egoless awareness*, which is a synonym for the egoless watcher. The egocentric watcher, in contrast, is the actor that takes the grasping actions of judgment, repression, attachment and following, and that as a result, causes itself to have dual awareness of all of the meanings it knows.

Given that egoless awareness refrains from grasping meanings in the course of having nondual awareness of them, this means that it also refrains from projecting a conceptual overlay onto those meanings in the process of knowing them. As a result, it knows the content of each meaning exactly as it is. *Awareness and meaning are mirror images of one another.* This is the sense in which nondual awareness is epistemologically nondual.

Given that nondual awareness is the only action that egoless awareness ever takes, this means that it allows the stream of consciousness to remain in its natural state. Egoless awareness does not try to alter the stream of consciousness in any way, and as a result, it allows the stream of consciousness to pursue its natural course and do whatever it is going to do.

In other words, egoless awareness behaves like a space through which the stream of consciousness flows unimpeded and unaltered. Egoless awareness allows the stream of consciousness to pursue its natural course and do whatever it is going to do on its own.

This is not a trivial detail. When the stream of consciousness is left in its natural state like this, egoless awareness has nondual awareness of all of the phenomena that appear in its stream of consciousness. As a result, they are all

13. Please see the section on causal phenomena below for a discussion of both dissolution and the activation of mind-films and moods.

transformed them into either egoless awareness or the nondual meanings of the egoless mind.[14]

Let's now take a look at an extraordinary passage from a lama interview that describes the space-like quality of egoless awareness and the transformations it engenders. This passage comes from an interview with Lopon Tenzin Namdak at his monastery outside of Kathmandu in March 1999. Lopon is one of the leading lamas of the Bön religion, and a profound human being who has the steadfast presence of a mountain.

Lopon and I actually work together in this passage to describe the qualities of egoless awareness in this interview. I started out asking Lopon some fairly mundane questions about the egocentric mind, and the next thing I knew Lopon had turned the tables and was interviewing me!

As you read the passage, it looks like Lopon must have decided that he wanted to see if I had in fact experienced egoless awareness, and the questions he asked led me to describe the basic experience of egoless awareness—which Lopon refers to as "the nature" in this interview. Then Lopon took over and had much more to say about egoless awareness.

In addition to being a vivid description of egoless awareness, this passage is also an excellent example of how a lama examines another person to see what they have actually experienced in meditation. Lopon's examination in this passage seems to include the asking of trick questions. For example, among several others in this passage, it was a trick question when Lopon asked me how I control and sustain the experience of egoless awareness.

The interview ends with Lopon taking the time to make the most important point of all about egoless awareness: it purifies and transforms the thoughts and emotions of the ego and transforms them into the *realizations* and *goodness* of the egoless mind.[15] This is what Lopon means when he says, "It liberates the thoughts."

This is also the principal virtue of egoless awareness: it allows every phenomenon that appears in the stream of consciousness, including the egopoietic phenomena, to transform themselves into various aspects of the egoless mind. This is an extraordinary passage. Please read it carefully[16] (Vyner, 2007).

HMV: The first thing I would like to do is present some of my own experiences to you and ask you if they are observable phenomena that you recognize from your own experience. Would that be OK?

LTN: OK.

14. These transformations are called the *nondual transformations*, and they will be described in the "Causal Phenomena" section of this chapter. Their role in the generation of the egoless state of mind will be discussed at length in Chapter 11.
15. Please see the coming section on nondual transformations, which is a subsection of the causal phenomena section, for descriptions of the phenomena of realization and goodness.
16. Lopon speaks his own idiosyncratic style of English. I've left this passage in his original English for three reasons: (a) Lopon's English is strong and compelling; (b) it gives you a feel who Lopon really is; and (c) his own words convey his meaning far better than any version edited into proper English could ever do.

HMV: My experience has been that when a person first starts meditating, that many thoughts, a stream of thoughts, will appear in a person's mind. Is that correct?

LTN: Sure. This is nature.

HMV: And then after a person has been meditating for a while, the thoughts begin to slow down.

LTN: Yes.

HMV: And sometimes they even disappear. Can that happen?

LTN: Yes.

HMV: Thank you. Eventually, it seems that gaps will begin to appear in the stream of thoughts. Periods of time occur when there are no thoughts appearing. And sometimes those gaps will be very long. In your experience, can that happen as well?

LTN: Yes. What do you mean by gap?

HMV: By gap I mean that there are no inner appearances—no thoughts or emotions—coming. Nothing appears.

LTN: Then what is there?

HMV: Nothing.

LTN: Nothing?

HMV: Well there is awareness there.

LTN: What is awareness?

HMV: It is just awareness.

LTN: What's it aware of? To be aware means that you are seeing or knowing something. Otherwise there is no awareness.

HMV: It is aware of space.

LTN: Space. OK. Who is it at that time that is knowing that empty space?

HMV: Egoless awareness, rigpa.[17]

LTN: Oh yes. This is the point you see. Is this egoless awareness the same thing as consciousness?[18]

HMV: No. It is not consciousness.

LTN: OK. Then what is egoless awareness?

HMV: It is just the awareness of empty space.

LTN: Just space.

HMV: Just space.

17. In the remainder of this passage, I will be translating the Tibet term rigpa as "egoless awareness." Rigpa is usually translated as simply "awareness." But it can also be translated as egoless awareness or nondual awareness because the term rigpa denotes an awareness that has nondual awareness of all of the phenomena that it knows.
18. This is another trick question. Lopon is using the term consciousness here in a very specific way. Given the translation history of the word "consciousness," many Tibetans, including Lopon, equate the term consciousness with dual awareness. So here Lopon is asking me if the rigpa, or egoless awareness, that I am describing is a dual moment of consciousness.

LTN: Nothing else?

HMV: Nothing else.

LTN: OK. Only space. Why do you call this awareness? Space itself cannot see anything or know anything. It is empty. Then what is it that is aware?

HMV: The awareness itself. It is aware of both the space and itself.

LTN: OK. Just aware. Then how do you control it at that moment? How do you stay in that state?

HMV: Well I don't try and control it.

LTN: You don't do anything?

HMV: Nothing.

LTN: OK. Completely empty space.

HMV: Completely empty.

LTN: OK. There is no awareness. Nothing to see. Nothing to know. Only space exists.

HMV: There is only space, but it does feel like there is an awareness within the space, and within this space, inner appearances can continue to appear.

LTN: Yes.

HMV: The inner appearances continue, but they dissolve as soon as they appear.

LTN: Yes they continue, but is something changing, or does the space go on?

HMV: The way it seems to me is that the space goes on.

LTN: Never changing.

HMV: Never changing.

LTN: OK.

HMV: It never changes, but sometimes individual inner appearances will come into that space.

LTN: Yes.

HMV: But as soon as they come into this space, they dissolve.

LTN: OK.

HMV: And then there is space again. Maybe for a long time.

LTN: OK.

HMV: And then another single inner appearance will come, and it dissolves, too. And then it's gone.

LTN: OK. Who sees?

HMV: Just the awareness. My experience is that when these single inner appearances arise, they come into the space and then immediately disappear.

LTN: Yes.

HMV: My experience is that when they dissolve, different things can then happen. For example, sometimes when a single inner appearance arises and disappears, light will come. Light appears.

LTN: What is light?

HMV: My eyes are closed. And inside, there is a field of light. The space is now filled with light. In your experience, can that happen?

LTN: [Long pause] Yes. The conditions for the thought come up. Or as you say light. Where does the light come from?

HMV: From the nature.

LTN: From the nature. So nature has some power.

HMV: Yes.

LTN: So if you have experienced this much, this space itself, if you don't touch anything, this space is not normal space. It has special quality.

HMV: What do you mean by special quality?

LTN: I'm going to tell you now. This is not normal space. Normal space is only space. Nothing is there. Now this space is special because it liberates thoughts. It liberates consciousness. It looks like space. You have to use words. But it is not real space. This condition has this special power. Everything, nirvana, samsara, happiness, sadness can spontaneously appear in this space. This nature is also completely pure originally. *You cannot take any negative actions in this space.* Therefore this space is called pure, or kadag.

HMV: Everything is pure in this space.

LTN: Yes. Whatever appears, you don't have to do anything. Good things can come. Bad things can come. Sometimes very bad emotions can come up. Sometimes good things come up.

HMV: Do the bad emotions change when they come into that space?

LTN: If you are able to keep without disturbing anything, if whatever comes up you don't care, if you are keeping into the space without disturbances, then you are OK. If you can do this, gradually all of the negative actions and emotions, all the negative things become weaker and weaker. Finally they disappear. Then good things will start coming spontaneously into that space without there being thoughts and emotions first. They come if you do not expect them to come.

This is profound stuff. Lopon is actually describing here the awareness that is the ground of the egoless mind. His culminating point is that when you abide in this egoless awareness, everything that appears in the inner space of that awareness will be saturated with, and transformed by, the goodness that is the nondual awareness of the egoless mind. "You cannot take any negative actions in this space."

It has been Lopon's experience that all of the ego's thoughts and emotions—no matter how egocentric or neurotic they might be—will be transformed into the nondual realizations, joy and goodness of the egoless mind when they are known within the space of egoless awareness. Beyond that, Lopon says that once the ego's thoughts and emotions stop appearing, egoless meanings will appear spontaneously on their own. "Good things will start coming spontaneously into that space without there being thoughts and emotions first."

When you add to Lopon's interview this following passage from an interview with Khenpo Tsewang Gyatso about empty awareness, which is another synonym for egoless awareness, the exact nature of egoless awareness becomes even clearer:

HMV: What is empty awareness?
KTG: Empty awareness[19] is the absolute true nature of mind.
HMV: Thank you. So it is egoless awareness.
KTG: Yes.
HMV: Would it be correct to say that empty awareness realizes the emptiness of all of the inner appearances[20] it knows?
KTG: Yes.
HMV: Would it be correct to say that it is an awareness that does not reject, accept or follow inner appearances?
KTG: Yes.
HMV: Is it an awareness that does not attribute a self to the appearances it knows?
KTG: Yes.
HMV: Is it a blissful awareness?
KTG: Yes.
HMV: Is it an awareness that is like space?
KTG: Yes.
HMV: Is it nondual self-awareness?
KTG: Yes.
HMV: Is it the same thing as wisdom self-awareness?[21]
KTG: Yes.
HMV: Thank you. Is abiding in empty awareness the same thing as abiding in the nature of mind?
KTG: Yes.
HMV: Thank you very much

One of the several points that Khenpo is making here is that empty awareness, which is once again a synonym for the egoless awareness, is the generative heart of the egoless mind. Egoless awareness is the heart of the egoless mind because when it has nondual awareness of the meanings it knows, this generates, in turn, the nondual transformations that create the entire egoless state of mind.

Egoless awareness has nondual awareness of all of the meanings that it knows because it allows the stream of consciousness to remain in its natural state. This, in turn, causes the meanings to go through a spontaneous process called *nondual transformation.* There are several different types of nondual transformation, and each of them is a process in which either primordial meanings or egopoietic meanings

19. Tib.: Rig tong.
20. Tib.: Nang-gyi nangwa.
21. Tib.: Rang-rig yeshe.

are spontaneously transformed into various aspects of the egoless mind: nondual realizations, nondual goodness, nondual joy and egoless awareness itself.

The means that the nondual transformations create a positive feedback loop, if you will, in which egoless awareness strengthens and regenerates itself over and over again by having continual nondual awareness of the meanings that appear in its stream of consciousness. Every single nondual transformation strengthens and stabilizes egoless awareness a little bit more.

As we will soon be seeing, the science of the stream of consciousness has identified and described several different kinds of nondual transformations.

III. Causal Phenomena

When a cold air mass collides with a warm air mass in the heat of summer, it causes a thunderstorm. Sustained high blood pressure can cause an enlarged heart, congestive heart failure, heart attacks and strokes. Gravity causes apocryphal apples to fall from trees.

In much the same way, when the watcher makes a response to a meaning that appears in its stream of consciousness, it causes changes to occur in the stream of consciousness. Every single action that the watcher takes causes new phenomena to appear in the stream of consciousness, and the phenomena produced by these actions are called causal phenomena by the science of the stream of consciousness. They are easy to observe, and their occurrence is predictable. For example, if the watcher represses an emotion, that emotion will invariably remain in awareness as a mood.

The phenomena that are generated by the watcher's actions fall into three categories: (1) mode of awareness; (2) the egocentric transformations; and (3) the egoless transformations. The next three sections will list and describe the causal phenomena in each of these categories:

A. Modes of Awareness

1. Dual awareness
2. Nondual awareness
3. Complex awareness
4. Simple awareness.

The mind can have either dual or nondual awareness of itself. The egocentric mind has dual awareness of itself in the sense that it has dual awareness of the meanings that appear in its stream of consciousness. This is one of the defining characteristics of the egocentric mind.

The egocentric mind causes itself to have dual awareness of meanings because it grasps them in the process of knowing them—that is, it projects concepts onto meanings by judging, repressing, attaching or following them.

This can be summarized as a simple causal sequence:

WATCHER GRASPS MEANING → DUAL AWARENESS OF MEANING

Dual awareness is as a mode of awareness in which (1) awareness and meaning remain ontologically, spatially and epistemologically separate because (2) awareness projects concepts onto meanings in the process of knowing them.

In contrast, the egoless mind does not grasp the meanings that appear in its stream of consciousness, and as a result, it has nondual awareness of meanings:

WATCHER DOES NOT GRASP MEANING → NONDUAL AWARENESS OF MEANING

Nondual awareness can be described as a mode of awareness in which (1) awareness and meaning dissolve into one another because (2) awareness does not project concepts onto a meaning in the process of knowing it. Nondual awareness is one of the defining qualities of the egoless mind.

This distinction between dual and nondual awareness is an important one. When your mind has nondual awareness of itself, you are able to know yourself as you really are, and this makes it possible for you to be your true self. On the other hand, when you have dual awareness of your mind, it is virtually impossible to know and be your true self.

Dual self-awareness precludes the possibility of knowing your true self because it creates a state of mind in which it is almost impossible to know the suchness of the meanings that your mind gives to the present moment: the primordial meanings and the nondual realizations. Knowing the suchness of the meanings you give to the present moment is an indispensable aspect of knowing your true self.

Dual awareness blocks a person's ability to know the meanings your mind has given to the present moment because it creates a state of mind called *complex awareness*. Complex awareness is a state of mind in which several layers of thoughts, emotions, mind-films and moods are present in the stream of consciousness at the same time.

Dual awareness creates complex awareness by setting into motion causal processes that cause the egocentric mind to routinely project three different types of meaning into its stream of consciousness that have nothing to do with the present moment: (1) the mind-films, (2) the emotions that enact self-judgment and (3) the moods.

When they are present in the stream of consciousness, these contrapuntal layers of egopoietic meaning clutter the stream of consciousness and obscure your ability to see, much less have nondual awareness of, the primordial meanings and realizations.

Here is an example. Suppose that you are trying to remember the names of all of the many dukes, lords and princes that Shakespeare had the Duke of Gloucester murder on his way to becoming King Richard III. It is a difficult task because he did away with quite a few people.

Then imagine that a single thought arises that recalls the name of Gloucester's brother, the Duke of Clarence. The murder of Clarence is the first one we see in the play, although not the first one that Glouchester's ambitions led him to commit.

If that single thought with Clarence's name appears in your stream of consciousness at the same time that a robust mind-film is cycling through your mind—let's say a stream of thoughts about how bad your memory has become, then that film will make it difficult for you to detect the appearance of that single thought that contains Clarence's name, much less have accurate knowledge of its content.

In this kind of situation, which is typical of the routine workings of the egocentric state of mind, the thought containing Clarence's name is there, but you are unable to know it because it is veiled by the thoughts and mood of the mind-film. If the thoughts are dense enough, you might not even know that the thought is there. Or your experience might be that Clarence's name "rolled off the back of my tongue."

It is much the same as trying to listen to a Bach cello suite in your living room while the Rolling Stones are playing a concert just down the street in a stadium. It would be just about impossible to hear the subtle sounds of the cello, much less appreciate the grandeur of Bach's composition.

The egoless mind, in contrast, has nondual awareness of the meanings that appear in its stream of consciousness. When the mind has nondual awareness of its stream of consciousness, it does not initiate causal processes that cause emotions, mind-films or moods to appear and remain in the stream of consciousness. The only phenomena that appear in the egoless stream of consciousness are the primordial meanings, the realizations and the nondual transformations, all of which dissolve in an instant.

This creates the state of mind called *simple awareness* in which it is a simple matter for the mind to know the suchness of the meanings it gives to the present moment.

When a primordial meaning appears in the stream of consciousness of the egoless mind, there are no other thoughts, mind-films, emotions or moods present to veil and obscure it. This clears the way for the egoless watcher to have non-conceptual and nondual awareness of that primordial meaning and know its content exactly as it is.

When the mind is clear of mind-films, moods and emotions, you might just find that you have no trouble remembering the Duke of Clarence's name, or the names of all of the other people with whom Richard III dispensed on his way to the throne. You might even remember the names of all of the mountain villages that you have trekked and doctored your way through in Nepal.

B. Transformations

A transformation, in the context of the science of the stream of consciousness, is a process in which one phenomenon is transformed into a different kind of phenomenon by an action of the watcher. Transformations are constantly happening all of the time in both the egoless and the egocentric mind.

There are two basic categories of transformation: the egocentric transformations and the nondual transformations. The egocentric transformations create egocentric phenomena, and the nondual transformations generate egoless phenomena.

The egocentric phenomena are created by the grasping actions of the egocentric watcher. The egoless phenomena, in contrast, appear when the mind has nondual awareness of a meaning and realizes its suchness.

1. The Egocentric Transformations

A. Mind-film activation
B. Mood activation

A. Mind-Film Activation: When the watcher grasps a thought or emotion, it can cause a mind-film to appear in the stream of consciousness. This is the phenomenon of *mind-film activation.* Mind-film activation is a process in which a single meaning is immediately transformed into a mind-film.

Suppose an old and dear friend that you haven't heard from in years calls out of the blue, and you have a great conversation that feels like you saw each other just the day before.

After the two of you hang up, a thought arises that reminds you of the many good times you and she once had together. The memory is so dear to you that you hold on to and savor that thought. Then you find yourself indulging in and continuing to think about your shared good times. A feeling of happiness arises within you, and you hold on to that too. This is a moment of mind-film activation in which a single happy thought was transformed into a happy mind-film.

The same thing can happen with an unwanted emotion as well. Suppose a moment of sadness arises within you, and that you quickly repress it. That repression can also cause a mind-film activation, and if it does, two things will happen simultaneously:

1. A sad mood will take up residence in your mind, and
2. A vigorous involuntary stream of sad thoughts will appear in your mind.

Whereas in the first example the attachment of a single thought transformed the thought into an enjoyable mind-film, in the second case, the repression of an emotion transformed that emotion into a painful mind-film.

Both types of mind-film activation are constantly occurring in the egocentric stream of consciousness. They are the proximate cause of the constant thought noise, or mind wandering, that we all have running through the back of our minds. This thought noise is a staple presence in the egocentric mind because mind-films are constantly being activated by the actions of the egocentric watcher.

The activation of a mind-film creates the state of mind we already know as *complex awareness*, which is the normal state of the egocentric mind. The egocentric mind spends most of its time in the state of complex awareness, but there are also moments when it is able to reside in *simple awareness* for short periods of time. Whereas the egoless mind spends most if not all of its time in the state of simple awareness.

B. Mood Activation: Modern psychiatry and psychology tell us that unwanted and painful moods like sadness and depression are caused by imbalances of neurotransmitters in the brain. First there was the catecholamine hypothesis of depression, and then the serotonin hypothesis of depression (Schildkraut, 1965; Coppen, 1967). But after sixty years of research, neither theory has even come close to being unequivocally confirmed (Kirsch, 2010).

From the perspective of the science of the stream of consciousness, neither theory has been confirmed because moods are not caused by the neurotransmitters. The study of the stream of consciousness leads one to the conclusion that moods are caused by the actions of the egocentric watcher. From this perspective, it seems more likely that the neurotransmitters might *mediate* the appearance of moods, as opposed to causing them.

We know that the ego creates moods because it is easy to observe the process by which it creates them. It is the grasping of emotions by the egocentric watcher that causes moods to appear in the stream of consciousness. Basically, when the watcher grasps an emotion it will remain in awareness as a mood. A mood is a transformation of an emotion, and once again it is an easy matter to see this transformation as it occurs.

Imagine that you are angling your way back down a mountain that you have just climbed, and that all of a sudden a huge black bear makes its way onto the ridge you are descending about ten feet in front of you. You feel fear, and that fear is the meaning you give to the experience of seeing this large growling mammal who might well attack at any moment because he is slobbering. Slobbering is said to be a sign that a bear will attack, and this bear is also beginning to feint charges. He comes toward you and then turns away, and then turns towards you and away from you several times again.

If you have nondual awareness of that fear in that moment, the fear will wash through you and its hold on you will be diminished. However, if you try to repress your fear and deny that it is there, it will almost certainly take you over and become a fearful mood that will hamper your ability to assess and handle the situation.

That fearful mood would be a transformation of the emotion of fear that was your first response to the bear. By repressing the fear, you cause it to become a mood and remain in awareness. This same kind of transformation can and does happen with all of the emotions.

2. The Nondual Transformations

A. Dissolution
B. Realization
C. Amused compassion
D. Nondual goodness
E. Nondual light
F. Nondual joy
G. Abiding joy and goodness.

When the mind has nondual awareness of a meaning, it will invariably cause that meaning to be immediately transformed into a different type of phenomenon. Nondual awareness will transform any meaning—be it a primordial meaning, an emotion or a mind-film—into either egoless awareness itself or a nondual egoless meaning.

Nondual awareness causes six different types of transformation, and as a group, the science of the stream of consciousness calls them the *nondual transformations.* They are called the nondual transformations because they occur when the watcher has nondual awareness of a meaning. Each type of transformation produces a different type of phenomenon, and each transformation is named for the phenomenon it produces. They are as follows.

A. Dissolution: The first nondual transformation is the phenomenon of *dissolution*, which has already been described: an individual moment of consciousness appears and then it immediately dissolves and disappears. When the phenomenon of dissolution occurs, a period of time will then follow in which thoughts and emotions cease to appear in the stream of consciousness.

A mind-film can also dissolve. Normally, when a mind-film appears in the ego mind's stream of consciousness, it will just run on and on. But if the watcher stops believing and living in a film, nondual awareness of that film will occur, and the film will dissolve and disappear.

The late Tulku Urgyen saw the phenomenon of dissolution as the experience of emptiness. Here is an exchange between Tulku Urgyen and myself that occurred at Nagi Gompa—Tulku Urgyen's monastery in the hills above Kathmandu Valley—in March of 1991. This exchange begins with Tulku Urgyen asking questions of me:

TU: Do you see anything when you look at your mind?
HMV: If you changed "see" to "experience," I'd say yes.
TU: What do you experience?
HMV: My own mind being mirrored back to me.

TU: (Lots and lots of laughter) Do you experience something?
HMV: No I don't experience things.
TU: So you don't experience things?
HMV: That's right. But I do experience appearances. And as soon as I become aware of an appearance, it dissolves.
TU: That's right! That's the experience of emptiness.

In addition, all of the other nondual transformations begin with the dissolution of a meaning as well. In each of those transformations, the dissolution of a meaning occurs first, and then the dissolution is followed by the appearance of another phenomenon.

B. Realization: For example, consider the nondual transformation of *realization.* In this type of transformation, a meaning is transformed into a realization in which you feel you have understood something that is both large and profound.

A moment of nondual realization begins with the dissolution of a meaning. Then, after that first dissolution occurs, a deep insight into one's own nature and/or the nature of the universe comes to your awareness spontaneously. The person having the insight simultaneously feels at peace and as though he or she has gained an understanding of something important. This is the nondual transformation of realization, and it can also be called an *epiphany.*

C. Amused Compassion: A third type of nondual transformation is the phenomenon of *amused compassion.* In this type of transformation, a meaning dissolves and is transformed into a combined feeling of amusement and compassion.

The phenomenon of amused compassion is experienced like this: once again, the transformation begins with the dissolution of a meaning. As the meaning dissolves, you become aware of its content, and you see that it was really a foolish idea. In this act of seeing the content of a meaning as it is, you spontaneously see that it is foolish and accept it; and in that moment, feelings of amusement and compassion arise in place of the original meaning.

D. Nondual Goodness, Nondual Joy and Nondual Light: The fourth nondual transformation is the phenomenon of *nondual goodness.* In this type of transformation the meaning that dissolves is transformed into the feeling of goodness.

The fifth nondual transformation is the phenomenon of *nondual joy.* In this phenomenon, a meaning is transformed into a feeling of joy. The experience develops in much the same way as the phenomenon of amused compassion. A meaning appears. Nondual awareness of that meaning occurs, and as a result it dissolves and a feeling of nondual joy arises in its place.

The sixth nondual transformation is the phenomenon of *nondual light.* In this phenomenon, a meaning is transformed into an appearance of inner light as it dissolves. The meaning dissolves, and a glow of colored light appears within the inner space of the mind for a moment, and then the light dissolves as well.

E. Abiding Joy and Abiding Goodness: The phenomena of *abiding joy* and *abiding goodness* are related to the nondual transformations, although they are not in and of themselves nondual transformations. As described earlier, as a person progresses in meditation and becomes more and more adept at allowing the dissolutions of the nondual mind to occur naturally, feelings of joy and goodness build up and become a stable presence within your mind.

As these feelings become a fixed presence in your mind, they actually becomes your awareness. This joyous awareness that is saturated with goodness is actually the egoless awareness that is the subjective aspect of the egoless mind. It is the egoless watcher because it allows the stream of consciousness to run free and it has nondual awareness of all of the meanings it knows.

Khenpo Tsewang Gyatso: The Nondual Transformations

Khenpo Tsewang Gyatso is a teaching lama at the Namdroling Monastery in South India. He is a brilliant scholar whose intellectual accomplishments are grounded in genuine spiritual accomplishment. As I know from interviewing the Khenpo, his brilliance includes (1) his ability to articulate and describe subtle states of mind and (2) the fact that he never abandons a line of thought in our interviews until he has made sure that I have understood what he is saying. In a word, he has both the clarity of mind to do these things, and he cares. He has been exceedingly generous with both his knowledge and time in the many interviews that we have done and have continued to do together since 1997.

Here is a passage from an interview the Khenpo and I did at Namdroling Monastery in February 2009 in which we discuss four of the nondual transformations (Vyner, 2018):

HMV: At one point yesterday, we were talking about the nondual awareness of primordial meanings. Now I would like to ask you about the actual experience of having those moments of nondual awareness.

KTG: OK.

HMV: In my own experience, I have identified what I think of as being four different types of moments of nondual awareness. I'd like to describe them to you and see what you think.

KTG: OK.

HMV: The first one is dissolution.

KTG: OK.

HMV: A single inner appearance arises and then it immediately dissolves. After it dissolves, there is, for a while, a complete cessation of the appearance of thoughts, emotions and the mind-films.

KTG: OK.

HMV: The second one is called joy. A single inner appearance arises, then quickly dissolves. Once again, there is a complete cessation of thoughts and emotions, and at the same time, a feeling of non-conceptual joy arises. And it feels like I am the joy. The joy and my awareness are one. The joy is my awareness.

KTG: OK.

HMV: A third type of momentary nondual awareness is amused compassion. Again, a single thought arises and dissolves, I see that the content of that thought is maybe foolish or stupid, and then a feeling of amusement and compassion for that thought arises within me. Then I become the compassion; my awareness becomes the compassion and at that time, there are no thoughts coming into my mind. Finally, the fourth type of nondual awareness is called realization. A single inner appearance arises, it dissolves, there is a cessation of thoughts and emotions and then some kind of large insight into either myself or the universe arises. When the insight arises, I have the feeling that I have learned something important. It also feels like the original inner appearance gets integrated into, made part of, that larger realization. Do you know what I mean?

KTG: Yes.

HMV: At the same time, it also feels like I am accepting the original inner appearance. So again, these are these four different kinds of moments of nondual awareness that I have noticed in my own mind stream. I'd like to describe each of these experiences again, one at a time now, and ask you some questions about them.

KTG: OK.

HMV: Thank you. The first one is dissolution. A single inner appearance arises, it immediately dissolves, and there is a cessation of thoughts and emotions. My first question is, would you be willing to call that a moment of nondual awareness?

KTG: Yes. Dissolution is a moment of nondual awareness. Everything is kind of dissolved.

HMV: Is that a definition of nondual awareness?

KTG: Yes. Everything dissolves and yet there is still a sense of awareness.

HMV: What do you mean by sense of awareness? Do you mean that awareness is present?

KTG: Yes.

HMV: What name would you give to this kind of dissolving experience?

KTG: This type of experience is the self-liberation[22] of thoughts.

HMV: So in a scientific sense, would it be correct to say that the criteria for identifying and defining the self-liberation of a thought are (1) an thought dissolves; (2) there is a complete cessation of all thoughts and emotions for a while; and (3) awareness remains present?

22. Tib.: rang drol.

KTG: Yes.

HMV: Are these the defining characteristics of the self-liberation of a thought?

KTG: Yes.

HMV: Could you say that this a moment of abiding in egoless awareness?

KTG: Yes.

HMV: Thank you. On to nondual joy then.

KTG: OK.

HMV: An inner appearance arises, it dissolves, there is a cessation of all thoughts and emotions, and then a non-conceptual blissful awareness remains. Would you be willing to call this a moment of nondual awareness?

KTG: Yes.

HMV: Do you, or the DzogChen tradition, have a name for this type of moment of nondual awareness?

KTG: This is self-liberation into empty bliss. Tey-thong rang-drol.

HMV: Is this a moment of abiding in egoless awareness?

KTG: Yes.

HMV: If this blissful awareness were permanent, would this be what the experience of the blissful dimension of the Buddha's mind, or sambhogakaya, would be like?

KTG: Yes. It would be close.

HMV: How would it be different? Are you thinking of something in particular?

KTG: No, no. The blissful aspect is perfection, but this is like a moment. So this is part of, or an aspect of, the blissful aspect of the Buddha's mind. That is what I mean by close. It is a glimpse of the blissful aspect of the Buddha's mind.

HMV: Thank you. Now amused compassion. Do you know what I mean by that?

KTG: Amused?

HMV: It means something is funny in a subtle way.

KTG: OK.

HMV: It means you are laughing at your self and having compassion for your self at the same time. A thought arises, and it dissolves. As it dissolves I see the content of that thought as it is. I see that it is stupid and I laugh at it and myself in a compassionate way. And then that non-conceptual compassion persists for a while. Would you be willing to call this kind of dissolution a moment of nondual awareness?

KTG: Yes.

HMV: Is there a name for this type of dissolution?

KTG: The self-radiance of compassion. Nyingjé rang-dang.

HMV: If that non-conceptual compassion were permanent, that is, if it was accompanied by a permanent cessation of dual minds, would that be the experience of the compassionate aspect of the Buddha's mind, the nirmanakaya?

KTG: Yes. It would be related to that.

HMV: Thank you. Finally, then, realization is the fourth type of moment of nondual awareness. Again, a single inner appearance arises and dissolves, there is a cessation of dual minds, and then a big understanding of some kind arises. It could be an understanding of either myself, the mind or the universe. And then that big picture dissolves right away. I remember it, but it just appears and dissolves like a flash of lightning.

KTG: Yes.

HMV: And at the same time, I feel like I have accepted the original inner appearance and integrated it into my mandala.[23] Would you be willing to call this a moment of nondual awareness?

KTG: Yes. All four of these four are experiences of moments of nondual awareness.

HMV: What would you call the nondual moment in which a large insight arises?

KTG: That is an experience of wisdom. It is the radiance of primordial wisdom.[24]

HMV: Thank you very much.

IV. Causal Sequences

Finally, we come to fourth category of phenomena that appear in the stream of consciousness: the causal relationships that exist between the watcher and the phenomena that appear in the stream of consciousness. The independent variable in these causal processes is always an action taken by the watcher.

Our interviews have shown that there are a number of well-defined causal relationships that exist between the watcher's actions and phenomena that appear in the stream of consciousness. The actions that the watcher takes consistently cause the same events to occur in stream of consciousness, and as such their effects are replicable and predictable.

Sometimes a single action by the watcher will initiate two causal sequences at once. For example, the repression of an emotion can cause a mood to appear by itself, or it can also cause a mood and mind-film to appear simultaneously in the stream of consciousness.

The causal sequences being presented here have been divided into three categories: (1) the egocentric transformations, (2) the nondual transformations and (3) the effects of meditation. The remainder of this chapter will now list and briefly explain, by category, many of the countless causal sequences that have been delineated to date.

23. I used the term mandala at the time of the interview. Mandala is a Sanskrit term that refers to a picture that represents the universe, and my purpose in using this term was to say to the Khenpo that in those moments, it feels like the insight is integrated into my worldview.

24. Tib.: yeshe rang dang.

A. The Egocentric Transformations

1. When the watcher grasps an iMoC, it causes a mind-film to appear in the stream of consciousness:

    GRASPING OF IMOC → MIND-FILM ACTIVATION

2. When the watcher attaches a single MoC, it causes a mind-film to appear in the stream of consciousness:

    ATTACHMENT OF IMOC → MIND-FILM ACTIVATION

3. When the watcher represses a single MoC, it causes a mind-film to appear in the stream of consciousness:

    REPRESSION OF IMOC → MIND-FILM ACTIVATION

4. When the mind follows, or believes, a mind-film that is already present and active in the stream of consciousness, that film will remain active in the stream of consciousness:

    FOLLOWING OF MIND-FILM → CONTINUATION OF MIND-FILM

5. When the mind grasps a meaning, whether it be a moment of consciousness, an emotion or a mind-film, it will have dual awareness of that meaning:

    GRASPING OF MEANING → DUAL AWARENESS OF MEANING

6. When the watcher attaches a meaning, it will cause itself to have dual awareness of that meaning:

    ATTACHMENT OF MEANING → DUAL AWARENESS OF MEANING

7. When the watcher represses a meaning, it will cause itself to have dual awareness of that meaning:

    REPRESSION OF MEANING → DUAL AWARENESS OF MEANING

8. When the mind grasps a thought, it will cause a plethora of thoughts to appear in the stream of consciousness:

    GRASPING OF SINGLE THOUGHT → COUNTLESS THOUGHTS APPEAR IN SOC

    Annotation: When the watcher grasps an emotion, it can cause either a mood, mind-film or both to appear in the stream of consciousness, as follows:

9. When the watcher represses an emotion, a mood that is identical to the emotion will appear in the stream of consciousness:

    REPRESSION OF AN EMOTION → APPEARANCE OF A MOOD

10. When the watcher represses an emotion, it can also cause a mind-film to appear in the stream of consciousness:

    REPRESSION OF AN EMOTION → APPEARANCE OF A MIND-FILM

11. When the watcher attaches an emotion, a mood that is identical to that emotion will appear in the stream of consciousness:

    ATTACHMENT OF AN EMOTION → APPEARANCE OF A MOOD

12. When the watcher attaches an emotion, it can also cause a mind-film to appear in the stream of consciousness.

    ATTACHMENT OF EMOTION → APPEARANCE OF MIND-FILM

B. The Nondual Transformations

13. When the watcher has nondual awareness of a moment of consciousness, it causes a nondual transformation of that moment of consciousness to occur. In general:

    NONDUAL AWARENESS OF IMOC → NONDUAL TRANSFORMATION

14. Nondual awareness can cause several different kinds of nondual transformation of a moment of consciousness. For example:
    a. NONDUAL AWARENESS OF IMOC → DISSOLUTION
    b. NONDUAL AWARENESS OF IMOC → REALIZATION
    c. NONDUAL AWARENESS OF IMOC → AMUSED COMPASSION
    d. NONDUAL AWARENESS OF IMOC → GOODNESS
    e. NONDUAL AWARENESS OF IMOC → NONDUAL INNER LIGHT
    f. NONDUAL AWARENESS OF IMOC → NONDUAL JOY
15. When the watcher has nondual awareness of a mind-film, it causes a nondual transformation of that film to occur. In general:

    NONDUAL AWARENESS OF MIND-FILM → NONDUAL TRANSFORMATION

16. When the watcher has nondual awareness of a mind-film, it can cause the occurrence of several different kinds of nondual transformation. They are as follows:
    a. NONDUAL AWARENESS OF MIND-FILM → DISSOLUTION
    b. NONDUAL AWARENESS OF MIND-FILM → REALIZATION
    c. NONDUAL AWARENESS OF MIND-FILM → AMUSED COMPASSION
    d. NONDUAL AWARENESS OF MIND-FILM → GOODNESS
    e. NONDUAL AWARENESS OF MIND-FILM → NONDUAL INNER LIGHT
    f. NONDUAL AWARENESS OF MIND-FILM → NONDUAL JOY

C. The Effects of Meditation

17. Meditation causes the diminution and/or cessation of the ISoC to occur:

    MEDITATION → DIMINUTION/CESSATION

18. When diminution of the involuntary stream of consciousness occurs, the mind experiences more moments of nondual awareness.

    DIMINUTION → INCREASED FREQUENCY OF MOMENTS OF NONDUAL AWARENESS

19. When the diminution of the involuntary stream of consciousness occurs, the mind experiences more moments of realization:

    DIMINUTION → INCREASED FREQUENCY OF MOMENTS OF REALIZATION

20. As you have more and more moments of nondual awareness, the watcher begins to experience itself as being a joyful nondual awareness saturated with goodness:

    INCREASING FREQUENCY OF MOMENTS OF NONDUAL AWARENESS → AWARENESS BECOMES A JOYOUS AWARENESS SATURATED WITH GOODNESS

If you pause and think about it for a moment, the existence of these causal sequences forces upon us a rather interesting and large theoretical conclusion.

We live in a time in which science, and most of the rest of us as well, have become mesmerized by the brain and the impact of biological variables on the mind. There is even a feeling abroad that we can completely understand the mind by simply understanding the brain. Indeed, it is sometimes said now that the mind and brain are one and the same thing.

Biological psychiatry, for example, is now the dominant paradigm of psychiatry. Biological psychiatry has two main tenets: (1) biological lesions, which are usually, although not always, conceived of as being abnormal levels of one or more neurotransmitters, are the primary cause of psychopathology; and (2) the best way to treat a psychopathology is to either give a patient a medication that will modulate the levels of neurotransmitters in their central nervous system, or administer another physical modality of treatment.

In other words, psychiatry is now operating on the premise that the best way to alleviate mental suffering and cultivate mental health is to manipulate biological variables. This means that should you go to see a psychiatrist for a problem, the treatment you will most likely receive will be either a medication, electroshock therapy, transcranial magnetic stimulation or perhaps even psychosurgery.

But if we look at the causal sequences listed above, we see clear evidence of the fact that mental variables play a crucial role in determining whether or not a person has a healthy mind.

If you repress a moment of the emotion of sadness, it will remain in your mind as a sad mood. If you have persistent nondual awareness of your thoughts, a reservoir of joy and goodness will build up inside of your mind. If you try to control your stream of consciousness, you will create duality and conflict within your mind, and so forth.

As the next several chapters are about to make clear, our findings establish that the variables that determine whether or not a mind is happy and healthy are psychological variables. Happiness and mental health cannot cultivated by taking a medication or by the magnetic stimulation of the brain. The healthy mind is an egoless mind that is able to become its true self and live in goodness and happiness because it has cultivated the ability to have persistent nondual awareness of itself.

Conclusion

Electrons mediate the phenomenon that we call electricity. Photons mediate and generate the electromagnetic waves we call light. Lymphocytes mediate the mammalian body's immune response to foreign matter.

The phenomena that appear in the stream of consciousness mediate the psychological processes by which the mind knows, controls and transforms its stream of consciousness. This is the functional identity of these phenomena.

Our observations of the phenomena that appear in the stream of consciousness, and the typology of phenomena that they have generated, are the foundation upon which the science of the stream of consciousness will be built; and in particular, they are also the observations from which our theory of the healthy mind has been derived.

Chapters 8 through 12 will describe how these phenomena mediate the processes that both generate and constitute the egoless and egocentric states of mind. Chapter 8 will start off by presenting the raw observations from which our maps of these states of mind have been derived. We will then map out both the egocentric and egoless states of mind, and we will conclude by evaluating whether or not they are healthy states of mind. But before we proceed to this progression, we will first take a look at the place of the stream of consciousness and the ego in nature.

References

Coppen, A. (1967). The biochemistry of affective disorders. *British Journal of Psychiatry*, 113, 1237–1264.

Kirsch, I. (2010). *The Emperor's New Drugs: Exploding the Antidepressant Myth*. New York, NY: Basic Books.

Schildkraut, J. J. (1965). The catecholamine hypothesis of affective disorders: A review of supporting evidence. *American Journal of Psychiatry*, 122(5), 509–522.

Smallwood, J., and Schooler, J. (2006). The restless mind. *Psychological Bulletin*, 132(6), 946–958.

Vyner, H. M. (2003). The descriptive psychology of Tibetan Buddhism and the nature of the healthy human mind. *Anthropology of Consciousness*, 13(2), 1–25.

Vyner, H. M. (2004a). *The Healthy Mind Interviews, Volume 1: Khenpo Nyima Wangyal*. Kathmandu: Vajra Books.

Vyner, H. M. (2004b). *The Healthy Mind Interviews, Volume 2: Khenpo Tsewang Gyatso*. Kathmandu: Vajra Books.

Vyner, H. M. (2005). *The Healthy Mind Interviews, Volume 3: Lopon Tekchog*. Kathmandu: Vajra Books.

Vyner, H. M. (2007). *The Healthy Mind Interviews, Volume 4: Dalai Lama, Lopon Tenzin Namdak, Lopon Tekchog*. Kathmandu: Vajra Books.

Vyner, H. M. (2009–2010). A preliminary theory of the defining dynamic of the healthy human mind. *Imagination, Cognition and Personality*, 29(3), 225–270.

Vyner, H. M. (In Press, 2018). *The Healthy Mind Interviews, Volume 5: Penor Rinpoche and Khenpo Tsewang Gyatso*. Kathmandu: Vajra Books.

PART III

The Egocentric Mind

7

THE PLACE OF THE EGO IN NATURE

The wolf runs down the lame and halt caribou. Your immune system keeps foreign matter from taking up residence in your body. The earth's atmosphere, the bloodstream of our planet, maintains constant volumes of nitrogen and oxygen. The planets all keep the same orbits around the sun.

Electrons maintain the same average position within an atom. The human body maintains constant blood levels of sodium, glucose, oxygen, and countless other substances within its bloodstream. Much of the natural universe is composed of self-regulating systems.

A self-regulating system is technically defined as a collection of "things" that relate to one another for the purpose of maintaining a steady state. This is an austere definition, but it is actually the state of the art. The key term here is steady state. A self-regulating system is a system that maintains a steady state.

A single animal cell is a system made up of protoplasm and cell organelles that work together to preserve the steady state that is the life of that cell. The Amazonian rainforest is a geological, biological and climatic niche in which a vast number of flora and fauna survive by maintaining an ecological balance that sustains the integrity of the chunk of nature in which they all live together. The human body is a system composed of seven different strata of subsystems—atoms, molecules, cells, tissue, organs, organ systems and so forth—layered one on top of the other, and they all work together to maintain the life that is the steady state of your body.

This notion of a self-regulating system has been bequeathed to us by the still relatively new science of systems theory. Systems theory says that there is a level of organization at which a single bacterium is just like a society, a galaxy is like a guided missile, and a forest at climax is like a single atom of gold.

The mind, like everything else in nature, is also a system. The cognitive sciences, for example, have recognized the systemic nature of the mind in that they proceed on the premise that the mind is an information processing system that works very much like a computer. Or is it the other way around?

The human mind is, however, much more than just a simple information processing system. To the extent that our mind is a computer, it is a computer that looks into a mirror and thinks that it is someone. A person with an identity. More than that, the human mind is a computer that goes through its whole life attempting to maintain the image that it sees in that mirror. That image, its imagined identity, is the steady state that the egocentric human mind maintains.

In other words, the mind is another one of nature's self-regulating systems, and as we will be seeing, the medium in which it maintains its steady state is the stream of consciousness. This also means that the human mind and the stream of consciousness are both natural systems, and that to the extent that they are natural systems, they can both be studied by science.

This chapter is going to demonstrate that the egocentric mind is a self-regulating system. It will do so by undertaking a comparative analysis of several self-regulating systems for the purpose of delineating the defining structure and dynamics of a self-regulating system, and then show that the mind has the same structure and dynamic. Most of all, this analysis will provide us with the means of exploring the place of the ego and the stream of consciousness in nature. Is the stream of consciousness a natural process? Is the ego part of nature?

The Tundra

Wolves are shrewd hunters. They are built to run for several hours at a time at speeds in the neighborhood of twenty miles per hour, which is how they hunt caribou. The wolves wear the caribou down by chasing them for hours on end across the tundra. They pursue the caribou herd until one or more of the caribou can no longer stand the pace.

A pack of wolves will begin a hunt by taking out after a herd of caribou. Their basic strategy is that they pursue the pack until a young or sick or elderly animal begins to fall behind. Then the wolves single out the straggler and bring it down to the ground. If the first hour of a hunt does not yield a straggler, the wolves simply give up the chase and wait for another herd to appear. And then they start all over again (Mech, 1981).

Wolves are carnivores, although they will eat grass upon occasion. The majority of their diet consists of mice, ground squirrels, rabbits and pocket gophers. The amount of caribou they consume will ultimately depend upon the number of compromised animals they turn up in the process of pursuing the massive herds of caribou that stream across the tundra.

Caribou herds can be huge, and they often run into the tens of thousands. The number of compromised caribou depends upon the carrying capacity of the tundra and the size of the caribou herd. When the herd exceeds the capacity of the tundra to feed them, there isn't enough food to adequately feed all of the animals in the herd, and this causes an increase in the number of unhealthy caribou. The undernourished caribou weaken, and they are the animals that are most vulnerable to the predatory tactics of the wolves.

This means that wolf predation helps maintain the caribou population at a steady state level that is commensurate with the ability of the tundra to feed them. By weeding out the unhealthy and aging caribou, the wolves help keep the size of the caribou herd at a level for which there is enough plant life to feed them.

In other words, the tundra can successfully feed but so many caribou, and wolf predation helps to maintain the caribou population at that level. This dynamic also helps maintain the tundra itself by preventing overgrazing and the destruction of the land. Taken as a whole, the wolves and the caribou and the tundra are a large self-regulating system in which a negative feedback cycle sustains the integrity of the tundra ecosystem by controlling the size of the caribou population.

The Human Body as a Self-Regulating System

The system to which your own survival as a human being is most intimately linked, your body, is also a self-regulating system. Like every other self-regulating system, the human body is a collection of things, if you will, that work together to maintain a steady state. The ultimate steady state that is sustained by the human body is life itself.

To maintain this ultimate steady state of life, the healthy human body must sustain a vast array of component steady states. All of the different "things" in the body—the heart, the pituitary gland, the kidneys, the individual cells, the molecules that are our hormones—work together to keep us alive by maintaining a whole galaxy of steady states within our bodies. Here is just a small sample of the steady states that the human body maintains:

1. Oxygen
2. Potassium
3. Calcium
4. Water volume
5. Blood pressure
6. Thyroid hormone
7. Bilirubin
8. Body temperature.

In addition, just as the human mind maintains a psychological identity, the human body as a whole maintains a steady state that is its biological identity. It maintains a biological identity in the sense that it eliminates from itself any biological material that it deems to be foreign material, material that has a different identity than itself. This is what the immune system does. It eliminates, for instance, viruses, bacteria and, if left unchecked, organ transplants.

Our bodies reject organ transplants because the biological identity of the transplanted organ does not match our own individual biological identity. A given body's identity is encoded into the molecular structure of the membranes of its cells. In other words, and this is interesting, a human being has both a biological identity as well as a psychological identity.

The immune system is the primary subsystem within the body that maintains our biological identity, and it does so by eliminating cells from our body that do not match the molecular identity that it recognizes as its own.

First the immune system detects cells and matter that do not match its biological identity, and when it does, it generates a whole cavalcade of biological processes that eliminate those cells that it deems foreign. By eliminating foreign cells from the body, the immune system permits only those cells that it identifies as being part of its own body to remain within it, and it is in this way that it maintains the biological identity of a human being.

The human mind creates a similar type of identity, or steady state, within itself. The mind is a self-regulating system, and the steady state it maintains is your psychological identity. Just as our body eliminates bacteria and transplants, the ego marshals a cascade of psychological processes to eliminate thoughts and emotions that it regards as being foreign to its identity. This is one of the principal functions of the ego, and we'll return to it.

Human-Made Self-Regulating Systems

There are also self-regulating systems that are made by human beings. A society, for example, is a self-regulating system that maintain several steady states.

The steady states maintained by a society include its collective reality, its ethos and the structure and function of its component institutions. A society tends to maintain, for example, the structure and function of its churches, bureaucracies and belief systems.

One of the archetypal examples of a human-made self-regulating system in the history of systems theory has been the very simple case of the centralized heating system in a house. Systems theory has often made use of the example of the heating system to illustrate the basic structure and dynamic of a self-regulatory system.

A heating system has three simple components: a furnace, a thermostat and the house in which they are both located. It has, in this way, a structure and dynamic that are identical to the structure and dynamic of the system that controls the caribou population—which is composed of the caribou herd, the wolves and the tundra itself.

The heating system is a subsystem of the larger house—just as the cardiovascular system is a subsystem of the human body. The function of the heating subsystem is, of course, to maintain a steady state temperature within that house. You go out dancing for the evening, and when you come home to go to sleep the temperature in your house is the same as when you left, just as the earth is always roughly ninety-three million miles from the sun because the curved gravitational field of the sun keeps it there.

The essential dynamic of a heating system is that the furnace heats the house, and the thermostat controls the house's temperature by turning the furnace off and on. If house temperature is lower than the temperature at which the thermostat is set, the thermostat will turn the furnace on. If house temperature is too high, the furnace is turned off. It is not at all complicated.

Our purpose in analyzing the central heating system is that it makes the essential elements of a self-regulating systems stand out in bold relief. It shows us that a self-regulating system has three defining structures: the whole system itself and a control subsystem that consists of two basic structures.

The two structures of which a control subsystem is composed are called the master and the servant in systems theory. The master controls the behavior of the servant for the purpose of maintaining a steady state within the larger system, and this is the defining dynamic of a self-regulating system.

In the case of the heating system, the larger system is the house. The master is the thermostat and the servant is the furnace. The thermostat controls the behavior of the furnace as a means of maintaining a constant temperature within the house. It is not the most interesting self-regulating system in the world, but its simplicity makes it possible to easily understand the basic structure and dynamic of a self-regulating system.

The structural heart of any self-regulating systems is this dyadic structure of master and servant, and the defining dynamic of a self-regulatory system is the regulatory process by which the master controls the servant to maintain a steady state of some kind.

This dyad and dynamic are the essence of all self-regulating systems. In the tundra, the wolves control the size of the caribou herd. They force the herd to run beyond the endurance of its young and infirm members, and then they take the stragglers down.

The lymphocytes of the mammalian immune system eliminate any foreign matter that manages to make its way into the body. They identify, isolate and destroy that foreign material. In a heating system, the thermostat controls the furnace. In our solar system, the mass of the sun controls the orbits of the planets, and so forth.

Table 7.1 identifies these essential elements of a self-regulating system as seen in five systems.

TABLE 7.1 The Structure of Self-Regulatory Systems

System	*Master*	*Servant*	*Steady State*
Tundra	Wolves	Caribou	Caribou Population
Human Body	Immune System	Foreign Matter	No Foreign Matter
House	Thermostat	Furnace	House Temperature
Solar System	Sun	Planets	Orbits of the Planets
Atoms	Nucleus	Electrons	Orbits of Electrons

Self-Regulating Systems and the Stream of Consciousness

The egocentric mind is a self-regulating system, too. We can see that the mind is a self-regulating system because it possesses the same dyadic structure and control dynamic that defines all of the other self-regulatory systems in nature.

Like the tundra, the human body, our solar system and each and every atom in the universe, the human mind is a natural system in which there is a master that controls a servant for the purpose of maintaining a steady state (Vyner, 2007–2008).

This is an empirical finding, and not a matter of speculation. The master and servant of the mind are both observable empirical entities. When you look at your mind, you can easily see the master and servant, and the self-regulatory dynamic that transpires between them.

To review, the basic structure of the mind's experience of itself is one in which there is a stream of consciousness and a watcher, or awareness, that knows the stream of consciousness. The basic dynamic that occurs between the watcher and the stream of consciousness in the egocentric mind is one in which the watcher controls the stream of consciousness. The watcher controls the stream of consciousness by both repressing and holding on to its thoughts, emotions and mind-films and by narrating and inserting mind-films into the stream of consciousness. Which brings us back to the self-regulatory dynamic of the mind.

These facts tell us that the watcher is the master of a self-regulatory dynamic in the egocentric mind, and that the servant it controls is the stream of consciousness. The watcher controls the stream of consciousness for the purpose of maintaining a steady state within the mind. Just as the immune system controls the contents of the human body, the mind controls the contents of the stream of consciousness. The steady state that the egocentric watcher tries to maintain is the ego's identity.

Indeed, the dialogue that takes place between the watcher and the stream of consciousness in the egocentric mind is all about maintaining identity. It is a dynamic in which the egocentric mind maintains its sense of identity by making your thoughts, emotions and sense of reality conform to that identity (Vyner, 2009–2010).

All of this is to say that just as the immune system maintains the biological identity of the human body by eliminating foreign biological material, the egocentric watcher governs the contents of the stream of consciousness for the purpose of maintaining a person's psychological identity.

Identity, Social Control and the Stream of Consciousness

The steady state identity that is maintained by the watcher is the identity that a person presents to their world. Your identity tells people who you are, or at least who you think you are. It is also an important component of the regulatory subsystem within the mind that governs your behavior.

The watcher maintains a person's identity by controlling the contents of their stream of consciousness, and it does so because this is the means by which the egocentric mind exercises social control over itself. An identity acts as a template against which your thoughts, emotions and behavior are measured so as to ensure that they fit into the expectations and rules of the social system, or society, to which you belong.

Just as the mass of the sun controls the behavior of the planets in our solar system, the watcher governs your mind and behavior by controlling your stream of consciousness. It governs your mind by making sure that your thoughts and emotions conform to your identity, which in turn shapes you into being a person that will fit into, and become an accepted member of your society.

If you are a Bedouin and have a genuine Bedouin identity, adhering to that identity should go a long way towards ensuring that your thoughts and actions fit in with the basic values, worldview and ethos of Bedouin society. If you are a professor of comparative literature at Yale, you know that your career will probably go further if you project the identity of being an erudite and urbane scholar. Although a touch of eccentricity would certainly be tolerated. If you play football for the New England Patriots, your identity as a professional football player will serve as a template that molds your behavior so that you will fit in with and maintain your stature with your teammates both in the locker room and on the field.

Whatever identity you think you have, the watcher will repress thoughts and emotions that do not match your identity; hold on to thoughts and emotions that do match it; and create mind-films that narrate stories that support your sense of identity.

For example, if you see yourself as a pacifist, your mind will probably tend to repress thoughts and emotions that could move you to violence. Or if your boss tells you that you handled a business situation brilliantly, you might hold on to the thoughts that remember that successful transaction and your boss's comments about them; which will cause them to become a self-complementary mind-film that plays over and over again in your mind.

This is actually the primary use to which the stream of consciousness is put in the modern human mind. It is the anvil upon which the mind shapes a human being into having the socially acceptable identity that they think they have.

To put it another way, the egocentric watcher controls the stream of consciousness to establish and maintain a harmonizing steady state between an individual person's behavior and the behavioral expectations of the larger social system to which they belong.

An identity contains the behavioral, cognitive and emotional rules, if you will, that guide a person into being a functioning and accepted member of their society. Different identities embody different rules. The watcher enforces those rules, and it is in this sense that the watcher is the ego of the egocentric mind. Once again, the watcher is the ego because it is the entity within your mind that controls your mind.

Systems Within Systems

This is, of course, precisely the way all of the self-regulatory systems in nature work.

The universe is a cascade of systems. Natural systems are composed of subsystems, which are in turn composed of subsystems, which are in turn composed of more subsystems. A single animal cell is composed of mitochondria, ribosomes, a cell membrane and a nucleus with chromosomes. A cell membrane is composed of molecules, which are composed of atoms, which are composed of electrons and of protons, and the protons are composed of quarks.

In much the same way, a society is composed of subsystems that are individual human beings that carry within them, in turn, the subsystem that is their individual mind, which is also composed of subsystems.

Furthermore, all of the component subsystems of any given natural system adapt to and coordinate with one another and with the larger systems to which they belong. For example, when an atom joins with other atoms to become part of a molecule, the electrons in those atoms adjust their orbits accordingly.

The universal mechanism by which systems and subsystems coordinate with one another is that they create and maintain steady states that establish a functional harmony between them.

For example, many of us consume and metabolize an immense amount of sugar every day, and our digestive and endocrine systems work together to ensure that our entire body has enough, but not too much or too little, glucose in our bloodstream. They work together to maintain a steady state glucose level of 70–110 milligrams in every deciliter of our blood. It is important to maintain this steady state level of glucose because if you have too much or too little glucose in your body, it can cause illness and of course even death.

It is the same with the steady state distance of the earth from the sun. If the earth and sun did not maintain a steady state orbit between them in which the earth is always approximately ninety three million miles from the sun, it would become either too cold or too hot for there to be life on earth.

In much the same way, the mind establishes a steady state harmony between an individual person's behavior and the expectations of their society, and it does so by controlling the thoughts and emotions in their stream of consciousness. This tells us, in turn, the function of the stream of consciousness and its place in nature.

Just as evolution created and selected for us an opposed thumb and the prefrontal cortex, it appears that the stream of consciousness was selected for because it provides humanity with a mechanism for maintaining social cohesion between individuals and their society; between a subsystem that is an individual human being and the social system to which he or she belongs.

The evidence that suggests and supports this hypothesis comes from the empirical study of the stream of consciousness, which clearly shows that this is the use to which the stream of consciousness is being put now in the modern mind. The data shows that the egocentric watcher judges, represses, attaches and follows the meanings and narratives of its stream of consciousness, and that it does so to maintain what it deems to be a socially acceptable identity. Or in some cases, a person might come to a point in their life where they prefer to instantiate and maintain a socially unacceptable identity. In both cases, a steady state is being maintained.

The Place of the Stream of Consciousness in Nature

Once it has been understood that the egocentric mind is a self-regulating system that establishes a steady state between individual human beings and the larger social system to which they belong, this leads, in turn, to several fundamental and fascinating insights into the place of both the ego and the egocentric stream of consciousness in nature.

For one, it shows us that a society and an individual human being—system and subsystem—meet and interact with one another in the stream of consciousness. The stream of consciousness is the place where a society and a human being create and continually renegotiate the steady state that establishes a smooth working relationship between them.

When you repress a thought or emotion in your stream of consciousness, or when you solidify your identity by creating a mind-film that helps you believe that you really do have that identity, you are doing two things simultaneously: (1) taking steps to maintain your own belief that you have the identity you think you have and (2) aligning your mind with the behavioral expectations of your society.

This means that the psychological processes that occur in the stream of consciousness are the self-regulatory processes by which the subsystem that is a single human being and the larger social system to which that human being belongs interact with one another to maintain a steady state that put system and subsystem in harmony with one another.

Think again of the thermostat and how it constantly monitors room temperature and turns its furnace off and on to maintain a steady state temperature.

The egocentric watcher works in the much same way. It is constantly monitoring the thoughts, emotions and feelings that appear in the stream of consciousness to ensure that they conform to your sense of identity in both thought and deed.

If your ego thinks that you are too angry, it will try to repress and tamp down your anger. If your ego thinks you are being lazy, it might push you to work harder. If you have been brought up to be a great athlete, and you are falling short, then your ego might create mind-films that tell you that you really are a great athlete.

The second implication of the fact that the human mind is a self-regulating system is that this means that the phenomena and processes that appear in the stream of consciousness are natural ones.

The phenomena that appear in the stream of consciousness are natural phenomena because they mediate the self-regulatory processes of a natural system: the human mind. The mind is a subsystem of the human body, which is of course a natural system too.

The self-regulatory processes that appear in the stream of consciousness are exactly the same kind of self-regulatory processes that occur in each and every self-regulatory system that exists in nature.

They are the processes that maintain the steady state of the human mind—just as the self-regulatory processes of the mammalian body, the tundra and so forth maintain a steady state within their respective systems. As such, the phenomena and processes that appear in the stream of consciousness are simply another group of natural phenomena that can be empirically studied by science.

Finally, this analysis also tells us the place of the stream of consciousness in nature. The stream of consciousness is an essential component of the mind's self-regulatory subsystem. The place of the stream of consciousness in this regulatory subsystem is that it is the medium in which the ego shapes an individual person's mind and behavior to bring them into conformity with the social system to which that person belongs.

It is tempting to conclude that this subsystem was retained by natural selection because it enhances the ability of both an individual person and their society to survive. It increases their ability to survive by maintaining a well-oiled and harmonious relationship between an individual's mind and their society, which enhances the ability of individuals to cooperate and live together with one another.

This leads us to one further conclusion. The ego is a core component of the mind's self-regulatory subsystem. The ego, which is once again the watcher in the egocentric mind, is the master in this subsystem, in the language of systems theory, and the stream of consciousness is the slave. The ego's constant self-regulatory labor is to control the stream of consciousness. Through that labor, it maintains a state of equilibrium between the individual mind and the social system to which it belongs by maintaining a steady state identity. This would appear to be its place in nature.

The Origin of the Stream of Consciousness

Let us consider now a brief aside about a theory of the origin of the stream of consciousness that is suggested by the findings of the science of the stream of consciousness.

It starts here: once you have become adept at meditating, there will be times when mind-films stop running through your mind. Completely. There is no noise. Just a bright and peaceful inner space in which primordial meanings, realizations and the other nondual transformations occasionally appear.

This kind of inner quiet can sometimes occur without meditation as well: perhaps when you are alone in nature, or making love, or have a deep sense of satisfaction about the course of your life.

When the films stop appearing in your mind, this gives you an opportunity to see what makes your thoughts start appearing again when they do return. When your mind is quiet, it is easy to see when a first thought or a flood of thoughts appear again. The contrast is stark, and it is possible to see exactly what happens. First there are no thoughts; then all of a sudden the involuntary streams returns and starts running through your mind again.

In these circumstances, it is possible to see that there are a couple of different things will make the thoughts return when you are meditating. For example, if you were to think to yourself, "There are no thoughts in my mind. I'm a great meditator on the way to getting enlightened," then the next thing you know, a lot of thoughts will start running through your mind. Anyone who meditates can tell you that this is an experience that they have had.

In this case, a stream of thoughts appears because you held on to, or attached, your thought that you were special because of the cessation of thoughts in your mind. Holding on to a thought is one action that will cause the stream of thoughts to reappear in your mind, but there are other acts as well that will cause the stream of consciousness to reappear out of silence.

For example, if you repress a single thought or emotion as it starts to appear in your mind, this too will cause a train of thoughts to start running through your mind again.

Once again, when you attach or repress a thought, you are doing what Buddhist psychology calls "grasping" a thought. When you repress a thought or emotion, you are grasping it to keep yourself from expressing it. When you attach, or hold on to a thought, you are grasping it to savor and enjoy the sense of desired identity that it creates within you.

It is the grasping of a thought or emotion that causes a stream of thoughts to reappear in the quiet of the meditating mind. Or if your mind is already noisy, grasping a thought will cause even more thoughts to appear and run through your mind.

These observations can be described as two simple causal sequences:

The Repression of a Thought → Stream of Thoughts Appears in the SoC

The Attachment of a Thought → Stream of Thoughts Appears in the SoC

In sum, these causal sequences tell us that there are two types of independent variable that can cause the appearance of a stream of thoughts in the modern mind: the repression or attachment of a thought.

Perhaps something similar happened when the stream of consciousness first appeared in the prehistoric human mind. For hundreds of thousands of years, the first hominids and human beings probably had no stream of consciousness, and then one day they did. What happened?

Let's consider a possible prehistoric scene on the African savannah. Suppose that before this scene occurred, that there has never been a stream of consciousness in the mind of a single human being anywhere on earth, and that the scene that follows describes the first time that a person ever experienced themselves as having a stream of thoughts in their mind.

After a day of unsuccessful hunting on the savannah, a single man returns to the campsite that he shares with his clan of twenty-four other *Homo sapiens sapiens*. As he enters the camp, and bear in mind that he is the strongest man in his clan, he sees that one of the weaker men in his group has had a successful hunt and is already cooking his catch with his mate. The strong man starts to make moves to take his kin's meat for himself, but then the whole clan reacts as one with disapproval. Of late, the clan has begun to frown upon the strong taking from the weak. A new ethic has developed within the clan that discourages such behavior.

As the strong man remembers this new sentiment, he represses his desire to take his kinsman's the meat, and moves on. And at that very moment, a stream of thoughts appears in his mind. It is an angry stream of thoughts in which he resents the new rule that protects the weak.

This fictional sequence of events replicates a causal sequence of events that occurs every day in our own modern minds. Living as we do in complex societies, we often find ourselves in situations in which we repress desires and thoughts, only to have them reappear, in turn, as a mind-film.

Perhaps this same mechanism caused the very first appearances of the stream of consciousness in the human mind, as it did for our fictional hunter. He repressed a thought of desire, and then the thought reappeared as a stream of thoughts. Herein lies a possible theory for the origin of the stream of consciousness in human beings.

The theory is this: the evolution of human social groups led to the development of social constraints that made it necessary for human beings to start repressing thoughts and desires, and these repressions, in turn, led to the appearance of the stream of consciousness within the human mind, just as repressions do today.

If this theory is correct, it means that the stream of consciousness first appeared in the mind in response to the inception of social control, and then, as it began to appear in all human minds, it was appropriated for, and evolved into, a sophisticated mechanism for exercising social control. In this scenario, the stream of consciousness was eventually coupled with the identity and the ego to create the highly evolved mechanism of social control that it has become in our own day.

Don't We Not Need an Ego?

Let's return now to our systems analysis of the ego. At first glance, this analysis would seem to leave the impression that human beings need to have an ego. As viewed through the lens of systems theory, the ego would appear to simply be an indispensable component of the self-regulatory system that the mind uses to socialize itself.

Seen in this light, it would seem that we need to have an ego because it is the entity within the individual mind that exercises social control over the mind. As we have just seen, the ego establishes social control over the mind by maintaining a steady state within the mind that harmonizes an individual person's behavior with the ethos and moral expectations of the social system to which that person belongs.

The ego maintains a steady state—its identity—by governing the stream of consciousness, just as the pancreas maintains a steady state level of glucose in our bloodstream by secreting insulin. Once again, the master in this egocentric self-regulatory system is the watcher, which is the ego. The servant in this system is the stream of consciousness, and the steady state maintained by the ego is its identity.

From this perspective, a human identity is just one of the countless steady states that exist in nature, and the ego is just another one of the entities that maintains a steady state within a natural system. From a systems point of view, the ego appears to be simply a normal and necessary component of the self-regulatory sub-system of the natural system we call the mind.

Furthermore, given that as individuals living in society we need to control our minds, this would seem to make the ego indispensable. A society needs to maintain order to sustain itself, and it does so by maintaining a steady state between itself and each of the individuals who live within it. Without the ego, it would seem that this would not be possible, and that life in society would be sheer chaos.

However, even though this analysis seems straightforward and obvious, it is not quite correct. Even though the ego is, to be certain, an essential component of the self-regulating subsystem of the egocentric mind, it is not the natural self-regulatory system of the human mind. Nor is it the only available means we have of socializing the mind.

We know that this is true because a different mechanism of social control emerges when mind is left in its natural state. We are already familiar with this natural mechanism of self-control in a different context. Let's now review the salient details of this dynamic.

The natural mechanism of self-control occurs when the ego leaves the stream of consciousness in its natural state. The egoless watcher leaves the stream of consciousness in its natural state in the sense that: (1) it does not judge, repress or attach meanings that appear in the stream of consciousness and (2) it abstains from narrating and living in mind-films.

When the watcher leaves the stream of consciousness in its natural state, it causes itself to have nondual awareness of all of the meanings that it knows.

LEAVE STREAM OF CONSCIOUSNESS IN ITS NATURAL STATE → NONDUAL AWARENESS OF MEANINGS

Nondual awareness, in turn, generates the occurrence of the nondual transformations:

NONDUAL AWARENESS OF MEANINGS → NONDUAL TRANSFORMATIONS

The continued occurrence of the nondual transformations engenders, in turn, an abiding state of joy and goodness within the mind, and then those feelings become your awareness:

CONTINUAL OCCURRENCE OF NONDUAL TRANSFORMATIONS → EMERGENCE OF AWARENESS THAT ABIDES IN JOY AND GOODNESS

The goodness generated by nondual awareness and the nondual transformations is the natural steady state of the mind. It is also the natural self-regulatory mechanism of the mind. Once again, as this goodness becomes a stable presence within the mind, it becomes the ground of everything a person says and does.

As such, this nondual goodness is also the mind's natural mechanism of socialization. Whereas the egocentric mind establishes socially acceptable modes of behavior by governing the contents of its stream of consciousness, the egoless mind establishes good will between people by instilling a stable sense of goodness within itself, a goodness that creates an ethos of good will between people.

Ultimately, this means that we do not need to employ the ego to govern our minds. The dynamics of the egoless mind provide us with a more reliable and healthier means of socializing the mind.

Once again, if the ego were the only mechanism available to us to control the individual mind and integrate it into the social system in which it lives, then so be it. But there is another self-regulatory mechanism available to the mind, and it is a far healthier one at that.

The next four chapters will now examine and compare the egocentric and egoless states of mind towards the end of seeing which one is a healthier state of mind.

References

Mech, L. D. (1981). *The Wolf: The Ecology and Behavior of an Endangered Species*. Minneapolis, MN: University of Minnesota Press.

Vyner, H. M. (2007–2008). The dialectical phenomena and processes of the mind. *Imagination, Cognition and Personality*, 27(2), 163–196.

Vyner, H. M. (2009–2010). A preliminary theory of the defining dynamic of the healthy human mind. *Imagination, Cognition and Personality*, 29(3), 225–270.

8

THE EGOCENTRIC STATE OF MIND

Science first got its hands on DNA in 1868, when the Swiss physician-chemist Friedrich Miescher isolated a substance that he called *nuclein* from the nuclei of white blood cells that he had recovered from pus-laden bandages. Nuclein is what we today call DNA, but at the time, Miescher had no idea, understandably, that nuclein was a macromolecule that carried our genetic code.

In fact, in 1868 the now fundamental idea that there is some kind of biological entity, if you will, that transmits hereditary information from one generation to the next did not yet exist. The accomplished Austrian monk and botanist Gregor Mendel had already done his studies of the inheritance of traits in green peas that he had planted at his monastery, and these studies had led him to be the first to propose that there are transmissible units of hereditary information that are passed from one generation to the next. However, being a monk, he published his findings in an obscure journal, and the larger European and world community of scientists did not rediscover and become aware of his work until 1900. As a result, his notion of transmissible hereditary entities had not yet taken hold at the time of Miescher's discovery.

In the meantime, research into the chemical composition of nuclein proceeded apace for several decades. By 1878, the German biochemist Albrecht Kossel had discovered that nuclein was an acid, and he changed its name to deoxyribonucleic acid (DNA). He had also determined that DNA contained phosphate, sugar, and four different nitrogen-containing bases: adenine, thymine, guanine and cytosine.

By 1919, the American physician-biochemist Phoebus Levene had discovered that DNA was composed of repeating nucleotide units, and by 1943 the first x-ray diffraction studies of the structure of DNA were beginning to be produced. The use of x-ray studies to understand DNA turned out to be crucial because they led, ultimately, to Watson and Crick's articulation of the structure of DNA.

But still, up until the landmark work of Watson and Crick, it had yet to be accepted that DNA was the molecule, the Mendelian entity, that transmits inherited characteristics from one generation to the next. Nor did the scientific community yet understand that the DNA molecule and the chromosomes that were being seen under a microscope were one and the same thing. These insights were neither garnered nor generally accepted until the 1950s.

Chromosomes were first discovered in 1879, when microscopes became powerful enough for the German microscopist Walther Flemming to observe that the nucleus of a cell contained thread-like structures that he called chromatin, which are the entities that we now call chromosomes.

In 1902, soon after the rediscovery of Mendel's work, the American geneticist and physician Walter Sutton proposed that this anatomical entity, the chromosome, was the entity that carried Mendel's genes—the biological entities that transmit hereditary traits from one generation to the next. Thomas Henry Morgan's work with fruit fly chromosomes then confirmed this hypothesis by 1915.

It was then generally accepted that chromosomes are the anatomical structure that carry genes, but still no one suspected that a chromosome was the same thing as a DNA molecule. The majority of the scientific community still believed that only proteins had the requisite complexity to be the molecules that carried genetic information from one generation to the next.

Then two ingenious experiments and a series of x-ray diffraction studies established that DNA is decidedly the molecule that transmits inheritance from one generation of an organism to the next.

First, Oswald Avery and his colleagues at Rockefeller University established, in 1944, that DNA was the molecule that transmitted the trait of *virulence* from a virulent strain of pneumococcal bacteria to a previously benign strain. This experiment, in and of itself, could have been seen as establishing that DNA was the molecule that carries genetic information, but once again, at that time many students of the matter still harbored the conviction that it must be proteins that carry genetic information.

Then in 1952, Hershey and Chase worked their way through a series of experiments with a virus that infects and reproduces itself within bacteria. The infecting virus was an exceedingly simple organism that contained only two types of molecules: protein and a tiny strand of DNA. Using radioisotopes, Hershey and Chase found that the virus's DNA was transferred to the newly reproduced viruses, but that its protein was not. This meant that it had to be the DNA that carried genetic information to the newborn viruses.

Finally of course, Watson and Crick used x-ray diffraction studies to establish the double helix structure of the DNA molecule, and this, in turn, finally made it clear that DNA had a complex structure that had the ability to encode a vast amount of genetic information.

Taken together, the cumulative effect of these discoveries led to a tipping point. The scientific community finally embraced the idea that DNA was the molecule that transmits genetic traits from one generation to the next, and it also became apparent that DNA molecules and chromosomes are one and the same entity. The DNA molecule was first discovered in 1868, but it took almost a century of biochemical, genetic and histological research to determine its chemical composition, structure and function.

The Sequence of Healthy Mind Insights

Our twenty-seven-year-long and counting study of the healthy mind and stream of consciousness has neither the length nor the import of the discovery of DNA, but we have gone through a comparably lengthy sequence of findings to (1) map out the structure and dynamics of the egoless and egocentric states of minds and (2) understand the salient differences between them. And the bulk of our work is still lies before us.

We had to start at the very beginning. To make accurate observations of the stream of consciousness, it was necessary to first understand the basic structure and dynamic of the experience of knowing the stream of consciousness. Who is observing the stream of consciousness? What is being observed? What could be more basic in a scientific inquiry?

Without the fundamental insights that provided answers to these questions, it would not have been possible to make accurate observations of the stream of consciousness. It is, after all, "one great blooming, buzzing confusion."[1]

When you first begin to make observations of the stream of consciousness, you find yourself in the midst of a stream of phenomena with your head underwater, as it were. It is as if you have been dropped into a huge medieval cast iron kettle of stew and asked to make observations of the constituents of the stew.

Meditation clarifies this situation. In the process of doing a simple concentration meditation on an object, your awareness separates itself from the stream of consciousness, and takes up a position on the side, if you will, of the stream. This awareness that sits on the side of the stream is the watcher.

From that position on the side of the stream of consciousness, the watcher is now able to systematically observe what is going on within the stream of consciousness. In our work, the resulting observations led to a sequence of fundamental insights and breakthroughs that made it possible to empirically understand the stream of consciousness, the egocentric mind, the egoless mind and the nature of the healthy mind. Here is a thumbnail sketch of that sequence of insights:

1. This is William James's description of a baby's experience of the world, but it is also an apt description of the normal state of the egocentric stream of consciousness. James's description of a baby's experience can be found in the original 1890 edition of *The Principles of Psychology* (James, 1890) on page 462.

1. Once again, the first step was to appreciate that the basic structure of the experience of knowing the stream of consciousness is one in which there is a stream of consciousness and a watcher that knows the stream of consciousness. This was a crucial advance because it made it possible to understand who was observing the phenomena that appear in the stream of consciousness, what was being observed and how those observations were being made.

   From a scientific perspective, the import of this insight is that it makes it clear, to the observer of the stream of consciousness, that (1) they are the watcher who is making observations of the stream of consciousness; (2) the phenomena that they are observing are the phenomena that appear in the stream of consciousness; and (3) they are describing those phenomena as they are experienced by the watcher.
2. The second step was to develop a typology of all of the dual, predual[2] and nondual phenomena that appear in the SoC. The fruit of this labor was the descriptive science of the phenomena of the stream of consciousness that was presented in the first three sections of Chapter 6, "Ode to the Stream of Consciousness." The delineation of these phenomena led over time to all of our other insights.
3. In the process of delineating these phenomena, a frame of reference emerged that made it possible to understand what is actually happening in the stream of consciousness. The frame of reference was this: shorn of all of its many complications, there is one simple dynamic that is occurring and recurring over and over again between the watcher and the stream of consciousness. That dynamic, which is the basic modus operandi of the stream of consciousness, is composed of recurring individual cycles in which three basic things happen in sequence. Each cycle is composed of a sequence of the following three events:
   a. The stream of consciousness presents meanings to the watcher in the form of thoughts, feelings, emotions, moods, mind-films, subtle thoughts and realizations.
   b. The watcher knows and responds to those meanings.
   c. The watcher's actions initiate causal sequences that cause new phenomena to appear in the stream of consciousness.

   The stream of consciousness is composed of an infinite series of these cycles of self-awareness. Each cycle is defined by the appearance of a meaning, a response

2. The meanings that appear in the stream of consciousness fall into three categories: dual, nondual and predual. A predual meaning is a meaning that is neither dual—in that it has not yet been conceptually grasped by the watcher, nor nondual—in that it has not yet dissolved into egoless awareness and become nondual. A primordial meaning is a predual meaning when it first appears in the stream of consciousness. If it is grasped by the watcher, it will become a dual meaning—a thought, emotion or a mind-film. If the primordial meaning is not grasped, it will become a realization—which is a nondual meaning. See Vyner (2005) pages 8–11 for further discussion of these distinctions.

to that meaning and the effects of that response. A fresh cycle commences with the appearance of a new meaning and the response to that meaning.

4. Once it was understood that the watcher's actions set in motion causal sequences, this led us, in turn, to identify and delineate as many as possible of the causal processes that occur routinely between the watcher and the stream of consciousness. These causal relationships play a crucial role in determining what happens in the stream of consciousness. They are a part of the descriptive science of the stream of consciousness, and they presented in the final section of Chapter 6.
5. As this process of delineating more and more phenomena and causal sequences proceeded, a larger picture emerged. It became apparent that (a) the phenomena that appear in the stream of consciousness mediate the processes of self-awareness and self-control and that (b) the human mind has two profoundly different modes of self-awareness/self-control: an egoless mode and an egocentric mode.
6. The import of understanding that there are two different modes of self-awareness is that it opened the door to making sense of how the egoless and egocentric states of mind are created. First, it became apparent that it is these two modes of self-awareness that generate these two completely different states of mind. The egocentric mode of self-awareness creates the egocentric state of mind, and the egoless mode of self-awareness generates the egoless state of mind. This made it possible to take the next steps, which were (a) mapping out the egoless and egocentric states of mind and (b) delineating the mechanisms by which the two modes of self-awareness generated these two different states of mind.
7. The penultimate step in our analysis of the healthy mind was to step back and compare the egoless and egocentric states of mind to see which one was healthier. This included, among many other things, coming to the understanding that (a) the routine functioning of the ego creates a group of normal pathologies that define the egocentric state of mind and (b) that these pathologies do not appear in the egoless mind.
8. Finally, once we understood how the egoless mode of self-awareness generated the egoless state of mind, that made it important to assess what has to be done to cultivate an egoless mind.

It has taken more than twenty-five years to work our way through this sequence, and once again, there is a lot more work to be done. Chapter 13, "The Future of the Egoless Mind: Science," will identify some of the essential issues for which further research would be productive and worthwhile, and propose a research agenda that will address those issues.

The Observations From Which These Insights Were Derived

These basic insights, including the descriptive science of the stream of consciousness itself, were gleaned from countless raw observations of the phenomena that appear in the stream of consciousness; observations that were made by the watcher from its position adjacent to the stream of consciousness.

To fully understand the psychological processes that appear in the stream of consciousness, and to gain the insights that they have afforded into the nature of the healthy mind, it was necessary to sift through and make sense of the white noise that is the average human stream of consciousness.

The first step in making sense of this turbulent cascade was to distill it. We distilled it by identifying and describing the many phenomena that participate in that "blooming, buzzing confusion." Once these basic phenomena had been delineated, it was then possible to derive from our observations of these phenomena descriptive theories of the egocentric and egoless minds.

To give you an idea of what the experience of empirically observing the stream of consciousness is like, this chapter is now going to present a comprehensive list of the raw observations that eventually led to the above sequence of discoveries.

The hope and intent in presenting this long list of observations is that it will make it possible for you to (1) understand what our research process has been like and (2) see for yourself that you are already familiar with, and have already made, many of the same observations yourself. They are as follows:

1. The watcher.
2. The stream of consciousness.
3. The watcher knows the phenomena that appear in the stream of consciousness.
4. The phenomena that appear in the stream of consciousness are meanings.
5. The stream of consciousness is a temporal sequence of meanings.
6. As defined by our colloquial categories, several different types of meaning appear in the stream of consciousness. They are:
    a. Thoughts
    b. Feelings
    c. Emotions
    d. Moods
    e. Epiphanies.
7. As defined by the form that in turn determines their causal relationships, meanings appear in the stream of consciousness in six different forms:
    a. Individual Moments of Consciousness (iMoC)
    b. Involuntary Stream of Consciousness (ISoC)
    c. Voluntary Stream of Consciousness (VSoC)
    d. Emotions
    e. Moods
    f. Realizations.
8. When the ISoC appears in the stream of consciousness, it appears as a recurring cycle of thoughts that narrate the same type of story over and over again.
9. These recurring thought narratives are often accompanied by a mood that matches the theme of the story.

10. The iMoC's give meaning to a single present moment. As they arise, you can see that they are creating meaning and intention in response to the experience that you are having in the present moment.
11. The iMoC's appear as either a single subtle thought or as a feeling; both of which will often dissolve right away.
12. The mind-films usually run on and on for long periods of time.
13. A given mind-film can run for as long as a minute, day or month.
14. Mind-films give contextual meaning to a person's experience for as long as they run. While they are active, events take on meaning by being assimilated into the narrative of the film.
15. The mind-films project stories, or realities, that are congruent with the mind's conception of its identity.
16. The watcher can and does respond to the thoughts, emotions, mind-films and so forth that appear in its stream of consciousness.
17. The watcher can and does respond to meanings in a number of different ways. They are as follows:
    a. The watcher judges thoughts, emotions and mind-films.
    b. The watcher represses thoughts, emotions and mind-films.
    c. The watcher attaches thoughts, emotions and mind-films.
    d. Sometimes, the watcher believes and lives in the stories that the mind-films narrate.
    e. Sometimes the watcher does not believe and live in the stories that the mind-films narrate.
    f. Sometimes the watcher is simply aware of its stream of consciousness and allows it to flow free and remain in its natural state.
18. Each of the actions taken by the watcher initiates a causal sequence of events that cause new phenomena to appear in the stream of consciousness.
19. For example, the repression of an emotion can cause that emotion to remain in awareness as a mood.
20. The repression of an emotion can also cause a mind-film to appear in the stream of consciousness.
21. The repression of an emotion can will sometimes cause a mind-film and mood to simultaneously appear together in the stream of consciousness.
22. The attachment of an emotion can cause that emotion to remain in awareness as a mood.
23. The attachment of a thought can cause a mind-film that is expressive of that thought to appear in the stream of consciousness.
24. The attachment of an emotion can cause a mind-film and its mood to appear simultaneously in the stream of consciousness.
25. When the watcher believes and lives in the narrative of a mind-film that is already active within the mind, that mind-film will continue to be active in the stream of consciousness.
26. Sometimes a single thought will dissolve in the moment that it appears.

27. Sometimes a single emotion will dissolve in the moment that it appears.
28. Sometimes an active mind-film will all of a sudden dissolve and disappear.
29. Thoughts, emotions and mind-films dissolve and disappear when the watcher does not act upon them—when it does not judge, repress, attach or believe them.
30. Sometimes, when a meaning dissolves—be it a thought, emotion or mind-film—nothing more will happen in the stream of consciousness, and meanings will cease to appear for a period of time. That period of time might be a second. It might be a week.
31. Sometimes when a meaning dissolves, a new phenomenon will appear in its stead.
32. Sometimes when a meaning dissolves a realization will appear in the stream of consciousness.
33. Sometimes when a meaning dissolves a moment of amused compassion will immediately appear in the stream of consciousness.
34. Sometimes when a meaning dissolves a moment of joy will immediately appear in the stream of consciousness.
35. Sometimes when a meaning dissolves a moment of goodness will immediately appear in the stream of consciousness.
36. Sometimes when a meaning dissolves a moment of light will immediately appear in the stream of consciousness.
37. Sometimes, in meditation, a feeling of joy will build up and remain present in awareness.
38. Sometimes, in meditation, a feeling of goodness will build up and remain present in awareness.
39. Sometimes, in meditation, a feeling of equanimity will build up and remain present in awareness.
40. Sometimes, in meditation, the ISoC will slow down and become a less intense presence within the mind.
41. Sometimes, in meditation, the ISoC will temporarily disappear.
42. Sometimes the mind's awareness will abide in and become the feeling of joy when you are meditating.
43. Sometimes that abiding feeling of joy will remain present in your mind after you have stopped meditating.
44. Sometimes the mind's awareness will abide in and become the feeling of goodness when you are meditating.
45. Sometimes that abiding feeling of goodness will remain present in your mind after you have stopped meditating.
46. Sometimes the watcher feels as though it is in conflict with its stream of consciousness.
47. At other times, the watcher feel as though it is not in conflict with its stream of consciousness.

48. Sometimes mind-films appear in the stream of consciousness, and at other times mind-films do not appear in the stream of consciousness.
49. Mind-films appear in the stream of consciousness immediately after the watcher represses an emotion.
50. Mind-films appear in the stream of consciousness immediately after the watcher attaches a thought.
51. Sometimes uncomfortable moods appear in the stream of consciousness, and at other times uncomfortable moods do not appear in the stream of consciousness.
52. Moods appear in the stream of consciousness after the watcher represses or attaches an emotion.
53. Sometimes the watcher will judge the meanings that appear in its stream of consciousness, and those judgments appear in the stream of consciousness as an emotion.
54. At other times the watcher does not judge the meanings that appear in its stream of consciousness.
55. Sometimes all emotions and thoughts dissolve as soon as they appear in the stream of consciousness.
56. At other times, emotions and thoughts remain in the stream of consciousness as moods and mind-films.
57. Sometimes the stream of consciousness is clear and not congested because only iMoCs or realizations are appearing in the stream of consciousness.
58. When the stream of consciousness is clear, the watcher is able to be effortlessly aware of the iMoCs and realizations throughout the entire course of a normal day.
59. At other times, mind-films and moods remain in the stream of consciousness, and the mind stream is congested. At these times, the watcher finds that it is rarely, if ever, aware of realizations and iMoCs.
60. When moods and mind-films remain present in the stream of consciousness and as a result it is congested and unclear, the mind feels as though it is unable to know itself as it is; that it is unable to know how it sees and feels about its experiences of the world moment to moment.
61. When the stream of consciousness is clear and not congested, that is when moods and mind-films do not remain in the stream of consciousness, the mind feels as though it is able to know itself as it is; that it is able to know how it really sees and feels about its experiences of the world moment to moment.
62. When the watcher becomes aware of a meaning as it dissolves, it feels as though it knows the content of that meaning exactly as it is.

The descriptive science of the phenomena of the stream of consciousness that was presented in Chapter 6 emerged from, and in turn made sense of, these raw observations. With these observations and the descriptive science in hand, it then became possible to piece together theories of how the egocentric and egoless minds work.

There was one key discovery that opened the door to understanding and mapping out the workings of the egoless and egocentric mind. It was the realization that the mind has two modes of self-awareness, each of which generates a different state of mind.

That insight came, interesting enough, from reading a passage from a text called *Treasury of Word and Meaning*, which was written by the fourteenth-century Tibetan meditator-scholar Longchenpa (Germano, 1992; Thondup, 1996). My reading of this passage was that Longchenpa was describing the two possible fates that await a primordial meaning[3] in the moment that it first appears in the stream of consciousness.

Longchenpa said in this passage that once a primordial meaning appears in the stream of consciousness, one of two possible things will happen to it:

1. If the mind has nondual awareness of a primordial meaning, the "true meaning" of the meaning is known, and it will then become an appearance of the primordial wisdom of the enlightened mind.[4]
2. On the other hand, if the mind has dual awareness of a primordial meaning, that meaning will be transformed into one of the dual meanings of the egocentric mind.[5]

And there you have it: this is a description of the rudiments of the two modes of self-awareness. There is one mode of self-awareness in which the mind has nondual awareness of meanings, which is the egoless mode of self-awareness.

There is a second mode of self-awareness in which the mind has dual awareness of the meanings that appear in the stream of consciousness, and this is the egocentric mode of self-awareness.

With this insight in hand, the main thrust of my research became the task of mapping out the two modes of self-awareness and the two different states of mind that they generate. This has been one of the principal foci of my twenty plus years of interviews with the lamas.

The remainder of this chapter is now going to describe the mechanics of the egocentric mode of self-awareness. This mode of self-awareness is the defining dynamic of the egocentric mind because it generates the egocentric state of mind.

To make this dynamic as visible as possible, I will be describing it in layers, starting at the bottom, if you will. Each of the remaining sections of this chapter

3. Tib.: gZhi nang. See *The Healthy Mind Interviews, Volume 3: Lopon Tekchog* (2005) pages 8–11 for further description and discussion of the primordial meanings.
4. Tib.: yeshe.
5. Tib.: sems.

will describe a separate layer of the egocentric mode of self-awareness, and at the beginning of each section there will again be a list of the phenomena that are involved in the processes that are described in that layer.

The Egocentric Mode of Self-Awareness

Layer I: The Foundation of the Mind's Experience of Itself

1. Watcher
2. Stream of Consciousness.

As with everything in the science of the stream of consciousness, our description of the egocentric mode of self-awareness begins with the structure of the mind's awareness of itself.

The watcher and the stream of consciousness are the two central actors in the egocentric mode of self-awareness. The stream of consciousness presents meanings to the egocentric watcher as thoughts, emotions and so on. The egocentric watcher is the subject that knows and responds to those meanings.

The observable events that give a person the impression that these two entities are indeed the empirical face of two different minds is that the egocentric watcher and stream of consciousness often want different things at the same time. The watcher can, for example, find itself struggling to repress an emotion and keep itself from expressing it. Or it can find itself struggling to withdraw its attention from a mind-film so that it can attend to and be present in the present moment.

The dynamic that unfolds between the egocentric watcher and stream of consciousness is the egocentric mode of self-awareness, and it is the defining dynamic of the egocentric mind because it generates the egocentric state of mind. As such, egocentric self-awareness is the foundation of the egoless mind, and this is why the watcher and stream of consciousness are being portrayed as the first layer of the egocentric mind.

Layer II: The Dynamic That Occurs Between the Watcher and Stream of Consciousness in the Egocentric Mind

1. The Watcher
2. The Stream of Consciousness
3. The Egocentric Watcher's Repertoire of Actions: Judgement, Repression, Attachment, Following
4. The Repertoire of Causal Sequences Initiated by the Watcher's Actions.

The second layer of the egocentric mode of self-awareness is the dialectic that is always unfolding between the watcher and the stream of consciousness. We described this dynamic earlier in this chapter, but here it is again as the second layer of the egocentric mode of self-awareness:

a. The stream of consciousness presents meanings to the watcher in the form of thoughts, emotions, moods, mind-films, subtle thoughts and epiphanies.
b. The watcher knows and responds to those meanings.
c. The watcher's actions initiate causal sequences that cause the appearance of new phenomena in the stream of consciousness.

As a scientist trying to observe the stream of consciousness, it is helpful to remember that no matter how many baroque layers of process may be coming and going in the stream of consciousness, that they are always elaborations upon this basic dynamic. If you keep this elementary dynamic in focus, then all of the other processes that transpire in the stream of consciousness will come into focus as well. With this basic dynamic in mind, the additional layers of egopoietic meaning can then be seen for what they are: as ornaments, if you will, that are layered on top of this basic process.

This recurring dynamic of appearance, response and causal sequence sits at the core of both the egocentric and egoless modes of self-awareness, although they are, as we will be seeing, profoundly different dynamics as well.

Interlude

There is, in the history of ideas, a large swathe of mind theory whose central concern is describing and analyzing this duality of watcher and stream of consciousness. These theories recognize the existence of this dual structure, give theoretical names to each of these entities and most of all, they analyze the dynamic that unfolds between them. These theories are the dialectical theories of the mind (Vyner, 2007–2008).

The dialectical mind theories are one of the three basic species of mind theory that appear in the history of ideas. The three basic types of mind theory are (1) the metaphysical theories, (2) the cognitive theories and (3) the dialectical theories. Each type of theory is defined by the central fundamental question that it seeks to answer (Vyner, 2003).

For example, the traditional concern of the metaphysical theories has been that of answering one and only one question about the nature of the mind: What is the nature of the stuff, or substance, that is the mind? Is it matter? Or is it something altogether different than matter? Spirit or soul, for example.

The cognitive theories address a different fundamental question. They attempt to understand how the mind knows what it knows. They are, essentially, theories of how the mind constructs and gives meaning to its experience. This includes the philosophical epistemologies and the theories of modern cognitive science.

The dialectical theories are theories of how the mind knows and controls itself. These are usually structural theories of the mind in which one substructure of the mind is depicted as controlling the behavior of a second substructure within the mind. The control dynamic described by these theories is a dialectic, if you will, in which the watcher and the stream of consciousness are constantly negotiating resolutions to the differences between them.

The first explicit dialectical mind-theory that we know of in the literature of the West is a theory put forth by Plato in the dialogue he titled *The Phaedrus*. In this dialogue, Plato employs the metaphor of a horse-drawn chariot to depict the dialectical dynamics of the human mind. In his image of the chariot, the charioteer is reason, and he is assigned the endless and somewhat thankless task of keeping in rein and controlling the two horses, or driving forces, of the mind: the spirit and the appetites.

In more recent times, there has been a profusion of clinical oriented dialectical theories of the mind in the twentieth century. The most conspicuous and influential of these clinical theories was, of course, Freud's psychoanalytic theory, which had a large impact upon the practice of psychotherapy for half of a century. Freud's theory is a dialectical model of the mind in which one structure within the mind, the ego, is portrayed as controlling another structure within the mind, the id, at the behest of the superego.

In Jung's analytic theory we find a dialectic in which just the opposite happens: the self controls the ego. In Laing's theory, the false self system controls the self system and so forth.

From the perspective of the science of the stream of consciousness, the dual structures that lie at the center of the dialectical theories of the mind—whether they be the ego and id, ego and self, master and slave and so forth—are theoretical representations of the watcher and the stream of consciousness. These theories typically give different names to these entities, and try to understand, each in their own way, the conflicted control dynamic that transpires between them.

For our purposes here, the import of the dialectical theories, both historically and empirically, is that they have been the theoretical medium in which the fields of psychology and psychiatry have attempted to describe and analyze the nature of both the unhealthy and healthy mind.

For the most part, the dialectical theories have been harnessed to the task of explaining the causes of psychopathology. The history of twentieth-century personality theory documents this trend. Freud, Jung, Klein, Hartmann, Winnicott, Kernberg, Kohut and many other clinical theorists advanced dialectical theories of the mind to describe the origins and causes of mental illness.

In contrast to this general trend, the research being presented in *The Healthy Mind* has put forth a dialectical theory of the mind whose central concern is the task of understanding the nature of the healthy mind.

The crucial point I want to make here is that the dialectical theories of the mind have been used to analyze and understand two sides of the same coin: the causes of mental illness and the nature of the healthy mind.

This raises an interesting question: why is it that the dialectical theories of the mind are germane to the task of understanding both the causes of psychopathology and the nature of the healthy mind?

The answer is this: the dialogue that occurs between the watcher and the stream of consciousness determines whether or not a given mind is healthy or unhealthy.

For example, the science of the stream of consciousness has found that there are two fundamental kinds of dynamic can and do occur between the watcher and the stream of consciousness: the egocentric mode of self-awareness and the egoless mode of self-awareness. Our finding is that one of these modes of self-awareness is indeed healthy, and that one of them is not (Vyner, 2009–2010).

Given that the description and analysis of this dialogue between the watcher and stream of consciousness is the domain of dialectical mind theory, it falls to the dialectical theories to describe both the healthy and unhealthy versions of this dynamic. This is why the dialectical theories can be and are used to describe and analyze both the healthy and unhealthy mind.

Our description of the egocentric mode of self-awareness is being presented in this chapter. The next chapter, Chapter 9, will describe the egocentric state of mind that is generated by the egocentric mode of self-awareness

Descriptions of the egoless mode of self-awareness and the egoless state of mind that it engenders will then be presented in Chapters 10 and 11, respectively.

Layer III: The Primordial Meanings

1. The Watcher
2. The Stream of Consciousness
3. The Individual Moments of Consciousness (iMoCs)
4. Grasping
5. Dual Awareness.

When the mind gives meaning to a single experience, that meaning appears in the stream of consciousness as a single moment of consciousness (iMoC). The ISoC, in contrast, gives the contextual meaning to many different moments of experience.

An iMoC might be a feeling of love. Or a thought that reminds you that *Uncle Vanya* is your favorite play by Chekhov. Or a moment of fear as you kayak out towards the waves that are breaking over the coral reef that lies between you and the open sea.

The iMoCs are the primordial meanings of the mind in the sense that they are the first meaning you give to an experience, and they tell you how you actually feel about and want to respond to the present moment.

The primordial meanings appear in the stream of consciousness of both the egoless mind and the egocentric mind, although they meet very different fates in the egoless and egocentric mind.

When a primordial meaning appears in the egocentric stream of consciousness, it is grasped by the watcher, and as a result the mind has dual awareness of the meaning. When the watcher grasps a primordial meaning, it projects a concept of judgmental identity onto the meaning in the course of knowing it. As a result, the egocentric mind knows that primordial meaning as an amalgam of primordial meaning and the projected concept of identity. Given that it is hidden within this amalgam, it is not possible for the mind to know the suchness of that meaning.

In addition, the primordial meanings that arise in the egocentric mind will almost invariably emerge into an environment in which layers of mind-films and moods are already active or present in the stream of consciousness. In the egocentric mind, new meanings emerge into a tangle of films and moods because the habitual grasping actions of the egocentric watcher cause the mind to abide in the state of complex awareness in which contrapuntal layers of film and mood are a constant presence.

In this environment, primordial meanings are known in tandem with the films and moods that are already present in the stream of consciousness, and thus they take on additional layers of meaning by being absorbed into their narratives and feeling tone. This is a second mechanism that causes the egocentric mind to have dual awareness of a primordial meaning.

When the egocentric mind has dual awareness of a meaning, it is not able to know its suchness. Given that the egocentric mind has ongoing dual awareness of the primordial meanings, it is unable to know itself as it is. It is unable to know its true self; the suchness of the meanings that it gives to the present moment.

In contrast, when a primordial meaning appears in the egoless stream of consciousness, the watcher has nondual awareness of that meaning. It appears solo in the stream of consciousness, without emotions, mind-films or moods; and it dissolves into awareness. As a result, the egoless mind is able to accurately know the content of the primordial meanings—the meanings it gives to the present moment, which in turn means that the egoless mind is able to know and be its true self.

In summary, the primordial meanings are the third layer in our description of the egocentric mode of self-awareness. The ego's actions in response to the appearance of a primordial meaning determines what happens next in the stream of consciousness, and in so doing, they create the next two layers of the egocentric mode of self-awareness.

Layer IV: The Actions of the Egocentric Watcher

1. Judgment
2. Repression
3. Attachment
4. Following.

In the egocentric mode of self-awareness, the watcher can and does make a number of different responses to the meanings that appear in its stream of consciousness, and these actions play a central role in generating the egocentric state of mind. The ego has at its disposal a repertoire of four basic actions with which it controls and alters its stream of consciousness, and they are the actions that are listed above.

The egocentric watcher takes these actions to preserve the ego's identity, and in the course of so doing they cause collateral damage, if you will. They do so by setting in motion causal sequences that give birth to the normal pathologies of the ego and create the complex state of mind.

Among the causal sequences that these actions set in motion are processes that activate the mind-films, emotions and moods that make it virtually impossible for the mind to know the suchness of the meanings that it has given to the present moment.

Layer Five: Causal Sequences Activated by the Actions of the Egocentric Watcher

The actions taken by the egocentric watcher initiate causal sequences that change the state of the stream of consciousness, and in so doing these actions create the egocentric state of mind. The independent variables in all of these causal processes are always actions that have been taken by the watcher. The dependent variables produced by these causal sequences fall into three basic categories. The actions of the egocentric watcher cause:

1. Dual awareness of the meaning upon which the action was taken.
2. New phenomena to appear in the stream of consciousness.
   a. There are numerous causal sequences that cause new phenomena to appear in the stream of consciousness. Different causal sequences cause the appearance of different phenomena.
   b. The causal sequences initiated by the actions of the egocentric watcher can cause three different types of phenomena to appear in the stream of consciousness: (1) mind-films, (2) moods and (3) emotions that attribute judgmental conceptions of one's self to a meaning.
3. The mind to abide in the complex state of mind.

Here is a representative list of the causal sequences that generate the phenomena and processes that create the egocentric state of mind:

A. Causal Sequences That Cause Emotions to Appear

1. When the watcher judges a meaning, it causes an emotion that expresses the judgment to appear in the stream of consciousness.

JUDGMENT OF A MEANING → EMOTION APPEARS

B. Causal Sequences That Cause Mind-Film Activation

1. When the watcher grasps an iMoC, it causes a mind-film to appear in the stream of consciousness. This is the phenomenon of film activation:

   ATTACHMENT OF AN IMOC → MIND-FILM ACTIVATION

2. When the watcher represses an emotion, it causes a mind-film to appear in the stream of consciousness:

   REPRESSION OF AN EMOTION → MIND-FILM ACTIVATION

3. When the mind follows a mind-film that is already present and active in its stream of consciousness, that film will remain active in the stream of consciousness.

   FOLLOWING → CONTINUATION OF MIND-FILM

C. Causal Sequences That Cause Mood Activation

4. When the watcher represses an emotion, a mood that is identical to the emotion will appear in the stream of consciousness:

   REPRESSION OF AN EMOTION → APPEARANCE OF A MOOD

5. When the watcher attaches an emotion, a mood that is identical to that emotion will appear in the stream of consciousness:

   ATTACHMENT OF AN EMOTION → APPEARANCE OF A MOOD

6. When the mind follows a mood, the mood will remain present in awareness:

   FOLLOWING A MOOD → MOOD REMAINS IN AWARENESS

D. Causal Sequences That Cause the Mind to Have Dual Awareness of a Meaning

7. In general, when the mind grasps a meaning, whether it be a moment of consciousness or a mind-film, it will have dual awareness of that meaning:

   GRASPING OF MEANING → DUAL AWARENESS OF THAT MEANING

8. When the watcher attaches a meaning, it causes itself to have dual awareness of that meaning:

   ATTACHMENT → DUAL AWARENESS

9. When the watcher represses a meaning, it causes itself to have dual awareness of that meaning:

   REPRESSION → DUAL AWARENESS

Layer Six: The Complex State of Awareness

The egoless mind abides in a state of mind that is called the simple state of awareness by the science of the stream of consciousness.

The egoless mind abides in the state of simple awareness because meanings dissolve and disappear as soon as they appear in the egoless stream of consciousness. They dissolve because the egoless watcher does not grasp meanings and as a result has, almost invariably, nondual awareness of them meanings it knows.

This means, that for the most part, there will be only one meaning in the egoless stream of consciousness at a given time.[6] A meaning appears, the mind has nondual awareness of it, and then that meaning dissolves and disappears.

This generates a state of awareness that is simple in the sense that it is devoid of the multiple layers of meaning that simultaneously appear in the egocentric stream of consciousness. Mind-films, emotions and moods appear but rarely within the egoless mind. They seldom appear because the egoless watcher almost never grasps the meanings that appear in its stream of consciousness. The egoless watcher does not judge, repress, attach or follow meanings in the process of knowing them.

In general, the only phenomena that appear consistently in the egoless stream of consciousness are the primordial meanings themselves, and the nondual transformations of those primordial meanings: dissolution, realization, amused compassion, nondual joy and nondual goodness.

If the nondual transformations cause a nondual phenomenon to appear, that appearance will dissolve immediately as well. The egoless stream of consciousness is an uncluttered and clear stream.

The egocentric stream of consciousness, in contrast, is a cluttered and opaque cascade of white water. In this state of mind, the primordial meanings are virtually unknowable because they appear in tandem with concurrent layers of emotions, films and moods. This cascade of contrapuntal meanings that obscures the mind's ability to know the present moment is called the complex state of awareness of the egocentric mind. Given that it abides in the state of complex awareness, the egocentric mind is virtually unable to have nondual awareness of meanings, and as a result the nondual realizations rarely appear, if at all, in the egocentric mind.

The egocentric mind abides in complex awareness because the egocentric watcher grasps the meanings that appear in its stream of consciousness.

When the egocentric watcher grasps meanings, it adds even more emotions, films and moods to an already busy stream of consciousness. Given that the ego grasps almost all of the meanings that appear in its stream of consciousness, there will often be more than one mind-film and mood active in the egocentric stream of consciousness at a time. This is the complex state of awareness.

6. Occasionally the egoless watcher will grasp a meaning, and a mind-film or mood will briefly appear in the egoless stream of consciousness. This can cause moments in which two or more meanings can be present at once; but it is not a frequent occurrence, and the film and/or mood will dissolve immediately.

The persistent contrapuntal presence of emotions, moods and multiple films in the egocentric stream of consciousness is the hallmark of complex awareness. It might also be one of the reasons that Bach's music is so compelling—it evokes and brings grace to the contrapuntal state of complex awareness that we all know so well.

Complex Awareness and the Normal Pathologies of the Ego

Complex awareness is the basic state of mind that is generated by the egocentric mode of self-awareness, and it is the sum total of the six layers of the egocentric state of mind that we have just described. The opacity and turmoil of the egocentric stream of consciousness, in and of themselves, make it difficult for the egocentric mind to know with any clarity any of the meanings that appear in its stream of consciousness, much less have nondual awareness of them.

Simple awareness, in contrast, is the lucid state of mind generated by the egoless mode of self-awareness. The vital import of the difference between simple and complex awareness is this: When the mind abides in simple awareness, it is able to have persistent nondual awareness of itself and thus know the suchness of the meanings that appear in its stream of consciousness. This is why the egoless mind is able to know and be its true self as it really is. In addition, the egoless mode of self-awareness does not generate the normal pathologies of the ego.

By comparison, the mind that abides in complex awareness is unable to know its true self. Basically, there are too many other meanings standing in the way. These layers of meaning cloud and distort the egocentric mind's ability to accurately know the content of the meanings it gives to the present moment, and most of all they preclude the mind's ability to have nondual awareness of those meanings.

Finally, the complex state of awareness is also the petri dish upon which the normal pathologies of the ego grow. The next chapter will not explore in greater detail the normal pathologies of the ego, and the state of mind they generate.

References

Germano, D. (1992) *Poetic Thought, the Intelligent Universe, and the Mystery of the Self: The Tantric Synthesis of DzogChen in Fourteenth Century Tibet.* Dissertation. Madison, WI: University of Wisconsin.

James, W. (1890). *The Principles of Psychology.* New York, NY: Henry Holt and Co.

Thondup, T. (1996). *The Practice of DzogChen.* Ithaca, NY: Snow Lion Publications.

Vyner, H. M. (2003). The descriptive psychology of Tibetan Buddhism and the nature of the healthy human mind. *Anthropology of Consciousness*, 13(2), 1–25.

Vyner, H. M. (2005). *The Healthy Mind Interviews, Volume 3: Lopon Tegchoke.* Kathmandu: Vajra Publications.

Vyner, H. M. (2007–2008). The dialectical phenomena and processes of the mind. *Imagination, Cognition and Personality*, 27(2), 163–196.

Vyner, H. M. (2009–2010). A preliminary theory of the defining dynamic of the healthy human mind. *Imagination, Cognition and Personality*, 29(3), 225–270.

9

THE VICISSITUDES OF THE EGO

Given that the egocentric mind is the type of mind that we all have, I realize that asking you to accept the hypothesis that it is an inherently unhealthy mind is asking a great deal of you. At first glance, it must seem akin to asking you to believe that having a head is unhealthy, or that owning a frying pan or a computer is unhealthy. After all, we all have egos. But I assure you that this hypothesis is empirically correct, and this chapter will demonstrate its truth to you without vilifying the ego.

One reason that it is important not to vilify the ego is that doing so would be an egocentric act. It would be the stance of an anti-ego ego, and, it would violate the defining processes of the egoless mind. The egoless mind abstains from attributing judgmental identities to the ego's thoughts and emotions, and for that matter everything else that appears in its stream of consciousness.

Vilification wouldn't be appropriate because it is also true that the ego means well. He thinks that he is simply helping you take your place in society. In his eyes, all he is doing is giving you a heroic identity of some sort that will help you get out of bed in the morning and become someone of worth. And in the bargain, he is also making sure that you don't step on anyone else's toes. What could possibly be wrong?

We shouldn't be fooled, though. One of the core problems with the ego, although not the only problem, is that it is a mask. To have an ego is to wear at least one mask, perhaps more, for your entire life. You might change masks from time to time, but you will always be wearing a mask that hides the face of the person you really are. The ego is a trickster who has many faces, and he tells many tales to make you believe that he is real.

In asking each of us to wear a mask, the ego is making it clear that he doesn't understand one of the basic verities of life: true happiness and goodness come from being one's true self. The ego doesn't understand that by asking you to don a disguise, he is asking you to give up the happiness and goodness that are the natural endowment of the mind.

If you live in an egocentric society, you are given a mask in your childhood, and in exchange for this mask you barter away your true self, your soul. The implicit bargain, we are led to understand, is that in return, you can expect to be given social acceptance, a secure place in society and love.

However, there is more to the bargain than this. The loss of one's true self is only one of four normal pathologies of the ego.

The egocentric mind that we have all been brought up to have, and that we live with day in and day out, creates a larger set of problems that appear to be universal to the experience of having an ego: the normal pathologies of the ego. Given that the routine dynamics of the egocentric mind create the normal pathologies, it appears likely that everyone with an egocentric mind lives with the normal pathologies and endures them day in and day out, either consciously or unconsciously.[1]

We tolerate these unhappy states of mind created by the normal pathologies because: (1) they are so common that we think they are a normal part of life and also because (2) we think we need to have an ego. However, when you empirically evaluate the egocentric state of mind and its normal pathologies, it becomes clear that not only do they create painful states of mind, they are also unnecessary states of mind. We can do better.

This chapter is going to demonstrate that the egocentric mind is an unhealthy mind by: (1) describing the normal pathologies of the ego and (2) describing the processes by which the ego creates the normal pathologies. In other words, we will establish that the ego creates these pathologies by showing you the mechanics of processes by which it creates them.

Empirically, this is much the same as establishing that the presence of the *Streptococcus pneumoniae* bacterium in the lung will cause a pneumonia by showing you the pathogenesis of a streptococcal pneumonia. The pathogenesis of a streptococcal pneumonia is the sequence of pathological steps that cause a pneumonia to develop when streptococcal bacteria are present in the lung: bacteria enter the lung's alveoli and multiply, the bacteria secrete toxins that break down the lining of the alveoli, inflammatory fluid pours into the alveoli and so forth.

Once you observe and map out the sequence of processes that lead to the creation of a *Streptococcus* pneumonia, you have proven that it is the presence of the *Streptococcus* in the lung that causes the pneumonia. This chapter will do the same for the ego and the normal pathologies of the ego.

First though, as a matter of clarity, I would like to give us a clear and simple definition of the egocentric mind: the egocentric mind is a mind that believes

1. Please see Chapter 13 for a discussion of the delineation of universals in science, and in particular in the study of the mind.

it has a permanent identity and that controls its stream of consciousness for the purpose of maintaining that identity.

In contrast, the egoless mind is a mind that does not believe it has a permanent identity, and that as a result allows its stream of consciousness to run free. By allowing its stream of consciousness to run free, the egoless mind engenders, and abides in, the natural state of the mind.

Secondly, before delving into our more technical discussion of the normal pathologies of the ego, I would like to first give us an experiential introduction to the normal pathologies. Here is a list of colloquial descriptions, if you will, of some of the symptoms that are generated by the normal pathologies of the ego:

1. The ego floods the mind with trains of thought. If you should ever find that your mind is full of thoughts, and as a result you are unable to focus and be fully present in the moment, this is a state of mind created by ego.
2. The egocentric mind is a mind that is invariably in conflict with itself. It resides in conflict because the ego divides the mind in two and turns it into what seem to be two competing selves: the ego and the true self. If you ever find that you are in conflict with your own mind, this is a state of mind that has been created by your ego.
3. The ego creates moods. It creates moods by repressing and/or holding on to emotions that appear in its stream of consciousness. This means, for example, that:
   a. If you ever find yourself stuck in an angry mood, this is a state of mind that has been created by your ego.
   b. If you ever find yourself stuck in a sad mood, this too is a state of mind created by the ego.
   c. If you ever find yourself stuck in a fit of jealousy, this is another state of mind created by the ego.
4. The mind with an ego is a mind that is constantly judging and evaluating itself:
   a. If you think you are better than someone else, this is ego.
   b. If you ever think that someone else is better than you, this too is ego.
   c. If you think that you are a superior person, this is ego.
   d. If you ever think you are a worthless person, this is ego.
   e. Even just the act of thinking that you are someone is ego.
5. If you ever feel you are betraying your integrity, or being dishonest with your self, the greater likelihood is that you feel this way because you have abandoned your true self to align yourself with and become your ego's identity.
6. Whenever you find yourself trying to control your mind, this is an egocentric act. Indeed, it is the essence of the ego. This means, for example, that:
   a. If you find yourself repressing your feelings, this is an action that is being taken by your ego.
   b. If you find yourself holding on to and savoring a stream of thoughts and emotions that cast you in a favorable light, this is an action that is being taken by your ego to preserve a favorable conception of your self.

7. When you believe and live in a story that is being narrated by a mind-film that is cycling through your mind, this is ego.
8. When you feel like you do not know who you are, or what you want to do with your life, this is more than likely a consequence of having abandoned your true self to become your ego.
9. If you believe that your truth is the only truth, this is ego.
10. If you feel intolerant of, and want to eliminate, truths that are different than your own, this is an act of your ego.
11. If you dislike or discriminate against people because you see them as being different than your self, this too is an act of the ego.

These phenomena and states of mind are, once again, symptoms of the normal pathologies of the ego.

There are two basic lines of evidence that lead to the conclusion that the normal pathologies of the ego are created by and unique to the egocentric mind. For one, we can observe the mechanisms by which the ego's control dynamic creates them. Secondly, they do not occur in the egoless mind.

As creations of the ego, the normal pathologies are the price we are paying, as a species, for institutionalizing the ego and making it part of our lives. By becoming an ego, we literally trade away our inherent happiness and goodness, and we do so to achieve the social acceptance and control that the ego affords us.

The ego is unhealthy in three fundamental respects: (1) it creates unpleasant states of mind that in and of themselves make a person unhappy; (2) it makes it virtually impossible for a person to realize the genuine happiness of knowing and being their true self; and (3) it creates a conflicted state of mind that generates interpersonal, and perhaps even sociopolitical, conflict in the world.

There are four normal pathologies of the ego for which we have sufficient data to establish that they exist and that they are created by the ego. Our findings describe these pathologies and the mechanisms by which the ego creates them. They are as follows:

1. Duality and Conflict
2. Loss of Self
3. Moods
4. Mind-Films and the Existential Ruts They Generate.

The remainder of this chapter is now going to discuss the normal pathologies of the ego one at a time. The first one that will be considered is the pathology of duality and the conflict that it engenders.

Duality and Conflict

Imagine that a National Geographic expedition has been sent to the Himalaya to look for the hidden utopian valley of Shambhala, and that as they searched they did indeed stumble into a deep semi-tropical valley in the middle of the mountains in which they found a young man, a Caucasian man, living in the valley all alone in a state of nature.

It turned out that this young man had come to the valley ten years earlier at the age of five with his adventurer-scientist parents—who had also been looking for Shambhala. One day his parents had disappeared, and he had never seen them or any other human being again until the expedition arrived. Survival had been relatively easy for him. Fruit grew on the trees, and the water in the valley's glacier-fed streams was pure.

What made the young man more than a little interesting was that he had somehow lost all sense of having an identity over the years. He had no concept of being someone, or of feeling that he should be someone. In the absence of human society, his embryonic childhood identity had simply faded away and disappeared. And yet, in the eyes of all who met him, he was a remarkably happy and healthy young man. To be sure, some people saw him as being a bit uncouth and irreverent at times, but nonetheless, everyone recognized that he was a radiant being who was filled with goodness.

On his return to civilization, a team of psychologists did a battery of tests on him and discovered, to their surprise, that the young man had no stream of consciousness. They found that he was not aware of his mind in any way. He did not even know what thoughts were.

It also turned out that he did not judge his mind. Without a stream of consciousness, there were no thoughts or mind-films to judge. Most surprising of all, the psychologists found that given that this young man had no identity or ego, he was just one person. He was just simply himself, and he never experienced himself as having any conflict about who he should or should not be.

When he was hungry he ate. When he saw rabbits slowly eating and loping their way around his garden, he felt a sense of joy in being a witness to their innocence. When he was tired he slept. When he saw the good in someone, he was drawn to it. He was never distracted by thoughts and moods because he did not have them. He lived in the moment.

However, after being back to North America for awhile, and after being reunited with his overjoyed relatives, he began once again, to take on an identity. It was only natural that living in society would cause him to become someone in his own eyes again. Now he began to think that he had an identity, as did everyone else as well. He was the young man who had been lost in the Himalaya for ten years.

As he took on his identity, a surprising and revealing thing happened: a stream of thoughts and emotions began to run through his mind, and as this happened, he of course became aware of his mind. He also began to judge his thoughts, and he even found himself having to make constant choices about whether or not he should express them.

Sometimes his thoughts bothered him. There were thoughts and moods he didn't like. Sometimes his thoughts brought him joy, and he would try to hold on to the thoughts that he liked. More often than not, though, he found himself in conflict with his thoughts and emotions, and then he began doing something that he had never done before—he began to repress thoughts and emotions that he didn't like.

Now the young man was like everyone else. He had become two people. On the surface, he was the person who was acting out his identity. But beneath the surface he found that he was also someone else—the person who thought and felt all of the things that were not in keeping with his identity.

Like this young man, we all have, as socialized human beings with an ego, two selves. One self is the ego—the person who believes in and adheres to your identity. The second self is your true self.[2]

When you have an ego, you aren't quite able to know and be your true self, but you do know that there is someone else there inside of you because you keep having wishes, thoughts and feelings that don't match the identity you think you have. This duality of self and ego is one of the fundamental dualities of the egocentric mind, and it is a duality brought to life by the presence of the ego within the mind.

Inevitably, these two selves come into conflict with one another when they want different things at the same time—both in the long run and the short run.

A healthy mind would be a mind that finds a harmonious way to integrate these two selves so that they can comfortably coexist with one another. This would be a mind that finds a means of allowing the two selves to become one nondual self in every moment.

However, the egocentric mind fails to find a way to integrate these two selves. Indeed, the only reason that these two selves seem to exist in the first place is that the presence of an ego both creates a second self, and then it does not allow the two selves to integrate with one another. We would not have two selves if there were no ego.

In other words, it is the presence of the ego that divides the mind into two selves. The ego divides the mind in two by reifying, or concretizing, both the watcher and the stream of consciousness. This reification turns them into the two seemingly separate and conflicted structural entities that appear at the core of our theories of personality. Ego and Id. Ego and Self. False Self and True Self.

The ego concretizes the watcher and stream of consciousness and turns them into separate entities by literally keeping them separate from one another. It keeps them apart by setting them in epistemological concrete, if you will. Here's how that happens.

2. The true self, as defined here, is the coalescence, in every moment, of egoless awareness and the nondual meanings that the mind has given to the present moment. Please see Chapter 11 for a more thorough discussion of the true self.

In the egoless state of the mind, meanings dissolve into awareness, and this makes the egoless watcher and the meanings that appear in its stream of consciousness nondual, both ontologically and epistemologically.

The meanings that appear in the egoless stream of consciousness dissolve because the egoless watcher does not grasp them. There are a number of different causal processes that allow these dissolutions to happen, but the general dynamic of all of these causal processes can be summarized as follows:

NON-GRASPING OF MEANING → DISSOLUTION OF MEANING

In the egocentric mind, however, the watcher does grasp the meanings that appear in its stream of consciousness. The thoughts and emotions that are grasped by the watcher do not dissolve, and as a result, they remain present in the stream of consciousness as mind-films and moods. This causes the meanings of the stream of consciousness to remain separate from the watcher, ontologically, epistemologically and in terms of intentionality.

This ongoing separation of the watcher and the stream of consciousness makes it seem as though they are two separate entities. These two entities become, in turn, the two selves of the egocentric mind. Their continuing presence creates the structural duality of the egocentric mind that is enshrined in the personality theory of the twentieth century. As we will be seeing, having created these two selves, the ego then proceeds to create a conflicted dynamic between them.

Once again, it is the ego's grasping actions that create and fortify this perception that there are two selves in our minds. These actions create this perception that we have two selves by causing meanings to remain present in the stream of consciousness. For example:

GRASPING OF THOUGHT → MIND-FILM ACTIVATION

GRASPING OF EMOTION → MOOD ACTIVATION

The first causal sequence tells us that when the watcher grasps a thought, it remains present in the stream of consciousness as a mind-film. The second one tells us that when the watcher grasps an emotion, it remains present in the stream of consciousness as a mood.

The persistent presence, and thus seeming permanence, of the resulting films and moods in the stream of consciousness creates the impression that the stream of consciousness is a permanent structural entity that is separate from the watcher. This impression, in turn, causes the egocentric mind, and our theoreticians of personality, to perceive the watcher and stream of consciousness as being two different selves.

Many of our theories of personality propagate this egocentric perception that we have two selves. They do so by casting them as the central actors in a conflicted dynamic that is the core dynamic of the egocentric mind.[3] Freud, once again, cast this conflict as a dialectic between two structures that he called the ego and id. Hegel, in his theory of self-awareness, saw it as a conflict between a master and a slave, and so forth.

In addition to creating this dyadic structure, the ego also creates the conflicted dynamic between these two selves. The conflict arises, of course, because the egocentric watcher tries to control the stream of consciousness. As we now know well, the egocentric watcher attempts to control the stream of consciousness for the purpose of preserving its identity. It controls the stream of consciousness by grasping—judging, repressing and holding on to—the meanings that appear in its stream of consciousness.

The grasping actions of the control dynamic generate conflict by creating situations in which the watcher and stream of consciousness want two different things at the same time. The ego's constant desire is to preserve its identity, but the meanings that arise in your stream of consciousness often express a desire that is at odds with that identity.

Jealousy might arise within you, but your ego will not want you to express that jealousy because it doesn't want to appear vulnerable. Or your ego might suppress a mind-film that is composed of a set of uncomfortable memories that you long ago suppressed because the events portrayed by the mind-film are not consistent with your conception of your identity.

Humanity has long recognized that there are two selves in the egocentric mind that live in more or less constant conflict with one another.

Here is Socrates using the metaphor of a horse drawn chariot to describe this primordial duality and conflict of the egocentric mind. It comes from *The Phaedrus*, which is one of Plato's dialogues (Plato, 1995):

> I divide the soul into three—two horses and a charioteer; and one of the horses was good and the other bad . . . The right-hand horse is . . . a lover of honor and modesty and temperance . . . he needs no touch of the whip, but is guided by word and admonition only. The other is a crooked lumbering animal . . . the mate of insolence and pride, shag-eared and deaf, hardly yielding to whip and spur.
>
> Now when the charioteer beholds the vision of love . . . and is full of the prickings and ticklings of desire, the obedient steed . . . refrains from leaping on the beloved; but the other, heedless of the . . . blows of the

3. In contrast, Buddhist theorists see this duality as a delusion. My guess is that Western theoreticians have tended to reify this dicentric structure *and see it as a structural element of the mind* because they have not been aware of the possibility of the egoless mind. To the best of my knowledge, there has not been, until recently, any explicit mention of the egoless mind in the history of Western mind theory. Western thought has seen the egocentric mind as being the only type of mind there is. In contrast, in the South Asian subcontinent, the egoless mind was in the air, if you will, and it was explored at length by several traditions.

> whip . . . runs away, giving all manner of trouble to . . . the charioteer, whom he forces to approach the beloved.

This conflict was a major issue in Saint Augustine's life as well (AD 354–430), and here he is describing his experience of what was for him a moral conflict in two different passages from the Eighth Book of his *Confessions* (Augustine, 2013):

> Thus did my two wills, one new, and the other old, one carnal, the other spiritual, struggle within me; and by their discord, undid my soul.
>
> There are two minds in us of two kinds, one good, the other evil.

Twenty-four centuries after Plato, Freud put this same conflict at the center of his theory of personality and described it as being a conflict between two structures within the mind that he called the ego and the id, between reason and animal desire (Freud, 1960):

> Thus in its relation to the id, (the ego) is like a man on horse back, who has to hold in check the superior strength of the horse; with this difference, that the rider tries to do so with his own strength while the ego uses borrowed forces. The analogy may be carried a little further. Often a rider, if he is not to be parted from his horse, is obliged to guide it where it wants to go; so in the same way the ego is in the habit of transforming the id's will into action as if it were its own.

Clearly, our history of ideas has long recognized that the egocentric mind that we all have is a mind that has two selves that are often in conflict with one another.

This is a conflict that we all know. We experience it as a feud, if you will, that we have with our desires, emotions, thoughts and moods. You might experience it as a struggle to suppress a moment of pride. Or you might know it as the need to temper a sense of superiority. Or you might, like Augustine, find yourself trying to turn away from your carnality so that you can live a spiritual life.

This conflict, and the structural duality from which it takes its birth, are both artifacts that are created by the machinations of the egocentric mind. We know that they are created by the ego because we can observe the processes by which the ego creates them. We also know that they need not happen because duality and conflict do not appear in the egoless mind.

This means that it is not necessary for us to endure the duality and conflict of the egocentric mind. They are preventable. If we did not have egos, we would not be in conflict with ourselves.

Indeed, the egoless mind does not create these conflicts because it is not in the habit of trying to either control the meanings that appear in its stream of consciousness or of altering the realities they create to make them conform to an identity.

Given that the egoless mind is not trying to maintain an identity, it abstains from grasping the meanings that appear in its stream of consciousness. This allows its thoughts and emotions to dissolve and become nondual with awareness in every moment. The egoless mind does not reify the meanings that appear in its stream of consciousness and turn them into a permanent entities, and this why there is no structural duality in the egoless mind.

The absence of structural duality also explains why there is no conflict in the egoless mind. Conflict does not arise in the egoless mind because it does not have two separate selves that could possibly be in conflict with one another. It does have two selves because for one, it does not create them in the first place. Secondly, there is no conflict because the egoless watcher does not try to control its stream of consciousness.

Conflict in the History of Ideas

Over the centuries, many different theorists have concurred with the egocentric mind's view of itself, and given us theories that portray the mind as having within itself two different selves that are in conflict with one another. These theories are, once again, the dialectical theories of the mind (Vyner, 2007–2008). They depict the mind, our egocentric mind, as being a mind that has two selves that are in perpetual conflict with one another.

Table 9.1 provides a sampling of some of the more salient dialectical theories that have been developed to frame, give names to and explain the conflict between the two minds that are, empirically, the watcher and stream of consciousness.

This long history is substantial evidence of the fact that the mind with an ego experiences itself as having two separate selves, and that it has done so since at least Plato and the Katha Upanishad, which is thought to date back to just before Plato at around 500 BC, and perhaps even earlier.

TABLE 9.1 The Dyadic Structures of the Dialectical Mind Theories

Theorist	*Master*	*Slave*
Plato	Reason	Spirit/Appetites
Upanishads	Intellect	Senses
Hegel	Master	Slave
Freud	Ego	Id
Jung	Ego	Self
Winnicott	False Self	Self
Rogers	Desired Self	Self
Laing	False Self System	Self System

Each different theorist has given the two selves different names, but it all amounts to the same thing: the mind with an ego experiences itself as being two selves, one of which tries to control the other. This is the fundamental duality of the egocentric mind.

These theorists have all described the two selves of the egocentric mind as being entities that constantly quarrel with one another.

The ego's traditional means of resolving the conflicts between the two selves it creates is to pretend that we are only one person. This is the ego's modus operandi. It tries to sustain, for itself, the illusion that each of us has but one self—which is the ego's identity—by controlling its stream of consciousness.

By taking this approach to resolving its duality and conflict, the egocentric mind cuts itself off from the feelings and thoughts that are its true self. In so doing, the ego turns a person into being a razor-thin cardboard cutout of a self that is predicated upon an identity.

This conflict is the primordial pathology of the egocentric mind. The control dynamic that the ego mounts to resolve this conflict between the two selves creates, in turn, the other normal pathologies of the ego. It is this primal duality and the normal pathologies to which it gives birth that make the egocentric mind an unhealthy mind.

Let's now briefly revisit the control dynamic before moving on to taking a look at the other egocentric pathologies that it generates.

The Second Control Paradox

We live our lives taking it as a given that we have to control our minds—and for good reason. We all know that it is better to leave unexpressed much of what happens in our minds. There is violence in the mind. Vanity. Superiority. Inferiority. Foolishness. Reckless desire. Naked ambition. Self-deception. Indifference to the needs and feelings of others. We see many of these sentiments in ourselves, and we see them in others as well. What could be more fundamental than the need to control all of this?

However, if we were able to consistently look at the ignoble contents of our mind through the lens of the natural and nondual goodness of the egoless mind, we wouldn't have to repress or control them because they would be transformed by that goodness.

But given that most of us have egos, we aren't able to see our minds through the lens of goodness all that often, if at all. We live in the midst of the judgments, emotions and stories created by the egos that have been bequeathed to us by centuries of biological and cultural evolution; and for the most part, the ego makes our basic goodness unavailable to us.

The principal dynamic problem with the ego is that, despite its good intentions, it works on the mistaken premise that the best way to socialize the mind is to control the stream of consciousness. Unfortunately, controlling the stream of consciousness obscures the fundamental goodness within us.

Nevertheless, we continue to lean on the ego's approach to socializing ourselves because we have not yet understood that the only reason we need to control our minds is that we control our minds in the first place. Let me say that again: we have to control our minds because we control our minds.

To be more precise, the actions that the ego takes to govern the mind generate the very emotions, films, and moods that we feel we need to control. Repressing emotions creates moods. Creating and living in ego stories breeds recurring conflict and dysfunctional relationships. And so forth. Control breeds the need for control.

This is the second control paradox of the mind. The first one involved the egoless mind: the egoless mind controls itself by not controlling itself. The second one involves the egocentric mind: the egocentric mind needs to control itself because it controls itself.

Sisyphus was condemned by Zeus, for his deceitfulness and hubris, to rolling a stone up a hill over and over again for eternity. The ego, like Sisyphus, is also condemned to a life of unsuccessful labor.

The ego spends its life trying to govern the mind by making its thoughts, emotions and behavior conform to its identity. It rolls the stone of identity up the hill over and over again, but it never quite succeeds in getting it to the top and making it stay there.

An identity is of course a concept. It is a concept that carves out a place in society for a person by ascribing to them an inherent and permanent character. To say that a person has an identity is to say that they have a character that is both permanent and causally independent of the rest of the universe.

To put it in simpler terms, an identity embodies the idea that a person has the same character all of the time. The ego is assigned the impossible and ultimately fruitless labor of trying to ensure that a person will indeed have the same character all of the time, even though we are all constantly changing, and even though we all have thoughts and emotions that do not match our identity.

We don't always think and behave in a way that is congruent with our identities. A conservative senator can be found in a public bathroom having sex with a young man. A loving mother might find herself angrily demeaning a child she loves dearly.

We often have thoughts and emotions that don't match our identity, or mind-films that take us away from the present moment when we want or need to be present in that moment. This is the nature of being a human being. There is nothing wrong about it.

Nonetheless, the ego works on the premise that this inconsistency is undesirable, and it tries to eliminate it. This is the reason that the ego controls the stream of consciousness. It constantly judges, represses and attaches the meanings that appear in its stream of consciousness for the purpose of trying to make them conform to its sense of identity. It also narrates stories and inserts them into the stream of consciousness for the purpose of creating realities that help you believe you have the identity you think you have.

And herein lies the rub with having an identity and an ego. As we have already begun to see, it is the actions that the egocentric watcher takes to control the mind that cause much of the psychological pain of our lives. It does so by generating the normal pathologies of the ego.

The actions of the egocentric watcher attempt to maintain an identity by controlling two fundamental aspects of the stream of consciousness.

1. The watcher determines which meanings will and will not be expressed. For example, if you repress a moment of anger when a policeman stops you to give you an unwarranted ticket, or if you repress a moment of attraction to your spouse's best friend, these repressions will probably keep you from expressing those emotions, at least in that moment anyway.
2. The watcher also controls the content of the meanings that appear in the stream of consciousness. It can, for example, delete thoughts that it does not like by repressing them, and it can, just as readily, hold on to thoughts that it does like; which turns them into mind-films that continue to appear in the stream of consciousness.

Once again, the watcher has a repertoire of four actions that it can and does take to exercise this control over the stream of consciousness: (1) judgment, (2) repression, (3) attachment and (4) creating and living in thought films.

These actions generate, in concert, the egocentric state of mind and its normal pathologies. They create the egocentric state of mind by engendering conflict, and also by inserting three of the principal components of the normal pathologies into the stream of consciousness: (1) emotions, (2) mind-films and (3) moods.

Here. once again, are three representative examples of the many causal sequences by which the watcher's actions generate the constituent elements of the normal pathologies:

WATCHER GRASPS THOUGHT → THOUGHT FILM ACTIVATION

WATCHER JUDGES MEANING → EMOTION APPEARS

WATCHER GRASPS EMOTION → MOOD ACTIVATION

The important thing to understand here is that the meanings produced by all three of these causal sequences are the proximate cause of the normal pathologies of the egocentric mind. They all play a significant role in generating the ego's pathologies and the unhappiness that they create.

The mind-films, for example, act as scripts that cause a person to act out and even seek out the same type of dysfunctional interpersonal relationships over and again. They cause other problems as well. In the next section, we will examine the several mechanisms by which the mind-films contribute to the creation of the normal pathologies of the ego.

Existential Ruts, the Present Moment and the Loss of Self

A. Summary: The Science of the Activation of Mind-Films

1. The egocentric watcher routinely activates mind-films. There are several mechanisms by which the actions of the egocentric watcher activate and sustain the presence of the mind-films in the stream of consciousness. Here are three of them:
   a. When the watcher attaches a thought, it causes that thought to remain in the stream of consciousness as a mind-film:

      WATCHER ATTACHES THOUGHT → MIND-FILM ACTIVATION

   b. When the watcher represses an emotion, that causes the simultaneous appearance of a mind-film and mood:

      WATCHER REPRESSES EMOTION → MIND-FILM ACTIVATION

   c. When the watcher follows, or believes the contents of, a mind-film, that film continues to be projected onto the stream of consciousness:

      WATCHER FOLLOWS MIND-FILM → MIND-FILM REMAINS IN STREAM OF CONSCIOUSNESS

2. In contrast, mind-films do not appear in the egoless mind because the egoless watcher does not grasp—repress or attach—any of the meanings that appear in its stream of consciousness:
   a. WATCHER DOES NOT GRASP MEANINGS → MIND-FILMS DO NOT APPEAR IN MIND-FILM REMAINS IN SoC

B. Evidence for the Existence of the Mind-Films

Roger Walsh, a psychiatrist who was a central figure in what was once the field of transpersonal psychology, published two papers in the late 1970s in which he described his experiences during his first three-month meditation retreat (Walsh, 1977; Walsh, 1978). One of his many observations was that there appeared within his mind "a frantic torrent of forceful, demanding, loud and often unrelated thoughts and fantasies."

This experience had taken him by surprise. He had not known that a robust involuntary stream of thoughts was constantly running through his mind before he began to meditate. In his own words, "The power and pervasiveness of these inner dialogues and fantasies left me amazed that we could be so unaware of them during our normal waking life" (Walsh, 1977).

This is a common experience among meditators. Most meditators will tell you that their mind routinely wanders in meditation, and that they were completely unaware that this torrent of thoughts and emotions existed in their mind before they took up the practice of meditation. If someone were to ever do a study of this phenomenon among meditators, I wouldn't be surprised if 95 percent or more of their subjects reported that a robust involuntary stream of thoughts routinely appeared in their mind when they first began to meditate.

Of relevance, is a 2010 study of mind wandering that was done by Killingsworth and Gilbert. They used computer technology to randomly call subjects on their iPhones to inquire about whether or not they were thinking about something other than what they were doing at the moment of the phone call (Killingsworth and Gilbert, 2010).

If you were at your office working when the call came, were you thinking about something else? Or if you were making love, presumably at home, were you thinking about something else, and so forth. They called 2,250 adults and found that 46.9 percent of their subjects were mind wandering when they were called (Killingsworth and Gilbert, 2010).

I'm going to venture a guess that this figure of 46.9 percent was almost certainly low. Why? Think of Roger Walsh. Mind wandering, the involuntary stream of consciousness, usually occurs subliminally. We are often not aware of it as it happens. Dr. Walsh was not aware that there was such a constant and robust cascade of fantasies in his mind until he began to meditate. In the same way, many of us mind wander without being fully aware that we are.

Just as you can tune out and not hear a background noise, let's say the ticking of a grandfather clock while you are reading a book, you can also tune out and not hear a steady stream of background thoughts in your own mind.

Meditation makes it just about impossible to tune out your involuntary stream of consciousness. The experience of meditation is one in which the involuntary stream of consciousness is a more or less constant presence in the mind, especially when you first begin meditating.

Thubten Jinpa, the Dalai Lama's longtime principal translator, and an important Buddhist scholar and teacher in his own right, has written that "Our default state of mind is that of mind wandering, and this mind wandering is a source of unhappiness" (Jinpa, 2015). He knows because he is of course a lifelong practitioner of meditation.

To return, though, to Killingsworth and Gilbert's findings, even if their prevalence figure of 46.9 percent turns out to be low, their findings are still remarkable. They have experimentally established that mind wandering is a prominent feature in the landscape of the human mind. Almost 50 percent of the subjects in their sample of 2,250 people were aware of the fact that as they go through their days they are often thinking about something else.

Killingworth and Gilbert's study of mind wandering is part of a burgeoning cottage industry of mind wandering studies (Callard et al., 2013). Over the last fifteen years, interest in the phenomenon has blossomed, and this vein of work leaves no doubt that mind wandering, which is called the involuntary stream of consciousness by the science of the stream of consciousness, is a prevalent phenomenon in the human mind. A plethora of imaging studies of the brain have even led to the suggestion that mind wandering might be the mind and brain's default mode of function (Richle, 2001; Fox et al, 2015).

Of perhaps greater import, the empirical study of mind wandering seems to have opened the door to the scientific study of the stream of consciousness. Mind wandering is, of course, a phenomenon that appears in the stream of consciousness; one of many. With the widespread advent of the study of mind wandering, the cognitive sciences seem to be nudging open the door to empirically studying the stream of consciousness. So far, it is only this one phenomenon of mind wandering, but it is a start.

C. Mind-Films and Being Present in the Moment

The science of the stream of consciousness has been drawn to documenting two of the unhealthy effects of the mind-films: (1) the loss of your ability to know your true self and (2) the creation of interpersonal ruts in which a person acts out the same small repertoire of mind-film narratives over and over again. We will come back to these effects in a moment.

The cognitive sciences, however, have been drawn to studying a different set of the effects of the mind-films, and I would like to begin our discussion of the negative impacts of the mind-films by drawing attention to one of their most important findings: the mind-films distract a person from paying attention to and being present in the present moment. A number of studies have experimentally established something that we all know as a matter of common sense: when an involuntary stream of thoughts is running through your mind, it draws your attention away from the present moment.

In general, this group of studies has established the existence of this divorce from the moment by showing that when mind-films are running through a person's mind, they were less competent at doing an assigned experimental task.

For example, Antrobus and Singer (Antrobus et al., 1966) did an experiment in which subjects were asked to listen to a series of tones that was composed of just two tones: one high tone and one low tone. The subjects were asked to respond to each tone by simply indicating whether it was the high tone or the low tone. That was their task.

Before they were led into the laboratory to do the experiment, subjects were left in a waiting room for fifteen minutes, and radio music was piped into the room. While one group of subjects was waiting, a mock news bulletin interrupted the music to announce that China had declared war on the United States because of our participation in the Vietnam War. A control group of subjects heard only music during their entire time in the waiting room.

Antrobus and Singer measured two things in this experiment: (1) the frequency of "task-irrelevant thoughts" that each subject had as they were doing the signal detection experiment and (2) how accurately each subject performed the task of discriminating the difference between the high and low tones.

They found two things: (1) the subjects who heard the fake war broadcast had a higher frequency of task-irrelevant thoughts while they were doing the signal detection task than the control group subjects and (2) the subjects who heard the fake war broadcast made more signal detection mistakes than the control group.

These results were interpreted as meaning that the increased presence of what they called task-irrelevant thoughts in the stream of consciousness caused subjects to give a less accurate performance in the signal detection tests.

These findings have since been repeated innumerable times in many different types of experimental settings. Subsequent studies of the deleterious effects of mind wandering on task performance fall into four basic categories of task: reading, sustained attention, working memory and intelligence testing. Here are some of those findings:

a. Mind wandering during reading comprehension tests decreases the ability to recall information from, and to make inferences about, the material that was read (Schooler et al., 2004; Smallwood et al., 2008).
b. The ability to successfully attend to a task that requires a response is reduced by mind wandering (Cheyne et al., 2009).
c. Mind wandering reduces working memory (Mrazek et al., 2012).
d. Mind wandering decreases performance on aptitude measuring tests (Mrazek et al., 2012).

These studies have been interpreted to mean that mind wandering causes a phenomenon that the field is calling *perceptual decoupling*—which is defined as a state of mind in which "attention to ongoing perceptual information is reduced, often in favor of the active consideration of internally generated thoughts and feelings" (Smallwood, 2011).

There is now an abundance of neurobiological evidence that supports this hypothesis. For example, imaging studies of the brain are showing that when mind wandering occurs, there is decreased cortical processing of external events (Smallwood et al., 2008; Barron et al., 2011).

In other words, mind-films cause a person to not be present in the moment. When mind-films are running through your mind, it draws you away from paying attention to the present moment. This is one of the negative effects of the mind-films.

D. Mind-Films and the Existential Ruts

One type of normal pathology that is caused by the egocentric narratives of the mind-films is that they create existential ruts in a person's life. They create ruts in the sense that they act as recursive scripts within the mind that cause a person to act out and become the central character in those scripts over and over again. In other words, when a film is being actively projected within the mind, a person will tend to become a character in that film.

For example, if an angry film is constantly running through a person's mind, that person will tend to act out those films by becoming angry, even when it makes absolutely no sense at all in the situation at hand. Or if a person has a proclivity for jealous films, they might tend to act out that jealousy and so forth.

Meditation provides a person with a sequence of experiences that make this connection between the mind-films and behavior apparent. First you become aware that there is an involuntary stream of thoughts and emotions constantly running through your mind. Then you realize that the involuntary stream tells stories.

The next step is that you realize that the same small repertoire of stories is running over and again in your mind, which is why the films create ruts. Given that the same stories are repeatedly running through your mind, a person acts out the same scripts out over and again.

Finally, at some point, it becomes apparent to you that there are times when you actually do act out these stories. You might notice, for example, that when a prideful film is active in your mind in tandem with a prideful mood, that you become inflated with pride and act out that pride. Or that when an inferiority film is playing that you act as if there is something is wrong with you. Or that when someone else is getting more recognition than you, that a jealous film begins to play within your mind, and that you will act out your jealousy by criticizing the other person.

The basic insight here is this: given that the same recursive mind-films tend to play over and over again in a person's mind, they generate repetitive patterns of both mentation and behavior.

There is a growing body of both laboratory research and clinical experience that confirms this causal connection between films and the expression of those films as recurring patterns of mentation and behavior. For example, there is now a small body of work that is beginning to show that mind wandering is related to patterns of mental illness (Kanske, 2016).

Kanske, in a fascinating recent study of the contents of mind wandering in four specific mental disorders found that:

> [E]ach condition was . . . associated with specific alterations in self-generated thoughts: While Borderline Personality Disorder patients showed strong fluctuations in how self- and other-related their thoughts were, Major Depression patients showed a rumination-like pattern with generally increased negatively valenced off-task thoughts about past events. Narcissism in contrast was associated with more positively valenced thoughts about the self, while the aggressive group reported more negatively valenced thoughts about

> others. The results suggest that different psychopathological conditions are associated with distinct patterns of self-generated thought content.
>
> (Kanske, 2016)

Cognitive behavioral therapists have also explored this relationship between mind-films, which they term automatic thoughts, and psychopathology. One of the central theoretical tenets of cognitive behavioral therapy is that mental disorders are caused by dysfunctional cognitive schemas and the automatic thoughts, or mind-films, that express those schemas.

Several decades of clinical experience have led cognitive therapists to conclude that the pathogenesis of the following disorders is mediated by automatic thoughts: depression, general anxiety disorder and a spectrum of personality disorders; antisocial personality disorder, borderline personality disorder, histrionic personality disorder, narcissistic personality disorder, dependent personality disorder, avoidant personality disorder, obsessive-compulsive personality disorder and passive-aggressive personality disorder (Beck et al., 2004).

Now let's take a look at the mechanisms by which the mind-films cause a person to lose access to their true self.

E. Mind-Films and the Loss of Self

Mercutio

I talk of dreams,
Which are the children of an idle brain,
Begot of nothing but vain fantasy . . .
And more inconstant than the wind . . .

Benvolio

This wind, you talk of, blows us from ourselves . . .

Romeo and Juliet, Act I, Scene 4

A second, more profound, normal pathology mediated by the mind-films is that they play a role in causing a person to lose their ability to know and be their true self (Vyner, 2009–2010).

To really know your true self without an overlay of egocentric meanings, one has to be able to abide in egoless awareness, which will, in turn, endow you with the ability to have nondual awareness of all of the meanings that appear in your stream of consciousness. This will, in turn, make it possible for you to know the suchness of the content of the meanings that you give to the present moment, which is the same as knowing your true self.[4]

4. Please see Chapter 11, "The Egoless State of Mind," for a thorough explanation of the crucial role that the nondual awareness of meanings plays in enabling the egoless mind to know its true self.

The key that opens the door to abiding in egoless awareness, is the ability to sense and become one with the goodness and joy that are egoless awareness. In addition, it is virtually imperative that your mind be able to see meanings clearly to have nondual awareness of them. The presence of mind-films in the stream of consciousness make both of these tasks virtually impossible.

In other words, the mind-films cause the mind to lose access to its true self by blanketing over and obscuring its ability to know the elements of one's true self: the primordial meanings of the mind, the nondual realizations generated by the nondual transformations and most importantly, egoless awareness itself.

The egocentric mind loses access to these elements of its true self because it swaddles itself in layers of identity-confirming mind-films and moods. Several films and moods can be present in the egocentric stream of consciousness at one time, and they make it exceedingly difficult for the mind to see itself clearly, which causes it to lose access to its true self.

There are several mechanisms by which mind-films cause the mind to lose access to its true self. They are as follows:

1. The presence of the mind-films in the stream of consciousness makes it difficult for the mind to even be simply aware of the primordial meanings that give meaning to the present moment, much less have nondual awareness of them. The films act as veils that obscure the primordial meanings.
2. The presence of multiple mind-films and moods in the stream of consciousness blocks the mind's ability to know, and thus makes it unfeasible for the mind to have nondual awareness of, the egopoietic meanings as well. For example, the films preclude nondual awareness of the emotions, moods and other mind-films.
3. The presence of the mind-films in the stream of consciousness makes it virtually impossible for the mind to sense, much less abide in, the joy and goodness that are egoless awareness.
4. By blocking the mind's ability to have nondual awareness of meanings, the mind-films also prevent the occurrence of the nondual transformations. This impedance of the nondual transformations blocks the generation of several crucial elements of the true self: a clear stream of consciousness, the nondual realizations and egoless awareness itself.

Ultimately, to know your true self, your mind must have nondual awareness of all, or almost all, of the phenomena that appear in its stream of consciousness. If you have consistent nondual awareness of your stream of consciousness, you will be able to know and be your true self because (1) you will be able to abide in egoless awareness, and as a result (2) you will have nondual awareness of the meanings you give to the present moment.[5]

5. Please see Chapter 11 for a systematic discussion of the role that nondual awareness plays in generating the egoless state of mind.

If, however, you are unable to have consistent nondual awareness of your stream of consciousness, you will not be able to know and be your true self. It is that simple, and this is the fundamental reason why the mind-films preclude self-realization. They obstruct the mind's ability to abide in egoless awareness and have nondual awareness of the meanings that appear in its stream of consciousness.

In contrast, the egoless mind does have nondual awareness of the phenomena that appear in its stream of consciousness, and as a result, the mind-films rarely appear in the egoless mind, if they appear at all. They do not appear in the egoless stream of consciousness because the egoless watcher does not repress or attach meanings.

On those rare occasions in which mind-films do appear in the egoless mind, the egoless watcher does not follow or live in the narrative of those films. The egoless mind has nondual awareness of the mind-films, which will cause them to dissolve and disappear on their own.

As a result, the mind-films are not a robust presence in the egoless mind, and they do not cause it to lose access to the abiding joy and goodness that are egoless awareness. This means that the egoless mind is able to (1) sense and abide in egoless awareness, (2) have nondual awareness of its stream of consciousness and (3) be its true self.

Moods and the Normal Pathologies

The empirical study of the stream of consciousness presents us with observations that provide straightforward evidence that the proximate psychological cause of the painful moods is the routine workings of the ego.

The data is stunning in its simplicity, and you can actually see the creation of a mood within the mind as it happens. The process of mood activation can be readily observed by the watcher.

Here's what you see, for example, when you witness the creation of an angry mood: a moment of anger arises, the watcher moves to repress the anger and that causes the anger to remain in the stream of consciousness as an angry mood. The same thing can happen with any emotion: pride, sadness, guilt, shame, jealousy and so forth.

The basic principle at work here is this: the egocentric watcher creates moods by grasping emotions. It really is that simple. The watcher creates a mood whenever it represses or attaches an emotion. It represses emotions that it does not like, and it holds on to emotions that it does like. Either way, a mood is created.

It is in this sense that the routine workings of the ego create moods. The egocentric watcher regularly represses and attaches emotions in the course of its day-to-day functioning.

In light of these observations of the creation of moods, it would be unscientific to deny that it is the ego's actions cause the appearance of moods in the mind.

Further evidence in support of this hypothesis is that moods do not generally appear in the egoless mind. Moods don't appear in the egoless mind because the egoless watcher does not grasp emotions. As a result, emotions dissolve and disappear in the moment that they appear in the stream of consciousness, instead of becoming moods.

The implication of these findings is that it might be possible to prevent mood disorders by teaching people to cultivate a state of mind in which they cease to repress and attach emotions by leaving their stream of consciousness in its natural state.

In this context, then, what are we to make of the studies that suggest that it is neurotransmitter imbalances that are the cause of mood disorders? Does this mean that they are incorrect? Not entirely.

The greater likelihood is that neurotransmitter imbalances might be the intervening variables that biologically mediate the pathogenesis of the moods that are caused by the actions of the egocentric watcher. Everything that happens in the mind—including the moods, the emotions and the repression of emotions—is of course mediated by the central nervous system.

But once again, even this hypothesis is not certain because as of yet, the major neurotransmitter theories of depression—the catecholamine hypothesis and the serotonin hypothesis—have not been proven to be correct.

Either way, our findings suggest that the negative moods are created by the machinations of the ego, and that as such they are one of the normal pathologies. They are a pathology in two senses. For one, they are painful in and of themselves. Second, they also play a central role in causing the development of the other normal pathologies. They cause the mind to lose access to its natural sense of peace, goodness and joy. In addition they also distort and obscure the mind's ability to know and have nondual awareness of the meanings that it gives to the present moment, just as the mind-films do.

In conclusion, here are the mechanisms by which the moods contribute to the creation of the normal pathologies of the ego:

1. The negative moods are problematic in and of themselves. Just their presence in the mind stream can be painful and cause a person to feel unhappy.
2. The negative moods also obscure the natural joy and goodness of the mind and make it all but impossible for awareness to feel and become one with them.
3. The moods also distort the content of the meanings that the mind gives to the present moment, and all other meanings as well. The moods tend to be intense, and they color and add another layer of meaning to whatever meanings appear in tandem with them. In so doing, they are like a colorful translucent wash that has been spread over the surface of a painting.
4. By coloring the meanings that you give to your experience, the moods also color a person's behavior. An angry mood will predispose to angry behavior and so forth.

The science of the stream of consciousness is hopeful, though, on this matter of the moods. It shows us that it might well be possible to cultivate a state of mind in which the mind does not create negative moods because it abstains from the acts of repressing and holding on to emotions.

Loss of Self

There is something about life that sometimes makes people feel as though they have lost their soul, or if you are of a more modern bent, that you have lost your true self.

One body of evidence for the prevalence of this feeling is the premodern belief in soul loss. This belief was and continues to be widespread, and it has had a long history that continues to this day in many regions of the world (Desjarlais, 1989).

However, the belief in soul loss is not only a premodern myth. With the advent of modern science, the belief in soul loss has taken on a new configuration. It remains with us in the form of the theory of the unconscious mind, which is a belief in the loss of a portion of one's mind.

What is it about the mind that causes human beings to feel as though they have lost themselves? Or as though they have lost their integrity?

The basic notion of soul loss, in premodern societies, is that every human being has a soul, or even several souls, and that on certain occasions a soul can leave its body and fail to return.

There is a lush mythology of soul loss in traditional societies, and it has appeared in many places on our planet. Sir James George Frazier recorded soul-loss beliefs in Scandinavia, Oceania, Africa and premodern Europe (Frazier, 1911). Mircea Eliade found that the belief in soul loss was a core element of the shamanic cultures of north and central Asia (Eliade, 1964). The possibility of losing one's soul has long been a widespread belief in the shamanic tribes of South America (Shepard, 2004). To this day soul loss is invoked to explain illness in Nepal (Kohrt and Harper, 2008).

Across the breadth of the world's mythology, there have basically been three occasions on which a person's soul is said to leave their body—all of them dangerous.

One of those occasions, of course, is the final departure of death. Needless to say, it has long been a Christian belief that the soul leaves the body at death and makes its way to either heaven, hell or purgatory. Hindus and Buddhists believe in reincarnation, which is the belief that the mind leaves the body at death and is then reborn in another body. The Bella Coola of British Columbia believed that the soul left the body at death, as did the Lapps of northern Scandinavia and so forth.

The second circumstance in which soul loss is said to occur happens every night: dreaming. Many traditional cultures have held the belief that when a person sleeps, their soul leaves their body and wanders around the universe. The idea is that the sleeping person "visits the places, sees the persons and performs the acts of which he dreams" (Frazier, 1911).

There is said to be much danger in these nocturnal travels of the soul. The soul can get lost and fail to find its way back home. Or a soul can be kidnapped and stolen by a malevolent spirit. Or another spirit might sneak up and occupy your body while your own soul is out wandering around.

The third circumstance in which a person might lose their soul is illness. It has been a widespread belief that the departure of a person's soul can cause sickness, insanity or death. The cultures that ascribe to the theory that soul loss is pathogenic are countless. The Yolmo Sherpa of Nepal still believe that soul loss causes illness (Desjarlais, 1989), as do the Kayabi of Brazil (Oakdale, 2005). The belief that soul loss is a major cause of illness has been prevalent in North and South America (Hultkrantz, 1967; Eliade, 1964), and among the peoples of central Asia (Eliade, 1964).

To the modern eye, these theories of soul loss seem, of course, implausible and unscientific. Nonetheless, we do still have a modern version of theory of soul loss that most of us accept as being empirically valid: the theory of the unconscious mind. This theory was first given to us in the early nineteenth century by the German Romantic movement, and it was then popularized and empiricized by Charcôt, Janet and Freud at the end of the century.

In essence, the theory of the unconscious mind holds that there are significant portions of the mind to which the average human being does not have conscious access. There are portions of the mind that are lost, if you will, to normal waking consciousness.

Given that the mind is the modern equivalent of the soul, the theory of the unconscious mind can be seen as a myth of partial soul loss. It is a theory in which part of the soul is lost—the unconscious mind. Like the traditional myths of soul loss that came before it, the theory of the unconscious mind has also been marshaled to explain the etiology of illness, both psychological and somatic. Given our widespread modern belief in the existence of the unconscious mind, it appears that the belief in soul loss and its pathogenicity is still with us today.

Another theory of the mind that can be read as a soul loss theory is the Buddhist theory of the nature of the mind.[6] The basic gist of this theory is that a person with an ego loses access to the state of mind that Buddhism calls the true nature of the mind, or the natural mind. In this theory, the mind is said to lose access to its true nature because it is covered over, and obscured by, the thoughts and emotions that are created by the ego.

Here is the contemporary Tibetan lama Tulku Thondup explaining that in the course of its normal operation, the ego, which he here calls the

6. Tib.: Sems nyid.

ordinary dualistic mind, obscures and covers over the true nature of the mind (Thondup, 2015):

> Our mind has two aspects: ordinary mind and enlightened mind. Ordinary mind, also known . . . as deluded mind, is conceptual, dualistic, and emotional. Enlightened mind—also known as the awakened state or Buddha-nature—is the true and pure nature of the mind. For most of us, the dualistic concepts, unhealthy emotions, and obsessive sensations . . . of our ordinary mind cover the enlightened aspect of our mind. These thoughts are like coverings that obstruct us from realizing and manifesting our true nature—like clouds covering the sun.

Like the theory of the unconscious mind, the Buddhist theory of the true nature of mind holds that one aspect of the mind is lost.

The findings of the science of the stream of consciousness support a similar hypothesis, which can be concisely articulated as follows: the egocentric mind loses access to its true self. Here's an overview of the relevant data.

The science of the stream of consciousness defines the true self as being the natural state of the mind; the state of mind that naturally emerges, moment to moment, when the ego ceases to control the stream of consciousness. The natural state of the mind is your true self because it is a state of mind in which you abide in egoless awareness and as a result have constant nondual awareness of the meanings that your mind gives to the present moment.

The natural state of the mind can be described as having three basic components: (1) the egoless awareness that has nondual awareness of all the meanings that appear in its stream of consciousness; (2) the nondual meanings that give meaning to the present moment; and (3) the phenomena generated by the nondual transformations that are brought to life by nondual awareness—dissolution, realization, nondual joy, nondual goodness and amused compassion.

In the natural mind, which is also the same as the egoless mind, primordial meanings arise in the stream of consciousness to give meaning and intention to the present moment, and then the mind has nondual awareness of them. When the mind has nondual awareness of a primordial meaning, it knows your true self as it is in that moment. Your true self is the coalescence, in every moment, of the meanings that your mind gives to the present moment and the egoless awareness that knows them as they are.

However, one cannot abide in a state of mind in which you realize your true self by having nondual awareness of only the primordial meanings. You must also have nondual awareness of all of the other meanings that appear in your stream of consciousness as well, including the emotions, mind-films and moods created by your ego.

If you were to have dual awareness of the meanings created by your ego, you would cause yourself to abide in the state of complex awareness, which as we know is a state of awareness in which it is virtually impossible to know your true self.

If, on the other hand, you have nondual awareness of the emotions, mind-films and moods, they will dissolve and be transformed into realizations, goodness, joy and compassion by the nondual transformations.

By having nondual awareness of everything that appears in its stream of consciousness, the egoless mind is able to know the suchness of the meanings it has given to the present moment. As a result, it does not suffer the loss of its true self, or partial soul loss, if you will.

Things work very differently in the egocentric mind, and as a result, the egocentric mind is virtually unable to know its true self. The routine workings of the ego create a state of mind in which you lose access to your true self because it all but disappears from view.

When you look at the way the egocentric mind works, it almost seems as though it was carefully designed by a master engineer whose purpose was to design a mind that would not be able to know its true self.

Why would humanity choose to create and live inside a mind that is unable to know and be its true self? Why would we choose to live with the albatross of an ego around our necks, and teach ourselves and our children to be someone other than our true self?

Answer: it makes it easier for us to turn away from our true self and take up our designated place in society by taking on and becoming both an identity and an ego.

If you don't have access to your true self, or even more, if you lose sight of the fact that you have a self that is different than their ego, it is much easier to abandon it and become your ego.

The egocentric mind causes a person to lose their true self by causing itself to lose access to the two fundamental dimensions of the egoless mind: (1) nondual egoless awareness itself and (2) the nondual meanings that are your natural response to the present moment: the primordial meanings and the nondual realizations.

This brings us back to the phenomenon of grasping. Grasping is the epistemological mode of the egocentric mind, and it is the root of the egocentric mind's loss of self. Grasping causes loss of self because it is the independent variable that sets in motion all of the causal processes that create complex awareness and make the egocentric mind lose access to both egoless awareness and the nondual meanings of the present moment. Let's take a look now at the mechanics of the processes that make each of these losses happen.

A. The Loss of Nondual Meanings

The egocentric watcher loses the ability to have nondual awareness of the meanings that it gives to the present moment because it routinely grasps all of the meanings that appear in its stream of consciousness in the process of knowing them. It judges, represses and attaches meanings for the purpose of preserving its identity. Each of these actions is a grasping action because it attributes a conceptual identity to a meaning in the process of knowing it.

By grasping a meaning, the egocentric watcher creates an amalgam of meaning and conceptual identity, and this amalgam is what the mind knows when it knows a meaning that has been grasped. It knows the meaning in combination with the conceptual identity it has attributed to it. This precludes the possibility of having nondual awareness of that meaning, and knowing its content exactly as it is.

To illustrate what this is like, imagine that you are about to meet someone for the first time, and that you have heard many good things about him. However, just before you are scheduled to meet him, a mutual friend who knows him well tells you that actually, he has done some pretty lousy things. Now you will see him through the lens of that different identity, and that will change the way you see this person when you meet him. It's the same with attributing an identity to a meaning. It adds another layer of meaning to, and changes the way you see, the original meaning to which it has been added.

This means that the ego's routine practice of grasping meanings makes it almost impossible for you to know your self as you really are in any given moment; which is to say that it is one of the several mechanisms by which the egocentric mind loses its ability to know its true self.

Here are three causal sequences that explain why the grasping of a meaning makes it impossible for the egocentric mind to know the suchness of the meanings that appear in its stream of consciousness:

1. When the mind grasps a meaning, you will have dual awareness of that meaning:

   GRASPING OF MEANING → DUAL AWARENESS OF MEANING

2. When the mind has dual awareness of a meaning, it knows that meaning in tandem with the concept of identity that it has projected onto it in the process of knowing if:

   DUAL AWARENESS OF MEANING → MEANING IS KNOWN IN TANDEM WITH PROJECTED CONCEPT OF IDENTITY

3. When you have dual awareness of a meaning, it is not possible to know the suchness of that meaning:

   DUAL AWARENESS OF MEANING → NOT POSSIBLE TO KNOW SUCHNESS OF MEANING

There is a second mechanism by which the ego's grasping of meanings makes it impossible for the mind to know the suchness of the meanings it gives to the present moment. When the egocentric watcher grasps meanings, it also causes more emotions, moods and mind-films to appear in its stream of consciousness.

In general, the presence of these additional meanings clutters the stream of consciousness and make it virtually impossible to know the suchness of any of the other meanings that might be present in the stream of consciousness at the same time, just as litter on the surface of a river would make it difficult to see what is happening in the water below the trash.

When the egocentric watcher grasps a meaning, it can cause three different types of egopoietic phenomena to appear in the stream of consciousness, and it is these meanings that distort and block the watcher's view of all of the other phenomena that are simultaneously present in the stream of consciousness.

The first one, as we have just seen, is that when the watcher grasps a meaning, it attributes to that meaning a judgmental identity. That identity appears in the stream of consciousness as an emotion. Once again, when that happens, the mind will now know the original meaning, let's say it is a primordial meaning, in tandem with that emotion. As a result, is no longer able to know that meaning as it really is.

But the cognitive situation gets far more complex than this. When the watcher represses or attaches a meaning, it will, of course, also cause mind-films and moods to appear in the stream of consciousness.

Here is a representative sample of the many causal sequences by which the various forms of grasping cause mind-films and moods to both appear in, and remain in, the stream of consciousness:

Attachment of Primordial Meaning → Appearance of Mind-Film

Repression of Emotion → Appearance of Mood Identical to Emotion

Belief of Active Mind-Film Narrative → Continued Projection of Mind-Film

The presence of the mind-films and moods make it exceedingly difficult for the egocentric mind to be aware of, much less have the nondual awareness of, the primordial meanings that give meaning to the present moment, or of any other meanings as well. They block the view, if you will.

When a primordial meaning appears in the egocentric stream of consciousness, it almost invariably emerges into an environment in which mind-films and moods are already present. In this state of complex awareness, it is virtually impossible for the mind to know the suchness of the primordial meanings because they are known in tandem with the other meanings that are already present in the stream of consciousness.

In addition, the moods and mind-films also complicate the task of having nondual awareness of other moods and mind-films. The mind must be aware of a meaning to have nondual awareness of it, and the presence of mind-films and moods at a time in the stream of consciousness makes it difficult for the mind to discern and thus have nondual awareness of any meaning clearly.

Here is an analogy to illustrate how grasping causes the egocentric mind to lose the ability to know the suchness of the meanings that it gives to its experience.

Imagine that you are watching a slide projector flash single slides onto a movie screen. The projector has been set up to allow each slide to remain on the screen for one second. In addition, it allows two seconds to elapse between each slide. One slide follows after another, and it is easy to see and discern the visual content of each slide, which are images of animals that live on the Serengeti. In this metaphor, each slide represents a primordial meaning.

Now imagine that the film technician turns on a second slide projector. The second projector projects single slides onto the very same spot as the first projector, and it does so at exactly the same time and rate. The second set of slides project colored fields, and they are projected on top of the animals of the first slides. You can still see the animals from the first slides, but their colors are changed now. The colored slides represent the emotions that are created by the ego's judgments.

Imagine further that as you are watching this contrapuntal progression of slides, the technician now turns on a movie projector. All at once, a movie about the animals that live on the Serengeti appears on the screen, while at the same time the slide projectors continue to project their slides.

With the layering of the movie on top of the slides, it has now become, of course, all but impossible to see the individual slides, much less accurately discern their content. The imagery of the movie makes it exceedingly difficult to see the individual slides. Occasionally, you are able to make out the content of a single slide, but now you see them as part of the narrative of the film.

Now imagine that a second film projected is turned on. This, of course, will make it entirely impossible to understand what's going on in either movie, much less discern the content of the slides.

The movies represent, of course, the mind films and moods of the egocentric mind, and the montage of films and slides is a metaphor for the state of complex awareness.

In much the same way that the film and colored slides would obscure your ability to see the images of the lions, wildebeests and zebra on the original animal slides, the appearance of the mind-films and moods within the egocentric mind stream veil and make it virtually impossible for the mind to either: (1) be aware of the primordial meanings that give meaning to the present moment or (2) have nondual awareness of them and know their suchness.

Finally, there is a third mechanism by which the egocentric mind loses access to nondual meanings: the loss of the nondual transformations.

The nondual transformations only occur, of course, when the watcher has nondual awareness of meanings. Given that the egocentric watcher grasps meanings, and as a result is virtually unable to have nondual awareness of the meanings that appear in its stream of consciousness, the nondual transformations almost never occur in the egocentric mind.

This causes the mind to lose access to several aspects of its true self, including the epiphanies that are generated by the nondual transformation of realization.

Given that the egocentric mind grasps its meanings, it is rarely able to know realizations. The loss of realizations is a significant one because they are one of the two types of nondual phenomena that give meaning to the present moment. The other one is of course the primordial meanings.

B. The Loss of Egoless Awareness

The virtual absence of both nondual awareness and the nondual transformations in the egocentric mind causes one further significant loss: the loss of egoless awareness itself.

In the absence of nondual awareness, the nondual transformations do not occur. As a result, the ego does not realize the dissolutions, nondual joy, nondual goodness and amused compassion that generate egoless awareness.

These nondual transformations routinely generate, nourish and strengthen the presence of egoless awareness within the egoless mind. Without the routine occurrence of the nondual transformations, egoless awareness ceases to be a constant and stable presence within the mind.

The loss of egoless awareness has, in turn, further consequences. Without egoless awareness, there is no egoless mind. Egoless awareness is the foundation of the egoless mind because it generates and regenerates both itself and the nondual meanings that are the mind's response to the present moment.

The loss of egoless awareness is the second of the two mechanisms by which the machinations of the ego cause the mind to lose access to its true self. The first mechanism involves the loss of nondual meanings beneath a cascade of emotions, mind-films and moods.

The second mechanism is one in which the proliferation of mind-films and moods buries the joy and goodness of egoless awareness beneath their baroque complexity. Egoless awareness itself disappears beneath the layers of film and mood that are generated by the grasping actions of the egocentric mind.

Here's another analogy to illuminate the mechanism by which the egocentric mind loses egoless awareness. Imagine that you are sailing in twenty-five knots of wind on San Francisco Bay in the middle of a summer afternoon. The sun is bright and warm. You can see San Francisco, the Berkeley Hills and the Golden Gate Bridge in of all their northern California glory.

Then, as often happens in San Francisco during the summer, a massive fog rolls in over the bridge and fills the western half of the bay in less than half an hour. Now you can no longer see the sun or feel its warmth, or see much of anything else either.

This is what it's like to lose access to the warmth, if you will, of egoless awareness. Just as you can no longer feel the warmth of the sun in the fog, you can no longer sense and become one with the goodness and joy of egoless awareness when they get buried beneath the clouds that appear in the egocentric stream of consciousness: the mind-films and the moods.

This loss of egoless awareness means, of course, that you will also lose your ability to have nondual awareness of the meanings that appear in your mind, just as you can no longer see other sailboats or the Berkeley Hills in the fog.

By losing access to the joy and goodness of egoless awareness, the egocentric mind loses access to the most fundamental aspect of the true self. Given that egoless awareness is the foundation of the egoless mind's ability to know the true self, the person who loses access to the natural joy and goodness of egoless awareness also loses their ability to see what is good and real in both their own self and in other people.

In view of the fact that we all have egocentric minds that cause us to lose our true self, it is difficult not to see the loss of the egoless awareness as a tragedy.

Perhaps it was the experience of going through this loss that led people to formulate the traditional myths of soul loss.

C. Soul Loss and the Sanctification of Identity

The loss of one's true self is by any standard a huge loss. To sacrifice your true self is to lose the most valuable thing you will ever have. Given its magnitude, we try to justify and accept this loss by convincing ourselves that the identities to which we have sacrificed our true selves are monumentally sacred.

We cover our identities with a veneer of sanctity to persuade ourselves that the sacrifice of our self to the deity of identity is worth our while. By sanctifying our identities, we attempt to make the loss of our natural happiness and true self seem acceptable.

To compensate ourselves for this lifelong sacrifice, we sanctify not only our individual identities but our collective identities as well. Our nation is sacred. Our religion is sacred. Our political party is sacred. Our football team is sacred. Our favorite rock and roll band is sacred and so forth. We bring a great deal of fervor to our beliefs that our identities are sacred, and once again, we need to do so to convince ourselves that the sacrifice we are making is justified.

Indeed our collective identities become so sacred that we are willing to do just about anything to protect and defend them. That can include brawling at sporting events, violating someone else's humanity because we want and need to think that their ethnicity is inferior to our own, and even going off to war to assert the sanctity of our national identity.

However, the findings of the science of the stream of consciousness suggest that our identities are not at all sacred entities. Once you strip away the romance, an identity is simply a part of the mechanism by which the ego exercises social control over our minds and behavior. This is, in essence, what an identity is: a Faustian exchange in which we sacrifice our true selves for an identity that we hope will bring us a place in society, acceptance and love.

The Eliminative Dynamic: The Contagious Nature of Egocentric Conflict

The egocentric mind is a mind that routinely eliminates thoughts, emotions, feelings and mind-films from its stream of consciousness by repressing them. It represses and eliminates all meanings that it deems to be non-self, which are meanings that it sees as being incompatible with its identity.

This eliminative dynamic is part of the egocentric mind's modus operandi. It is the inherent nature of the egocentric mind to eliminate things that are different than its identity from both itself and the larger world in which it lives.

The handmaiden of this eliminative dynamic is the ego's quest for superiority, which seems to be inherent to the functioning of many egocentric minds. Indeed, the egocentric mind operates on the implicit premise that one portion of its mind is better than, or superior to, the remaining portion of its mind.

By eliminating films, emotions and moods that do not match its identity, the ego commits itself to a posture of superiority in which its identity is superior to the meanings it eliminates. The egocentric mind operates on the implicit premise that one portion of itself is better than the rest of itself.

One sees the replication of the ego's inner eliminative dynamic and its sense of superiority in its relationships with other people.

The egocentric mind has a tendency to take the stance that it is better than people who are different than its own identity. We see both historical and present-day evidence of this phenomenon in the occurrence of racism and racial superiority.

For example, throughout much of their history, the Han Chinese have seen themselves as being superior to the Japanese, Korean and Vietnamese people, whom they have regarded as uncivilized. Mao Zedong coined the term Han Chauvinism for this phenomenon, and he criticized it. There have long been, and there still are, Caucasians who see themselves as being superior to people of African descent. This perception made it morally acceptable to enslave black people; and even now this sense of superiority is still moving some Caucasian people to deny equality to people of African descent.

Another sociopolitical expression of this eliminative dynamic is that egocentric people will often take the stance that a religion that is different than their own religion is heresy. In history, we see that people of different religions have gotten into a few protracted struggles with one another: the Thirty Years' War in Germany in which Catholics fought Protestants; the Crusades in which Christians fought Muslims; the slaughters that occurred between Muslims, Sikhs and Hindus at the time of Independence and Partition on the Indian subcontinent; the conflict between Buddhists and Muslims in Myanmar as I type.

Another eliminative phenomenon is, of course, the genocides in which one people have tried to eliminate a different people from the face of the earth. In our own time, for example, we have seen the Armenian genocide, the Holocaust of World War II, and the Rwandan genocide.

And then finally there is organized warfare itself. Organized warfare is a situation in which one nation tries to defeat and eliminate another nation of people, a people who are perceived, once again, as being different than one's self.

These conflicts of racial superiority, religious intolerance and nationality are all identity-based conflicts in which a people of one identity try to cast themselves as being superior to a people of a different identity. They are conflicts in which one people try to subjugate, and even eliminate, people whom they regard as non-self, just as the egocentric mind eliminates thoughts and emotions that it regards as non-self.

Ultimately, sociopolitical conflicts have a structure and dynamic that is homologous to the conflict that sits at the center of the egocentric mind. The egocentric mind eliminates thoughts, feelings and emotions that it regards as divergent from its individual identity. Egocentric human beings eliminate human beings and belief systems that they regard as being divergent from their group identity.

It is indeed tempting to conclude that all of these inner and outer identity-based conflicts are made of the same fabric; that our sociopolitical conflicts are caused by the identity-based conflict that sits at the center of the egocentric mind. The homologies between our psychological and sociopolitical conflicts strongly suggest that the sociopolitical conflicts are simply replications of the conflict that is one of the normal pathologies of the egocentric mind.[7]

Indeed, it seems obvious that the ego breeds and gives birth to all of these interpersonal conflicts based on identity, and yet we cannot just assume that it is true. It will be both necessary and helpful to do a body of research to determine if this hypothesis is empirically valid.

Once again, the most elegant way to address this issue would be to study the people on a planet where everyone is brought up to be egoless to see if they practice racial superiority, religious intolerance, genocide or organized warfare. But of course, no such planet exists, at least to the best of our knowledge. So other means will have to be found to explore this issue.

These are important questions to investigate for at least two reasons: (1) if systematic research were to show that the structural conflict and eliminative dynamic of the egocentric mind generates the eliminative conflicts of racial supremacy, religious intolerance and so forth, this would be further evidence that the egocentric mind is an unhealthy mind; and (2) if we were to find that the egoless mind does not generate the eliminative conflicts of politics and religion, it would provide us with the possibility of preventing the contagious spread of the egocentric mind's conflict with itself to the sociopolitical realm.

Perhaps, if it were established that the egoless mind is humanity's healthy mind, and people were not brought up to have egos, we would see a significant

7. Please see Chapter 14 for further discussion of the dynamic and structural homologies between the egocentric mind's conflict with itself and sociopolitical conflict.

diminution in the number of identity-based conflicts. It might even present us with the possibility of a feasible psychology of peace.

Furthermore, if research were to show that the structural conflict of the egocentric mind is contagious, and that it does indeed export this inner conflict to its affairs in the world, it would lend greater urgency to going forward with doing a body of research that will investigate and confirm one way or the other our preliminary finding that the egoless mind is a healthier mind than the egocentric mind.

Let us now take a look at the egoless state of mind.

References

Antrobus, J. S., Singer, J. L., and Greenberg, S. (1966). Studies in the stream of consciousness: Experimental enhancement and suppression of spontaneous cognitive processes. *Perceptual Motor Skills*, 23, 399–417.

Augustine. (2013). *Confessions: St Augustine*, trans. Fr Benignus O'Rourke O.S.A. London: DLT Books.

Barron, E., Riby, L. M., Greer, J., and Smallwood, J. (2011). Absorbed in thought: The effect of mind wandering on the processing of relevant and irrelevant events. *Psychological Science*, 22(5), 596–601.

Beck, A. T., Freeman, A., and Davis, D. D. (2004). *Cognitive Therapy of Personality Disorders*. New York and London: The Guilford Press.

Callard, F., Smallwood, J., Golchert, J., and Margulies, D. S. (2013). The Era of the wandering mind? Twenty-first century research on self-generated mental activity. *Frontiers in Psychology*, 4, 89.

Cheyne, A., Solman, J. A., Carriere, G.J.F., and Smilek, D. (2009). Anatomy of an error: A bidirectional state model of task engagement/disengagement and attention-related errors. *Cognition*, 111, 98–113.

Desjarlais, R. (1989). Sadness, soul loss and healing among the Yolmo Sherpa. *Himalaya, the Journal of the Association for Nepal and Himalayan Studies*, 9(2), Article 5.

Eliade, M. (1964). *Shamanism*. Princeton, NJ: Princeton University Press.

Fox, K. C. Spreng, R. N., Ellamil, M., Andrews-Hanna, J. R., and Christoff, K. (2015). The wandering brain: Meta-analysis of functional neuroimaging studies of mind-wandering and related spontaneous thought processes. *NeuroImage*, 111, 611–621.

Frazier, J. G. (1911). *Taboo and the Perils of the Soul: Golden Bough, Part II*. London: Macmillan and Co.

Freud, S. (1960). *The Ego and the Id*. New York, NY: W. W. Norton.

Hultkrantz, A. (1967). *The Religions of the American Indians*. Berkeley and Los Angeles, CA: University of California Press.

Kanske, P. (2016). *Profiles of Mind Wandering Activity in Psychopathology*. Talk presented at 50th Congress of the German Society for Psychology (DGPs). Leipzig, Germany.

Killingsworth, M. A., and Gilbert, D. T. (2010). A wandering mind is an unhappy mind. *Science*, 330, 932.

Kirsch, I. (2014). The emperor's new drugs: Medication and placebo in the treatment of depression. *Handbook of Experimental Pharmacology*, 225, 291–303. doi:10.1007/978-3-662-44519-8_16.

Kohrt, B. A., and Harper, I. (2008). Navigating diagnoses: Understanding mind—body relations, mental health, and stigma in Nepal. *Culture, Medicine and Psychiatry*, 32, 462–498.

Mrazek, M. D., Smallwood, J., Franklin, M. S., Chin, J. M., Baird, B., and Schooler, J. W. (2012). The role of mind-wandering in measurements of general aptitude. *Journal of Experimental Psychology: General*, 141(4), 788–798.

Nolen-Hoeksema, S., Wisco, B. E., and Lyubomirsky, S. (2008). Rethinking rumination. *Perspectives on Psychological Science*, 3, 400–424.

Oakdale, S. (2005). *I Foresee My Life: The Ritual Performance of Autobiography in an Amazonian Community*. Lincoln: University of Nebraska Press.

Plato. (1995). *Phaedrus*, trans. A. Nehamus and P. Woodruff. Indianapolis, IN: Hackett Publishing Company.

Richle, M. et al. (2001). A default mode of brain function. *PNAS*, 98(2), 676–682.

Schooler, J. W., Reichle, E. D., and Halpern, D. V. (2004). Zoning out while reading: Evidence for dissociations between experience and metaconsciousness. In D. T. Levin (ed.), *Thinking and Seeing: Visual Metacognition in Adults and Children*. Cambridge, MA: MIT Press, pp. 203–226.

Shepard, G. H. (2004). Central and South American Shamanism. In M. N. Walter and E.J.N. Friedman (eds.), *Shamanism: An Encyclopedia of World Beliefs, Practices and Culture*, Volume 1. Santa Barbara: ABC-CLIO, pp. 365–370.

Smallwood, J. (2011). Mind-wandering while reading: Attentional decoupling, mindless reading and the cascade model of inattention. *Language and Linguistics Compass*, 5(2), 63–77.

Smallwood, J., Beach, E., Schooler, J. W., and Handy, T. C. (2008). Going AWOL in the brain: Mind wandering reduces cortical analysis of external events. *Journal of Cognitive Neuroscience*, 20, 458–469.

Smallwood, J., Fitzgerald, A., Miles, L. K., and Phillips, L. H. (2009). Shifting moods, wandering minds: Negative moods lead the mind to wander. *Emotion*, 9, 271–276.

Smallwood, J., McSpadden, M., and Schooler, J. W. (2008). When attention matters: The curious incident of the wandering mind. *Memory & Cognition*, 36, 1144–1150.

Thondup, T. (2015). *The Heart of Unconditional Love: A Powerful New Approach to Loving-Kindness Meditation*. Boston: Shambhala Publications.

Thubten Jinpa. (2015). *A Fearless Heart: How the Courage to Be Compassionate Can Transform Our Lives*. New York, NY: Hudson Street Press, p. 90.

Vyner, H. M. (2007–2008). The dialectical phenomena and processes of the mind. *Imagination, Cognition and Personality*, 27(2), 163–196.

Vyner, H. M. (2009–2010). A preliminary theory of the defining dynamic of the healthy human mind. *Imagination, Cognition and Personality*, 29(3), 225–270.

Walsh, R. (1977). Initial meditation experiences: Part I. *Journal of Transpersonal Psychology*, 9, 151–192.

Walsh, R. (1978). Initial meditation experiences: Part II. *Journal of Transpersonal Psychology*, 10, 1–28.

PART IV
The Egoless Mind

10

THE GOODNESS OF THE NATURAL MIND

The Control of No Control

There is a mirror within the mind, and when you look into that mirror you see your thoughts and emotions, just as you see your face when you look at the surface of a physical mirror. The mind's mirror is the stream of consciousness. When you look into that mirror, you know your mind as the thoughts, emotions, mind-films and epiphanies that appear in your stream of consciousness.

There is a charming and profound story about this mirror of the mind that appears in the biography of Huineng, a Zen teacher who was one of the patriarchs and great masters of the Chan school of Chinese Buddhism.

Chan Buddhism first appeared in China in the sixth century AD, and it is the historical antecedent of Zen Buddhism. Chan took on the name of Zen when it migrated to Japan in the thirteenth century, and Zen is simply the Japanese rendering of Chan.

Chan and Zen both emphasize and cultivate the sudden attainment of enlightenment in a single blazing moment of nondual realization, whereas there are many other traditions in Buddhism that emphasize the gradual attainment of enlightenment after years of study and meditation. Huineng, himself, became enlightened after only eight months of doing nothing but pounding rice as a laborer in the monastic kitchen in which he worked—or so the story goes.

The founder of Chan Buddhism was Bodhidharma, an Indian monk who migrated to China in the sixth century. He was the first Patriarch of Chan. The sixth and final Patriarch was Huineng.

The story of how Huineng became the sixth Patriarch is the story I want to retell here. It is the story of a man who became enlightened even though he was a common laborer in a monastery, and even though he was seen as an illiterate barbarian by everyone else in the monastery. The full and original story can be found in the Platform Sutra (Yampolsky, 1967), which is "the fundamental text of Ch'an Buddhism."

The head monk at Huineng's monastery was nobody less than the fifth Patriarch of Chan Buddhism. One day the fifth Patriarch summoned all of the monks in his monastery to a meeting. He bid them to look into their own true nature and compose a verse that would display their understanding of the original nature of the mind. This was to be a contest in which the writer of the best verse would become the sixth Patriarch.

Huineng, who was working in the kitchen, was completely oblivious to the Patriarch's charge to his disciples. It didn't matter anyway because only one of the monks, Shen-hsiu, who was the head teacher at the monastery, submitted a verse. All of the other monks abstained from writing verses out of deference to their teacher.

Here is the verse that was composed by Shen-hsiu:

> The body is like a Bodhi tree,
> The mind is like a bright mirror stand,
> Time and again brush it clean,
> And let no dust alight.

In essence, this verse expresses the view that the work of a Chan monk seeking enlightenment is to constantly cleanse the mirror of the mind in meditation and keep it free of dust. To be enlightened, in this vision of the Buddhist path, is to keep the mirror in one's mind clean and free of dust.

The fifth Patriarch called the teacher-monk who had written this verse to his chamber and said to him, "The verse that you wrote shows that you have not yet seen your original nature. You are still outside the gate."

The Patriarch suggested that he think it over for a couple of days and see if he could come up with a better verse, but after that the teacher-monk's mind was paralyzed with agitation, and he was stuck in a bad mood. He found himself unable to write another verse.

During this period of time when the teacher was struggling to write a better verse, a young monk came walking by the threshing room where Huineng was pounding rice, and as he walked by he was chanting the teacher's unsuccessful verse. Huineng heard him, and knew right away that the writer of the verse was not enlightened. This common laborer working in the kitchen knew that the writer of this verse had not yet realized his own original nature.

He asked the chanting monk who had written the verse, which led the chanter to explain that the Patriarch had called upon his monks to write a verse to show their understanding of the original nature of mind.

Huineng decided to compose his own verse, and because he could neither read nor write, he asked an official at the monastery to write the verse on the same wall upon which the first verse, the teacher's verse, had been written. Here is Huineng's verse:

> Originally Bodhi has no tree,
> The bright mirror has no stand.
> Originally there is not a single thing:
> Where can the dust alight?

Shortly thereafter, the fifth Patriarch saw the verse on the wall, realized that Huineng was enlightened, and Huineng the barbarian in the kitchen became, although secretly at first, the sixth Patriarch-designate.

The central teaching of Huineng's verse is that neither the mirror nor the thoughts that appear in that mirror exist in the Buddhist sense. "Originally there is not a single thing." He was saying that neither the mirror nor anything else has a permanent identity that is causally independent of the workings of the universe.

The story of Huineng also presents us with two different metaphors for how to keep the mirror in your mind free of dust so that you can see your mind as it really is. One metaphor says that you have to constantly dust the mirror off and keep it clean. The second metaphor makes the liberating claim that the mirror is already clean and that it has always been clean, if you look at it right.

This second metaphor is another way of stating the primary teaching of this parable: the enlightened mind of Buddhism is a mind that realizes that the mirror in the mind is already clean. It is already free of dust, and it has always been free of dust, once you realize that both the mirror and the images that appear in the mirror have no permanent identity. In the language of Buddhism, they are all empty of identity.

Indeed, the mirror has dust on it in the first place only because the mind with an ego thinks that the mirror and the images that appear in the mirror do have a permanent identity, or self-concept. The motes of dust on the mirror are these conceptions of identity.

As long as you think that the images in the mirror have an identity, dust will accumulate on your mirror and distort your view of the images that appear in the mirror. Indeed, this is what causes the dust to appear. This is also why the author of the first verse thinks that the mirror needs constant cleaning. His mind is still putting dust on the mirror, so he is in constant need of cleaning it. This is the first lesson of the story of Huineng.

A second lesson of the parable is that the human mind has two modes of self-awareness; two different ways of knowing itself. There is one mode of self-knowledge in which dust is constantly accumulating on the mirror; and a second mode of self-knowledge in which there simply is no dust.

Huineng's verse depicts the mirror of self-knowledge as being a mirror upon which dust does not alight. When the mind looks into an egoless mirror that is unsullied by dust, it can see itself exactly as it is. This is the mirror in which the egoless mind knows itself.

What then is this dust that appears on the senior monk's mirror? This dust is composed of the concepts of identity that are created by the ego. The ego grasps and attributes an identity to each of the thoughts and emotions that appear in its stream of consciousness, and that causes them to remain on the mirror as dust. To remain in the stream of consciousness as moods and mind-films.

In contrast, when thoughts and emotions appear in Huineng's egoless mirror, the mirror does not grasp or hold on to them by attributing a conceptual identity to them. Indeed, mirrors don't generally do that. This is why dust doesn't accumulate on the mirror of the egoless mind.

Because there is no dust on Huineng's mirror, it is a mirror in which the mind can see itself exactly as it is in every moment. There is no dust to distort or obscure the reflections that appear in his mirror. It is an egoless mirror, if you will.

The mirror that Shen-hsiu the teacher-monk describes is a very different one. It is an egocentric mirror. It is a mirror that grasps your thoughts and emotions, and thinks that they have an identity. This causes dust to accumulate on the mirror of the egocentric mind, and as a result, it is the mirror that needs constant cleaning.

The dust that accumulates on this mirror also keeps the mind from clearly seeing the images that appear in the mirror. As a result, a person with an egocentric mind cannot know their mind as it really is in every moment. You cannot realize your true self in the mirror in which the egocentric mind sees itself.

In summary, the parable of Huineng tells us that the mind has two different ways of knowing itself. It has two different modes of self-awareness. The mirror on which dust accumulates is called the egocentric mode of self-awareness by the science of the stream of consciousness. The mirror on which there is no dust is called the egoless mode of self-awareness. The realizations that the mind has these two basic modes of self-awareness has been one of the key findings of the science of the stream of consciousness (Vyner, 2009–2010).

Goodness and the Control of No Control

The processes of self-awareness and self-control are inextricably bound up with one another in the human mind (Carver and Scheier, 1998; Goleman, 1997; Vyner, 2007–2008). For example, when the watcher becomes aware of a moment of anger in its stream of consciousness, this is a moment of self-awareness. If the watcher then decides that it does not want to express that anger and represses it, this is an instance of self-control. It is in this basic sense that the processes of self-awareness and self-control are entwined with one another.

This action of repressing an emotion is one of the means by which the egocentric mind controls itself. The egoless mind, on the other hand, does not repress emotions.

In other words, the two different modes of self-awareness, the egoless mode and the egocentric mode, employ very different mechanisms of self-control (Vyner, 2009–2010). We have already seen how the egocentric mode of self-awareness marshals the actions of judgement, repression, attachment and following to control the mind. Let's now investigate how the egoless mode of self-awareness controls the mind.

The egoless mind is, if you will, a tiny little mental factory that specializes in manufacturing joy and goodness moment in and moment out, day in and day out. Living in the reservoir of joy and goodness that this factory manufactures changes everything in a person's life.

This natural joy and goodness of the egoless mind is something that you initially begin to discover (in small doses at first) in meditation. It is a state of mind that you can begin to experience in moments while you still have an ego.

The first thing that you will notice is that sometimes a feeling of joy will arise within your mind when you meditate. The next thing you will notice, as your skill in meditation grows, is that there will be times when that joy will remain in your mind even after you stop meditating.

As your meditation continues to mature, that joy will build up and at times it will remain as a constant presence within your mind. As you become more familiar with that joy, it will become apparent that it is mingled with goodness as well. Basically, it feels like the joy and goodness are mixed together as one and the same feeling.

Finally, at some point you will find that these feelings of joy and goodness are actually becoming you. Once again, they become you in the very literal sense that they unite with and become one with your awareness. This joyous awareness is egoless awareness, and its import is that it has nondual awareness of all of the meanings that appear in your stream of consciousness. It knows meanings without layering the dust of self-conceptions on top of them.

When egoless awareness knows itself, it knows itself as this nondual joy and goodness. It is your awareness, and it knows itself as the feelings of joy and goodness. Nonetheless, these feelings and the awareness that knows them are nondual, as observed by Mipham in a short text called *The Nature of Mind:* (Mipham, 2016)

> In seeing it, there is no separate one who sees . . .
> Even looker and looking are one and the same.

Meditation generates this joyous awareness that is saturated with goodness because it allows the stream of consciousness to run free and remain in its natural state. This is once again a scientific statement. It is a simple and verifiable causal sequence that the science of the stream of consciousness articulates as follows:

ALLOW THE STREAM OF CONSCIOUSNESS TO RUN FREE → ABIDING SENSE OF JOY AND GOODNESS WILL BUILD UP WITHIN THE MIND

This causal sequence has the same empirical status as the statement that the sun heats the earth, or the statement that neutrons are composed of quarks. Indeed, several meditation techniques and traditions have been founded upon the success of this basic principle.

The empirical validity of this causal sequence can be assessed because it describes a testable prediction: if you learn to allow your stream of consciousness to run free and remain in its natural state in meditation, you will find that slowly but surely a reservoir of joy and goodness will build up within your mind.

Try it and see for yourself. Once you learn to let your stream of consciousness run free, you will find that it will instill palpable feelings of goodness and joy within your mind.

Once again, there are several meditation techniques that cultivate a state of mind in which the stream of consciousness is left in its natural state.

For example, there are several Buddhist meditation traditions in which allowing the mind to remain in its natural state, which Buddhism calls resting in the nature of the mind, is the central purpose of their meditations. This includes, for example, the DzogChen and Mahamudra traditions of Indo-Tibetan Buddhism and the Shikantaza meditation technique of Soto Zen Buddhism.

A key component of allowing your stream of consciousness to run free is to cease judging your thoughts and emotions as they appear in your stream of consciousness. In this regard, this state of mind is the same as mindfulness as it has been defined by Jon Kabat-Zinn: "Mindfulness is awareness that arises through paying attention, on purpose, in the present moment, non-judgmentally" (Kabat-Zinn, 1994). Ruth Baer elaborates upon this definition by specifically applying it to the stream of consciousness. She says that mindfulness is, "the non-judgmental observation of the ongoing stream of internal and external stimuli as they arise" (Baer, 2003).[1]

One of the rewards of letting your stream of consciousness run free, for lack of a better way to put it, is that the feelings of joy and goodness it generates will in and of themselves make you happy. Simply enough, it feels good to be filled with feelings of joy and goodness.

There is more to be gained though from the accretion of these feelings of goodness and joy. They become the nondual lens through which you see everything in your mind and world. Seen through this nondual lens of joy and goodness, your emotions and mind-films dissolve and become egoless mind.

However, living in this reservoir of joy and goodness is not just a source of happiness. It is also a profoundly moral thing to do. Once you abide in the

1. There has been an interesting discussion about whether or not these contemporary definitions of mindfulness are correct and in keeping with traditional Buddhist definitions of mindfulness. See, for example, Wallace and Bodhi (2006).

goodness of egoless awareness, that goodness becomes the foundation of everything you say and do.

Over and over again, you will find yourself acting out of goodness, as opposed to acting out of the selfish concerns and scripts of your ego. You will manifest this goodness without trying to do so, and it will often take you by surprise. As an added reward, it is fun as well.

In other words, the egoless mode of self-awareness and self-control presents humanity with a different means of cultivating within ourselves the morality and decency that we need to have to live together with one another in a society. As we will seeing, it is also a healthier means of cultivating morality.

The egocentric mind, as we now well know, governs and socializes itself by establishing an identity and controlling the contents of the stream of consciousness so that they conform to that identity. It represses thoughts and emotions it thinks it should not express. It holds on to thoughts and mind-films that flatter its sense of identity, and so forth.

The egoless mind, in contrast, makes itself fit for life in society by allowing its stream of consciousness to run free, which instills a sense of goodness within itself. This goodness is the source of its morality.

This disparity in approach to morality and the stream of consciousness is a reflection of the differing dynamics that define the principal difference between these two types of mind:

1. The egocentric mind is, in essence, a mind that socializes and governs itself by maintaining an identity via the means of controlling its stream of consciousness.
2. The egoless mind is a mind that socializes itself by instilling a sense of goodness within itself. It instills this goodness allowing its stream of consciousness to run free and remain in its natural state, which it is able to do because it does not believe it needs to maintain a permanent concept of identity.

If we compare the two states of mind generated by these two different approaches to the stream of consciousness and socialization, it becomes clear that one of them is a healthier state of mind.

The problem with egocentric mind, once again, is that its mode of self-control engenders the normal pathologies of the ego. The normal pathologies create a state of mind in which people are unable to realize their true self, and in which they live in and act out a miasma of contagious conflict, moods and mind-films.

The egoless mode of self-control, in contrast, generates a state of mind in which a person is moved to realize their true self moment to moment. As we have already seen, it also instills morality and goodness within a person while at the same time being a fount of genuine happiness. Finally, it is a state of mind in which the normal pathologies of the ego do not arise.

Wait a Minute: Don't We Need to Have an Ego? II

At first glance, any suggestion of dispensing with the ego would seem to be a preposterous idea because the ego appears to be utterly indispensable to those of us who have one. It is, after all, the psychological foundation of civilization as we know it. Living with egos as we all do, most of us thoroughly believe that it is nothing less than human nature to have one.

We believe that we would not be able to live either civilized or accomplished lives if we were to somehow wake up tomorrow morning and find that we no longer have egos.

Once again, the ego is the implement we use to accomplish two of the psychological tasks that lie at the very core of being a civilized human being. For one, the ego is the instrument we use to give direction to our lives. It is the tool we use to motivate ourselves to achieve great things, and to guide ourselves in our more prosaic quests to become the kind of mothers, fathers, husbands, wives and children that we have been brought up to be.

Most of all, though, we think that we need to have an ego because it is the tool we use to control our minds and behavior. As social animals, we know deep down that if people are to live together in harmony with one another that we need to control ourselves. Our societies work on the understandable premise that if we didn't control our behavior, we might find ourselves living in a treacherous and amoral human jungle.

After all, no one wants to wake up one morning and find that their gun-toting neighbors have occupied their kitchen and basement and are refusing to leave because they say they need more space. Or that a dictator has taken control of our country and that armed militias are roaming the streets eliminating "undesirable" people, and that we are no longer living in a civil society. Nor do we want to live in a society in which it is acceptable for someone living upstream to pollute the water that the rest of us are drinking downstream.

Thus it is, as a species, that we have clearly found it indispensable to govern both our minds and our behavior. It is an inherent part of living within a social contract. One of the requisites of life in society is that it is incumbent upon those of us living in a society to find shared levels of decency so that we will treat one another well.

Ultimately, of course, we socialize ourselves by controlling our minds. This makes perfect sense given that it is the mind that generates our behavior. Once a group of human beings commits itself to the idea of living together, it becomes inevitable that they will also have to control the workings of their minds.

This is not the end of the discussion, though. The next question, which is a question to which we need to give more thought, is this: what is the healthiest way to control the mind?

Humanity has, to date, displayed a distinct lack of creativity when it comes to this question of governing the mind. Even though human beings have evolved an extravagant number of diverse cultures, we have utilized but one fundamental means of controlling the mind: the ego. We have made the ego more fundamental to the project of being a human being than culture.

All of the societies of which we are aware teach their young to both cultivate an identity and develop an ego that preserves that identity. The Irish have egos. Bengalis have egos. The Tukano of the Ecuadorian Amazon do. The Nuer of the southern Sudan do. Millennials do. It even happens in societies that adhere to religions that call for the abandonment of the ego. As matters stand now, we are all brought up to have egos.

This is a reflection of the fact that we all live in egocentric societies: societies that are organized around the ego, and that propagate the ego from one generation to the next.

But given that the ego governs the mind by constraining the stream of consciousness, and given that this well-intended dynamic creates the normal pathologies of the ego, and that it is probably the ground from which more serious personal and societal pathologies take growth as well, should we not be looking to find a healthier way to "control" our minds and behavior?

As both nature and nurture would have it, it turns out that there is a far healthier way to create decency and harmony between people. We have just seen that one of the fundamental findings of the science of the stream of consciousness is that the egoless mind uses a different means of self-control than the egocentric mind. It controls itself by not controlling itself, and this dynamic, in turn, generates a healthy state of mind that is simultaneously a profoundly moral mind.

How, you might ask, could a human being possibly be a moral person if they allow their thoughts and emotions to run free? This proposition raises two questions that we considered earlier in Chapter 2:

1. Does advocating the cultivation of a state of mind in which the stream of consciousness runs free mean that a person with an egoless mind would act out and express every thought and feeling that comes to mind? Once again, the answer to this question is no, of course not.
2. If science and society were to accept the notion that the egocentric mind is an unhealthy mind, and thus abandon the ego, does this mean that humanity would altogether abandon self-control and even the very notion of a social contract? Once again, the answer is no.

As was said earlier, allowing your stream of consciousness to run free is not at all the same thing as expressing everything you are thinking and feeling. These are two completely different realms of action.

The thought can cross your mind that you would like to tell a person that they are speaking absolute racist nonsense, and that they should shut up, without you actually saying that. Or you can allow the feeling to fully arise within you that you'd like to make love to your wife right here and now, without actually walking on stage and doing it because she is in the midst of giving a brilliant and inspiring lecture.

Nonetheless, to many if not most of us, it will seem at first glance that the idea of allowing our thoughts and emotions to run free is a preposterous thing to do, not to mention counterintuitive. Our fear will be that if we do not control our minds, we will become immoral beings.

As we are already beginning to see, though, it turns out that allowing your stream of consciousness to run free is a profoundly moral and healthy thing to do. Why? We already know the answer to this question. When the stream of consciousness is allowed to run free, the mind spontaneously generates within itself an abiding sense of goodness.

When this natural goodness settles into place, it is no longer necessary to have an ego that controls the stream of consciousness because everything you say and do will be grounded in that goodness. Whereas the actions of an egocentric person are grounded in the emotions, moods and stories created by their ego, the egoless mind is grounded in the goodness that is the natural state of the mind.

A River in Tibet

There is a Buddhist river in Tibet that is famous for its flying fish. There are some people who say the river is Taoist, and yet others who say it is a Bön river. Some say the river is just a metaphor. The river doesn't seem to care; perhaps it is pleased and grateful that Buddhists monks have long come down to the river to learn how to get enlightened.

The Tibetan name for the river translates into English as the Stream of Awareness. As is well known in eastern Tibet, there is much that a fisherman can learn from this river.

There are spots along the river where fish two feet long will jump out of the water and land in your lap if you sit there patiently enough by the stream's edge. Sometimes, the fish that jump into your lap are so large that it is impossible to measure them.

One of the spots where the biggest fish jump out of the water is a quiet and hidden place that is known as "The Fishing Hole with No Name." Then there is a second spot that draws hordes of tourists and fishermen who wear fancy new clothes from L. L. Buddha and fish with the latest gear. That spot is called "The Place of the Greatest Fishermen."

The fishermen who go to the Hole with No Name come and sit peacefully by the river and do nothing at all except take non-judgmental delight in the view. They sit there with empty minds and watch the river go by. The sky is big and blue at the Hole with No Name, and the fishermen who go there feel as big and open as the sky. Innocent rabbits, deer and elk are always sauntering by the Hole with No Name for those who have eyes to see them.

The fishermen who go there always come home with enough fish for all of their friends.

The fishermen who go to the Place of the Greatest Fishermen are different. They go there to become famous. They stand by the river adorned with the latest fishing gear and clothing. They wade into the river with hip boots made by L. L. Buddha, and they stomp around scaring off fish as they cast their lines. They play loud music on their boom boxes, and when a tourist comes by, they never fail to tell them in loud and boasting voices what great fisherman they are. They always claim to have caught the biggest fish ever caught there. But in truth, they almost never catch anything.

When someone comes by and tells them how many fish are being caught up at the Hole with No Name, the great fishermen get very, very angry. They say threatening things to those people and force them to go away. Sometimes, when they have no audience, they talk out loud anyway and tell themselves stories about what great fishermen they really are. They even tell themselves these stories when other people are around.

In Tibet, the fishermen who go to the Hole with No Name are known as the "Fishermen with No Ego." Not surprisingly, the fishermen who go to the Place of the Greatest Fishermen are called "The Fishermen with Egos Bigger Than Their Fish Stories."

Long ago the inhabitants of the area recognized that these two different types of fishermen were actually metaphors for the egoless and egocentric mind. They knew that the egoless fisherman who sat by the edge of the river and waited for the fish to jump into their laps were just like the watcher of the egoless mind. They both do nothing and allow nature to take its course.

And everybody understood that the fishermen who wade into the river in their fancy clothes, tell tall tales and drive off messengers who bring unwanted news are just like the watcher of the egocentric mind.

The descendants of the people who lived in the region close to the Stream of Awareness were not at all surprised when eight centuries later they heard that the science of the stream of consciousness had finally discovered that the qualities that define the difference between the egoless mind and the egocentric mind are precisely the same qualities that define the difference between the egoless fishermen and the fishermen with big egos.

They nodded at one another knowingly when the translations of this new science made their way into the bookstores of their remote little Tibetan towns, and they immediately understood when they learned that this new science had discovered that the mind actually has two different ways of knowing and controlling itself.

After reading one of the new books that contained this science that resembled their ancient wisdom in so many ways, they made a copy of one of the charts they found in that book. The chart summarized the crucial characteristics that define the differences between the egoless mode of self-awareness and the egocentric mode of self-awareness. They had the chart cast onto a bronze plaque

TABLE 10.1 The Two Modes of Self-Awareness

	Egoless Mode of Self-Knowledge	*Egocentric Mode of Self-Knowledge*
Goal	Self-Realization	Maintain Identity
Actions	Nondual Awareness	Judgement, Repression, Attachment, Following
Mode of Awareness of Phenomena that Appear in the SoC	Nondual Awareness	Dual Awareness
Mode of Self-Control	Control of No Control	Control of Stream of Consciousness by Repression, Attachment and Mind-Films
Self-Concepts	Does Not Attribute Self-Concepts to Meanings That Appear in its SoC	Does Attribute Self-Concepts to meanings That Appear in its SoC
State of Awareness	**Simple Awareness:** Only primordial meanings and nondual transformations appear in the SoC. No mind-films or moods appear.	**Complex Awareness:** Primordial meanings appear in tandem with mind-films and moods. Nondual transformations do not occur often.
Nondual Transformations	Frequently	Almost Never
Normal Pathologies of Ego	No	Yes

in both Tibetan and English, and then they placed that plaque on a rugged stone column in the square at the center of their town so that everyone would remember the wisdom it contained.

A multitude of prayer flags flutter over the plaque to this day. Mountaineers come by and read it on the way to losing their egos as they climb the nearby peaks. In Table 10.1 is the English version of the chart that was inscribed on the plaque.

In essence, the chart tells us that in the egoless mode of self-awareness, the watcher has nondual awareness of the meanings that appear in its stream of consciousness. This means that it does not grasp—judge, repress, attach or follow—its thoughts and emotions, and that as a result, the egoless mind is a mind that (Vyner, 2009–2010):

1. Has nondual awareness of the meanings that appear in its stream of awareness and knows them exactly as they are.
2. Lives in a constant state of self-realization in which it able to know and become its true self moment to moment.
3. Abides in a state of simple awareness in which only primordial meanings and the nondual transformations appear in the stream of consciousness.

4. Abides in the joy and goodness that are egoless awareness and the natural state of the mind.
5. Does not generate the normal pathologies of the ego.

In contrast, the egocentric watcher responds to meanings by judging, repressing, attaching and following them when they appear in its stream of consciousness. As a result, the egocentric mind is a mind that (Vyner, 2009–2010):

1. Has dual awareness of its thoughts and emotions.
2. Is, for the most part, unable to know or be its true self.
3. Generates a state of complex awareness in which many layers of moods, mind-films, thoughts and emotions are simultaneously appearing in its stream of consciousness.
4. Does not generate nondual transformations.
5. Does not abide in the joy and goodness that are egoless awareness.
6. Creates the normal pathologies of the ego.

The importance of understanding the two modes of self-awareness is that they give birth to two very different states of mind. The egoless mode of self-knowledge generates the egoless state of mind. The egocentric mode of self-knowledge generates the egocentric state of mind.

We have already seen how the egocentric mode of self awareness generates the normal pathologies of the ego and an unhealthy state of mind. In the next chapter, we will now take a look at the state of mind that is generated by the egoless mode of awareness.

References

Baer, R. (2003). Mindfulness training as a clinical intervention: A conceptual and empirical review. *Clinical Psychology: Science and Practice*, 10(2), 125–142.

Carver, C. S., and Scheier, M. F. (1998). *On the Self-Regulation of Behavior.* New York, NY: Cambridge University Press.

Goleman, D. (1997). *Emotional Intelligence: Why It Can Matter More than IQ.* New York, NY: Bantam Books.

Kabat-Zinn, J. (1994). *Wherever You Go, There You Are.* New York, NY: Hyperion.

Mipham. (2016) *On the Nature of Mind*, trans. Adam Pearcey. www.lotsawahouse.org/tibetan-masters/mipham/nature-of-mind

Vyner, H.M. (2007–2008). The dialectical phenomena and processes of the mind. *Imagination, Cognition and Personality*, 27(2), 163–196.

Vyner, H. M. (2009–2010). A preliminary theory of the defining dynamic of the healthy human mind. *Imagination, Cognition and Personality*, 29(3), 225–270.

Wallace, A., and Bodhi, B. (2006). *The Nature of Mindfulness and Its Role in Meditation.* shamatha.org/sites/default/files.Bhikku Bodhi Correspondence.pdf

Yampolsky, P. B. (1967). *The Platform Sutra of the Sixth Patriarch: The Text of the Tun-Huang Manuscript With Translation, Introduction and Notes.* New York, NY: Columbia University Press.

11

THE EGOLESS STATE OF MIND

The first four times I asked a Tibetan lama named Khenpo Thubten if nondual meanings ever appear in the stream of consciousness, he said no. The fifth time I asked him the very same question, he simply said yes.

The late Khenpo Thubten had a small and admirably primitive monastery up in the mountains overlooking the Kullu Valley in northern India hard by the western border of Tibet. The Khenpo had left Tibet, moved to the Kullu Valley and built his monastery with his own hands after the Chinese invaded Tibet in the 1950s.

The Kullu Valley is a mid-Himalayan valley in northern India that is famous for its apple orchards, the intricate pastel-colored shawls that its women weave by hand and the fine wool jackets that its tailors make for men. Those jackets fall over the hip, and they can keep you plenty warm should you ever be shepherding goats high in the mountains, and they will also do just fine at a party or a lecture in Boston or San Francisco.

You have to hike about an hour from the nearest road over a couple of gentle ridges to get to Khenpo Thubten's monastery, and once you get there, you are treated to unobstructed views of the nearby snow-covered peaks of the high Himalaya lying to the north and east. The name of his monastery is Pongong Gompa, and it is the kind of monastery where there is no indoor plumbing, toilets or electricity. Life is simple there. That simplicity is a reflection of the Khenpo's own simplicity. He had no need for ostentation. There was no vanity.

When it was time for a young reincarnate lama who was studying with the Dalai Lama to do serious study of the writings of the seminal fourteenth-century lama Longchenpa, His Holiness would send the young lama to work with Khenpo Thubten. It is a ten-hour bus ride on a listing and derelict old bus over a sometimes single-lane, sometimes two-lane road that meanders through hills, villages and the occasional market town to get from Dharmasala to the Kullu Valley.

I, myself, first met Khenpo Thubten at DzogChen Monastery in south India in the winter of 1992. I had never heard of him before then. He was not a well-known lama in Western circles, if you will; but I would have to been blind to not see right away that he was unquestionably the real thing. To be around the Khenpo was to feel like you were in the presence of a mountain. He was ancient and immovable, and he didn't care about anything but enlightenment. For myself, I have deep respect for someone like that right away.

Khenpo Thubten granted me permission to interview him, and we did three interviews together that first winter at DzogChen Monastery before he went back north to his own monastery in Kullu. Over the years I visited Pongong Monastery several times to do more interviews with him there before he passed away in 2000.

Looking back, it amuses me that Khenpo Thubten said no the first four times I asked him if there was such a thing as nondual meanings that appear in the stream of consciousness of the egoless mind. Especially since the fifth time that I posed the very same question to him, the answer was yes!

But at the time it was perplexing. For one, I was fairly certain, from my own experience, that nondual meanings do appear in the stream of consciousness. I was also fairly certain that having nondual awareness of the meanings that appear in one's own stream of consciousness is an absolutely essential, as well as an everyday aspect of, the egoless mind.

More than that, I thought that nondual meanings are, as we will be seeing, one of the defining aspects of the egoless mind. That is why I continued asking Khenpo Thubten, with no disrespect intended, about nondual meanings; even though the Khenpo kept saying there were none.

It was by no means an oversight or accident that Khenpo responded with a "no" those first four times. There was a good reason, and I think that we were both well aware of it.

Actually there could have been several reasons. Maybe the Khenpo thought that I might not properly understand a straightforward answer to my question. Or perhaps he might have thought that I was asking the question for the wrong reasons. Or that I might jump to several wrong conclusions if he told me the truth right away and said yes. Or that I might write a book about it some day! Or that it wasn't right to answer such a profound question because I was not a student of his.

Or perhaps he may have wanted to first assess whether or not I understood what I was talking about. To be honest, I never asked the Khenpo why he said no the first four times. Nor did he blink, or show any sign of awkwardness, when finally, after the fifth time, he said yes. Nor did I.

There was no blinking to be done because we both knew, without ever having to say it to one another, that for whatever other reasons he might have had, there was really one principal reason that the Khenpo had said no the first four times: there is virtually a taboo against talking about the experience of nondual awareness in the Buddhist tradition.

Nondual awareness is a synonym for the sacred experience of what is called "emptiness" in Buddhism, and the theory of emptiness, for those of you who aren't familiar with it, is one of the cornerstones of Buddhist philosophy.[1] To be enlightened, for example, is to realize the emptiness of one's own mind. To describe the experience of nondual awareness is no less than describing the experience of having an enlightened mind. If nothing else, it is not something to be shared lightly.

I myself already knew, at the time of these early interviews, that the taboo existed, as I had seen many a lama refrain from talking about the experience of emptiness. I had, for instance, seen several lamas abstain from answering questions at public talks about the experience of emptiness. This happens all of the time. Furthermore, in my interviews, there had already been many a time when lamas had, especially at first, been reluctant to answer any questions I might ask about nondual awareness.

I also knew that there were understandable reasons for this reluctance. For one, there is a feeling abroad in the Buddhist world that it is the better part of wisdom to refrain from talking about one's own experiences of emptiness and nondual awareness. That attitude is grounded in the belief that if you talk about your experiences of emptiness, you will lose the wisdom and realization that those experiences have granted you.

There was, in addition, a fundamental philosophical rationale for the lamas' reluctance to talk about the experience of emptiness. There is a sword of Damocles, if you will, that hangs over one's head when the subject of talking about nondual awareness and emptiness arises, and it is aptly articulated by a dictum from Nagarjuna that that is found in his *MulaMadhyamakakarika*:[2]

> The victorious ones have said
> That emptiness is the relinquishing of all views.

This famous verse has been taken, by many, to mean that the realization of emptiness, which is regarded as the experience that makes you enlightened, has no content. It has no "view," as Nagarjuna says. The implied assertion here seems to be that the experience of emptiness is the experience of nothingness. Therefore, there is nothing to talk about.

1. Many thick and turgid volumes have been written about emptiness over the centuries. But a quick introduction to the meaning of the term is that it means that neither a person nor a phenomenon has a permanent identity, or essence. In the language of Buddhism, both people and phenomena are said to be *empty* of having a static identity.
2. Nagarjuna. (1995). *The Fundamental Wisdom of the Middle Way: Nagarjuna's Mulamadhyamakakarika*, trans. J. Garfield. New York: Oxford University Press.

This is one of the predominant interpretations, although not the only one, of Nagarjuna's dictum that "emptiness is the relinquishing of all views," and it is an interpretation that has had an outsized influence on the history of Buddhist philosophy.

Nagarjuna, for those of you who are not familiar with the history of Buddhism, founded the Middle Way school of philosophy, and the Middle Way school is roundly regard by Buddhists as the most advanced and influential school of Buddhist philosophy.

No serious Buddhist would contradict the Middle Way's fundamental positions, although there are different subschools of the Middle Way school that give different interpretations to Nagarjuna's seminal theory of emptiness.[3]

Ultimately, the notion of emptiness means that neither a human being nor a phenomenon has a permanent essence, or identity. Let me just repeat that for emphasis: neither a human being nor a phenomenon have a permanent essence that can be articulated as an identity or self-concept. A person, for example, is said to be empty of identity.

The underlying rationale, in Buddhist philosophy for this theory of emptiness, is the assertion that neither a human being nor any of the other phenomena in the universe has a permanent character that is causally independent of the rest of the universe.[4] From this perspective, any personal identity that you might think you have is an illusion.

Emptiness means that neither you nor the book that you are holding in your hand right now has a permanent identity. Both you and the book are impermanent because both of you are always changing in dependence upon your causal interactions with the rest of the universe. If you were to leave this book in the bow of a sailboat berthed in a tropical marina for a year, you would find it mildewed on your return.

The importance and centrality of the theory of emptiness in Buddhism, and the unassailability of the Middle Way school that produced this theory, derives from the fact that one of the core tenets of Buddhism is that the act of thinking that you have a personal identity is the ultimate cause of unhappiness among all human beings.

Indeed, the foundation of the Buddhist path is this belief that human beings suffer and are unhappy because we think we are someone. In the words of the Dalai Lama: "All our suffering is rooted in the grasping of an independent self." (Dalai Lama, 2015)

The solution to the problem of suffering, from this perspective, is to realize that your identity is an illusion, let it go and cultivate an egoless mind.

3. However, there are also important schools of Buddhist thought that take the position that the experience of emptiness does have content; that there is something there.
4. This perspective is expressed and epitomized in the Buddhist doctrine known as "The Twelvefold Chain of Dependent Origination," an explanation of which can be found in just about any text on Buddhist philosophy. See for example Harvey (1990).

If, like Khenpo Thubten, you have accepted as correct the Middle Way theory that people and phenomena are empty of having a permanent self, this would probably mean that you have also accepted Nagarjuna's view that emptiness has no views, no content.

This would, in turn, mean that there could not possibly be anything to say about the nondual experience of emptiness. In this analysis, there is nothing there in the experience of emptiness that one could talk about. And this explains why many lamas, including Khenpo Thubten, will often not answer questions about nondual awareness and the experience of emptiness.

But then why did the Khenpo say yes the fifth time around? And why have so many other lamas been willing to discuss and describe the egoless state of mind in our interviews once we got to know one another? Indeed, this is, in fact, what happened.

Furthermore, here I am in the midst of writing a chapter that proposes to describe the egoless state of mind. Is that possible? Is it possible to do so without violating Nagarjuna's dictum? Is it a helpful thing to do? If you were given accurate descriptions of the egoless state of mind, would it help you understand the egoless mind? Would it help you better understand how to cultivate an egoless mind? The answer is yes on all counts.

Is There Anything to Be Learned?

There are, indeed, a few important things that one human being can learn from another human being about the egoless mind that will help them understand how to cultivate an egoless mind. This is, of course, one of the reasons that Buddhist practitioners write and read books. Describing the egoless mind is also essential to the scientist investigating the nature of the healthy mind.

Here is an example of what can be learned: imagine that you are talking with a wise and elderly Tibetan lama, a lama who is roundly regarded as being enlightened. Let's say that the lama is the late 16th Karmapa.[5] Imagine further that in the course of answering a question that the Karmapa tells you that the egoless mind is a mind that knows that the contents of its thoughts, emotions and mind-films are not true. He says that the egoless mind knows that the contents of its thoughts, emotions or mind-films are not real because it understands that they are illusions created by the ego, just as the reflections of mountain in a lake are not really the mountain itself.

If you were to think, for a moment, that you were seeing an airplane sitting on top of Mount Everest, a moment of reflection will tell you that your

5. The Karmapa, like the Dalai Lama, is a reincarnate lama. He is a reincarnate lama in the Karma Kagyu lineage of Tibetan Buddhism, and the sixteenth Karmapa was roundly regarded as being enlightened.

thought could not possibly be true. For the egoless mind, it is the same for all of the emotions, moods, and stories that the ego creates. It knows they are not true.

Coming from a trusted source like the Karmapa who really knows the egoless mind, this piece of information could be very helpful. If you were to believe and take to heart this counterintuitive description of the workings of the egoless mind, it would change the way you relate to your own mind. You would stop believing that the contents of your thoughts, emotions and so forth are real. You would see a recursive mind-film that is critical of someone else, or a bad mood, as a product of the judgmental machinations of your ego and not believe them. And this would take you a long way towards developing an egoless mind.

Why? Because, this is exactly what the egoless mind does: it does not believe that the realities depicted by the ego's thoughts, emotions and mind-films are real. It knows that they are fictions created by the remnants of your ego, and it lets them flow by unbelieved. In contrast, the egocentric mind does believe the emotions and films it creates.

This understanding has important consequences. If you don't believe that your thoughts are real, it opens the door to not grasping them. If you see a pink elephant in your backyard, you won't turn and run in fear. It is the same with thoughts and emotions. If you know they aren't real, you won't repress or hold on to them. You will, instead, let them flow by, and as a result, you will have nondual awareness of them and realize their suchness as they dissolve.

Here's a second example of how information about the egoless mind can be useful and have practical consequences. You will find it familiar. Suppose an enlightened person told you that nondual meanings really do appear in the stream of consciousness of the egoless mind. This would be helpful too. Why? Because then you would know that there are nondual egoless meanings that you can express in action and words without indulging or strengthening your ego.

Then the question arises: How would you recognize a nondual meaning? How would you tell the difference between a nondual and dual meaning? Here is a passage from an interview with Lopon Tegchoke in which we discuss this issue. In response to one of my questions, Lopon Tegchoke asked me to describe the attributes of a nondual inner appearance, which is the same as a nondual meaning. As I described the qualities of a nondual meaning, he then confirmed them (Vyner, 2005):

HMV: Given that it is possible to have nondual awareness of an inner appearance, is it also possible to have nondual awareness of an outer appearance?

LTC: When you say nondual, what do you mean?

HMV: Well, let's talk about that.

LTC: OK.

HMV: When I talk about nondual appearances, what interests me most, are the nondual inner appearances. And for me, Lopon, a nondual appearance is, for one, an appearance that has not been grasped. It is an appearance that has not been accepted, rejected or followed.

LTC: OK.

HMV: Two, it is an appearance that has dissolved.

LTC: Oh yes.

HMV: And three, as a result of its dissolution, you will experience either a moment of egoless awareness or a moment of primordial wisdom. This is what I mean by nondual awareness of an inner appearance.

LTC: Yes. That's acceptable.

With this kind of information in hand, it becomes easy to tell the difference between dual and nondual meanings. If you have not yet become completely egoless, this is helpful because dual meanings created by the ego will still be appearing in your stream of consciousness.

Once you learn how to differentiate between nondual and dual meanings, you can free yourself to express nondual meanings when they appear and dissolve. At the same time, you will then be able to allow dual meanings to flow by without expressing them because you know they are just egocentric meanings.

This does not, however, mean that you would or should repress dual meanings and hold on to nondual meanings. This would just be more ego process.

What you would do, however, is permit your stream of consciousness to run completely free, and when nondual meanings appear, simply go ahead and express them. On the other hand, egocentric dual meanings will, at some point, cease to appear in your stream of consciousness, and when that happens, it will no longer be necessary to discern which meanings are nondual.

Here is yet another description of the egoless mind that is a good example of how describing the egoless mind can be helpful. It comes from a text named the "Ganga Mahamudra Upadesa" by Tilopa, an eleventh-century Indian practitioner of a Buddhist tradition called Mahamudra[6] (Tilopa, 2015):

> Look directly into one's own mind, until awareness is revealed in its bare nakedness.
> Let the polluted pool of mental activity clear itself. Merely watch the flow, just as it is.
> Do not engage with appearances as they arise, for (the enlightened mind) is beyond acceptance and rejection . . .
> Let the mind rest in itself, spacious and un-preoccupied with thought.
> When the mind is not possessed by aims, that is Mahamudra.
> When this is realized, that is Great Enlightenment!

6. Tilopa is a historically important practitioner and teacher of Mahamudra. This passage is from his famous instructions to a student named Naropa, who was himself a seminal figure in the Mahamudra tradition.

This is a straightforward set of instructions. Here Tilopa is saying that if you "merely watch the flow" of the stream of consciousness and abstain from "acceptance and rejection," that "the polluted pool of mental activity (will) clear itself." He adds that when you "Let the mind rest in itself, spacious and un-preoccupied with thought . . . that is Great Enlightenment!"

This passage would be helpful to someone wanting to cultivate an egoless mind in a number of ways. In essence, it tells the reader that to cultivate an egoless mind, all that has to be done is leave your thoughts in their natural state. Do not judge them negatively and repress them. Nor should you judge them in a positive light and hold on to them.

This passage also tells us much more in what it leaves unsaid. It tells you that there are so many things that you don't have to do to cultivate an egoless mind. For example, it tells you that ultimately there is no need to:

1. Analyze your thoughts.
2. Determine if a given thought is an expression of your ego or your true self.
3. Try to understand why you are thinking the particular thoughts you are thinking, as we often do in Western psychotherapy.

Here is the focus of this pedagogical passage: it teaches its readers that the primary skill that they have to develop to cultivate an egoless mind is to learn to do nothing; to do nothing to their thoughts and emotions and allow them to go wherever they will go.

It also tells you that there is something else to let go of as well. When you find that you are doing something to your thoughts—for example, repressing an emotion or holding on to a thought, just let your actions go as well; which will allow your thoughts and emotions to remain in their natural state. If you can just do this, "the polluted pool of mental activity (will) clear itself."

Once again, this is a crucial aspect of cultivating an egoless mind. If you really do abstain from judging, repressing, attaching and following your thoughts and emotions, then you will have nondual awareness of them.

Nondual awareness will, in turn, initiate the nondual transformation of those meanings, and those transformations will, in turn, give birth to egoless awareness and the nondual meanings of the egoless mind.

This brings us back to Khenpo Thubten and the question of why he said no four times, and then said yes the fifth time.

The Risk Inherent in Describing the Egoless Mind

Even though receiving a description of the egoless mind can be helpful to a person trying to cultivate an egoless mind, there is, to be sure, a risk in being presented with a description of the egoless mind.

The risk that one takes, in receiving a description of how the egoless mind works, is that you could end up cultivating an egocentric mind. You could turn the described state of mind into a state of mind that you would seek to cultivate and preserve, just as the egocentric mind cultivates and preserves an identity.

One of the defining qualities of the egoless mind, is that unlike the egocentric mind, it does not seek to either attain or maintain any predefined states of mind. The egoless mind, as emphasized by Longchenpa and others in their descriptions of self-liberation, is a mind that leaves its stream of consciousness in its natural state, and in so doing, it is a mind that abstains from seeking a predefined state of mind. If you try to cultivate a specific state of mind, you will not become egoless.

By allowing its stream of consciousness to run free and seek its own natural end, the egoless mind creates and recreates itself over and over again in every moment. Allowing the stream of consciousness to run free generates and regenerates the goodness and joy of egoless awareness, and at the same time, it simultaneously creates moments in which the mind realizes its true self.

The egocentric mind, in contrast, does seek to abide in a predefined state of mind, and the usual state of mind that it strives to create and perpetuate is an identity. As we have seen, the ego nourishes its sense of identity by governing its thoughts, emotions, films and behavior so as to ensure that they will conform to its identity. The is one of the defining differences between the egoless and egocentric minds.

One could, however, make the case that the egoless state of mind is actually an egocentric mind because it seeks a predefined state of mind, too. You could argue that the state of mind sought by the egoless mind is one in which the stream of consciousness runs free and has perpetual nondual awareness of itself.

This is an adroit analysis, but it is not quite correct.

It is, to be certain, true that the egoless state of mind can be described, and that one essential aspect of that description is that it is a state of mind in which the mind stream runs free and that as a result the egoless mind has constant nondual awareness of all of the meanings that appear in its stream of consciousness. In a sense, this could be construed as the egoless mind's identity.

However, the egoless mind is not an egocentric mind for one simple and profound reason: it does not control its stream of consciousness to attain the egoless state of mind. It cultivates the egoless state of mind by allowing its mind stream to run free. This is the crux of the matter, and it is the defining dynamic of the egoless mind.

If the egoless mind tried to control its stream of consciousness, it would not be an egoless mind. This would be true for three principal reasons: (1) it would not abide in egoless awareness (2) it would not be able to know its true self and (3) it would generate the normal pathologies of the ego. In other words, it would become an egocentric mind.

However, by leaving its stream of consciousness in its natural state, the egoless mind is egoless because it is able to (1) abide in egoless awareness (2) live in a series of moments of nondual awareness in which it knows its true self and (3) abstain from generating the normal pathologies of the ego.

Remember, the cause of nondual awareness is letting the stream of consciousness run free and remain in its natural state. The only way you can have persistent nondual awareness of the meanings in your stream of consciousness is to let your mind stream run free, which allows you, in turn, to know the suchness of your own mind:

ALLOW SoC TO RUN FREE → NONDUAL AWARENESS OF MEANINGS

NONDUAL AWARENESS OF MEANINGS → KNOW THE SUCHNESS OF YOUR MIND

By virtue of allowing its stream of consciousness to run free, the egoless mind abstains from the act of trying to cultivate a predefined state of mind. This is why it is not an egocentric mind. The egoless mind abstains from enacting the control dynamic that defines the egocentric mind and its pursuit of a permanent identity. Nor does the egoless mind divide itself into good and bad moral moieties.

However, this still leaves the danger that I mentioned earlier. The danger is this: if you articulate a description of the egoless state of mind, either for yourself or others, you definitely run the risk of creating a situation in which you turn the egoless mind into an egocentric mind. Once again, the risk is that you would turn the described state of mind into a goal that is to be sought after, just as an egocentric mind pursues its identity.

Here's an example of how that could happen. Suppose you were taught that an egoless mind is a mind in which thoughts never appear, and that as a result, you make this a goal of your meditation practice. Your goal would be to cultivate a state of mind in which thoughts cease to appear.

Here is how a person with this goal in mind could turn this state of mind into an egocentric identity: they would repress thoughts when they appear in their stream of consciousness, and they would try to hold on to those moments when thoughts have ceased to appear.

This would be a case of turning a (mistaken) description of the egoless mind into an egocentric state of mind. In this situation, the cessation of thoughts has become an identity that you are seeking to maintain because you are trying to control your stream of consciousness so that thoughts will cease to appear.

This, then, is the real danger of articulating a description of the egoless state of mind. A person trying to cultivate an egoless mind might turn the described state of mind into an egocentric goal—an identity, if you will.

However, if you really understand that the crux of the cultivating the egoless state of mind is to allow your stream of consciousness to run free, this would not be a danger.

Indeed, this is an excellent reason to describe the egoless state of mind. If the description is done well, it will bring its recipients to the understanding that the crux of cultivating an egoless mind is to abandon the ego's Sisyphean control dynamic and simply learn to let your stream of consciousness run free. This may well be why Longchenpa explained the import of allowing the mind stream to run free and self-liberate so often in his writings.

Let's now move on to describing the egoless state of mind in more detail.

The Simplicity of the Egoless Mind

The egoless mind is a profoundly simple state of mind. Those who have realized the egoless state of mind often marvel at just how simple it really is. The egocentric mind, in contrast, is a most complicated mind.

The egoless mind is so simple that one can capture and completely describe the appearing aspect of the egoless state of mind by making but two assertions.

The first one is that the egoless mind is simply a series of moments of nondual awareness. It is a series of moments in which the mind has nondual awareness of each and every meaning that appears in its stream of consciousness.

A thought appears. The egoless mind has nondual awareness of the thought, and the thought dissolves and disappears. An emotion appears. The mind has nondual awareness of the emotion, and the emotion dissolves and disappears. Occasionally, a mind-film will arise, and the egoless mind will have nondual awareness of it as well, which will cause the film to dissolve and disappear too.

The second assertion is that the egoless mind is a series of moments of nondual transformation. Indeed, the egoless mind abides in a constant state of nondual transformation.

As thoughts and emotions dissolve in the light of nondual awareness, they are spontaneously converted into different aspects of the egoless mind by a nondual transformation. Sometimes thoughts and emotions are transformed into nondual meanings, and sometimes they are transformed into egoless awareness itself.

A single thought might be transformed into a moment of amused compassion. A mind-film in which you are imagining what other people think of you might be transformed into a moment of goodness, a moment of doubt might be transformed into a moment of nondual realization and so forth.[7]

One can plausibly make the case that this is a complete description of the dynamics of the egoless mind. It is simply a state of mind in which the nondual transformation of meanings is constantly occurring because the mind has constant nondual awareness of them.

This simplicity of the egoless state of mind is promising. It tells us that all that needs to be done to cultivate an egoless mind is develop a state of mind in which you have nondual awareness of each of the meanings that appear in your stream of consciousness. If you can learn this one skill, everything else will take

7. It should also be said that nondual realizations can also appear on their own as a moment of nondual awareness, without their first being a transformation of a pervious dual or predual meaning.

care of itself. The transformations that create the egoless state of mind will follow automatically on their own.

How does one cultivate the nondual awareness of meanings? This is simple too, at least in theory. Once again, all that needs to be done is stop judging and controlling your stream of consciousness and allow it to pursue its own natural course. This is the independent variable that causes nondual awareness. The resulting moments of nondual awareness will, in turn, generate the goodness and self-realizations of the egoless mind. There is nothing more to be done.

I can almost hear the fourteenth-century Tibetan lama Longchenpa laughing as I write. Longchenpa, who captures the letter and spirit of the self-liberating mind as well as anyone in his writings, would from time to time exalt and take delight in about just how simple the enlightened mind really is. Well-meaning authors—including Longchenpa himself—have written tome after lengthy and complicated tome about the enlightened mind, and those tomes make it seem as though the egoless mind is a complicated state of mind that is difficult to attain. But actually, as Longchenpa likes to emphasize, it is really simple.

Here is Longchenpa laughing at the simplicity of the natural mind in a poetic text called *Naturally Liberated Mind, the Great Perfection* (Thondup, 1996):

> Since everything is but an illusion,
> Perfect in being what it is,
> Having nothing to do with good or bad,
> Acceptance or rejection,
> One might as well burst out laughing!

Longchenpa is saying here that the egoless mind is simply a state of mind in which the watcher allows the stream of consciousness to remain in its natural state. In essence, the egoless watcher is totally open to its stream of consciousness. It refrains from judging, repressing, attaching or even believing any of the meanings that appear in its stream of consciousness. In Longchenpa's words, the egoless mind has nothing to do with "good or bad, acceptance or rejection."

He affirms here that ultimately, all one has to do to develop an egoless mind is cultivate the egoless awareness that allows your stream of consciousness to remain in its natural state and thereby transform itself into egoless mind in every moment.

Cultivating this egoless mode of awareness is, thus, the central task on the path to developing the egoless mind. Egoless awareness is an awareness that is saturated in the joy, goodness and compassion that are generated by the nondual transformations; but most of all, once it becomes a stable presence in the mind, it continues to generate the egoless state of mind over and over again in every moment.

Egoless Awareness

The mind has but one awareness. The awareness that knows the world in which we live is the same awareness that turns inward and knows your thoughts and feelings. If it is not apparent to you that this is true, close your eyes for a moment and look at your mind, and then open them and look around. That should make it clear.

When this singular awareness looks at its stream of consciousness, it is called the watcher by the science of the stream of consciousness. The two terms awareness and watcher can be used interchangeably.

Self-awareness, the mind's awareness of itself, occurs when the watcher knows the phenomena that appear in its stream of consciousness.

Given that the watcher has two modes of self-awareness—an egoless mode and an egocentric mode—there are also two types of watcher: an egoless watcher and an egocentric watcher.

The two types of watcher respond differently to the stream of consciousness, and as a result, they have a different type of awareness of the meanings that appear in the stream of consciousness. The egoless watcher has nondual awareness of the stream of consciousness, and the egocentric watcher has dual awareness of the stream of consciousness.

The egoless watcher is thus the subjective aspect of the egoless mind. The nondual phenomena it knows are its objective aspect. The remainder of this chapter will now describe egoless awareness and its experience of the egoless state of mind it creates.

The Experience of Egoless Awareness

A. Goodness

Awareness is able to know itself. Egoless awareness knows itself as the nondual feelings of joy and goodness that are generated by the nondual transformations. When these feelings of joy and goodness become a stable presence in the mind, they unite with, and thus become nondual with, awareness itself. This is the experience of abiding in egoless awareness.

When these feelings of joy and goodness become nondual with awareness, the resulting awareness is nondual in a second sense as well. It has nondual awareness of the phenomena that appear in their stream of consciousness.

Even though egoless awareness is an unmistakable feeling of goodness, it is virtually impossible to explain how you know that this feeling is goodness. Nonetheless, when you feel it, there is no doubt in your mind that it is goodness. You just know that it is.

One of the reasons that you know that this feeling is goodness, or as the Dalai Lama says a "warm heart," is that you'll find yourself consistently meaning well in the world. You will often find yourself spontaneously acting out of a manifest goodness without consciously willing it. You will also feel like you could not possibly try to hurt another human being, animal or your self. This feeling is noticeably different than the egocentric emotions of anger and jealousy that can move you to want to hurt someone.

Another reason that you know it is goodness is that you will naturally find yourself wanting to see what is real and good in everyone else and yourself. If, as you look at your mind, you see the foolishness of your ego, for example, you will look through the foolishness to see the true self that lies within it. You will see everyone else in exactly the same light as well.

You will find yourself automatically looking through your own ego, and everyone else's ego as well, to see what is real and good beneath the surface. All of this will come spontaneously. When you are abiding in the goodness of egoless awareness, you don't have to make an effort to see things in this light.

A delightful bonus of living in this goodness is that it just simply feels good. It genuinely feels good to be effortlessly good to other people. It also feels good because the goodness also contains feelings of peacefulness and equanimity. You feel at peace, and you feel that there is no need to do anything to change yourself when your mind is grounded in these feelings.

Finally, the goodness of the egoless mind is invariably mingled with a sense of joy. It's a joy that makes you feel glad to be alive; glad to just be your self; glad to have the opportunity to share your goodness with other people; and glad to touch that which is genuine and good in each and every one of them.

This goodness—and the joy and equanimity with which it is saturated—is egoless awareness. Sometimes it appears for just a moment. Sometimes it might stay with you for months at a time.

B. The Intensification and Stabilization of Egoless Awareness

The egocentric watcher, as we now well know, creates the normal pathologies of the ego by grasping the meanings that appear in its stream of consciousness in the process of knowing them. Grasping initiates the bundle of causal processes that create both the normal pathologies and the state of complex awareness.

As the egocentric watcher grasps thoughts and emotions, it causes mind-films and moods to appear and take up residence within the stream of consciousness. When this happens, the stream of consciousness becomes very busy. The films and moods generated by these egocentric causal sequences cover over and hide the natural goodness and joy that are egoless awareness and make it unknowable, like a cloud covering the sun.

Meditation changes all of this. It unravels the complications of the egocentric state of mind, and in so doing, it reveals the mind's natural goodness.

The first step in restoring the mind to the simplicity of egoless awareness is to do a concentration meditation that distracts the watcher from its routine of grasping meanings. As you concentrate on an object in meditation, you will sometimes become so focused on the object that you will stop paying attention to and grasping thoughts and emotions. For example, if your attention is tightly focused on your breath, there will be moments when you stop attending to your thoughts, and as a result, you will forget to judge and grasp them as well.

These first moments in which the watcher abstains from grasping its thoughts are the beginning of a crescendoing process that engenders the goodness and joy that eventually become a stable egoless awareness.[8]

Here's how it works: when the watcher abstains from grasping thoughts and emotions in meditation, it causes itself to have spontaneous nondual awareness of the meanings that it knows in those moments. Here is just one example of the many causal sequences that shows how the mind causes itself to have nondual awareness of itself the meanings that appear in its stream of consciousness:

WATCHER DOES NOT GRASP THOUGHT → WATCHER HAS NONDUAL AWARENESS OF THOUGHT

When the watcher has nondual awareness of a thought, emotion or mind-film, it will often trigger the immediate occurrence of a second causal sequence in which a nondual transformation occurs.

It is these nondual transformations that cause the first moments of nondual joy and goodness to begin to dawn in the stream of consciousness. It is possible, as we already know, to observe and describe each of the nondual transformations that engender the goodness and joy of egoless awareness within the mind. Here are a few examples of the several causal sequences that describe the nondual transformations that bring to life the abiding goodness and joy of the egoless mind:

NONDUAL AWARENESS OF → NONDUAL TRANSFORMATION OF ANGER JOY OCCURS

NONDUAL AWARENESS OF A MIND-FILM → NONDUAL JOY

NONDUAL AWARENESS OF THE EMOTION OF ANGER → DISSOLUTION

NONDUAL AWARENESS OF A FLATTERING THOUGHT → NONDUAL GOODNESS

As the mind becomes more and more adept at having nondual awareness of its meanings, the nondual transformations will occur more often. As they become more frequent, that is when the reservoir of goodness and joy builds up within your mind.

It actually feels as though there is a deep well of joy and goodness within you, and it also feels as if it is getting fuller and fuller.

As the reservoir swells and fills, your experience of that joyful awareness becomes palpably stronger in two senses. First, it grows in intensity and becomes

8. The mechanism by which meditation causes the cessation of grasping will be described at length in Chapter 13.

more apparent. It is the same as if a weak light were to become brighter. As the strength of the joy increases, it becomes brighter and more visible.

Second, it becomes stronger in the very specific sense that it becomes a more stable and durable presence within the mind. It becomes more and more resistant to disappearing.

When the mind first begins to experience the goodness and joy of egoless awareness, they aren't stable. Egoless awareness might disappear for a moment, or an hour or a day if, for example, a strong emotion arises and becomes a mood that covers it over; or if you get caught up in believing a mind-film. In other words, the goodness will often disappear in the presence of a mood or mind-film.

Eventually, though, the goodness and joy become so strong that they won't disappear when an emotion or film appears, and this is the second sense in which this joyful awareness becomes stronger.

As the joy and goodness become more apparent and durable, they become the stable egoless awareness of the egoless mind. This egoless awareness has, of course, nondual awareness of whatever meanings appear in its stream of consciousness, and the increasing occurrence of nondual awareness will, in turn, strengthen egoless awareness even more by causing the more frequent occurrence of the nondual transformations that generate realizations, compassion, joy and goodness.

Egoless awareness begets more egoless awareness.

C. Egoless Awareness as Space

The egoless awareness that is generated by the nondual transformations behaves like a space.

When a solid object moves through a physical space—be it a jet or a solid ball dropped from the Tower of Pisa—it seems to us, for the most part, that space does not interfere with the movement of these objects. Leaving aside general relativity and the effects of the curvature of space on the movement of large astronomical objects, the physical space in which we live our lives does not appear to have an effect upon the movement of the everyday objects that pass through it.

The same is true of egoless awareness. It is a space through which the stream of consciousness flows unimpeded. The egoless stream of consciousness flows through egoless awareness unhindered and unaltered, like a wild river that has not been dammed.

In comparison, egocentric awareness is not at all like a space. The egocentric stream of consciousness is impeded in many ways as it flows past the egocentric watcher. Remember, the egocentric watcher is forever and always trying to alter the movements and contents of its stream of consciousness to make them match its identity.

Unlike the egocentric watcher, the egoless watcher does nothing at all to the meanings that flow by in its stream of consciousness. It does not repress moments of anger, pride, jealousy or sadness. It does not narrate and live in mind-films that allow you to take delight in and pretend to have done great thing you haven't actually done. Nor does it create or indulge in moods.

Egoless awareness does nothing because it feels no need to be anybody. It is not in the business of being or preserving an identity. It just sits peacefully on the riverbank beside your stream of consciousness and watches that stream flow by. Paradoxically enough though, by doing nothing, the egoless watcher generates the egoless state of mind.

The import of this space-like quality of egoless awareness is that it is the independent variable that causes the occurrence of both nondual awareness and the nondual transformations that give birth to the egoless state of mind.

The nondual transformations do a number of things to foster the egoless state of mind. They reveal and sustain the joy and goodness of egoless awareness. They allow the emotions, moods and mind-films of the ego to dissolve and clear the stream of consciousness. They engender the growth of compassion. And they grant a constant stream of nondual realizations to the person who has an egoless mind.

Here is a description of the transformative qualities of egoless awareness that comes from an interview with the Bön lama Lopon Tenzin Namdak. This passage is part of a larger passage that was presented earlier in Chapter 6, but I'm presenting it again, because it is a very unique and special description of transformative space-like quality of egoless awareness. In this passage, Lopon Tenzin Namdak describes how egoless awareness is a space within which self-liberation, which is the Tibetan term for the nondual transformations, occur as the mind has nondual awareness of itself (Vyner, 2007):

HMV: The nature of mind knows itself. Does it not?

LTN: Ah yes. Then how to know it?

HMV: When the nature of mind[9] knows itself, is that self-awareness?[10]

LTN: Yes. Self-knowing. Clear. Knowing means knowing something precisely right. No mistake. How does it know itself? You yourself can't make a prescription. You know it by your self. No method. We have a saying: Sharp knife does not cut itself. Then how do you know?

HMV: That's what I want to talk to you about. [Shared laughter] My first question today is a follow-up on one of the interviews we did eight years ago. In that interview you were talking about the space that is the nature of mind.

LTN: Um hm.

HMV: And you said, "You cannot take any negative actions in that space."

LTN: Yes. [Emphatic]

9. The technical term nature of mind (Tib.: sems-nyid) is a synonym for egoless awareness.
10. Rang-rig is the Tibetan term that is being translated here as self-awareness.

HMV: "Therefore, this space is also called pure, or kadag."

LTN: Um hm.

HMV: What do you mean when you say that you can't take any negative actions in that space?

LTN: Negative actions are taken by consciousness.[11] So this nature is completely beyond all of the consciousnesses and senses. It doesn't care about negative actions, positive actions. Good, bad or nothing. So that is the meaning.

HMV: Are you saying that all of the appearances that arise in that space are self-liberated?[12]

LTN: Sure. Sure. So this nature is very special. You can't compare it to any other space. [That space] itself is clear to itself. [That space] itself is empty, and empty is clear. No separation. We only create separate terms so we can understand each other. Unification. Everything is the natural state. No separation. So nondual awareness, rigpa is also called clarity.

HMV: Does clarity refer to appearances?

LTN: You can't say that the nature has qualities.

HMV: OK.

LTN: Space cannot be changed. When clouds come, it is not changed. Space is space. Whatever is coming and going, space does not stop the clouds, or wind or storms. Whatever comes, let them come. Let them disappear. But space is there. All the consciousnesses, thoughts, senses, everything can come, but it doesn't do anything to change the basic nature.

HMV: Would it be correct to say that this nature that is like space doesn't follow the consciousnesses that come, and that as a result, they dissolve and self-liberate?

LTN: Sure. The thoughts, the consciousnesses, are coming from the nature. They themselves are nature because whatever bubble comes from water, they are visible, but they are water. Bubbles, reflections, everything, comes from water. Into water and it is water. Everything is an empty form.

HMV: Are empty appearances nondual appearances?

LTN: Yes. If you realize that, then you don't need to do anything, only do more and more practice . . .

HMV: When a thought is self-liberated, what happens to the thought?

LTN: Well nothing happens. It comes from the nature into nature. The thought itself is nature. It's like a reflection in water. When you see a reflection, it is all as water. You can see them, but it is water. It is an empty form, but it comes from nature, into nature and is never separated from the nature. So if

11. Once again, Lopon is using the term "consciousness" here to refer specifically to individual dual minds such as thoughts, emotions and so forth.

12. Self-liberation is a technical term in DzogChen, and the cultivation of self-liberation is the defining principle of DzogChen practice. In addition, the egoless mind is a mind in which self-liberation is constantly occurring. The Tibetan term for DzogChen is "rang-drol." The phenomena that the science of the stream of consciousness calls the nondual transformations are equivalent to the self-liberations of DzogChen.

a great practitioner is clearly knowing, and he doesn't care about whatever comes, that's the watcher. Whatever comes spontaneously will stay a little while, disappear and be liberated back into the nature. It doesn't go away from the nature at all.

HMV: So there are appearances.

LTN: Yes. If you look at the thoughts as they disappear, afterwards, you can see things, hear things. Don't judge, that state is clarity. Explaining it is not right. You must have the experience. That is wisdom self-awareness, or the natural state.

In this passage, Lopon makes it clear that in his experience, egoless awareness behaves like a space, a space that has the ability to transform the thoughts and emotions that flow through it.

Indeed, when you close your eyes and look at your mind through the lens of egoless awareness, you experience your mind as being an inner space through which the stream of consciousness is able to flow unimpeded.

As Lopon Tenzin Namdak says in the passage above, that space is also experienced as a place within which all of the meanings that appear in the stream of consciousness dissolve and are transformed into the elements of the egoless mind.

D. The Foundation of the Egoless Mind

Egoless awareness is the foundation of the egoless mind because in addition to being the psychological space within which nondual awareness and the nondual transformations occur, the nondual transformations that it generates also give birth to the other healthy qualities of the egoless state of mind.

In sum, the nondual transformations of egoless awareness generate the egoless state of mind in the sense that they:

1. Engender and sustain egoless awareness.
2. Transform pre-dual primordial meanings into the nondual primordial meanings of the egoless mind.
3. Generate the nondual realizations.
4. Know the suchness of the meanings the mind gives to the present moment, which makes it possible for the mind to realize its true self.
5. Give birth to the simple state of awareness in which the egoless mind abides.
6. Prevent the creation of the normal pathologies of the ego.

The Experience of the Nondual Transformations

A. Nondual Transformations and the Realization of True Self

The egoless state of mind is a series of moments of nondual awareness. Each moment is composed of the appearance of a meaning, the subsequent nondual awareness of that meaning and the resulting nondual transformation.

An egoless moment will often begin with the appearance of a primordial meaning that gives meaning to the present moment by articulating a response to the experience you are in the midst of having.

When a primordial meaning appears in the stream of consciousness, egoless awareness will, of course, have immediate nondual awareness of the meaning. As a result, the primordial meaning will immediately dissolve and disappear.

This dissolution is an indication that nondual awareness has occurred, and in and of itself, it is also a nondual transformation. It is a metamorphosis in which a primordial meaning is transformed into nothingness—the absence of any phenomena in the stream of consciousness:

NONDUAL AWARENESS OF PRIMORDIAL MEANING → DISSOLUTION

In the moment that the primordial meaning dissolves, it becomes a nondual meaning and the mind knows the content of that meaning as it really is. When the mind knows the suchness of a primordial meaning in this way, it knows its true self in that moment. It tells you exactly how you see and feel about the moment in which you are presently immersed.

The dissolution of a primordial meaning will sometimes be immediately followed by another nondual transformation that produces the second type of nondual meaning that gives meaning to the present moment: a nondual realization.

NONDUAL AWARENESS OF PRIMORDIAL MEANING → REALIZATION

Once again, a realization is experienced as a large insight (Vyner, 2005). It could be an insight into how to structure this chapter. It could be an insight into the nature of the egoless mind. It could be an insight in which you understand that the cement that binds President Trump and his base together is a narcissistic collusion (Mika, 2017).

Given that a realization is a nondual meaning that the egoless mind gives to the present moment, it is another type of moment of awareness in which a person knows their true self.

B. Nondual Transformations and the Fate of Egocentric Meanings in the Egoless Mind

However, unless you are completely egoless, the egoless mind will not always have nondual awareness of the meanings that appear in its stream of consciousness.[13]

13. A completely egoless mind is a mind that lives in egoless awareness all of the time and as a result has nondual awareness of every single meaning that appears in its stream of consciousness. However, the attainment of a completely egoless mind is difficult and rare. A completely egoless mind is equivalent to the enlightened mind of Buddhism.

There is, however, a more attainable egoless state of mind that is also a healthy mind: the partially egoless mind (PESoM). The primary difference between the completely egoless state of mind (CESoM) and partially egoless states of mind is that even though the partially egoless mind abides in egoless awareness for a majority of the time, it is not able to do so all of the time, as the completely egoless mind does.[14]

There will be, in the partially egoless mind, occasional moments in which the watcher grasps a meaning. That grasping, in turn, will initiate causal processes that generate the appearance of dual egocentric meanings. That dual meaning could be, for example, an emotion, a mind-film or a mood.

When the watcher of the partially egoless mind grasps a meaning, it often happens unconsciously. For the most part, you won't be aware that you are grasping a meaning in the moment that you grasp it.

What will happen, though, is that you will become aware of the appearance of a film or an emotion, and this will tell you that you have just grasped a meaning.

If your egoless awareness is stable, you will not believe the egocentric meaning that has been produced by an isolated moment of grasping. If this is indeed the case, you will have swift nondual awareness of the dual meaning in question, and it will dissolve.

These moments in which the mind has nondual awareness of egocentric meanings will also produce nondual transformations. As we already know, there can be nondual transformations of the emotions, moods and mind-films. These transformations will be more likely to generate and regenerate egoless awareness, although they can also give birth to nondual meanings.

These transformations regenerate egoless awareness by creating momentary appearances of different aspects of egoless awareness. This would include nondual joy, nondual goodness, amused compassion, dissolutions and the appearance of inner light.

The nondual transformations that continue the process of generating egoless awareness are the same ones that we cited in our analysis of how meditation generates egoless awareness in the first place. Here, again, is a representative sample of those nondual transformations:

NONDUAL AWARENESS OF MIND-FILM → NONDUAL JOY

NONDUAL AWARENESS OF EMOTION → NONDUAL GOODNESS

NONDUAL AWARENESS OF MIND-FILM → AMUSED COMPASSION

NONDUAL AWARENESS OF MOOD → DISSOLUTION

14. For further discussion of the partially egoless mind, and the differences between it and the completely egoless mind, please see the "Overview" section of Chapter 12.

Given that egoless awareness tends to have nondual awareness of all or most of the meanings that appear in its stream of consciousness, the bulk of the phenomena that appear in the egoless mind stream will be primordial meanings and their nondual transformations.

A primordial meaning appears, the mind has nondual awareness of that meaning, the meaning dissolves and a nondual transformation occurs. Then the next primordial meaning appears, and this begins the next moment.

However, on those occasions in which the watcher does grasp a meaning, the emotions and films that appear as a result will, in the usual course of affairs, dissolve right away. In other words, if the egoless awareness of a partially egoless mind is reasonably stable, it will have prompt nondual awareness of them as well.

The consistent occurrence of these dissolutions produces a clarity of mind. The egoless stream of consciousness is a clear and uncluttered stream of consciousness because given that the films, emotions and moods usually dissolve as soon as they appear, they do not remain in the stream of consciousness and clutter it up.

The absence of grasping in the egoless mind, whether it be total or almost total, allows all of the silt to settle to the bottom of the stream, and this makes it possible for the mind to see clearly all of the phenomena that continue to appear in the stream as they give meaning to the present moment.

In contrast, the egocentric stream of consciousness is cluttered and opaque because the egocentric watcher routinely grasps the meanings that appear in its stream of consciousness. As a result of these grasping actions, the egocentric stream of consciousness is usually clogged with contrapuntal layers of emotions, moods and multiple mind-films. This makes it difficult to either be aware of, or accurately discern the content of, individual meanings.

C. The Nondual Transformations in DzogChen Mind Science

It is worth noting, for a moment, that the DzogChen traditions of Tibetan Buddhism and Bön both recognize and confirm the existence of the nondual transformations. The nondual transformations are called self-liberations by DzogChen mind science.

Self-liberation and the nondual transformations are the same phenomena in the sense that they are both processes in which nondual awareness transforms a meaning into egoless mind. They can transform meanings into either egoless awareness itself or a nondual meaning.

Here is a passage from an interview with Khenpo Tsewang Gyatso in which the Khenpo confirms that empirically, self-liberation is the same phenomenon as the process that is termed a nondual transformation by the science of the stream of consciousness. In this passage, he confirms that nondual awareness can transform both primordial meanings and emotions into egoless mind, and he calls both of these transformation self-liberations (Vyner, 2018):

HMV: When nondual awareness recognizes a primordial meaning as a self-appearance[15] and primordial wisdom appears, is that self-liberation?[16]

KTG: Yes.

HMV: Thank you. When nondual awareness recognizes the emptiness of anger, and the anger becomes the mirror-like wisdom[17] it has always been, is that also self-liberation?

KTG: Yes. Yes. [Emphatic.]

HMV: So they are both self-liberation.

KTG: Yes.

HMV: In general then, when a primordial meaning becomes the primordial wisdom that it has always been, is that self-liberation?

KTG: Yes.

HMV: And in the same way, when nondual awareness recognizes the emptiness of an emotion and it becomes the primordial wisdom that it has always been, this is also self-liberation.

KTG: Yes.

The interesting thing to notice about DzogChen discussions of self-liberation is that they assert that allowing the stream of consciousness to run free is all that one need do to cultivate nondual awareness and the nondual transformations.

The unmistakable flavor of DzogChen discussions of self-liberation is that they emphasize, and indeed take delight in pointing out, that all you have to do to cultivate an egoless mind is nothing. The idea is that by doing nothing your stream of consciousness will run free and spontaneously self-liberate and transform itself into egoless mind in every moment.

Here is a verse from the DzogChen master Jigme Lingpa's *Vajra Verses on the Natural State* in which he describes the simplicity of self-liberation (Lingpa, 2015):

> Good thoughts, bad thoughts, and those in between,
> Without slipping into any such categorization,
> Are freed upon arising, without any agent to make distinctions.

15. Tib.: rang-nang.
16. This is a description of a nondual transformation in which nondual awareness transforms a primordial meaning into a realization. For further discussion of realizations, please see the section titled "Nondual Meanings: Primordial Wisdom" in Vyner (2005).
17. Tib.: melong yeshe. This is another question in which I describe a nondual transformation and ask the Khenpo if this is an example of self-liberation. In this transformation the mind has nondual awareness of an emotion, and that emotion is transformed into egoless awareness, which is called mirror-like wisdom here. This is a nondual transformation, and once again, Khenpo says that it is an instance of self-liberation.

> As long as awareness does not lose its own ground,
> There is no need for anything more than this.

"There is no need for anything more than this." All you have to do to realize the egoless mind is give up the dualistic labor of categorizing thoughts into "good thoughts, bad thoughts, and those in between."

The assertion here is that if you cease judging your thoughts and leave your stream of consciousness in its natural state, everything else will take care of itself. Nondual awareness and the nondual transformations will occur spontaneously, and they will generate the compassion, joy, goodness and self-realizations of the egoless mind in every moment.

Ultimately, of course, it is egoless awareness that allows the stream of consciousness to run free, and this is why it is the foundation of the egoless mind. The egoless mind is the state of mind that develops naturally when the egoless watcher allows the stream of consciousness to run free.

We have already seen that allowing the mind stream to run free generates moments of nondual awareness, the nondual transformations, nondual meanings and egoless awareness itself. In the remainder of this chapter, we will now explore further this egoless state of mind that is generated by egoless awareness and its nondual transformations.

First, we will establish that the egoless mind does not cause itself to suffer as the egocentric mind does. We will do so by showing that the workings of the egoless mind do not engender the normal pathologies of the ego.

Then the final sections of the chapter will systematically explain how egoless awareness and the nondual transformations create a state of mind in which a person becomes their true self in every moment.

The Diminution of Endemic Suffering

The routine workings of the egocentric mind cause unhappiness and psychological pain. This pain is both indigenous to, and unique to, the egocentric mind.

There are two broad mechanisms by which the ego causes pain: (1) it creates states of mind that are painful in and of themselves and (2) it blocks the mind's access to egoless awareness, which would otherwise prevent the formation of the egopoietic states of mind that are painful.

The unhappiness of the egocentric mind is, of course, caused by the normal pathologies of the ego. Here are some examples of the mechanisms by which the normal pathologies cause pain and the loss of happiness:

1. The emotions and moods created by the ego can be, in and of themselves, painful.
2. The structural conflict of the ego causes a person to fight with and lose their ability to be their true self. This can cause confusion and the loss of peace of

mind. Most of all it causes a person to lose the joy of knowing that they are being the person they really are.
3. The recurring mind-films created by the ego are scripts that propel a person into the dysfunctional and painful relationships.
4. The ego's emotions, moods and films blanket over, and cause the mind to lose access to, the joy and goodness that are egoless awareness.

The normal pathologies of the ego are brought to life, as we have seen, by the grasping actions that the egocentric watcher takes to control its stream of consciousness. Once again, repressing an emotion causes that emotion to remain in awareness as a mood. Holding onto a thought causes the thought to remain in the stream of consciousness as a mind-film. Repressing thoughts and feelings that give meaning to the present moment, creates a conflict between the watcher and the stream of consciousness. These are all routine consequences of the ego's control dynamic.

The egoless mind, in contrast, does not grasp the meanings that appear in its stream of consciousness. It has instead nondual awareness of all of the meanings that it knows. As a result, the normal pathologies of the ego do not generally occur in the egoless mind, nor is pain an endemic presence in the egoless mind. Unpleasant emotions can appear in the egoless mind, but given that egoless awareness has nondual awareness of them, they dissolve in in the moment that they appear.

Most of all, though, the egoless mind abstains from egopoietic suffering because it lives in the joy and goodness that are the natural state of the mind. In the absence of grasping, and in the absence of the films and moods that the ego inserts into the stream of consciousness, the egoless mind abides and lives in the joy and goodness of egoless awareness, which in and of themselves make life a delight—even in the face of adversity.

The Natural State of the Mind

The natural state of the mind is the state of mind that is generated when the stream of consciousness is allowed to run free. When the mind stream is allowed to pursue its own natural course, the silt of the stream of consciousness—the mind-films emotions and moods—settle into awareness and dissolve. This will generate a state of mind in which:

1. The mind abides in egoless awareness.
2. The mind has nondual awareness of all of the meanings that appear in its stream of consciousness.
3. Nondual transformations occur constantly in every, or almost every, moment of awareness.
4. The mind is able to know and express its true self.

This state of the mind is natural in the sense that it is the state of mind that develops spontaneously on its own when the ego stops controlling the stream of consciousness.

In the natural state of the mind, meanings dissolve as soon as they appear. A mind-film appears, and in that instant it immediately dissolves and is transformed into joy. A subtle thought that is a primordial meaning dissolves and is, without delay, immediately transformed into a realization. A moment of desire dissolves and becomes a moment of goodness.

This means that in the natural state of the mind, which is the same as the egoless mind, all of the meanings that appear in your stream of consciousness are transformed into either joy, goodness, compassion or realizations in the moment that they arise within the mind. If you do not have an ego, the mind becomes a mechanism that is perpetually producing a constant stream of dissolutions and nondual transformations.

The egoless awareness that allows this nondual dynamic to unfold is also the natural state of the mind. It too, appears naturally within the mind when the ego leaves the stream of consciousness in its natural state. Nothing else has to be done to make it appear, and at the same time you cannot make it appear.

Empirically, egoless awareness and the nondual meanings it knows are inseparable; they are nondual if you will. They are both epistemologically and ontologically nondual. Meanings become epistemologically nondual only when the mind has nondual awareness of them, and the mind has nondual awareness of meanings only when they dissolve into, and become ontologically nondual with, awareness. Nondual meanings become nondual when they are known by egoless awareness.

Finally, egoless awareness engenders both itself and the entire natural state of the mind. By allowing the mind stream to run free, it initiates the nondual transformations that generate the joy and goodness of egoless awareness and perpetuate the natural state of the mind.

In sum, as the watcher gives up the Sisyphean labor of trying to control the stream of consciousness and allows the natural state of the mind to develop, it causes egoless awareness, nondual meanings and the nondual transformations to appear spontaneously within the mind. Left to its own devices, a free flowing stream of consciousness will, on its own, generate all of these elements of the egoless state of mind.

Life is the natural state of the human body. The egoless state of mind is the natural state of the human mind.

True Self as Nondual Awareness of the Meanings Given to the Present Moment

The primary virtue of the egoless mind is that, unlike the egocentric mind, it gives a person the ability to know and be their true self moment to moment, and to experience the joy and goodness that come with being their true self.

For the egoless mind, the self is neither an identity, nor a concept of who you are, as the self is for the egocentric mind.

For the egoless mind, knowing the true self is a matter of knowing the suchness of the meanings that you give to each and every present moment in that moment itself. The egoless mind is able to know the suchness of the meanings that it gives to the present moment because it has nondual awareness of them as they appear in the stream of consciousness.

Knowing and being your true self begins—and I want to stress the word "begins"—with knowing the suchness of the two types of meaning that the mind gives to the present moment: the primordial meanings and the nondual realizations.

To know the suchness of a primordial meaning is to know its content accurately, to know it as it really is. To know the suchness of a primordial meaning one must (1) refrain from projecting any egocentric constructs onto it in the process of becoming aware of it and at the same time (2) have nondual awareness of it.

The first step in knowing the suchness of a primordial meaning is to abstain from grasping it, which keeps the mind from superimposing other meanings onto it.

To put it another way, to know the suchness of a primordial meaning, that meaning must be known by itself, and not in tandem with other meanings. To know a primordial meaning by itself is to know it without there being any emotions, moods or mind-films present in the stream of consciousness at the same time.

In the absence of these egopoietic meanings, spontaneous nondual awareness of a primordial meaning will occur, and this is the second step of knowing the suchness of a meaning.

Here is a rough analogy that begins to explain what it means to know the suchness of a meaning. The analogy is rough because it uses using external phenomena, whereas meanings, of course, are inner phenomena.

Suppose you are climbing a mountain with a friend, and your friend is leading as you are climbing a wall through a whiteout. The temperature is minus 20 degrees, and the wind is blowing 40 knots—which makes it difficult for the two of you to hear one another. Your friend realizes she is getting hypothermic, and she decides that she should let you know. She yells down to you, "I am getting too cold." But the words are difficult to hear because the wind is both noisy and blowing her words off course.

If you hear your friend say, "I'm getting too old," you have definitely not heard the suchness of her words. If you hear her say "I'm getting too cold," and if you have also understood her precise intent in saying these words, you have heard their suchness.

Knowing the suchness of the primordial meanings is one aspect, again just one aspect, of knowing your true self. They are a person's true self because they give meaning to a present single moment, and in so doing, they create intention in response to that moment. To know the suchness of a primordial meaning is to consciously know exactly how you see and feel about, and how you want to respond to, the present moment.

A primordial meaning might be the feeling of taking delight in the innocence of a bird singing in the early morning as you wake up. Or it might be a single subtle thought that tells you to check the weather and see if there is enough snow up on the pass to go skiing.

Here is a passage from an interview with Khenpo Tsewang Gyatso in which he explains that having nondual awareness of a primordial meaning is the same as knowing one's self. The Khenpo also confirms, in this passage, that various aspects of the enlightened mind—the primordial meanings, primordial wisdom and the three aspects of the enlightened mind[18]—are indeed one's self; although they are not a self that is equivalent to the "self-characterized" self, or self-concept, of Western discourse and the egocentric mind:

HMV: Here is a quote from the interview we did two days ago. You said, "Recognizing a primordial meaning as one's self[19] is the primordial wisdom of egoless awareness."[20]

KTG: Yes.

HMV: One of the things that intrigues and interests me here is your use of the word self: "recognizing a primordial meaning as one's self." At first glance, that sentence sounds like it is not a Buddhist sentence. Buddhism says that human beings and phenomena don't have a self. I don't have a self. These flowers don't have a self. And so forth.

KTG: Yes.

HMV: What did you mean by saying that recognizing a primordial meaning is one's self?

KTG: One's self does not mean that it is a self-characterized self.[21] It means that the self is not other than the primordial meaning. Nor is it other than primordial wisdom. Not other than the three aspects of the Buddha's enlightened mind.[22]

HMV: Would it be correct to say that recognizing your self is the same as recognizing your Buddha nature?

KTG: Yes.

HMV: Would it be correct to say that your self is your Buddha nature?

KTG: Yes.

18. Tib.: sku sum.
19. Khenpo is basically saying, in this quote, that when the mind has nondual awareness of a primordial meaning, this is a moment of enlightened, and thus egoless, mind. He describes a moment of nondual awareness, here, as being a moment in which awareness recognizes a primordial meaning as being an appearance of one's self. (Tib.: rang nang) What is most intriguing here is that Khenpo is also saying that a primordial meaning is actually an aspect of one's self.
20. Tib.: rigpa'i yeshe.
21. By saying here that the genuine self is not a "self-characterized self," Khenpo is saying that the self is not a conceptualized self, or identity. The self to which the Khenpo is referring here is the true nature of the mind. It is not a conceptual self that has been constructed by the ego.
22. Khenpo is saying here that various aspects of the enlightened mind—the primordial meanings, primordial wisdom and the three aspects of the enlightened mind (Tib.: sku sum)—are the self.

HMV: That is fair?

KTG: Yes.

HMV: Thank you.

Given that knowing the suchness of your primordial meanings is one aspect of knowing your true self, a second dimension of knowing your true self is to know the suchness of your realizations, or as the Khenpo says here, primordial wisdom. Once again, realizations are the second type of meaning that the mind gives to the present moment.[23]

Realizations are a nondual transformation of a primordial meaning, and they arise in the immediate wake of having nondual awareness of a primordial meaning. When the mind has nondual awareness of a primordial meaning, the nondual transformation of realization occurs:

NONDUAL AWARENESS OF PRIMORDIAL MEANING → NONDUAL REALIZATION

The nondual realizations gives meaning to the present moment by showing you the larger significance of a moment. A realization shows you what that moment reveals about how you see your self, your life and the larger world in which you are living. It reveals a piece of the larger vision, or personal cosmology if you will, in which you live. This is a second aspect of your true self.

True Self as Nondual Awareness of Everything Else as Well

To consistently know and be your true self, it is not enough to have nondual awareness of just the meanings you give to the present moment: the primordial meanings and nondual realizations. To have sustained knowledge of your true self, one must also have nondual awareness of all of the other meanings that appear in your stream of consciousness as well. This includes, most of all, the egopoietic meanings.

If, instead, you were to have dual awareness of the other meanings that appear in your stream of consciousness—the egopoietic meanings—it would cause you to lose your ability to have nondual awareness of the primordial meanings and realizations. Here's why.

The watcher has two basic options in regards to the way it knows any meaning that appears in its stream of consciousness. It can either grasp a meaning and have dual awareness of it, or it can abstain from grasping and as a result, have nondual awareness of a meaning (Vyner, 2005).

23. Tib.: de khona nyid togpa'i yeshe. This term translates as "suchness primordial wisdom," and it is equivalent to the nondual phenomenon that is called "realization" by the science of the stream of consciousness. Please see Chapter 6 for a thorough discussion of the phenomenon of realization. Please see Vyner (2005) or Chapter 6 for a thorough description and discussion of realizations.

When the watcher grasps and has dual awareness of a meaning, it causes emotions, moods and films to both appear and remain present in the stream of consciousness. We have already seen many of the causal sequences that make this happen. To review, here are some examples of those sequences once again:

Repression of an Emotion → Appearance of a Mood

Attaching a Thought → Activation of a Mind-Film

Belief in the Content of → Continued Projection of A Mind-Film

The important thing to understand here is that if you grasp the emotions, thoughts and films that appear in your mind, they will remain present in your stream of consciousness and create a residual multilayered weave of meanings within your stream of consciousness. As a persistent presence in the mind, this contrapuntal fabric of residual meanings will block your ability to have nondual awareness of the meanings that give meaning to the present moment: the primordial meanings and the realizations.

These emotions, moods and films preclude nondual awareness because they form an opaque epistemological wall, if you will, between the watcher and whatever new meanings might appear in the stream of consciousness to give meaning to the present moment. This wall makes it impossible for the egocentric mind to clearly discern, much less have nondual awareness of, both the primordial meanings and realizations, and the egopoietic meanings as well.

However, if you have nondual awareness of all of the meanings that appear in your stream of consciousness, or at least most of them, that epistemological wall will not be erected in your mind. When you have nondual awareness of the egopoietic meanings, they will of course dissolve and disappear, which makes it possible, in turn, for you to clearly see and have nondual awareness of the primordial meanings and realizations.

This, then, is the reason that it is imperative for the watcher to have nondual awareness of the egopoietic meanings as well. For the mind to know its true self by having nondual awareness of the meanings it gives to the present moment, it is essential that the emotions, moods and mind-films not become an abiding presence within the stream of consciousness. For this to happen, the mind must have nondual awareness of all of the egopoietic meanings as well.

When the mind does have nondual awareness of its egopoietic meanings, they do not remain present in the mind because they will dissolve in the moment that they are known. This causes the bricks of the ego's epistemological wall to vanish before they can be cemented into place, and as a result, the mind is able to have nondual awareness of, and thus realize the suchness of, the primordial meanings and realizations that give meaning to the present moment. This in turn, makes it possible for a person to know and be their true self.

Nondual Transformations and the Realization of the True Self

The nondual transformations are another indispensable aspect of one's true self. They are indispensable because they generate two of the essential elements of the egoless mind.

The first element is the nondual realizations. We have already taken note, in the previous section, of how the realizations are generated by the nondual transformations, which are, again, one of the two types of constructs that the mind creates to give meaning to the present moment. If the nondual transformation of realization did not occur, the mind would have nondual realizations.

Secondly, the nondual transformations do something even more fundamental. They generate and continually regenerate egoless awareness. It is essential to continually regenerate egoless awareness because only then will it be a stable presence in the mind.

It is essential that egoless awareness be a continual presence in the mind because it is the foundation of the egoless mind's ability to know its true self. It is the subject that has nondual awareness of, and thus knows the suchness of, all the meanings that appear in the stream of consciousness; and as such it is also the agent that generates the nondual transformations. If egoless awareness were not a persistent presence in the mind, it would not be possible for the mind to know its true self with any consistency, or in any larger sense.

The nondual transformations create and recreate egoless awareness by causing the nondual goodness and joy of egoless awareness to appear and increase within the mind. Here are two by now familiar examples of the many different causal sequences that reveal egoless awareness:

NONDUAL AWARENESS OF EMOTION → NONDUAL TRANSFORMATION OF GOODNESS

NONDUAL AWARENESS OF MIND-FILM → NONDUAL TRANSFORMATION OF JOY

In other words, when the mind has nondual awareness of its emotions, moods and films, it sets in motion a dynamic that at first creates and then later adds to the reservoir of joy and goodness that becomes egoless awareness. These resulting nondual transformations strengthen, stabilize and make more resilient the egoless awareness that knows your true self. This is the second reason that the nondual transformations are an indispensable component of the egoless mind.

The Natural State of the Mind Is the Egoless Mind

We have just seen that the egoless mind is able to know its true self because it has nondual awareness of all of the phenomena that appear in its stream of consciousness. The sustained nondual awareness of one's own mind is the cornerstone of realizing your true self.

Nondual awareness is the cornerstone of self-realization because it initiates an ongoing nexus of causal processes that generate and regenerate the egoless

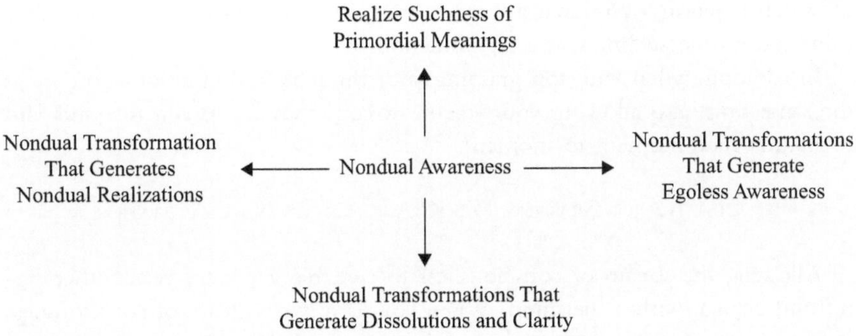

FIGURE 11.1 The Causal Nexus of Nondual Awareness

state of mind in which a person is able to constantly know their true self moment to moment. Figure 11.1 is a schematic diagram of the nexus of causal processes generated by nondual awareness.

This diagram summarizes all of the causal processes initiated by nondual awareness that make it possible for the egoless mind to know its true self. They generate:

1. Realization of the suchness of the primordial meanings.
2. The nondual transformations that create the nondual realizations.
3. The nondual transformations that generate and regenerate egoless awareness itself.
4. The clarity of mind that makes the ongoing occurrence of nondual awareness possible.

However, this still leaves us with an important underlying question: what is the independent variable that causes the mind to have the ongoing moments of non-dual awareness that grant a person the ability to know and express their true self?

We already know one answer to this question: the principal cause of dual awareness is grasping, and the principal cause of nondual awareness is the cessation of grasping.

If the mind does not grasp a meaning that has appeared in its stream of consciousness, it causes itself to have nondual awareness of that meaning:

Cessation of Grasping → Moments of Nondual Awareness

The cessation of grasping is the key that unlocks the door to nondual awareness and knowing your true self.

Nonetheless, the cessation of grasping is not, in and of itself, the same phe-nomenon as nondual awareness. The cessation of grasping is a halting of a class of watcher actions. Nondual awareness is a mode of awareness in which the mind knows the suchness of a phenomenon.

In addition, when you stop grasping your thoughts and emotions, you are at the same time, also allowing your stream of consciousness to run free and find its natural state moment to moment:

CESSATION OF GRASPING → SoC ABIDES IN ITS NATURAL STATE

Allowing the stream of consciousness to run free generates yet another significant change within the mind. When you leave your stream of consciousness in its natural state, it generates the natural state of the mind:

SoC IS ALLOWED TO RUN FREE → NATURAL STATE OF MIND DEVELOPS

Indeed, this is the definition of the natural state of the mind. The science of the stream of consciousness defines the natural mind as being the state of mind that spontaneously develops on its own when the ego stops controlling the stream of consciousness. It is the state of mind that emerges naturally when the watcher stops judging, repressing, attaching and indulging in the meanings that appear in its stream of consciousness. And this is, of course, a very different state of mind than the egocentric state of mind.

Think of it this way. Before the Colorado River was dammed, it would flow from its source beneath La Poudre Pass in the Rocky Mountains of northern Colorado all the way to its mouth at the north end of the Gulf of California in Mexico. However, the river has not been in its natural state for more than half a century now. Dams and aqueducts have been built in abundance, and large volumes of water are lost to domestic consumption, irrigation, the formation of lakes and the generation of electricity.

As a result, the river no longer reaches the Gulf of California. In most years, the last hundred miles of the riverbed are dry. The Colorado River is no longer in its natural state.

Now imagine what would happen, though, if all of the dams and aqueducts on the Colorado River were removed. The river and its surrounding ecosystems would return to their natural state, and the river would flow all the way to the Gulf of California.

The same is true of the mind. When the ego stops controlling the stream of consciousness, the mind returns to its natural state. The state of mind that automatically develops when the stream of consciousness is allowed to pursue its natural course is the natural state of the mind. Once again:

SoC IS ALLOWED TO RUN FREE → SPONTANEOUS DEVELOPMENT OF THE NATURAL STATE OF MIND

The spontaneous state of mind that develops when the stream of consciousness is allowed to run free is one in which the mind:

1. Abides in egoless awareness.
2. Realizes the suchness of the meanings it gives to the present moment.
3. Has nondual awareness of all of the meanings that appear in its stream of consciousness.
4. Generates nondual transformations of the meanings that appear in its stream of consciousness.

If you think about this list for a moment, it tells us that the egoless mind and the natural state of the mind are one and the same state of mind.

For one, they both have the same cause. They are both the state of mind that naturally and spontaneously develops when the watcher abstains from grasping and controlling the stream of consciousness. They are both the state of mind that develops when the mind allows stream of consciousness to run free and pursue its natural course.

Secondly, both states of mind are composed of the same constituent elements and processes. Both minds: (1) abide in egoless awareness (2) have nondual awareness of, and thus realize the suchness of, the meanings it gives to the present moment (3) have nondual awareness of all of the other phenomena that appear in its stream of consciousness as well (4) generate nondual transformations of the meanings that appear in its stream of consciousness and (5) have an uncluttered and clear stream of consciousness.

Finally, the natural mind and the egoless mind are both states of mind in which a person is able to realize their true self. More than this, the constituents of the true self are also the constituents of the egoless mind and the natural mind. They are all one and the same. In other words, the natural state of the mind *is* a person's true self.

The egoless awareness, nondual awareness, nondual transformations, primordial meanings and nondual realizations that arise when the mind is left in its natural state also constitute a complete list of all of the elements of your moment-to-moment true self. To know the elements of the natural state of your mind is to also know the elements of your true self. The egoless mind, the natural mind and the true self are all one and the same state of mind.

Given that allowing the stream of consciousness to run free is the foundation of the egoless state of mind in which one is able to know and be one's true self, our final step in understanding the healthy mind will be to determine how to cultivate a state of mind in which the mind stops grasping itself and allows the stream of consciousness to remain in its natural state. This is the subject of our next chapter.

References

Dalai Lama. (2015). *18 Great Stages of the Path (Lam Rim) Commentaries*. https://www.dalailama.com/videos/18-great-stages-of-the-path-lam-rim-commentaries-2015.

Harvey, P. (1990). *An Introduction to Buddhism*. Cambridge: Cambridge University Press.

Jigme Lingpa. (2015). *Vajra Verses on the Natural State*, trans. Adam Pearcey. www.lotsawahouse.org/tibetan-masters/jigme-lingpa/vajra-verses-on-the-natural-state.

Mika, E. (2017). Goes Trump? Tyranny as a triumph of narcissism. In B. Lee (ed.), *The Dangerous Case of Donald Trump*. New York, NY: St. Martin's Press.

Nagarjuna. (1995). *The Fundamental Wisdom of the Middle Way: Nagarjuna's Mulamadhyamakakarika*, trans. J. Garfield. New York, NY: Oxford University Press.

Thondup, T. (1996). *The Practice of DzogChen*. Ithaca, NY: Snow Lion Publications.

Tilopa. (2015) *Ganga-Mahamudra-Upadesa of Sri Tilopa*, trans. The Dharma Fellowship, verses 22–23. https://kagyu-sfla.org/sri-tilopa/.

Vyner, H. M. (2005). *The Healthy Mind Interviews, Volume 3: Lopon Tegchoke*. Kathmandu: Vajra Books.

Vyner, H. M. (2007) *The Healthy Mind Interviews, Volume 4: The Dalai Lama, Lopon Tenzin Namdak & Lopon Tegchoke*. Kathmandu: Vajra Books.

Vyner, H. M. (In Press, 2018). *The Healthy Mind Interviews, Volume 5: Penor Rinpoche & Khenpo Tsewang Gyatso*. Kathmandu: Vajra Books.

12

MEDITATION

The Cultivation of the Egoless Mind

Meditation Is a Mind Ritual

A mind ritual is a rite that a society or individual creates and practices for the purpose of changing the structure and/or dynamics of the mind.

Many of the world's societies have developed mind rituals that are vital threads in the fabric of their culture. The Kalahari !Kung Fire Dance is a mind ritual (Katz, 1964). The Vision Quest of the Plains Indians (Benedict, 1922) is a mind ritual, as is Haitian voodou (Bourguignon, 1976). The exorcisms practiced by the medieval Catholic church were mind rituals (Ellenberger, 1970), as is the cognitive behavioral therapy of modern psychotherapy, to name just a few.

There are four fundamental types of mind ritual: (1) rituals of catharsis, (2) rituals of identification, (3) rituals of transformation and (4) rituals of nonduality. Meditation is a ritual of nonduality.

Each type of mind ritual is defined by the distinctive strategy it employs to address and heal the somatic and psychological symptoms that are caused by the pathogenic contents of the unconscious mind.

Rituals of Catharsis

Rituals of catharsis, for example, are rites that facilitate the release and expression of repressed unconscious material.[1] Thoughts, emotions and even whole sub-personalities that have been repressed in the day-to-day course of social life can

1. There was, in the second half of the nineteenth century, a line of clinical research that suggests that the psychological equivalent of the anatomical lesion, the lesions that cause psychopathology, are the unconscious *idée fixe* and the complexes they form when they aggregate with one another. Contributors to this work included Charcôt, Janet, Freud, Breuer and Jung. Their findings also suggest that the unconscious material released by the rituals of catharsis are the *idée fixe* and the complexes.

be released and de-energized by a ritual of catharsis. This is the mechanism of action that defines the rituals of catharsis.

Hypnosis is a mind ritual that can be used for more than one psychological purpose. It can, for example, be used as either a ritual of catharsis or a ritual of transformation.

Hypnosis is a ritual of catharsis when it is used to place a person in an altered state of consciousness for the purpose of having that person uncover and express troublesome secrets and memories of which they themselves have been unaware.

For instance, take a patient named Marie whom the French psychologist Pierre Janet presented in one of his famous case studies. Several of Marie's symptoms centered around her menstrual period. Here is part of Janet's description of those symptoms (Ellenberger, 1970):

> At the time preceding her menstruations, Marie's character changed; she became gloomy and violent . . . things went on almost regularly during the first day, but hardly 20 hours after the beginning, the menstruation stopped suddenly and a great tremor seized the whole body; then, a sharp pain ascended slowly from the abdomen to the throat, and a great hysterical crisis ensued. The attacks, although they were very violent, never lasted a long time, and never had resembled epileptoid tremors; instead, there was a very long and severe delirium.

Janet asked Marie to recount her memories of her first menstruation, but she said she couldn't *remember* anything about it. After a long period in which there was no clinical progress, Janet hypnotized Marie, and when he did, she recounted the whole experience of her first menstruation: she had tried to stop her first period by dousing herself in ice cold water because she was ashamed of her period. This remembering of a traumatic memory is the cathartic aspect of Janet's treatment of Marie with hypnosis.

However, it was not this catharsis, in and of itself, that cured Marie. Janet, who was the first to recognize that unconscious fixed ideas cause psychopathology, sometimes treated patients by using hypnosis to transform a pathogenic fixed idea. In Marie's case, he used hypnosis to transform her memory of her first menstruation. In her new memory, everything went well and she had a normal period. This entirely cured Marie of her symptoms.

Breuer and Freud, in contrast, used hypnosis solely as a ritual of catharsis. They employed hypnosis for the purpose of eliciting previously unconscious fixed ideas. However, unlike Janet, they did not modify those ideas once they had become apparent.[2]

2. Before Freud developed free association, the mind ritual that became the principal therapeutic technique of psychoanalysis, he and Josef Breuer employed hypnosis to both study and treat the neurosis that was then called hysteria. This work was the point of departure for all of Freud's later work.

Breuer and Freud had found that when a hypnotized patient expressed previously unconscious memories of a traumatic experience, that sometimes the symptoms of their illness would spontaneously disappear. This led them, like Janet before them, to conclude that these unconscious memories, or unconscious fixed ideas, were the cause of the symptoms of what was then called hysteria.

In keeping with this analysis, they treated a number of patients with hypnosis, which they used to uncover and cathartically release pathogenic unconscious ideas. Here is a brief description of how Breuer used hypnosis as a ritual of catharsis in the treatment of a patient named Anna O. In this passage, Freud describes how Breuer resolved two of her symptoms: a paralysis of her left arm and the loss of her ability to speak German (Freud and Breuer, 2004):

> Finally, the last symptom was traced back to an incident that occurred while she was nursing her sick father; she had had an hallucination of a black snake, had been upset, and had muttered a prayer in English, the only one that came to mind. As soon as Anna had recovered that memory, the paralysis left her arm, and she was (once again) able to speak German.

However, Anna was not cured by this catharsis. Her symptoms reappeared in a new form, as described in this passage from Henri Ellenberger's *Discovery of the Unconscious* (Ellenberger, 1970):

> In a seminar given in Zurich in 1925, Jung revealed that Freud had told him that (Anna O.) had actually not been cured. In 1953, (Ernest) Jones published a version of the story that differs notably from that given by Breuer. According to it, Freud had told Jones that at the time of the alleged termination of the disease, the patient was far from cured, and was in the throes of hysterical childbirth after a phantom pregnancy, that Breuer had hypnotized her and left the house in a cold sweat, whereupon he left for Venice to spend a second honeymoon, which resulted in the conception of a daughter, Dora. The patient Anna O. was admitted to an institution in Gross Enzerdorf where she remained ill for several years.

In other words, when hypnosis is used as only a ritual of catharsis, it seems to have only a temporary curative effect. Janet, in contrast, used hypnosis as a ritual of transformation, and as a result had more therapeutic success. Marie was cured.

Another ritual of catharsis is Haitian voodou. Voodou is the folk religion of Haiti, and possession by gods and spirits is a central element in its rituals.

Voodou is a syncretic religion, a synthesis of Catholicism and the religious traditions of west Africa. It was created by African slaves after they were brought to the French colony of St. Dominique in the eighteenth century, and the vast majority of Haitians practice voodou to this day.

In the words of the late anthropologist Erika Bourguignon, a longtime student of Haitian voodou and the anthropology of consciousness, voodou is a possession ritual that allows:

> " … the possibility of expressing and ventilating some unconscious stresses and conflicts and of deriving some satisfactions and compensations within the ritual framework."
>
> (Bourguignon, 1976)

For example, she describes one all-night voodou ceremony in which a large cast of people went into possession together, including a man who brought to the surface and expressed an unconscious personality by going into possession: "Victor's brother, Sino, a little man usually humble and deferential, was possessed by Papa Loko. He now acted like royalty, full of dignity and ceremony" (Bourguignon, 1976).

Finally, there are many mind rituals in which catharsis is combined with one or more of the other mechanisms employed by the mind rituals to modify the workings of the mind. Janet's use of hypnosis is an apt example of a mind ritual that uses more than one mechanism: he used hypnosis as a ritual of catharsis to first elicit unconscious ideas, and then as a ritual of transformation to reshape the contents of those ideas.

Rituals of Identification

Rituals of identification are a type of mind ritual in which a person strengthens their sense of identity. The virtue of fortifying one's identity, from an egocentric perspective, is that it strengthens a person's ability to repress troublesome contents of the unconscious mind.

The late British anthropologist Victor Turner has described in great detail an Ndembu[3] healing ritual that he called the Ihemba rite (Turner, 1970). This is a rite that is primarily, although not solely, a ritual of identification. As described by the Turner, the Ihemba rite is both a ritual of catharsis and a ritual of identification.

The patient in the Ihemba rite that Turner chronicles was a man named Kamahasanyi who was having both health and marital problems. Kamahasanyi sought out a healer named Ihembi to help him cure himself of his troubles.

Ihembi's diagnosis of Kamahasanyi's problems was that the primary cause of his symptoms was that Kamahasanyi was, by Ndembu standards, an overly effeminate man. He was deemed effeminate in the very specific sense that his behavior did not embody the traditional Ndembu male ideal of the strong and

3. The Ndembu people are horticulturalists and fishermen who live in the northwest corner of what is now Zimbabwe.

aggressive hunter. Kamahasanyi had not, in Ihembi's judgment, sufficiently identified with the Ndembu ideal of manhood.

Ihembi put together a healing ritual for this man that lasted an entire day. As Turner describes it, it was a theatrical event that included multiple bloodlettings, seizures, and a participating Greek chorus that was composed of almost everyone in Kamahasanyi's village. The entire village gathered around as a participating audience in the ritual.

The rite was, at its core, a multifaceted identification ritual in which almost everyone present seemed to identify with something or someone. Kamahasanyi, for one, identified with his male ancestors and the fierce ideal of the Ndembu hunter that they had embodied. Throughout the course of the day, he openly declared over and over again his intention to firmly adhere to these same ideals.

His wife Maria, in contrast to her previous infidelity, ritually identified with the role of being a proper and faithful Ndembu wife. The whole village identified with Kamahasanyi, the welfare of their village and the entire Ndembu tradition. It was as if Emile Durkheim, the French sociologist who took the theoretical position that religion is the means by which a society sanctifies and worships itself, had written the script for the ritual.

The Ihemba rite worked. Turner reports that Kamahasanyi's symptoms were still completely gone a year later.

A second but very different ritual of identification is the Tibetan Buddhist meditation practice that is called deity yoga.[4] Deity yoga is a meditation technique in which a person visualizes an image of a Buddhist deity. The ultimate purpose of this meditation is to cultivate a blissful nondual awareness, which means that it is, at its core, a ritual of nonduality.

However, one of the essential dynamics of this meditation technique is that the meditator identifies with the deity he or she is visualizing. Deity yoga is thus a ritual of identification as well. Given that the visualized deities of deity yoga are symbols of different aspects of the egoless mind, this means that deity yoga is, paradoxically, a ritual in which a person identifies with the identity of egolessness.

There are many different rituals of identification that are woven into the fabric of our lives. Rites of passage, for example, are rituals of identification in which a person confirms their transition from one identity to another. Religious pilgrimages are rituals of identification in which a person confirms their commitment to their religious identity. Even going to weekly or daily services at one's church, synagogue or mosque can be understood as a ritual of identification, as can going to a sporting event, or a political convention, rally or demonstration.

4. Tib.: lha'i nal 'byor.

Rituals of Transformation

The third type of mind ritual is the ritual of transformation. These are mind rituals in which unconscious material is first expressed and then transformed, as we saw in Janet's treatment of Marie. In contrast, a ritual of catharsis is a ritual in which unconscious material is simply expressed.

The unconscious material that is brought to the surface in a ritual of transformation is often modified by transforming it into a pre-existing cultural form. For example, a dream or a vision might be interpreted as a story that is an integral part of the existing mythology of a person's culture, or a repressed personality that is brought to life by a possession ritual might be interpreted as being a possession by a god or goddess.

The Yaje Ceremony of the Tukano tribe that we discussed in chapter one is a graphic and beautiful example of a ritual of transformation (Reichel-Dolmatoff, 1975). It is a shamanic ritual, and like many shamanic rites, it is a ritual of transformation.

Yaje is a hallucinogenic vine that grows throughout the entire Amazonian basin. For the Yaje Ceremony, the Tukano make up a large cauldron of a cold Yaje potion, and then they stay up all night drinking their potion, singing and dancing.

The Tukano say that the purpose of the Yaje ritual is to seek and receive the hallucinations that the Yaje brings to them. They believe that these hallucinations are direct communications from their gods.

Whenever a hallucination comes to a celebrant in a Yaje ceremony, that person will describe it out loud so that all will hear, and then they work together to interpret and giving meaning to that hallucination; just as a modern Analyst might interpret a dream for a Psychoanalytic patient.

In Reichel-Dolmatoff's experience, the Tukano give their hallucinations meaning by integrating them into their mythology, and this tells us the essence of a ritual of transformation. It is a mind ritual in which the unconscious contents of a single person's mind are transformed into cultural myth. This same dynamic occurs in the Peyote Hunt of the Huichol (Myerhoff, 1974), the Vision Quest of the Plains Indians of North America (Benedict, 1922) and Haitian voodou (Bourguignon, 1976), among many others. Hypnosis, when used as a ritual of transformation, is an occasion on which the transformation of the contents of the unconscious mind are understood in terms of a mythology that our civilization calls psychological theory.

Rituals of Nonduality

We now come to meditation and the cultivation of the egoless mind.

Meditation, in most of its many forms, is a ritual of nonduality. Rituals of nonduality are rites that cultivate nondual awareness, or more precisely, nondual self-awareness. Meditation is the prototypical ritual of nonduality.

Nondual self-awareness is a mode of self-awareness in which the mind has nondual awareness of the meanings that appear in its stream of consciousness. Whereas the egocentric mind has dual awareness of meanings, the egoless mind has nondual awareness of the meanings that appear in its stream of consciousness. The virtue, once again, of nondual self-awareness is that it allows the mind to know itself as it really is; to know its true self.

Even if you only practice meditation occasionally, you will from time to time realize moments of nondual self-awareness. If you develop a disciplined meditation practice, it will generate a state of mind in which you have more and more frequent moments of nondual self-awareness.

One of life's delights is that there are many other means of generating moments of nondual awareness as well. For example, rock climbing, mountain climbing, skiing, making love, dancing and playing music—especially improvisational music—can transport a person into fleeting glimpses of nondual awareness in which they are unequivocally rooted in the present moment. So can seeing a bear up close on a trail, or for that matter, any situation that unequivocally demands that you be present in the moment because survival itself is at stake.

Nondual awareness of one's own mind has many virtues. We have already discussed two of them: (1) consistent nondual self-awareness will generate the egoless state of mind, which mediates a person's ability to know and be their true self and (2) nondual self-awareness abstains from causing the normal pathologies of the ego.

There are countless meditation techniques in the Buddhist tradition that cultivate nondual awareness. For one, there are the concentration meditations in which a person tries to focus their mind on one object. That object could be your breath, a candle or an image of a deity that represents an aspect of the enlightened mind.

The concentration meditations are not unique to Buddhism, and they have been very important in the Hindu and Jain traditions as well. Yoga, for example, can be practiced as a concentration meditation (Bryant, 2009).

Another group of Buddhist meditation techniques are the insight meditations in which the goal is realize what Buddhist philosophy calls the emptiness of phenomena, which is the same as having nondual awareness of phenomena. When you realize the emptiness of a phenomenon, you know it as it really is, without projecting any concepts of identity or stories onto it in the process of knowing it.

There are also Buddhist meditations whose primary purpose is to cultivate compassion, and other meditations that cultivate loving-kindness. There are meditations that involve the visualization of the channels, energies and energy centers of the sacred anatomy and physiology of the body as it is envisioned by Buddhist tantra.

Finally, there are Buddhist meditations in which the technique is to do nothing. The purpose of practicing a technique in which one does nothing is to cultivate the ability to allow the mind to remain in its natural state. The trekchö meditation of the DzogChen traditions of Tibet, and the shikantaza meditation of the Soto school of Zen Buddhism are both natural mind meditations.

To the best of our knowledge, the formal practice of meditation appears to have taken birth in the Indian subcontinent. The earliest record of meditation that we have is a clay seal, or medallion, that is from the Indus Valley Civilization. It has been dated to 2500 BC, and it seems to show a man sitting in a meditation posture, although some scholars dispute that interpretation.

Meditation went on to take a prominent place in the Hindu, Jain and Buddhist religions of the Indian subcontinent, and each of these traditions has its own distinctive meditation techniques. As meditation spread further, it also became a vital part of the Taoist tradition of China.

Meditation is also practiced in the Sufi tradition of Islam. There are many forms of meditation in Sufism, and a well-known one is Sufi Whirling, which is an active form of meditation in which the meditator spins in place. Another type of active meditation is the practice of walking meditation, which is found in several schools of Buddhism.

Meditation has also long been practiced by monastics in the Christian tradition as well. The Christian practice of meditation dates back to the Desert Fathers a group of ascetics who began living in the Egyptian desert in the fourth century AD (Merton, 1960). Their practices spread to and became influential in the Benedictine, Franciscan and Augustinian orders of medieval Europe, and in some of the monastic communities of the Eastern Church as well.

Finally, there appear to be many other mind rituals that are not meditations per se, but that might, upon further investigation, prove to be rituals of nonduality. The Kalahari !Kung Fire Dance, for example, comes to mind.

Richard Katz's research on the Fire Dance is excellent work, and to my mind, it suggests that the Fire Dance might well be a ritual of nonduality (Katz, 1984). However, the information in Katz's descriptions of the Fire Dance is not quite the information one would need to be able to conclude that it is a ritual of nonduality. I would have to know more about the inner experiences that the !Kung have as they do the Fire Dance. The same can be said as well, for many other mind rituals that have been described in the anthropological literature.

Meditation: The Cultivation of the Egoless Mind

Meditation can be practiced for many different purposes. In its traditional south Asian setting, for example, it was and still is used to cultivate attention, the cessation of thoughts, compassion, equanimity and the realization of emptiness.

In modern settings, its repertoire of applications has been expanded. Meditation is being marketed now in the West, and it has been marketed as a means of relaxing, reducing stress, reducing blood pressure, coping with pain and making a person more competitive in the marketplace, to name but a few.

In the remainder of this chapter, we are going to explore one of the traditional uses of meditation. We will describe one specific approach to using meditation for the cultivation of the egoless mind.

The essence of this approach to cultivating the egoless mind is summarized in its name: "The Cultivation of the Goodness that is Egoless Awareness by Abiding in the Natural State of the Mind." This approach involves learning to let the stream of consciousness run free and remain in its natural state, which is, as we have seen, a powerful generator of nondual goodness, nondual awareness and the nondual transformations.

This particular means of developing the egoless mind is centered around the cultivation of the goodness that is egoless awareness, the ground of the egoless mind. The means of cultivating nondual goodness that is being presented here involves practicing a series of three meditations.

Each meditation will progressively teach you how to cultivate the natural state of the mind, and how to abide in the nondual goodness that it generates. Living in this goodness will open the door to knowing and accepting your own mind exactly as it is, and to expressing goodness in much of what you say and do.

Goodness can be defined in many ways.[5] Here, it is defined as being a simple feeling: the unmistakable feeling of goodness. It can also be defined as the feeling that transforms awareness into egoless awareness by uniting with, and becomes nondual with, awareness.

When a person lives in this feeling of goodness, they find themselves wanting everyone else to live in this same goodness so that they too can have the happiness of knowing and being their true self.

Expressing this nondual goodness requires no effort. It is not like a moral teaching to which one has to make an effort to adhere. Once you abide in this feeling of goodness, you will find yourself spontaneously manifesting that goodness to everyone, including yourself.

One of the more interesting things about this nondual goodness is that it is probably the natural state of the mind. This goodness emerges spontaneously when your ego stops grasping your stream of consciousness. There is nothing else that you have to do, or that you can do, to make this goodness manifest. It simply happens on its own when you stop grasping your thoughts and emotions. This is what makes it seem as though it was already there in your mind and is thus its natural state.

The three meditation techniques that will be described in this chapter are a sequence of meditations that cultivate both the goodness and joy of egoless

5. I am using the term goodness because this is what egoless awareness feels like. This feeling of goodness can, at different times, also feel like, and express itself as: compassion, love and equanimity. I see the term goodness as a non-literal translation of the Sanskrit Buddhist term "bodhicitta," which is usually translated as "awakened mind." The contemporary Tibetan lama Tulku Thondup Rinpoche translates bodhicitta as loving-kindness.

awareness, and the moment-to-moment self-realization that it confers upon a person. The series of meditations begins with a simple concentration meditation on the breath, and ends with a meditation in which you rest in the goodness and joy of egoless awareness and simultaneously allow your stream of consciousness to run free.

Basically, these meditations will take you through a progression. The progression begins with the experience of knowing the natural goodness of the mind in moments, and ends with that goodness becoming a stable presence within your mind.

Once nondual goodness becomes an enduring presence in the mind, it becomes the subjective aspect of the egoless mind; the subject that has transformative nondual awareness of all of the meanings that appear in your stream of consciousness.

We are going to be looking at three aspects of this meditative path to egoless awareness: (1) the meditation techniques themselves, (2) the experiences that one has while applying them to the cultivation of egoless awareness and (3) the mechanics of the processes by which meditation cultivates egoless awareness.

To begin, let's first look at an overview of the process of cultivating egoless awareness with meditation.

Overview

The process of cultivating an egoless mind is, in its totality, one in which you use the mind ritual of meditation to cultivate egoless awareness. Once you cultivate a stable egoless awareness, everything else will take care of itself. Egoless awareness is both the necessary and sufficient condition for generating the egoless mind. Indeed, it is the egoless mind.

Egoless awareness will take care of everything in the sense that once it is a stable presence in the mind, it will continually generate the entire egoless state of mind anew in every moment. The nondual transformations that it sets in motion generate and regenerate the joy, goodness, compassion and nondual meanings that are the egoless mind.

Just as the grasping actions of the egocentric watcher generate the egocentric state of mind, egoless awareness creates the egoless state of mind. Egoless awareness generates the egoless mind moment to moment by having nondual awareness of the meanings that appear in its stream of consciousness.

The principal qualities of egoless awareness are captured by their synonyms, and they are as follows:

1. *Nondual awareness*: Egoless awareness has nondual awareness of the phenomena that appear in its stream of consciousness.
2. *Empty awareness*: Egoless awareness realizes the emptiness, or suchness, of the phenomena that appear in its stream of consciousness.
3. *Nondual self-awareness*: Egoless awareness is a mode of self-awareness in which the mind has nondual awareness of itself.

4. *Space-like awareness*: Egoless awareness is like a space in the sense that it allows the stream of consciousness to pass through it unaltered, just as physical objects appear to pass through space unaltered.

Egoless awareness is not a theoretical entity. It is an empirical entity that can be readily observed and experienced. Egoless awareness is the watcher of the egoless mind, and it appears to itself as the feelings of nondual goodness and joy. Egoless awareness experiences itself as a blend of goodness and joy, that is also accompanied by the feelings of love, peace and equanimity.

This sense of joy and goodness is something that is easy to discover in meditation. The first thing you notice will be that sometimes a moment of joy will appear in your mind as you meditate. Then, as your meditation progresses, they will arise more and more often.

As you spend more time meditating, the feeling of goodness and joy will both accumulate and become a more constant and stable presence within your mind. Then at some point you will realize that they have merged with your awareness and become you. This nondual union of joy, goodness and awareness is egoless awareness.

This joyful awareness that is saturated with goodness becomes you in the very literal sense that it becomes the subject of your experience. It becomes the lens through which you see and give meaning to both your world and your mind.

When the joy and goodness of egoless awareness become a stable and permanent presence within your mind, then you have become completely and irreversibly egoless.

When egoless awareness becomes stable, it is stable in three principal respects: (1) it has nondual awareness of all of the phenomena that appear in your stream of consciousness; (2) it is never overwhelmed or obscured by emotions and moods; and (3) it never gets caught up in the narrative of a mind-film, should one ever appear in your mind.

To abide in egoless awareness all of the time is to have a *completely egoless mind* (CESoM).

The completely egoless mind is an uncluttered state of mind because for the most part only one meaning appears in the egoless stream of consciousness at a time. A meaning will appear, and then the mind will have nondual awareness of that meaning. As a result, that meaning will dissolve, and it will metamorphose into one of the phenomena that are created by the nondual transformations: the realizations, nondual joy, nondual compassion and goodness of the egoless mind.

The completely egoless mind is able to constantly abide in the egoless state of mind because:

1. It never grasps meanings.
2. It abides in egoless awareness all of the time.
3. It always allows its stream of consciousness to run free and remain in its natural state.

4. It is an unbroken series of moments of nondual awareness in which the mind has nondual awareness of all of the phenomena that appear in its stream of consciousness.
5. All of the phenomena that appear in its stream of consciousness undergo immediate and spontaneous nondual transformation.
6. Only nondual meanings appear in the egoless stream of consciousness.

A more complete description of the completely egoless mind would also include the fact that given that it never grasps meanings, the following egocentric phenomena never appear in the completely egoless stream of consciousness:

1. Dual awareness.
2. The moods and the mind-films.
3. The grasping actions of the watcher: judgment, repression, attachment and following.

As a result, the completely egoless mind is able to know and be its true self in every moment. In addition, it is a profoundly moral mind because everything it does is saturated in the goodness of egoless awareness.

The completely egoless state of mind is, however, a very difficult state of mind to attain because it is equivalent to the enlightened mind.

There is, however, a more attainable egoless state of mind: the *partially egoless mind* (PESoM).

The partially egoless mind is like the completely egoless mind in many respects. It abides in the goodness and joy of egoless awareness much of the time; it has nondual awareness of most of the meanings that appear in its stream of consciousness; it is able to be its true self much of the time; and most of all, it does not generate the normal pathologies of the ego. As such, it is still a far healthier mind than the egocentric mind.

The principal difference between the completely egoless mind and the partially egoless mind is that even though the partially egoless mind abides in egoless awareness the majority of the time, it is not able to do so all of the time, as the completely egoless mind does.

The partially egoless mind is unable to abide in egoless awareness all of the time because it still believes and thus grasps *some* of the thoughts, emotions and films created by its ego, which causes it to oscillate back and forth between being an ego and being egoless.

However, the partially egoless mind is also a healthy mind because the joy and goodness of egoless awareness are a strong and stable presence within it. To put it another way, the egoless awareness of the partially egoless mind will for the most part not vanish when an emotion or mind-film appears in its stream of consciousness, although it will upon occasion become obscured.

This means that the partially egoless mind will tend to remain grounded in egoless awareness, and that it will generally have nondual awareness of the mind-films and moods if and when they appear in its stream of consciousness. As a result, the partially egoless mind spends most of its time in the egoless state of mind in which it abides in goodness and is able to have nondual awareness of itself and realize its true self.[6]

The import of the partially egoless mind is that it is a healthy state of mind that is easier to attain than the completely egoless mind.

Either way though, the work of cultivating either the completely egoless mind and the partially egoless mind is the work of cultivating a strong and stable egoless awareness.

The Cessation of Grasping

There are many different meditations that can be used to cultivate egoless awareness. The path being described here is just one of many approaches to cultivating egoless awareness, and it is a simple one at that.

In the context of developing egoless awareness, meditation can be seen as a tool that transforms the egocentric watcher into being an egoless watcher. It is essential to transform the egocentric watcher because the normal pathologies of the ego are all generated by its grasping actions. It is the watcher that grasps the meanings that appear in the egocentric stream of consciousness.

When the watcher grasps meanings, it initiates the causal sequences that cause the pathologies of the egocentric mind to come to life. These causal sequences generate the normal pathologies by causing the constituent elements of the normal pathologies to appear in the stream of consciousness.

For example, grasping causes the mind to have dual awareness of itself. It also sustains and extends the ego's belief that it has a permanent personal identity. Finally, it causes the emotions, moods and mind-films to both appear in, and remain present in, the stream of consciousness.

Here is a sample of the several causal processes in which the grasping of meanings causes the elements of the normal pathologies to appear within the stream of consciousness:

REPRESSING OR ATTACHING THOUGHTS, EMOTIONS AND FILMS → DUAL AWARENESS

REPRESSING OR ATTACHING AN EMOTION → MOOD ACTIVATION

REPRESSING OR ATTACHING A THOUGHT → MIND-FILM ACTIVATION

6. For further discussion of the partially egoless mind, see the section titled "A Reservoir of Goodness" below.

Given the central role that the ego's grasping actions play in the creation of the egocentric state of mind, one crucial thing to understand about the meditations that we will be describing in this chapter is that they all have a common mode of action. These meditations all work by creating situations within the mind that cause the watcher to stop grasping the phenomena that appear in its stream of consciousness.

The three meditations being described cause the mind to stop grasping in different ways at different stages in the process of cultivating egoless awareness. At the beginning, a concentration meditation is used as a means of distracting the watcher from grasping. In the final stages, a different meditation is used to create a state of mind in which the watcher understands there is no need to grasp anything because there is nothing to grasp.

The import of ceasing to grasp one's own mind, is that as you stop grasping the meanings that appear in your stream of consciousness, not only will you stop creating the elements of the ego, you will also begin to have spontaneous moments of nondual awareness. With continued meditation, the moments of nondual awareness become more and more frequent, and as they become more frequent, they create the egoless state of mind.

Concentration Meditation: Opening the Door

There must be hundreds of different concentration meditations. Each type of concentration meditation is a technique in which the assigned meditative task is to focus your attention, your awareness, on one specific object.

Typically, as you try to focus on an object—let's say it's your breath—thoughts will arise in your mind and you will get lost in those thoughts instead of paying attention to your breath. A robust streams of thoughts will keep appearing in your mind as the ISoC, and you will get lost in those thoughts over and over again.

There will be times when you get so absorbed into your thoughts that you will completely forget that you are supposed to be meditating on an object. You might get lost in your thoughts for a minute, ten minutes or an hour before you realize you are no longer focused on your object. This is an archetypal experience that happens to everyone who meditates, and for many, it dominates the experience of meditating.

However, another archetypal experience in meditation is that in the midst of all of this thinking, you will at some point realize that you have abandoned your meditation object, and return your attention to it. In a concentration meditation, this will happen over and over again; and you will often suppress your thoughts as you return to your object.

In the scheme of things being presented here, a concentration meditation is the first step in cultivating egoless awareness. It is the beginning of the process of tutoring the watcher to stop grasping the phenomena that appear in its stream of consciousness. In the bargain, it will also grant you equanimity and occasional moments of nondual awareness.

A concentration meditation lulls you, if you will, into not grasping meanings. It works by distracting the watcher from its habit of grasping everything that appears in its stream of consciousness. It is much like giving an infant a pacifier to stop him from crying. It becomes impossible for a child to continue crying as long as it exercises its sucking reflex on the pacifier.

It's essentially the same with a concentration meditation. When you focus your attention on an object in meditation, you will be drawn away from attending to and grasping meanings. At first this only happens once in a while, but as time passes, you will begin to abstain from grasping your thoughts more and more often.

In those moments in which you manage to forgo grasping a meaning, you will begin to experience your first moments of nondual awareness. This is where real progress begins to occur. It is in these first moments of nondual awareness that you begin to see and feel what is possible.

One of the first new experiences that you will have, as you stop grasping your thoughts and emotions, is that your stream of consciousness will begin to clarify. If you don't stir up the bottom of a creek, the water in the creek will become clear as its silt drops to the bottom and stays there.

In much the same way, if you don't grasp your mind, you won't stir up the silt of mind-films and moods. As less and less moods and films appear in your stream of consciousness, the stream will become clearer. This is the phenomenon of diminution:

Decreased Grasping by Watcher → Diminution of Emotions, Moods and Mind-Films

This diminution, in turn, makes it easier for you to see the meanings in your mind as they really are.

The emotions, moods and films that the egocentric mind projects onto the stream of consciousness act as conceptual veils that make it difficult to accurately know the content of whatever meanings are present in your stream of consciousness, including the primordial meanings.

These veils will begin to disappear, to some extent in a concentration meditation as the phenomenon of diminution begins to occur. Diminution will, in turn, begin to make it easier to see and have nondual awareness of the meanings that appear in your stream of consciousness:

Diminution → Increased Frequency of Moments of Nondual Awareness

But there is more. As you begin to have more and more moments of nondual awareness, the nondual transformations will begin to occasionally occur. As your thoughts and emotions dissolve in the light of nondual awareness, moments of nondual joy and goodness will start appearing in your stream of consciousness:

NONDUAL AWARENESS → THE NONDUAL TRANSFORMATIONS OF JOY AND GOODNESS OCCUR

At first, you will find that you have an inclination to hold onto the resulting moments of joy and goodness. Holding on to them is a mistake, although an understandable one. They feel good, but holding on to them is simply a form of grasping.

It is important to let the moments of joy and goodness go so that they can pursue their own natural course and dissolve. If you hold on to those moments of joy, they will become an ego that brings to life the usual mischief that an ego causes. If you let the moments of joy and goodness go, more of them will arise.

These first fleeting moments of abiding joy will sometimes give rise to further moments of nondual awareness. They will also leave you with the feeling of equanimity, which is helpful because given that it feels good, it becomes a potent incentive to persevere and continue on with your meditation practice.

With the continued practice of concentration meditation, you will eventually begin to notice that sometimes the joy produced by the nondual transformations will briefly become an abiding presence within your mind. It will stick around.

At this point, the process of cultivating egoless awareness has really gotten underway. You have begun to cultivate the joy of egoless awareness, and you have also begun to stop getting involved with and believing your mind-films. This happens because when you succeed in keeping your mind focused on your object, you are simultaneously keeping yourself from getting involved with, and believing, your ego's mind-films. But still, this is just the beginning.

A Reservoir of Goodness

The next step on the path to the egoless mind is to do a meditation that allows the goodness that becomes egoless awareness to naturally grow and strengthen its presence within your mind.

A meditation in which you concentrate on an object while at the same time allowing your stream of consciousness to run free is a good method for encouraging the growth of nondual goodness, and allowing it to well up and become a stable presence within your mind.

Whereas in a simple concentration meditation, the tendency is to suppress your thoughts when you return your awareness to your object, in this type of concentration/openness meditation you do not suppress your thoughts. You allow them to flow free and remain in their natural state as you focus your attention upon your object. You focus on your meditative object, but not too tightly.

By allowing your stream of consciousness to run free and pursue its natural course as you concentrate on an object, you are now developing the habit of not grasping your thoughts and emotions as they flow by. At the same time, you are also learning to simultaneously stay in the present moment by keeping your mind focused on your breath, or whatever object it might be.

By focusing on an object while your stream of consciousness runs free, you are keeping yourself from repressing, attaching or believing any of the thoughts, emotions or films that appear in your stream of consciousness. You are refraining from getting involved with thoughts and emotions as they appear, and as a result, you won't believe or follow the narratives or ideas they are presenting to you.

However, if you do find, while doing this meditation, that you have gotten lost in your thoughts, which will still happen, then the thing to do is simply return to your object without repressing your thoughts. This will, once again, allow your thoughts to remain in their natural state and do whatever they are going to do.

Most importantly, permitting your thoughts to run free without getting involved with them will, in and of itself, intensify the feelings of joy and goodness that are now beginning to wax within your mind. It does so by allowing more and more moments of nondual awareness to spontaneously occur.

The moments of nondual awareness that are generated by allowing your stream of consciousness to run free will engender, in turn, the nondual transformations that will lead to the development of egoless awareness. Here are some of the causal processes that give rise to the elements of egoless awareness:

Nondual Awareness of Thoughts, Emotions, Moods or Films → Nondual Goodness

Nondual Awareness of Thoughts, Emotions, Moods or Films → Nondual Joy

Nondual Awareness of Thoughts, Emotions, Moods or Films → Dissolution

Nondual Awareness of Thoughts, Emotions, Moods or Films → Amused Compassion

Nondual Awareness of Thoughts, Emotions, Moods or Films → Equanimity

As these nondual transformations happen more and more frequently, that reservoir of joy, goodness and peace will increasingly well up within your mind. As these feelings grow, they will become a stable presence within your mind, and as they do so, this is the point at which they will begin to become you. They will do so by uniting with, and becoming nondual with, your awareness; which will transform awareness into an egoless awareness that will see, without any effort, the goodness in everyone.

The virtues of this abiding goodness are, first of all, that it is goodness. As it becomes a stable presence within your mind, it will permeate your thoughts and deeds, and make them an expression of that goodness.

It is also fun and gratifying to see yourself acting out of goodness, and at its best, it will take you by surprise. Once again, you will find yourself making spontaneous acts of utter goodness that you did not know were in you. Acts of goodness that you had not thought of, or planned beforehand, just pop out of you.

You will also extend that goodness to yourself. As the goodness grows within you, you will find yourself accepting and transforming, over and over again, thoughts, emotions and insights that you might normally judge and reject, which makes it possible for you to somehow now see them in a new and positive light.

Another quality of this abiding goodness is that it can refract into different feelings, as appropriate, in different situations. For example, the goodness can morph into a simple joy; joy at seeing a happy and unencumbered child in a Nepali alley. Joy at seeing the simple clarity of the slanting sunlight just before sunset.

The goodness can also be transformed into and known as compassion. It might be compassion for yourself as you see yourself rushing for no good reason at all for the twentieth time today. Or it might be compassion for someone else when you see them making themselves suffer by trying to pretend they are important. Or compassion for someone who is exasperated and getting angry at everyone as a result.

The goodness can also manifest as amused compassion: compassion mingled with amusement at how foolish you are being in the exact same way for perhaps the hundredth time.

Finally, this goodness seems to mingle and coexist with equanimity. As the goodness grows, it sits there in your mind in a calm repose, and you find yourself no longer feeling a need to change your self.

You no longer feel the need to control your thoughts and emotions because you know that if you simply let them go they will transform themselves into egoless mind, and that everything will be okay without your interference.

When you have reached this point on the path to egoless awareness, you are now beginning to feel at home in the goodness of egoless awareness. The goodness is growing stronger, and there will now be times when you can effortlessly rest in the goodness for long periods of time.

However, your ability to live in egoless awareness will still be intermittent at this point. You will find yourself moving back and forth between those times in which you are living in the goodness of egoless awareness, and at other times slipping back into your being your ego.

There are several mechanisms by which you can slip back into being your ego. You might get caught up in the narrative of one of your ego's mind-films. Or you might judge a thought relative to an aspect of your ego's identity in which you still believe. Or you might get stuck in a bad mood that embodies a negative conception of your self.

You might repress some of your thoughts and emotions because they seem inconsistent with your goal of becoming egoless. Or you might hold on to a sense of detachment because you think it makes you seem egoless. Or perhaps you will hold on to thoughts that will make you appear to be an old identity that you haven't quite let go of yet.

In other words, the reason that you move back and forth between the goodness of egoless awareness and being your ego at this stage is that you are still judging and grasping some of your ego's thoughts and emotions.

When you grasp a thought or emotion, you become your ego again. On the other hand, if you do not grasp your thoughts and emotions, you will have nondual awareness of them, and in those moments, you will be both egoless and your true self.

This brings us, then, to the next step: developing the ability to stop grasping the specific thoughts and emotions that you still have a propensity to judge and grasp. The task at hand now is to identify and correct the underlying reason that pushes you to keep grasping the meanings you still grasp.

Seeing the Remnants of Ego Through the Nondual Lens of Goodness

Empirically, it is a simple matter to explain why the goodness of egoless awareness is still only an intermittent presence in your mind at this point: the feeling of goodness is still getting covered over at times by meanings that are created by your ego—the judgmental emotions, moods, mind-films and so forth.

In these moments in which the natural goodness of your mind gets obscured by your ego, you are not able to feel that goodness or experience the nondual awareness that it would otherwise mediate when it is not obscured. Once you have known and lived in the equanimity and goodness of the egoless mind, it is immediately obvious to you when it is no longer there. You feel different.

The underlying, yet easy to understand, reason that the natural goodness of your mind is still getting veiled by your ego is this: some of the emotions and films created by your ego have been so deeply ingrained in your mind that you still believe them when they come up. When they appear in your stream of consciousness, you still see them as being expressions of how you really feel about the present moment.

In other words, you still believe that some, not all but some, of the words that the monkey on your back is chattering into your ear are your own truth, and those moments of believing put you back into being your ego again. You continue to believe them even though you know intellectually that they are just fictions that have been created by your ego to maintain your identity.

You might still feel, for example, that you are a worthless person, which will predispose you to grasping and settling into a mood of despair when that feeling arises. Or you might feel just the opposite: that you are better than everyone else, which will set you up to buy into and live in that superiority film that sometimes cycles through your stream of consciousness. In other words, there are still a few specific meanings and conceptions of identity that you believe even though you know better.

Believing that these last few realities are true is a curable predicament, and it defines the final stage of this path to the egoless mind. The next step is to find a way to stop believing the egocentric meanings that you are still believe are true.

The problem with believing that some of your ego's films and moods are true is that when you believe them, you will grasp them. This will, of course, take you away from abiding in egoless awareness because when you grasp a meaning by repressing or attaching it, it will remain present in your stream of consciousness. A thought remains as a film; an emotion remains as a film or a mood.

The meanings that remain in your mind stream will, in turn, obscure your awareness, just like they always have, just as a smudge on a mirror will block your ability to see your self in the mirror. Most of all, they will block your ability to feel the natural goodness of your mind. As always, it becomes difficult to feel the goodness of egoless awareness when it is covered over by films and moods.

When films and moods remain in your stream of consciousness, you become the egocentric watcher again. Without access to the goodness of egoless awareness, you revert to being an ego, to being immersed in and acting out the emotions, films and moods of your ego.

However, given that you are now abiding in egoless awareness much or most of the time, this means that you have stopped believing many of the films and emotions that appear in your stream of consciousness. You have already come a long way. You have seen some of your films and judgments so many times that you have realized that they are simply illusions that are empty of reality, and as a result, you do not believe in or grasp them anymore.

If you see a plane sitting on the summit of Everest, you don't call your travel agent and book a flight. You know it is an illusion.

At this point in your development, it is the same with most of the films, emotions and moods created by your ego. You have seen them so many times before, that you now know that they have nothing at all to do with how you really see or feel about the present moment. You stop believing them because you know that they are figments of your ego's imagination; that they are just tricks being played by the ego to try and keep you in its fold.

But it would be a mistake to think that the meanings created by the ego are either useless or a dead end. They are not to be disposed of. That is what an ego would do with them.

If you don't grasp these egocentric meanings when they appear, you will have spontaneous nondual awareness of them; and as we now well know, every time you have nondual awareness of a meaning, it will dissolve and be transformed into egoless mind by a nondual transformation. This will bring you back to the goodness of egoless awareness, and as that meaning dissolves, you will also know its suchness.

You are always just a moment away from restoring yourself to the egoless mind. At this point on the path especially, it is always close at hand.

This, then, tells us the mechanism that causes you to oscillate back and forth between being either an ego or the natural goodness of your mind. When you believe and as a result grasp any of the meanings that appear in your stream of consciousness, this will cut you off from your goodness and you will become an ego again in that moment. When you have nondual awareness of meanings, you become one again with the natural goodness of the egoless mind.

In the context of this analysis, there are, at this point, two factors that are keeping you from abiding in egoless awareness all of the time: (1) your ego is still fabricating meanings and (2) you still believe that some of those meanings are your true self and as a result, you identify with and believe them.

If you didn't believe any of the meanings created by your ego, everything would be okay. You would not grasp them, and they wouldn't remain in your stream of consciousness. This would, in turn, make egoless awareness a stable and constant presence in your mind.

In sum, all of this means that the remedy for intermittent egoless awareness is to (1) find a way to stop believing the remaining egocentric thoughts, emotions, moods and films that you still believe are true so that (2) you will stop grasping them and making them stay in the mind stream.

Once you stop believing the remaining meanings that keep you oscillating back and forth, you will have nondual awareness of them whenever they appear, and they will dissolve. In those moments, you will remain united with egoless awareness, and in the long run, this will allow the feelings of joy and goodness to grow stronger and become a more stable presence within your mind.

Ultimately, the overall goal, in cultivating an egoless mind, is to develop a state of mind in which you abide in the goodness and joy of egoless awareness all of the time.

To reiterate, given that the impediment to abiding full time in egoless awareness is that you still believe that some of the ego's meanings are real, the final step is to find a way to realize that all of the meanings that you still believe and get stuck in are just fabrications created by the ego to maintain its sense of identity.

Once you fully realize that they are empty of reality, you will refrain from grasping them. In the absence of grasping, the moods and films that obscure egoless awareness will no longer appear in the stream of consciousness, and you will live in the union of goodness and egoless awareness more and more of the time.

The Third Meditation: Abiding in the Goodness of Egoless Awareness

One approach to accomplishing the complete cessation of believing in and grasping meanings created by the ego is to do a meditation in which you simply rest in the goodness that is the natural state of the mind—the goodness that is egoless awareness. This is the third meditation.

To rest in the goodness of egoless awareness, you simply locate and settle down into the feeling of goodness. You become one, if you will, with the feeling of goodness.

As you rest in egoless awareness, you will have nondual awareness of most of the meanings that appear in your stream of consciousness. However, moments will also come in which you will grasp and get stuck in one of the moods or mind-films that you still believe are true. This will cause you to oscillate back and forth between having an ego and being egoless.

When you get stuck in a mood or film, there are two possible ways to get unstuck and let the films and moods dissolve. One involves conscious effort, and the other happens spontaneously.

If the films and moods that occur in oscillation obscure the goodness of egoless awareness, it is necessary to make a conscious effort to dissolve them. Once again, you will experience this obscuration as the literal loss of that feeling of goodness and the egoless awareness it mediates.

In those moments when you realize that the goodness is gone, the thing to do is to simply bring your awareness to the film or mood in question, and notice that it is just ego and thus not real. You might even say that to yourself, if you find it helpful, "this is just ego."

This will almost always cause a film to dissolve and disappear in an instant. Sometimes it might take a few moments for a mood to dissolve. As they dissolve, you are actually letting them go and ceasing to believe that their illusory content is real. Once they dissolve, you will find yourself resting in the goodness of egoless awareness once again. The veils that had been obscuring it are now gone.

Conscious effort is not required, however, if the goodness of egoless awareness does not disappear when the films and moods appear. In this circumstance, the films and moods appear, but you remain firmly rooted in the nondual goodness of the egoless mind.

If you remain in the goodness of egoless awareness when the films and moods appear, they will simply dissolve and disappear immediately. This will usually happen spontaneously, and it will automatically return you to egoless awareness and the present moment.

As you repeatedly work your way through this process of letting go of these recalcitrant films, emotions, judgments and moods, you will stop believing them; just as you have already stopped believing that most of the other meanings created by your ego are true.

As a result, you will stop repressing and holding onto these meanings, and this is the solution to the issue of still believing some of the meanings created by your ego. As you learn to stop believing the remaining egocentric meanings, the oscillations between being an ego and being egoless will slow down and perhaps even disappear.

In addition, the dissolution of these meanings will further strengthen and stabilize egoless awareness by catalyzing further nondual transformations in the very next moment: more moments of joy, goodness, realization, amused compassion and so forth will arise in your mind.

In the long run, as you continue to let go of your ego over and over again, several lasting changes will occur in your state of mind.

One of those lasting changes is that you will find that all of the meanings that appear in your stream of consciousness will start feeling dramatically lighter and subtler. Their weight, if you will, will decrease. Moods and emotions will come to feel like feathers.

As the meanings become lighter, it will become easier and easier to let them go and stop believing them. This includes, of course, all of the meanings created by your ego.

Eventually, your egocentric meanings will become so subtle, that there will be nothing left to believe or disbelieve, and you will stop grasping them. The final development will be that the meanings will become so subtle that they will simply stop appearing in your stream of consciousness.

There is an old Tibetan adage that captures this state of affairs: "Thoughts are like thieves. When they find that there is nothing to steal in a house, they stop coming around."

This process is like the calving of a glacier. As the warmth and goodness of your egoless awareness grows, and as the meanings created by your ego stop coming around, pieces of your ego break off and dissolve into the goodness that is your awareness never to appear again, just as pieces of a glacier dissolve into the Gulf of Alaska.

As more and more pieces of your ego cease to command your belief, the goodness that is egoless awareness will become increasingly stable within your mind. That goodness will become more and more resistant to getting lost in and obscured by mind-films and moods, and as this happens, it becomes a stronger and more persistent presence in your mind. You will find yourself spending more and more time abiding in the nondual goodness of egoless awareness.

This goodness has no inclination to grasp the meanings that appear in its stream of consciousness. It is steeped in an equanimity that is content to know those meanings exactly as they are by allowing them to remain in their natural state.

As you abide in the natural goodness of the egoless mind, your mind will have nondual awareness of all of the meanings that appear in your stream of consciousness. Obscurations will cease to arise, and you will dwell increasingly in the joy, goodness, compassion and realizations of the egoless mind. And as you do so, you will know your true self in every moment.

References

Benedict, R. (1922). The vision in plains culture. *American Anthropologist*, 24(1), 1–23.
Bourguignon, E. (1976). *Possession*. San Francisco, CA: Chandler and Sharp.
Bryant, E. F. (2009). *The Yoga Sutras of Patanjali*. New York, NY: North Point Press.

Ellenberger, H. (1970). *The Discovery of the Unconscious.* New York, NY: Basic Books.
Freud, S., and Breuer, J. (2004). *Studies in Hysteria.* Translated by Nicola Luckhurst. London: Penguin Books.
Katz, R. (1984). *Boiling Energy: Community Healing Among the Kalahari Kung.* Cambridge, MA: Harvard University Press.
Merton, T. (1960). *The Wisdom of the Desert: Sayings From the Desert Fathers of the Fourth Century.* New York, NY: New Directions Books.
Myerhoff, B. G. (1974). *Peyote Hunt: The Sacred Journey of the Huichol Indians (Symbol, Myth and Ritual).* Ithaca, NY: Cornell University Press.
Reichel-Dolmatoff, G. (1975). *The Shaman and the Jaguar.* Philadelphia, PA: Temple University Press.
Turner, V. (1970). *Forest of Symbols.* Ithaca, NY: Cornell University Press.

13

THE FUTURE OF THE EGOLESS MIND

The Science

Our research has established, to my own satisfaction, that the egoless mind is a far healthier mind than the egocentric mind. However, it is also true that it will be necessary to do perhaps decades of further research to put together a body of data that will confirm our preliminary findings and convince the larger scientific community that they are valid. This is as it should be.

For one, the notion that the egocentric mind is an unhealthy mind is a large counterintuitive pill to swallow. In addition, the science of the stream of consciousness is a new field of inquiry that reports on a realm of phenomena that are beyond the boundary of what is currently considered fair game for the scientific method; although with the burgeoning scientific investigation of mind wandering and the work being presented in this book, the boundary is beginning to shift.

There are two principal rationales for concluding that the egocentric mind is an unhealthy mind. One is that the egocentric mind creates and immerses itself in the normal pathologies of the ego. The second one is that the egocentric mind loses its ability to be its true self, and in doing so, it alienates itself from the joy and goodness that are the natural state of the mind.

Then there is the additional question of whether or not the structural conflict of the egocentric mind is a contagious conflict.

Does the egocentric mind's conflict with itself predispose egocentric human beings to having conflicts with other people? Does the ego's conflict with itself, a conflict in which the mind must take the stance that it is better than itself, push egocentric people to take a similar stance of superiority vis-à-vis classes of human beings that they regard as being different than themselves?

Our research has convinced me that the ego's internal conflict, as well as all of the other normal pathologies, are universals in the sense that they are a product of the routine workings of the ego and that they are present in all minds that have an ego.

The lamas that I have been interviewing described both the egoless and egocentric states of mind in our interviews, and I am convinced that we have established a good first draft of the universal structure and dynamics of the egocentric mind and the egoless mind as well.

To understand why I have concluded that the properties of the egoless and egocentric minds that we have delineated to date are their universal properties, let's take a look at how science has traditionally established the existence of universals.

If you were to do a single study of mitochondria from rat liver cells, as Albert Lehninger and his graduate student Eugene Kennedy did in 1949, and discover that the mitochondria you studied were the cell organelles that store biochemical energy in ATP through the processes of respiration and oxidative phosphorylation (Kennedy and Lehninger, 1949), you could have reasonably extrapolated from that one study that all mitochondria synthesize and store biochemical energy in ATP, and the scientific community would have embraced this assertion.

However, it was not necessary for Lehninger and Kennedy to make the assertion of universality. Everyone understood that this was the case. When biology studies an organism, an organ or an organelle, it works on the assumption that its valid findings are universals.

What is true for the study of mitochondria, would also be true for the study of the structure of the human heart. If you were Andreas Vesalius, the sixteenth-century Flemish anatomist, and you had carefully dissected a few human hearts and found that they each had four chambers, against the prevailing Galenic orthodoxy that asserted that the heart had but two chambers, it would be reasonable for you to extrapolate from those dissections that all human beings have four-chambered hearts. And you would, of course, have been correct.

But being a good scientist, you would probably have dissected several more human hearts to make certain that your hypothesis was correct; or as Popper points out, to make certain that your hypothesis could not be proven to be incorrect. As history has it, Vesalius did do countless human dissections, and he even did public dissections to teach and demonstrate the validity of his findings. In this case, the dissection of a few hearts sufficed to establish a universal.

The field of paleoanthropology provides us with an extraordinary example of how a universal can even be inferred from the discovery of a single extremely partial specimen.

The field of paleoanthropology has discovered, over the last century, several extinct species that belong to the same genus as modern human beings: the genus *Homo*. This would include *Homo erectus*, *Homo heidelbergensis* and *Homo neanderthalensis*, among several others. The existence of these species is inferred from the discovery of bones, and more often than not, the existence of a species is inferred from the discovery of partial skeletons. This is routine practice in the field of paleoanthropology.

The delineation of a new species from a partial skeleton reached new heights with the discovery of the Denisovan hominin. The Denisovan hominin is either an extinct species or subspecies[1] of the genus *Homo*, and it was only recently discovered in a cave in the Altai mountains of southwestern Siberia in 2008.

The existence of this species was extrapolated from the discovery of a scant four fossils: a fragment from a single finger bone and three molar teeth. The analysis of DNA from these fossils led to the conclusion that they all came from a single *Homo* species or subspecies that is closely related to both us (*Homo sapiens sapiens*) and the Neanderthals (*Homo neanderthalensis*) (Krause et al., 2010). Once again, the existence of this extinct human species was inferred from the discovery of but one bone fragment and three teeth.

Nonetheless, this inference about the existence of the Denisovan hominin was valid because nature does create biological universals, and the four fossils provided enough evidence to establish that they had all come from a previously unknown hominin. They all come from a species of hominin whose members are believed to have universally carried the same genome as the DNA found in the fragmentary fossils that were unearthed in the cave in Siberia.

For much the same reason—the existence of biological universals, it was also valid for science to conclude that all mitochondria have the same function as the mitochondria studied by Lehninger and Kennedy. Indeed it would have seemed preposterous to us if further research had found that other rats and mammals had dissimilar mitochondria.

And of course, the same logic would apply to Vesalius. It was reasonable for Vesalius to conclude from his limited sample of dissections that all human hearts have four chambers, which is of course correct.

In sum, it is in the nature of the sciéntific method to conclude from a few specimens that they represent a universal phenomenon or a universal law because we know that nature creates universals. It would be an extraordinarily unusual event if science were to somehow find that about forty percent of all human beings have a Galenic heart with but two chambers.

Science's ability to discern universals also depends upon our ability to discern when it is not appropriate to apply this law of universals. If one person told a social psychologist that they identify with Erik Erikson, the psychologist would not, of course, conclude that all human beings identify with Erik Erikson. If an archeologist found parched wheat grain in the ruins of a Neolithic dwelling in Anatolia, he or she would not conclude that all Neolithic human beings grew and consumed wheat. Rice and millet were the staple crops of Neolithic humans in eastern Asia, as were corn and beans in the Americas.

Our investigations of the structure and dynamics of the egoless and egocentric minds have also proceeded on the premise that we have been studying universals. The human mind, like the human body, has universal structures and dynamics,

1. As of yet, there is not sufficient evidence to determine if the Denisovan hominin is a different species than *Homo sapiens sapiens* or a subspecies of *Homo sapiens sapiens*.

and we have described some of the universal features of the stream of consciousness and the states of mind they create.

Just as the human body has universal structures and dynamics—we all have brains and livers; insulin promotes the movement of glucose into cells in all of our bodies—the human mind has universal structures and dynamics as well. The mind has universal characteristics precisely because it is a manifestation of our biology. The mind is, of course, mediated by a biological entity: the brain.

Here is the philosopher of mind John Searle making the obvious case that consciousness, and thus the stream of consciousness, is a biological phenomenon that can be and should be studied by science (Searle, 2000):

> Consciousness is entirely caused by neurobiological processes and is realized in brain structures. The essential trait of consciousness that we need to explain is unified qualitative subjectivity. Consciousness thus differs from other biological phenomena in that it has a subjective or first-person ontology, but this subjective ontology does not prevent us from having an epistemically objective science of consciousness.

Given that the stream of consciousness, and the mind in general, are created by the biological processes of our bodies, we can expect that just as the study of the body leads to the discovery of universals, the empirical study of the stream of consciousness will lead us to the discovery of universals as well. However, as we have already seen in comprehensive depth, the universal properties of the human mind are not its contents.[2] Not everyone believes that it is polite to burp after a meal. The universal properties of the phenomena that appear in the stream of consciousness are their form, structure and dynamics.

Universals Asserted by Our Healthy Mind Research

Another way to argue that the mind has universals is to give you some incontestable examples of phenomena that most, if not all of us, would agree are phenomena that appear universally in all minds. To say the obvious, everyone has thoughts. Everyone has emotions. Everyone represses emotions and thoughts from time to time. We all have a stream of consciousness.

These phenomena are all universals, and their existence confirms that just as there are universals in all other biological systems, there are phenomena and processes that appear in the stream of consciousness of all human beings.

Our research on the stream of consciousness and the healthy mind has delineated a great number of phenomena and processes that appear to be

2. I am referring here to the discussion of the two modes of knowing the phenomena that appear in the stream of consciousness—the empirical mode and the subjective mode—that appeared in Chapter 5.

universals. Our candidates for stream of consciousness universals fall into three categories:

1. Phenomena and processes that appear in all streams of consciousness.
2. Phenomena and processes that are unique to, and appear universally in, the egocentric stream of consciousness.
3. Phenomena and processes that are unique to, and appear universally in, the egoless stream of consciousness.

It is my assessment that further research will establish that most, if not all, of the phenomena and causal sequences that were described in the descriptive science of the stream of consciousness that was presented in Chapter 6 will prove to be universal phenomena that belong to one of the these three categories.

In addition, we have also delineated universal characteristics of the egocentric and egoless states of mind. Here is a list, by category, of the universals that are relevant to assessing the nature of the healthy mind:

General Observations

I. The human mind has two modes of self-awareness: the egocentric mode and the egoless mode.
II. The egocentric mode of self-awareness generates the egocentric state of mind.
III. The egoless mode of self-awareness generates the egoless state of mind.

The Egocentric Mind

IV. In the egocentric mode of self-awareness, the mind grasps the meanings that appear in its stream of consciousness.
   a. The egocentric mind has a repertoire of four actions that it can and does take to grasp meanings: judgment, repression, attachment and following.
V. The grasping actions of the ego initiate a number of causal sequences that create the egocentric state of mind. They are as follows:
   a. Grasping → Dual Awareness of the Grasped Meaning
   b. Grasping of an Emotion → Mood Activation
   c. Grasping of an Emotion → Mind-Film Activation
   d. Grasping of a Thought → Mind-Film Activation
   e. Consistent Grasping of Meanings → Complex State of Mind
      1. The Complex State of Mind is one in which multiple layers of meanings often appear simultaneously in the stream of consciousness.
      2. The meanings that appear in the Complex State of Mind include two categories of meaning:
         a. Phenomena that give meaning to the present moment: primordial meanings and the nondual realizations.
         b. Phenomena that are egopoietic meanings that give narrative and contextual meaning to large temporal swathes of experience: mind-films and moods.

f. THE CONSISTENT GRASPING OF MEANINGS → THE MIND IS NOT ABLE TO KNOW THE SUCHNESS OF THE MEANINGS IT GIVES TO THE PRESENT MOMENT

g. THE CONSISTENT GRASPING OF MEANINGS → THE MIND ABIDES IN AND SEES THE WORLD THROUGH THE LENS OF THE EMOTIONS, MOODS AND MIND-FILMS CREATED BY THE GRASPING ACTIONS OF THE EGO.

VI. In addition, the generalized grasping of meanings generates the normal pathologies of the ego: duality and conflict, loss of self, moods, the mind-films and the existential ruts that the mind-films create.

The Egoless Mind

VII. In the egoless mode of self-awareness the mind has nondual awareness of the meanings that appear in its stream of consciousness.

VIII. The nondual awareness of meanings initiates a number of causal sequences that create the egoless state of mind. They are as follows:

a. NONDUAL AWARENESS OF MEANING → THE NONDUAL TRANSFORMATIONS
  1. NONDUAL AWARENESS OF MEANING → DISSOLUTION OF MEANING
  2. NONDUAL AWARENESS OF MEANING → TRANSFORMATION INTO JOY
  3. NONDUAL AWARENESS OF MEANING → TRANSFORMATION INTO GOODNESS
  4. NONDUAL AWARENESS OF MEANING → TRANSFORMATION INTO AMUSED COMPASSION
  5. NONDUAL AWARENESS OF PRIMORDIAL MEANING → TRANSFORMATION INTO NONDUAL REALIZATION

b. THE CONSISTENT NONDUAL AWARENESS OF MEANINGS → SIMPLE STATE OF AWARENESS

c. THE CONSISTENT NONDUAL AWARENESS OF MEANINGS → THE MIND KNOWS THE SUCHNESS OF THE MEANINGS IT GIVES TO THE PRESENT MOMENT

d. THE CONSISTENT NONDUAL AWARENESS OF MEANINGS → THE MIND ABIDES IN, AND SEES THE WORLD THROUGH THE LENS OF, THE GOODNESS AND JOY THAT ARE GENERATED BY THE NONDUAL TRANSFORMATIONS OF THE EGOLESS MIND.

IX. The egoless mode of self-awareness, with its consistent nondual awareness of meanings, does not generate any of the normal pathologies of the ego.

These, then, are the universals that have been delineated by the twenty plus years of interviews that I have been doing with the lamas in our study of the nature of the healthy mind.

Given that there is, to date, virtually no modern science of the phenomena that appear in the stream of consciousness, it is clear that it will be necessary to develop an especially robust body of data to verify the validity of these findings.

It will be important to develop an especially robust body of data because it will be necessary to accomplish two tasks at once: (1) demonstrate that our preliminary findings are valid and (2) convince the scientific community that it is possible to do valid empirical studies of the phenomena that appear in the stream of consciousness. It is not unlikely that this might take at least one, if not three, more decades of research.

From this perspective, I would like to see the next round of research on the stream of consciousness focus, for one, on replicating, evaluating and expanding upon the descriptive science of the phenomena that appear in the stream of consciousness that has been generated by our research.

Second, I think it would be both crucial and helpful to do further research to evaluate the validity of the two basic hypotheses that have been generated by our healthy mind research:

The Egoless Mind is a Healthy Mind
The Egocentric Mind is an Unhealthy Mind

The Feasibility of Cultivating the Egoless Mind

When I first began to do the lama interviews, I would often ask lamas how many people they had known in their lifetime who had attained enlightenment, which is the same as attaining a completely egoless mind.

If you were sitting here with me, I would, for the fun of it, ask you to guess what their answers were. Their answers were surprising, surprisingly uniform and, if you will, enlightening.

The lamas would almost invariably say that they had known three to five enlightened people in their lifetime. And then without my asking, they would almost always name those people, and then explain why they thought they were enlightened: "He never gets angry." "I always feel better when I am in his presence."

These men[3]—all of whom had lived their whole lives in communities in which the entire purpose of life is to seek enlightenment and teach others how to do the same, and who had spent all of their days seeking enlightenment—had only known or heard of three to five people in their entire lives who they thought were enlightened.

If these figures are anywhere near correct as an estimate of the prevalence of enlightenment in a monastic society dedicated to its pursuit, and I have no reason to think they are not correct, this can only mean that it must be extremely difficult to cultivate and attain an enlightened state of mind. It is the epitome of a religious ideal.

If further research were to confirm that the egoless mind is a substantially healthier mind than the egocentric mind, this raises an obvious question: If it

3. The great majority of lamas are men, but there definitely are women lamas as well.

really is so difficult to become enlightened, could we possibly expect that the members of a general population could be raised to become egoless as a matter of public health?

A favorable answer to this question lies in appreciating the difference between the completely egoless mind—which is once again, equivalent to the enlightened mind—and the partially egoless mind.

Remember, as discussed in Chapter 12, the partially egoless mind might well be a healthy state of mind that is far easier to attain than the completely egoless state of mind. It is a mind that is healthy in the sense that (1) it empowers a person to become their true self and (2) it does not generate the normal pathologies of the ego.

Furthermore, the possibility arises that if children were raised to be partially egoless from birth, this might well solve the entire problem of feasibility. Just as it is easy to teach a child to have an ego from birth, it might be equally as easy to teach a child to be egoless if one were to start in infancy.

I am raising this issue now, before further research confirms that the egoless mind is the healthy mind, because it is the elephant in the room, if you will. We know intuitively that the cultivation of a completely egoless mind is very difficult, and that it would probably not be an appropriate or feasible goal for a society.

However, it may well be that raising children from birth to be partially egoless is entirely feasible, and determining whether or not this is the case would be an important second realm of further research on the egoless mind.

If indeed further research establishes that the egoless mind is a healthier mind than the egocentric mind, it would then become incumbent upon us to pursue answers to the following questions about the partially egoless mind:

1. Is the partially egoless mind a healthy mind?
2. Does the partially egoless mind facilitate the realization of one's true self?
3. Is it a mind that abstains from generating the normal pathologies of the ego?
4. Is it a state of mind that could be readily taught to a general population?

Here then is the next realm of research that I would like to see us pursue if and when it is confirmed that the egoless mind is the healthy mind.

Let's now move on now to consider one last (for now) area of possible research on the egoless mind.

References

Kennedy, E. P., and Lehninger, A. L. (1949). Oxidation of fatty acids and tricarboxylic acid cycle intermediates by isolated rat liver mitochondria. *Journal of Biological Chemistry*, 179, 957–972.

Krause, J., Fu, Q., Good, J. M., Viola, B., Shunkov, M. V., Derevianko, A. P., and Pääbo, S. (2010). The complete mitochondrial DNA genome of an unknown hominin from southern Siberia. *Nature*, 464(7290), 894–897.

Searle, J. R. (2000). Consciousness. *Annual Review of Neuroscience*, 23, 557–578.

14

THE FUTURE OF THE EGOLESS MIND

A Psychology of Peace

Charles Darwin marshaled several lines of evidence to support his theories of evolution and natural selection. The most important among them were as follows:

1. Extinct species: The fossil record already showed, by Darwin's day, that there were species that had gone extinct, that extinction does occur.
2. Artificial selection: The argument here was that given that human beings could breed livestock for specific traits, that certainly nature could do the same: natural selection.
3. Nested geographic distributions: Species that live on islands were found to be very similar to species that live on a nearby mainland, which suggested evolution.
4. Structural homologies, which we will now discuss.

A homologous structure, in biology, is a structure that appears, with variations, in several different species because they have a common ancestor.

For example, a human arm, a cat's leg, a whale's flipper, and a bat's wing all share the same basic bone structure. For this reason, the human arm and the whale's flipper are structural homologues of one another. It is easy to discern, by looking at them, that they all have the same basic configuration of bones.

Homologies were noted by Aristotle. The French naturalist and diplomat Pierre Belon noted the similarities between human and bird skeletons in 1555. The German Naturphilosophie movement was aware of homologies and saw them as a demonstration of the unity of nature. The French zoologist Etienne Geoffroy Saint-Hilaire noted in 1818 that fish, reptiles, birds and mammals shared similar structures and so on (Panchen, 1999).

Darwin's theory of evolution explained the existence of these structural homologies as being the result of their descent from a common ancestor (Darwin, 1859). The idea is that human beings, cats, whales and bats all had a common ancestor that bequeathed to all of them a common body plan that included homologous structures.

The point I want to make here, in preparation for our discussion of dynamic homologies, is that the uncovering of homologous structures pointed to the discovery of the causal process that created them. Indeed, it led to the discovery of one of nature's most fundamental causal processes: the evolution of species as it is shaped by natural selection.

The structural homologies were evidence of the fact that as a distant common ancestor evolved into several different species, it could pass on to its descendants a single anatomical structure that evolved into different forms in different ecological niches.

Dynamic Homologies

With these structural homologies in mind, I want to now bring to our attention a set of dynamic homologies and propose that like the structural homologies of evolution, these dynamic homologies point us towards the existence of another fundamental causal process in nature.

To explore these dynamic homologies and the causal relationships between them, I am going to:

1. Define dynamic homology.
2. Describe the set of dynamic homologies that exists between the conflicted dynamic of the egocentric mind and the conflicted sociopolitical processes that occur between egocentric people who see themselves as having different identities.
3. Propose that a causal relationship exists between the structural conflict of the egocentric mind and the conflicted sociopolitical relationships that occur between people.
4. Propose a mechanism that explains how that causal relationship works.

As we will be seeing, there are striking dynamic homologies between the workings of the egocentric mind and the dynamics of the identity-based sociopolitical conflicts that occur between egocentric individuals and groups. These homologies suggest the following hypothesis:

> The identity-based conflicts that occur between sociopolitical groups of different identities are replications of the identity-based conflict that occurs between the egocentric watcher and its stream of consciousness. The gist

> of this hypothesis is that it asserts that the conflicted dynamic of the egocentric mind is the psychological cause of identity-based sociopolitical conflicts.

This hypothesis proposed here is that just as the base sequence of a DNA molecule is replicated in preparation for every mitosis and meiosis of a cell, the structural conflict that occurs between self and non-self in the egocentric mind is replicated every time an egocentric person forms a conflicted relationship with an individual or a group of people that it sees as having an identity that is different than its own.

The mechanism that this hypothesis proposes to explain how these replications occur is a simple one: the ego uses the same basic type of eliminative process every time it forms a relationship with an entity that it regards as being non-self, whether that entity be a thought, emotion, person or group of people that it sees as having an identity that is different than its own.

If this hypothesis turns out to be correct, the egocentric mind would not be the only natural system that uses the same tactics to eliminate more than one type of non-self entity. Our immune system, for example, deploys the same basic immunological processes to remove bacteria, fungi and parasites from our body, just as the egocentric mind appears to use the same eliminative process to remove thoughts from its mind and people from its life.

Dynamic Homologies: Identity Based Conflicts

A dynamic homology is, by way of definition, analogous to a structural homology. If a structural homology is a situation in which two natural systems have a structure that is anatomically similar, a dynamic homology is a situation in which two natural systems have dynamics that are physiologically similar, if you will.

Two different dynamics are defined as being homologous if they employ the same spectrum of actions to reach similar goals. In addition, dynamic homologies and structural homologies often occur together with one another in the same system.

For example, many animals species have immune systems that are both structurally and dynamically homologous to our own immune system; that is, they have immune systems in which cells called lymphocytes are deployed to both ingest and create antibodies against disease causing organisms.

However, even though their dynamics are similar, the details of the processes by which these different immune systems work in different species varies from amphibians to reptiles to birds and to mammals. In other words, their immune systems exhibit dynamic homology. They use very similar but also slightly different processes to accomplish the same ends.

The endemic conflict of the egocentric mind and the sociopolitical conflicts that occur between egocentric human beings also have demonstrable dynamic homologies.

To establish the existence of these homologies, let's begin by reviewing the salient features of the control dynamic of the egocentric mind:

1. The egocentric mind controls the meanings that appear in its stream of consciousness for the purpose of establishing and maintaining its identity.
2. The egocentric mind exercises this control by judging, repressing, attaching and following the meanings that appear in its stream of consciousness.
3. When the ego represses meanings, it tries, in effect, to eliminate thoughts, emotions and so forth that do not match its identity. This eliminative dynamic cultivates a state of mind in which the mind tends to:
   a. Eliminate meanings who expression would generate actions that violate its sense of identity.
   b. Eliminate meanings that create realities that are inconsistent with its identity.
4. The ego judges and holds on to, or attaches, those meanings that do match its identity. This self-confirming dynamic cultivates a state of mind in which the mind tends to:
   a. Express only those meanings that are congruent with its sense of identity.
   b. Accept and believe only those meanings that depict realities that are consistent with its sense of identity.
5. The ego narrates and lives in mind-films that create realities that confirm its sense of identity. This includes films that establish both a person's superiority and inferiority vis-à-vis people with different identities.

Now let's take a look at a social group that exhibits the same type of eliminative, self-confirming and self-aggrandizing dynamics as the egocentric mind.

A Political Party

Imagine for a moment that there was an American political party that sought, in all of its policies, to preserve the goodness of the traditional American way of life, as they envisioned it. That they wanted to preserve that kind of small-town life where no one felt any need to lock their doors, where kids were innocent and respectful and could roam about town safely, where business was always brisk and there wasn't much poverty, where the men would work hard at manly jobs and go fishing and hunting on weekends, where marriages lasted until death do us part and where everyone knew their place. It was important, to the members of this party, to preserve a man's ability, if he had the gumption, to start a business and get rich without any rules and regulations fettering his potential to grow his business.

This party was built of people who felt that this traditional way of life was under threat, and they yearned to protect and restore it.

Some of them had not felt threatened by the civil rights movement at first. They believed in equality as an ideal. But as the welfare state grew, they began to resent the idea of supporting masses of people who looked to them like lazy ne'er-do-wells. They bore witness to inner-city crime and worried that it might leap the moat of law enforcement that had been constructed around the ghettos, and somehow reach them in their towns and suburbs.

Then came the Vietnam War. They believed strongly in the righteousness of America, and they did not like having their patriotism or America's good intentions called into question.

Then came environmentalism, which they felt encroached upon their freedom to do business and recreate and play in the woods as they saw fit. Then came feminism, which called into question their prerogatives and notions of manhood.

Then industries began to disappear from the American landscape as industrial jobs fled to countries where people worked for wages that were mere minuscule fractions of American wages.

Hispanic people began to flood across the border to find work and a better way of life in the world's largest economy. They settled in the United States and formed their own burgeoning communities, and many of them did so without properly applying for American citizenship. And then . . . the country elected an African-American president.

As each of these events transpired, they weighed heavily upon a certain kind of American manhood. Men lost their jobs, their prerogatives, their way of life, their health, their sense of self, their sense of freedom and even their sense of safety.

These men, and the people who loved them and shared their way of life with them, became the base of our aforementioned political party that sought to preserve their old way of life.

Their desire to preserve that way of life was, in and of itself, understandable and in many respects honorable.

But the means they chose to attain their goals were divisive and destructive because they adopted an egocentric approach to pursuing them. Whatever it was that might have been good in their intentions was distorted by the egocentric tactics that they chose to achieve them.

It is in this party's use of egocentric tactics that we see the existence of dynamic homologies between the actions of the egocentric mind and the actions of a group of egocentric people—in this case, a political party. The actions that the party took against the groups of people that it saw as having identities different than its own are exactly the same kind of actions that the ego takes against the thoughts, emotions and feelings that it perceives as being non-self in its own mind.

This party and their base replicated egocentric tactics in three fundamental respects:

1. *The eliminative dynamic*: The party's members took measures to eliminate the prerogatives, equality and even the presence of people whose way of life that they saw as being at odds with their own way of life; just as the ego eliminates thoughts, desires, emotions and mind-films that are inconsistent with its sense of identity.
2. *Establishing superiority*: The party and its members sought to establish, through their policies and statements, that their way of life was not only good, but the only good way of life. They attempted to establish the superiority of their values by mounting sustained and disdainful criticism of people whose values and way of life they saw as being different than their own, just as the ego criticizes and establishes a sense of superiority over thoughts, desires, emotions and mind-films that it sees as being non-self.
3. *Self-confirming fictions*: The party and its members created, believed and held on to a group of self-confirming fictions that they deployed to justify their actions and establish the superiority of their own way of life; just as the ego creates fictional mind-films to confirm and establish the sanctity and superiority of its identity.

Here are a few examples of the eliminative actions that this party has either taken, or wants to take, against groups of people whom they see as being threats to their way of life:

1. Disenfranchising African American voters by making it difficult for them to vote.
2. Deporting all undocumented Hispanic immigrants.
3. Not granting visas to travelers from Muslim nations.
4. Dismissing environmental scientists from positions at the EPA.
5. Eliminating modes of health care for women that they see as being supportive of lifestyles that are at variance with the way they want women to behave.

Here are a few examples of positions that this party has taken to allege the inferiority of people they see as having different identities than their own:

1. Vilifying Mexican immigrants by claiming that they are criminals.
2. Supporting and empowering white supremacists and white nationalists.
3. Mounting a sustained campaign to claim that Barack Obama was a Muslim and a socialist who was born in Kenya.
4. Mounting sustained, disdainful and dismissive criticism of people they perceive as liberals.
5. Dismissing news, journalists and even whole news organizations that publish or broadcast news that is at odds with their views.

Here are some examples of self-confirming beliefs that this party and its base have promoted:

1. Anthropogenic global warming does not exist.
2. There has been massive voter fraud.
3. Evolution did not happen.
4. The Russians did not interfere in the 2016 election.
5. Reducing taxes on the wealthy stimulates economic growth.

In sum, this political party and its members have been behaving just like an ego. One of its basic operating principles is that it seeks to eliminate non-self. Like an ego, it also creates fictions to sanctify itself and justify its eliminative actions; and like an ego, it establishes its superiority by alleging the inferiority of people who are different than they are.

Conflict and the Mind

These dynamic homologies suggest a simple hypothesis: the egocentric mind relates to human beings it perceives as being non-self with precisely the same tactics that it uses to relate to the non-self portions of its own mind. Sometimes this leads to constructive behavior, but more often it leads to destructive behavior.

The simplicity of this hypothesis is that it merely posits that given that the ego has two realms of operation—its own mind and the world—it behaves in precisely the same manner in both realms.

The ego divides the mind into self and non-self on the basis of its identity. It eliminates thoughts, impulses, films and emotions that it sees as non-self. It creates fictions in the form of mind-films to both justify these actions, and to create the belief that its identity is sacred. Most of all, its eliminative dynamic engenders the attitude that it is superior to those elements of its mind that it sees as non-self.

The ego does much the same thing in its relationships with the world. For example, the political party that we have just analyzed does not shrink from making systematic attempts to remove people it regards as non-self from both society and politics. It has also created fictions to justify its ideology of elimination, and it holds in contempt truths that are different than their own. Finally, like the egocentric mind, it goes to great lengths to sanctify its identity by ascribing to a range of beliefs that assert that they are superior to groups of people that it sees as being different than itself.

The hypothesis being put forward here is that this party is emblematic of a larger dynamic. They are certainly by no means the only political actors to have ever taken an egocentric approach to creating and resolving conflict with people they regard as having a different identity than themselves. Indeed, this is my point.

The hypothesis here is that many, if not most, of the actors who participate in our world's sociopolitical conflicts act out the eliminative actions of the ego. The dynamic homologies that exist between the ego and political conflict suggest that the sociopolitical replication of the ego's dynamics is simply the way things work in an egocentric world.

Once again, examples are easy to come by. Think of the purges and propaganda of the Soviet Union. Think of the genocide of World War II and its ideology, and of the Cultural Revolution that took place in the People's Republic of China. Or look at the culture war that defines life and politics in the United States as I write.

It should be made clear that not all egocentric people and groups manifest extreme eliminative behavior. Many people and groups succeed in ameliorating the eliminative and self-aggrandizing tendencies of the ego, and in so doing, they live lives in which they accept people who are different than themselves.

The hypothesis here is not that everyone with an ego indulges in extreme versions of the ego's destructive eliminative behavior. Rather, the hypothesis here is that when racism, terrorism, religious intolerance and warfare do occur, they are expressions of the eliminative behavior of the ego.

In the context of determining the nature of the healthy mind, this is an important issue that merits investigation. If the dynamics of the egocentric mind were found to cause identity-based sociopolitical conflict, this would have to be part of the equation of evaluating whether or not the egocentric mind is a healthy mind.

It would also provide us with insight into the causes of sociopolitical and international conflict, and most of all, a possible means of preventing them.

Given that the egoless mind does not generate conflict with itself, or imbibe in an eliminative dynamic, it seems entirely possible that it might not generate eliminative conflicts with people who have different beliefs, ethnicities or ways of life.

This would be in keeping with the principle of dynamic homology that we have seen at play in the egocentric mind. In other words, just as the egocentric mind generates relationships that replicate its conflict with itself, the greater likelihood is that the egoless mind will create relationships that replicate its unconflicted relationship with itself.

This, then, is another issue that would profit from investigation. If we were to find that people with egoless minds are not interested in either creating conflict, or in eliminating people who are different than themselves, we will have found a state of mind that is more peaceful than the egocentric mind—which is a mind that seeks out and even takes delight in conflict and establishing its superiority.

We already have in hand a body of data that establishes that at a personal level, the egoless mind is a healthier mind than the egocentric mind. It is a mind that fosters genuine happiness and goodness by allowing a person to become their true self. It is also a mind that abstains from creating the psychological pain caused by the normal pathologies of the ego.

The same may be true at an interpersonal level as well. It may well be that the egoless mind is a mind that forgoes the egocentric mind's propensity for conflict. After all, it does not create conflict within itself. The egoless mind may be, unlike the egocentric mind, a mind that seeks harmony with other human beings.

Which brings us back to 9/11. I feel certain that the terrorist attacks of 9/11 would not have happened in a world of egoless people and egoless societies. The greater likelihood is that in a world of egoless societies, people of one religion would not hate people who ascribe to a different religion.

The egoless mind works on the premise that there are many truths and many ways of life; and it believes that truth is relative. From the perspective of the egoless mind, there is no need to claim that one's own worldview and ethos are superior to someone else's, or that your truth and way of life are the only valid or righteous ones.

An egoless person has no wish to believe that their way of life is superior to other ways of life. He or she believes that all ways of life are valid if: (1) they are a genuine expression of one's true self and (2) they refrain from doing harm to, or advocating the elimination of, people who are different than one's self.

In the end, truth is a paradox for the egoless mind, as is one's true self as well. Truth and self are a paradox in the sense that both of them are simultaneously relative and absolute.

Your truth is absolute if it is a genuine expression of the way you see the world; and the same is true of your true self as well. They are absolute in the sense that they are the only authentic truth and self you have.

However, one's truth and self are also relative in the sense that each of us has our own unique truth and true self.

References

Darwin, C. (1859). *Origin of Species*. London: John Murray.

Panchen, A. L. (1999). Homology—History of a concept. *Novartis Foundation Symposium*, 222, 5–18.

INDEX